T0134052

Introduction to
NETWORK EMULATION

Introduction to
NETWORK EMULATION

Razvan Beuran

PAN STANFORD PUBLISHING

Published by

Pan Stanford Publishing Pte. Ltd.
Penthouse Level, Suntec Tower 3
8 Temasek Boulevard
Singapore 038988

Email: editorial@panstanford.com
Web: www.panstanford.com

British Library Cataloguing-in-Publication Data
A catalogue record for this book is available from the British Library.

Introduction to Network Emulation

ISBN 978-981-4310-91-8 (Hardcover)
ISBN 978-981-4364-09-6 (eBook)

Printed in the USA

To Yuki

Contents

List of Acronyms   xvii

Preface   xxi

1 Introduction   **1**

    PART I THE INS AND OUTS OF NETWORK EMULATION

2 Network Emulation 101   **7**

  2.1 What is Network Emulation?   7

      2.1.1 Background   7

      2.1.2 Definition   13

          2.1.2.1 Methodology   15

          2.1.2.2 Possible points of failure   15

      2.1.3 Evaluation   16

  2.2 What is Emulation Good For?   19

      2.2.1 Equipment Assessment   19

      2.2.2 Application Assessment   21

      2.2.3 Protocol Assessment   23

      2.2.4 Complex Scenarios   25

  2.3 Emulation vs. the Others   27

      2.3.1 Analytical Modeling   27

          2.3.1.1 Methodology   28

          2.3.1.2 Possible points of failure   28

          2.3.1.3 Evaluation   29

      2.3.2 Network Simulation   30

          2.3.2.1 Methodology   30

          2.3.2.2 Possible points of failure   31

          2.3.2.3 Evaluation   32

      2.3.3 Real-World Testing   33

          2.3.3.1 Methodology   34

		2.3.3.2	Possible points of failure	35
		2.3.3.3	Evaluation	35
	2.3.4	Comparison		37

3 Emulators in the Wild — **41**

3.1 What is Out There? — 41
3.2 Emulator Classification — 49
   3.2.1 Availability — 50
   3.2.2 Implementation Manner — 51
     3.2.2.1 Software emulators — 51
     3.2.2.2 Hardware emulators — 52
     3.2.2.3 Network testbeds — 54
   3.2.3 Emulation Level — 55
     3.2.3.1 Link-level emulators — 56
     3.2.3.2 Topology-level emulators — 57
   3.2.4 Model Complexity — 59
     3.2.4.1 Low-complexity emulators — 60
     3.2.4.2 Medium-complexity emulators — 60
     3.2.4.3 High-complexity emulators — 61
   3.2.5 Summary — 63
3.3 Carrying Out Emulations — 63
   3.3.1 Emulation Execution — 64
     3.3.1.1 Centralized emulation — 64
     3.3.1.2 Distributed execution — 66
   3.3.2 Running Applications — 71
     3.3.2.1 One application instance per host — 73
     3.3.2.2 Multiple application instances per host — 73
     3.3.2.3 Multiple applications per host — 75
     3.3.2.4 Application traffic generation — 75
   3.3.3 Performing Experiments — 77
     3.3.3.1 Experiment management — 77
     3.3.3.2 Management tools — 78

PART II   NETWORK EMULATORS TO REMEMBER

4 Free Network Emulators — **83**

4.1 Dummynet — 83
   4.1.1 Implementation — 84

	4.1.2	Configuration	85
	4.1.3	Discussion	88
4.2	NIST Net		89
	4.2.1	Implementation	90
	4.2.2	Configuration	91
	4.2.3	Discussion	92
4.3	NetEm		93
	4.3.1	Implementation	94
	4.3.2	Configuration	95
	4.3.3	Discussion	97
4.4	Comparison		99

5 Commercial Network Emulators   103

5.1	Shunra		103
	5.1.1	Shunra VE Appliance	104
		5.1.1.1 Implementation	105
		5.1.1.2 Configuration	106
		5.1.1.3 Discussion	108
	5.1.2	Shunra VE Cloud	111
		5.1.2.1 Implementation	112
		5.1.2.2 Configuration	112
		5.1.2.3 Discussion	113
	5.1.3	Shunra VE Desktop	113
		5.1.3.1 Shunra VE Desktop Standard	113
		5.1.3.2 Shunra VE Desktop Professional	114
		5.1.3.3 Discussion	114
	5.1.4	Discussion	115
5.2	PacketStorm Communications		117
	5.2.1	PacketStorm Series	118
		5.2.1.1 PacketStorm 4XG	118
		5.2.1.2 PacketStorm E series	120
	5.2.2	Hurricane Series	121
		5.2.2.1 Configuration	121
		5.2.2.2 Discussion	122
	5.2.3	Tornado	122
		5.2.3.1 Configuration	123
		5.2.3.2 Discussion	123
	5.2.4	Discussion	123
		5.2.4.1 Comparison	123
		5.2.4.2 Other tools	125

5.3   Simena   126
      5.3.1   Overview   127
              5.3.1.1   General features   127
              5.3.1.2   Configuration   130
      5.3.2   PTC Series   133
      5.3.3   NE Series   133
              5.3.3.1   NE3000 and NE2000   133
              5.3.3.2   NE100   134
      5.3.4   Discussion   135
              5.3.4.1   Comparison   135
              5.3.4.2   Other tools   137
5.4   Apposite Technologies   138
      5.4.1   Linktropy Series   139
              5.4.1.1   Linktropy 10G   139
              5.4.1.2   Linktropy 7500 PRO   142
              5.4.1.3   Linktropy 5500   144
              5.4.1.4   Linktropy Mini2   144
      5.4.2   Netropy Series   145
              5.4.2.1   Netropy 10G   145
              5.4.2.2   Netropy N80   148
              5.4.2.3   Netropy N60   148
      5.4.3   Discussion   148
5.5   Anue Systems   153
      5.5.1   XGEM   154
              5.5.1.1   Configuration   155
      5.5.2   GEM   157
              5.5.2.1   Configuration   157
      5.5.3   Discussion   158
              5.5.3.1   Comparison   158
              5.5.3.2   Other tools   159
5.6   Comparison   160

6   Emulation-Capable Network Simulators   169
6.1   Ns-2 Network Simulator   169
      6.1.1   Emulation Support   171
              6.1.1.1   Architecture for emulation   171
      6.1.2   Operation Modes   172
      6.1.3   Emulation Components   174

6.1.4   Discussion   177
6.2   OPNET Modeler   178
    6.2.1   Feature Overview   178
    6.2.2   System-in-the-loop Module   180
    6.2.3   Emulation Scenarios   181
        6.2.3.1   Live-Sim-Live   181
        6.2.3.2   Sim-Live-Sim   182
        6.2.3.3   Complex scenarios   183
    6.2.4   Discussion   184
6.3   QualNet Developer   186
    6.3.1   Components   186
    6.3.2   EXata Emulator   187
        6.3.2.1   EXata features   188
        6.3.2.2   EXata components   189
        6.3.2.3   EXata/Cyber   191
    6.3.3   Discussion   191
6.4   NCTUns   194
    6.4.1   Emulation Features   195
    6.4.2   Basic Methodology   196
    6.4.3   Additional Features   199
    6.4.4   Discussion   200
6.5   Comparison   201

7   Network Emulation Testbeds   205
7.1   Emulab   205
    7.1.1   Overview   206
    7.1.2   Architecture   208
        7.1.2.1   Control servers   208
        7.1.2.2   Experiment hosts   209
        7.1.2.3   Connectivity   211
        7.1.2.4   Other components   212
    7.1.3   Node Virtualization   213
        7.1.3.1   Basic support   214
        7.1.3.2   Xen-based virtualization   216
    7.1.4   Wireless Network Testbed   217
        7.1.4.1   Features   218
        7.1.4.2   Configuration   219
    7.1.5   Discussion   221

7.2   PlanetLab   222
      7.2.1   Overview   222
      7.2.2   Features   223
      7.2.3   Architecture   226
              7.2.3.1   Slices   226
              7.2.3.2   Design challenges   228
      7.2.4   Discussion   229
7.3   ORBIT   231
      7.3.1   Overview   232
      7.3.2   Architecture   234
              7.3.2.1   ORBIT hardware   235
              7.3.2.2   ORBIT software   237
      7.3.3   Emulation Features   240
              7.3.3.1   Network topology emulation   240
              7.3.3.2   Mobility emulation   243
      7.3.4   Discussion   244
7.4   Comparison   245

8   More to Consider   251
8.1   Network Emulation Issues   251
      8.1.1   Realism   252
      8.1.2   Scalability   255
      8.1.3   Flexibility   256
      8.1.4   Other Issues   259
8.2   Network Emulator Research   260
      8.2.1   Time Flow   261
      8.2.2   Network Protocols   262
      8.2.3   Network Interfaces   263
      8.2.4   Network Conditions   264
              8.2.4.1   Uncontrolled real conditions   265
              8.2.4.2   Controlled real conditions   266
              8.2.4.3   Modeled conditions   268
8.3   Discussion   269

PART III   A CASE STUDY: QOMB

9   QOMB Overview   277
9.1   Motivation   278
      9.1.1   Internet Access   278

9.1.2 Smart Environments   279
9.2 Requirements   280
9.2.1 Background   280
9.2.2 Large-Scale Wireless Emulation   281
9.3 Design Outline   283

10 QOMET   **285**
10.1 Overview   285
10.2 DeltaQ Library   287
10.2.1 Scenario Representation   288
10.2.2 Wireless Communication   288
10.2.2.1 Wireless network technologies   289
10.2.2.2 Wireless network antennas   291
10.2.2.3 Propagation models   292
10.2.3 Node Mobility   293
10.2.4 Synthetic Environments   293
10.2.5 ΔQ Description   294
10.3 Wireconf Library   294
10.3.1 Overview   294
10.3.2 Network Configuration   295
10.3.2.1 Link-layer emulator actions   295
10.3.2.2 Wireconf actions   297
10.4 Chanel Library   298
10.5 Command-Line Tools   299
10.5.1 Qomet Executable   299
10.5.2 Do_wireconf Executable   300
10.6 Discussion   301

11 StarBED   **303**
11.1 Overview   303
11.2 Infrastructure   305
11.2.1 Experiment Hosts   306
11.2.2 Switches   308
11.3 SpringOS   309
11.3.1 Host Reservation   310
11.3.2 Management Server   310
11.3.3 Experiment Hosts   311
11.3.4 Scenario File   312

11.3.5	Experiment Execution	313
11.4	RUNE	314
11.4.1	Scenario Elements	315
11.4.2	Architecture	316
11.4.3	Experiment Execution	318
11.5	Discussion	319

12   QOMET on StarBED   **321**

12.1	Experiment Features	321
12.2	QOMB Architecture	323
12.3	Integration with SpringOS	325
12.3.1	Alternatives	325
12.3.2	Example Experiment	327
12.3.2.1	QOMET scenario	327
12.3.2.2	SpringOS script	329
12.3.2.3	Shell script	332
12.4	Integration with RUNE	334
12.4.1	Ubiquitous Network Devices	334
12.4.1.1	Control space	336
12.4.1.2	Communication space	336
12.4.2	Example Experiment	337
12.4.2.1	RUNE definition file	337
12.4.2.2	Experiment execution	340
12.5	Discussion	341

13   QOMB Experiments   **345**

13.1	WLAN Experiments	345
13.1.1	VoIP Performance Assessment	346
13.1.1.1	VoIP requirements	346
13.1.1.2	User-perceived quality	347
13.1.1.3	Experiment overview	348
13.1.2	Motion Planning for Robots	349
13.1.2.1	Robot assumptions	350
13.1.2.2	Evaluation methodology	350
13.1.2.3	Experiment overview	351
13.1.3	Routing Protocol Evaluation	353
13.1.3.1	OLSR protocol	353
13.1.3.2	Experiment overview	354

13.2   Active RFID Tag Experiments   356
  13.2.1   Pedestrian Localization System   356
    13.2.1.1   Prototype system   357
    13.2.1.2   Real-world trials   357
  13.2.2   Emulation Framework   358
    13.2.2.1   Communication space   359
    13.2.2.2   Control space   360
    13.2.2.3   Time flow   361
  13.2.3   Experimental Results   361
    13.2.3.1   Emulation framework validation   362
    13.2.3.2   Prototype system analysis   362
    13.2.3.3   Parameter selection   363
    13.2.3.4   Large-scale experiments   364
    13.2.3.5   Experimentation procedure   365
13.3   Discussion   366

14   Concluding Remarks   367
14.1   Summing It All Up   367
  14.1.1   The Ins and Outs of Network Emulation   367
  14.1.2   Network Emulators to Remember   368
  14.1.3   A Case Study: QOMB   370
14.2   Practical Advice   372
  14.2.1   Small Company   372
  14.2.2   Large Company   374
  14.2.3   Research Group   376
    14.2.3.1   When modeling comes first   376
    14.2.3.2   When scale comes first   378

Bibliography   379

Index   389

List of Acronyms

ADSL	asymmetric digital subscriber line
AODV	ad hoc on-demand distance vector routing
ARP	Address Resolution Protocol
BER	bit error rate
BGP	Border Gateway Protocol
CBQ	class-based queuing
CBR	constant bit rate
CDMA	code division multiple access
CPU	central processing unit
CRC	cyclic redundancy check
CSV	comma-separated values
CTS	clear to send
DHCP	Dynamic Host Configuration Protocol
ECN	explicit congestion notification
EFS	error-free seconds
ERM	electronic records management
ERP	enterprise resource planning
FER	frame error rate
FIFO	first in first out
FPGA	field programmable gate array
FTP	File Transfer Protocol
GIS	geographic information systems
GPRS	general packet radio service
GPS	global positioning system
GSM	global system for mobile communications
GUI	graphical user interface
HDD	hard disk drive
ICMP	Internet Control Message Protocol
ICT	information and communication technology

IDE	integrated drive electronics
IETF	Internet Engineering Task Force
IP	Internet Protocol
IPTV	Internet Protocol Television
ISO	International Organization for Standardization
ISP	internet service provider
IT	information technology
ITU	International Telecommunication Union
JGN	Japanese Gigabit Network
JPGIS	Japanese Geographic Information Systems
LAN	local area network
LCD	liquid crystal display
LHC	large Hadron collider
LTE	long-term evolution
MAC	media access control
MAN	metropolitan area network
MANET	mobile ad hoc network
MOS	mean opinion score
MPEG	Motion Picture Experts Group
MPLS	multi-protocol label switching
NFS	network file system
NIC	network interface card
NICT	National Institute of Information and Communications Technology
NIST	National Institute of Standards and Technology
NSF	National Science Foundation
OLSR	optimized link state routing
OMF	ORBIT Management Framework
OML	ORBIT Measurement Library
OS	operating system
OSI	open systems interconnection
OSPF	open shortest path first
PAN	personal area network
PC	personal computer
PER	packet error rate
PESQ	perceptual evaluation of speech quality
PEVQ	perceptual evaluation of video quality
PHY	physical layer

PLC	PlanetLab Central
PPP	Point-to-Point Protocol
QA	quality assurance
QoE	quality of experience
QoS	quality of service
RAM	random access memory
RED	random early detection
RF	radio frequency
RFC	request for comments
RFID	radio frequency identification
RIP	Routing Information Protocol
RSSI	received signal strength indicator
RTP	Real-Time Transport Protocol
RTS	request to send
SAN	storage area network
SATA	serial advanced technology architecture
SCSI	small computer system interface
SIP	Session Initiation Protocol
SNMP	Simple Network Management Protocol
SNR	signal-to-noise ratio
SQL	structured query language
TCL	tool command language
TCP	Transmission Control Protocol
ToS	type of service
UDP	User Datagram Protocol
UML	Unified Modeling Language
UMTS	Universal Mobile Telecommunications System
UPQ	user-perceived quality
USB	universal serial bus
USRP	Universal Software Radio Peripheral
VLAN	virtual local area network
VM	virtual machine
VoIP	voice over IP
VPN	virtual private network
VTC	video teleconferencing
WAN	wide area network
WLAN	wireless local area network
XML	Extensible Markup Language

Preface

When the prehistoric people crafted their first tools, they had to test them in the real world. A knife that would not cut would serve no purpose; it would have to be discarded or improved. *Real-world testing* was the first experiment technique to be ever used.

Tens of thousands of years later, mathematicians used the power of thought to evaluate systems by what is now called *analytical modeling*. Reality was thus replaced by mathematical models, and its properties inferred from the properties of these models. Nevertheless, the results would only be as good as the models themselves, and over the years the process of modeling proved to be difficult for complicated systems.

In the modern era, computers provided an alternative experimentation technique: *simulation*. This technique is also based on creating logical models of systems. One, then, runs these models in a computer environment so as to simulate system behavior. Using computing power for model execution makes it possible to evaluate more complex systems in more detail, including network devices, applications, and protocols.

Emulation is a hybrid experimentation technique intended to bridge the gap between simulation experiments and real-world testing. The key idea of emulation is to reproduce in real time and in a controlled manner the essential functionality of a system, so that it can interact with other real systems that can thus be evaluated.

The *network emulation* methodology applies the technique of emulation to the field of networks both for network equipment, whose behavior is reproduced, and for the communication conditions between devices, which are modeled and reproduced in a controlled way in the emulated network, thus providing flexibility and repeatability. These emulated components are used in a setup together with the real network equipments and applications under test. Therefore, the experimental results are close to reality, and the observations are directly applicable to real situations. Hence, network emulation is a powerful tool for evaluating network equipment, protocols, and applications, for research and education purposes, as well as for pre-deployment assessments.

To facilitate its understanding and promote its usage, we shall attempt to thoroughly describe in this book the technique of network emulation and compare it with the other experimental approaches: the scholarly analytical modeling, the popular network simulation, and the demanding real-world testing. To emphasize the practical aspects related to emulation, we shall also give a large number examples of network emulators on the market, as well as provide an in-depth analysis of a case study, the wireless network emulation testbed called QOMB.

One key feature of this book is the fact that we discuss not only the emulation of wired networks, which is perhaps an easier task, but also that of wireless networks (WLANs, active RFID tags, IEEE 802.15.4). Given that wireless environments are more exposed to external influences, the technique of network emulation is even more useful in such cases. Hence, more people will be willing to adopt it once it becomes sufficiently usable, reliable, and accurate. An evidence in this sense is the fact that all currently widely used network simulators, such as Ns-2, QualNet Developer, or OPNET Modeler, do offer now the possibility of emulation as an optional feature.

Thus, by writing this book we intend to provide our readers with an instrument for understanding the differences between the various experiment techniques and for mastering the various approaches that are available for network emulation, both for the wired and wireless cases. Therefore, this book will be useful for the following categories of readers:

- students, researchers and ICT specialists, who can use it as a guidebook to make informed choices of the methodologies they use at different stages of their activities and to know all they need to know in order to successfully set up a network emulation testbed and to reliably perform emulation experiments

- developers of network emulators, who will get insightful hints for the future development of such systems

This book would not have been possible without the contribution and valuable advice of many people. I would like to list them here in alphabetic order: Prof. Dr. Vasile Buzuloiu, Assoc. Prof. Dr. Ken-ichi Chinen, Dr. Matei Ciobotaru, Prof. Dr. Neil Davies, Assoc. Prof. Dr. Mihai Ivanovici, Dr. Khin Thida Latt, Dr. Brian Martin, Dr. Catalin Meirosu, Dr. Toshiyuki Miyachi, Dr. Junya Nakata, Dr. Lan Tien Nguyen, Takashi Okada, Prof. Dr. Yoichi Shinoda, Dr. Stefan Stancu, Prof. Dr. Yasuo Tan, and Dr. Saber Zrelli.

R. Beuran

Chapter 1

Introduction

Computers were first created with the purpose of making calculations. Processing data using computers helped people do various
tedious tasks faster and also made it easier to avoid mistakes. As
computers became more versatile and more widely spread, they
became part of information systems, and the corresponding field
started being called IT (information technology).

It is generally agreed that the first person to discuss the idea
of a calculating engine was Charles Babbage, in 1822. But the first
functional digital computer, ENIAC, was completed more than 100
years later, in 1946. Still, it was only 22 years after that when
ARPANET, the first computer network, started being used in 1968.
Since then, information is being communicated in an ever easier and
more reliable manner, which translated into technical terms means
with higher bandwidth, lower delay, and lower loss.

As today's society moves at a faster rate than it used to some
decades ago, information is rendered obsolete very quickly. This
is perhaps why in recent years the communication aspect (and
network connectivity) became more important than the computing
aspect for most of us when talking about computers. Although some
people still own powerful desktops, we all use mobile devices in
our everyday lives. Such mobile devices don't typically have much

Introduction to Network Emulation
Razvan Beuran
Copyright © 2013 Pan Stanford Publishing Pte. Ltd.
ISBN 978-981-4310-91-8 (Hardcover), 978-981-4364-09-6 (eBook)
www.panstanford.com

processing power, but they are able to provide us with a function that became almost vital: connecting us to the world. This is why IT has turned into ICT (information and communication technology).

As communications and networks became so important, the infrastructure that supports such services, and the associated applications, became more diverse. New or improved network systems, applications, and protocols appear very frequently as technology evolves. This leads to the need of being able to quickly test such systems, applications, and protocols, so that they can be marketed as soon as possible.

At the moment, in the field of networks, simulation is the most widely used technique for performing network-related experiments during the research and development phase. Although this approach allows for controlled, reproducible experiments, the lack of any real components in a simulation setup leads to a lack of realism of the results. This is why prototypes and products must necessarily be tested in real-world environments before deployment, even if simulation was extensively used for their development.

The technique of network emulation is intended to bridge the gap between simulation experiments and real-world testing. Emulation inherits reproducibility and control from simulation, but makes possible direct experiments with the real components under test, thus increasing the realism of the results. In this respect, emulation can be seen as *aurea mediocritas*, the golden mean between simulation and real-world trials that trades off reproducibility and control for realism.

Although a significant number of emulation platforms and testbeds exist, we believe that this technique is not yet sufficiently well understood or widely spread, and not yet sufficiently well presented. In this book we attempt to give a thorough introduction to network emulation, so that its advantages and disadvantages compared with other experiment techniques can be better assessed for each particular situation.

The term "network emulation" is not well established yet, and there is still some amount of confusion and disagreement surrounding it. Thus, we have noticed this term being used for several techniques that nevertheless differ from each other, and we have also noticed the term "network simulation" being used in its place, although the technique described is clearly that of emulation. Therefore, in the first part of this book, titled "The Ins and Outs of Network Emulation," we start by defining network emulation and discussing its usage, as well as compare it to the other experimentation techniques: analytical modeling, simulation, and real-world testing (Chapter 2). Following that, in Chapter 3 we briefly review most of the existing emulation tools and then provide a comprehensive classification method that is intended to help readers put some order in the crowd of miscellaneous emulators and understand what characterizes each of them. To this end we also describe the various approaches to network emulation and compare them with each other.

A description without examples would be dry, and hence, in the second part of the book, titled "Network Emulators to Remember," we provide several examples of emulators that are in use at this time. Thus, we introduce existing tools for network emulation, such as the most used open-source ones, Dummynet, NIST Net, and NetEm, presented in Chapter 4. The most used commercial emulators, from companies such as Shunra, PacketStorm Communications, Simena, Apposite Technologies, and Anue Systems, are described in Chapter 5. Then in Chapter 6 we introduce the emulation features of widely used network simulators, such as Ns-2, OPNET Modeler, QualNet Developer, and NCTUns. For each tool we analyze its strengths and weaknesses from several points of view (realism, usability, etc.) and compare them to each other. The second part of the book continues with Chapter 7, in which we present several emulation testbeds that are available for R&D in various organizations all over the world. At the end we include a chapter dedicated to discussing several issues raised in the second part of the book (Chapter 8) and talk about the current research related to network emulation. Thus, the second part of the book represents a thorough analysis of the current state of the art for network emulators.

I first started working on network emulation in 2003, while being a project associate at CERN, the European Laboratory for Particle Physics, in Geneva, Switzerland. Our team was one of the first in the world to work in this field, using both software and hardware platforms, and ever since, network emulation has been my main research topic. Over the years we have accumulated significant hands-on experience in this field, and we would like to share it with our readers.

The third part of this book, "A Case Study: QOMB," is intended to provide a pragmatic view on network emulation by discussing all the practical issues related to setting up an emulation environment and to running emulation experiments. For this purpose we present a wireless network emulation testbed, to the development of which we contributed significantly, while with the National Institute of Information and Communications Technology in Japan namely QOMB. After a general overview on QOMB (Chapter 9), we proceed to introduce its two main components, the wireless network emulation set of tools QOMET, and the large-scale network experiment environment StarBED, in Chapter 10 and Chapter 11, respectively. The following chapter, Chapter 12, discusses how the two components were actually integrated to create QOMB. Finally, we illustrate the effective use of the technique of network emulation with several examples of experiments that we carried out on QOMB (Chapter 13). Since these experiments are related to employing emulation in connection with wireless networks, they perhaps best demonstrate the power and usefulness of network emulation. This presentation will help readers understand what are the effective steps that need to be undertaken in connection with network emulation experiments. The examples will also illustrate the wide range of possible applications of network emulation.

The book ends with a series of concluding remarks in Chapter 14. There we first sum up the entire book to provide an overview on its content, and thus a global view on network emulation. Then we provide detailed practical advice that applies the information included in this book to a series of application cases.

PART I

THE INS AND OUTS OF NETWORK EMULATION

Chapter 2

Network Emulation 101

In this chapter, we define the key concepts related to network emulation, and we explain what it can be used for. Then we give a summary of the other experimental techniques and conclude with a comparison of all these approaches.

2.1 What is Network Emulation?

Let us start by looking more deeply into the origins of network emulation and its place in the family of network testing techniques.

2.1.1 *Background*

Emulation as such is not a new concept in computer science, and not even in a wider sense, since this approach is already well established in several domains, as noted in [32].

One area in which emulation is widely used is that of training, especially for high-risk activities such as airplane flying, nuclear power plant operation, surgery, etc. In these fields it is necessary to provide a realistic environment in which training can take place without endangering human lives or risking damage to

Introduction to Network Emulation
Razvan Beuran
Copyright © 2013 Pan Stanford Publishing Pte. Ltd.
ISBN 978-981-4310-91-8 (Hardcover), 978-981-4364-09-6 (eBook)
www.panstanford.com

expensive equipment. The flight simulators used for training pilots are probably the most well-known example in this category.[1]

Another example of emulation usage, this time in the field of computer science, is the emulation of old personal computers, such as the Commodore Amiga, Atari, or ZX-Spectrum platforms, or for operating systems of handheld devices, such as Palm OS. In all these cases the functionality of one piece of hardware, such as an Atari computer or a Palm OS device, is reproduced on a different hardware platform, typically a modern PC, so that the same specific software for the emulated device can be run in real time on the emulation platform. A related tool is QEMU, which emulates a standard PC, so that a full-grown operating system can be run inside another operating system. QEMU is defined by its author as "a generic [...] machine emulator and virtualizer" [9].

The use of emulation in connection with networking is tightly related to the field of network testing, and more precisely to that of network experiment techniques, a concept that we define below.

Definition 2.1. A *network experiment technique* is a methodology by which the characteristics of a network system, application, or protocol are assessed so as to determine its performance, conformance to design or product specifications, etc.

The field of *network emulation* is not very new either. Perhaps the very first emulation experiments were performed in 1980, although in a very primitive manner, and they were related to the testing of the then relatively new TCP/IP protocol.[2] This methodology was made public in 1987 in a memo describing "some of the procedures, scoring, and tests used in the TCP and IP bake offs" [89]. Although the technique used at that time may be considered "primitive" by today's standards, it did play a significant role in network testing; its description in the memo is as follows:

---

[1]Although the name used is "flight simulator," according to the definitions we shall give later in this section a more appropriate name is probably "flight emulator," since pilots interact with the system in real time, often by using real airplane cockpits as the interface between them and the computer that executes the flight simulation program.

[2]TCP/IP was first proposed by Vint Cerf and Bob Kahn in 1974.

Some tests are made more interesting by the use of a "flakeway." A flakeway is a purposely flakey gateway. It should have control parameters that can be adjusted while it is running to specify a percentage of datagrams to be dropped, a percentage of datagrams to be corrupted and passed on, and a percentage of datagrams to be reordered so that they arrive in a different order than sent.

Although network emulation refers here only to effects such as dropping, erroring, and reordering, and parameters such as delay and bandwidth are ignored (although we now know how important they are for TCP/IP performance), the work mentioned clearly indicates that by doing alterations to the normal operation of the network one is able to do "more interesting" tests. By extending the concepts expressed above, we can say that the first emulation setup appeared because of the need to control the *network quality degradation* so as to perform reproducible tests with network protocols that were under development at that time.

Some readers may ask what network quality degradation actually is and where does it come from. To put it simply, network degradation appears because of the laws of physics. Because of, at minimum, signal propagation, network traffic will always be received later than it is sent (hence, with *delay*), including with a potential variation in the inter-packet gaps (hence, with *jitter*). Moreover, traffic interacts with all the network devices on the communication path. Hence it is subjected to their limitations; therefore, there will be bounds on the total amount of data being communicated (i.e., *throughput*), and potential loss of information (i.e., *packet loss*). This property can be formalized as follows.

Definition 2.2. Network quality degradation is the decline of the network performance parameters that occurs while traffic is transiting a communication network.

Davies was one of the first researchers to put forward the concept of network quality degradation and its inexorableness ("Quality is only ever lost") and to use network quality degradation in connection with quality provisioning in communication networks [24]. We follow his work and denote the network quality degradation by ΔQ.

Figure 2.1. Controlling the network quality degradation between two devices.

To summarize, for the very first emulation experiment that we previously mentioned researchers needed and built a way to control network quality degradation in order to make reproducible experiments with network protocols. Their experimental setup can be conceptually depicted as shown in Fig. 2.1, where A and B are two network devices, for example two PCs running the network protocol under test, and the "ΔQ Controller" is a system that can control the network quality degradation on the link between the two devices (i.e., the "flakeway" mentioned before).

The next notable emulation experiments were done in 1995, and it is not surprising that they were also related to the evaluation of a variant of the TCP/IP protocol. In these experiments, Ahn *et al.* used, in parallel with real-world testing, a wide area network (WAN) emulation testbed for comparing a variant of TCP/IP protocol called TCP Vegas, against its competitor called TCP Reno [1]. The testbed consisted of a dozen of workstations, and an operating system patch made it possible to assign to each link the desired characteristics in terms of bandwidth, propagation delay, bit error rate, and output-buffer size. Basically, we can say that the authors of [1] managed to integrate a "ΔQ Controller" into the end nodes, by modifying the operating system of those PCs, and thus introduced the possibility of creating in a local area network (LAN) conditions similar to those that would appear in a large global network.

Thus the WAN emulator presented in [1] became the first network emulator in a modern sense. The motivation given by its authors for building such a system, and the gains of using it, are the following:

> The fact that Vegas offers higher performance under normal network conditions, does not guarantee better performance under extraordinary ones. [...] [We managed] to study Vegas' ability to cope with severe and swiftly changing congestion, to evaluate

how Vegas and Reno compete for available network bandwidth, and to contrast Vegas and Reno performance as path buffer capacity increases. In the experiments summarized here, the network frequently reached 100% utilization. As the network was saturated, our experiments tested Vegas' stability, not its throughput gains.

This quote summarizes very well why researchers felt that a technique such as network emulation is needed. This feeling was not isolated, since, not long after, one of the first emulation tools that is still in use today, Dummynet, was made public in 1997 [94]. Dummynet was included by default in the FreeBSD operating system in 1998. In about the same period, more precisely in 1997, was founded one of the first companies that are still involved in commercial applications of network emulation, Shunra [99].

By extending the concepts presented above, we can say that emulation appeared due to the need to transform a physical testbed (e.g., the PCs A, B, and C in Fig. 2.2 that are all connected to each other by a network switch and located in a single area) into a virtual testbed which is globally distributed, similar to the one shown in Fig. 2.3, while avoiding the cost and effort needed to effectively create the global testbed. In this hypothetical scenario, the technique of network emulation is used to recreate the network quality degradation that occurs in the wide area communication networks on the physical testbed at hand.

Despite the fact that the idea of network emulation appeared almost 30 years ago, and that network emulation as such has existed for a more than 10 years, there is still no full agreement upon what network emulation should be defined as, and there is often confusion with the related technique of network simulation. Most researchers seem to agree that emulation involves real elements used together with simulated components. However, additional properties are required in some works. For example, Guruprasad *et al.* present "running in real time" as a defining property of emulators [34]. This view is shared by Nicol *et al.* [72]. Nevertheless, the more recent work of Gokturk recognizes that time is only another part of the reality that can be simulated in an emulation experiment [32]. To support this statement the paper mentions the

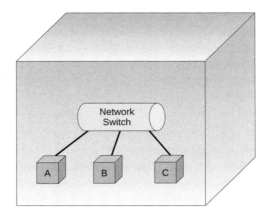

Figure 2.2. A physical network testbed consisting of PCs interconnected by means of a network switch, with all the elements being located in a single area.

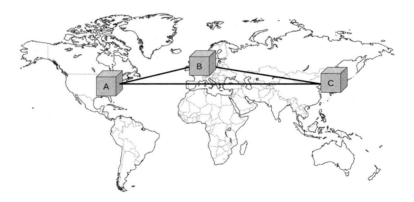

Figure 2.3. A globally distributed virtual testbed built upon a physical testbed by employing the technique of network emulation.

PC emulators that allow running the emulated PCs slower or faster than they would do in real time, while still having the properties of an emulator, since they do continue to run unmodified real programs in an identical fashion to the original platform.

We agree with the stance of Gokturk and further emphasize that sometimes being in full control of time may increase the value of an emulation platform. Being able to run an application slower or faster than real time makes it possible to observe effects that may otherwise go unnoticed, or speed up execution of lengthy operations.

Note that, although some of the ideas presented in this book can be used in general for experiment techniques in any field, unless noted otherwise, from this point we shall restrict our discussion to the area of networking.

2.1.2 *Definition*

Now that we have reviewed the historical background of network emulation, let us define it more formally, so that we can later compare it to other experimental techniques. Before defining it, though, we need to introduce two concepts that are necessary for this purpose.

Definition 2.3. An *analytical model* (also called "mathematical model") is a model that uses mathematical equations to describe a system.

For example, in order to describe a queuing system, one needs to consider mathematical models and to make assumptions for several aspects such as

- interarrival time distribution (basically the pattern of arrival of items into the queue)
- service time distribution, i.e., the pattern of servicing queue items
- number of servers that service the queue
- system capacity, i.e., the total number of slots in the queue
- calling population, i.e., the total number of incoming items
- service discipline, meaning in what order the queue items are served, usually compared with their arrival time

Distributions can be, for example, deterministic, exponential, general (arbitrary), and the number of servers can be 1, multiple, or even infinite. System capacity and calling population are also usually assumed to be infinite. The service discipline is typically first-in, first-out (FIFO).

Another type of model that is used in computer science and that may be built on the basis of analytical models is defined below.

Definition 2.4. A *computer model* is a computer representation of a system in which the physical components of the system are represented by virtual components.

Note that a computer model may contain analytical models to describe system functioning, but this is not necessary. For instance, modeling a network protocol can be done by implementing as a computer model the behavior of the protocol according to its specifications. In this sense the computer model is just another implementation of the protocol, similar to its real implementation, but specific to the model execution environment. However, some aspects of a network system functioning may need to be modeled analytically, such as, for instance, the physical error rate in Ethernet communication (e.g., random errors with a certain probability) or the effect of shadowing in wireless networks (e.g., Gaussian distribution with a certain variance).

Definition 2.5. *Network emulation* is a network experiment technique that employs an experimental setup containing *both* real[3] network components, be it either hardware or software, and components that are reproduced virtually through computer models.

In Fig. 2.4 we show a representative emulation setup. As before, and without losing any generality, we assume that the devices of interest are three PCs, denoted by A, B, and C. These PCs are connected to each other through a virtual network, which can be built by modeling the equivalent physical network over which communication is studied. This virtual network reproduces the communication characteristics of the physical one by means of computer models. However, the traffic flowing through the virtual network is real, being generated by the end PCs, and sometimes by the virtual PCs too.

---

[3] In this context "real" is equivalent in meaning to "that is used in the physical reality." A real network component may be a physically existing network device that is real, or a network application or protocol implementation that can be run on a physical computing platform.

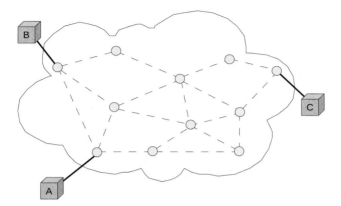

Figure 2.4. Typical emulation setup: the real network devices of interest are connected through a virtual network.

2.1.2.1 Methodology

When performing a network emulation experiment, one attempts to recreate the network conditions that correspond to a certain network scenario and assumes that the real components included in the emulation experiment will interact with the emulated ones as if they were placed in the equivalent real-world setup.

Note that this effectively contrives the emulated part of the network as a *black box*, for which only the input, output, and transfer characteristic are of importance. The transfer characteristic of a network is actually the network quality degradation ΔQ introduced in Definition 2.2. Therefore, in an emulation experiment, one effectively assumes that by recreating the end-to-end ΔQ of the emulated network it is possible to reproduce realistically a network scenario.

2.1.2.2 Possible points of failure

Considering the network as black box may pose problems, depending on the additional assumptions that are made about its transfer function. One may consider the equivalent ΔQ as constant, which may be true as long as the input and output are very low compared to the congestion threshold. A variation of ΔQ depending on the input requires real-time model calculations that may impede experiment execution.

2.1.3 *Evaluation*

In order to be able to compare emulation with the other experiment techniques, we need to use some clear criteria. Therefore, let us discuss next the most important points for evaluating such a methodology.

First of all, when thinking about an experimentation technique, one of the issues that comes to mind is *cost*. One aspect is the financial cost related to acquiring all the tools and equipment needed to make the experiment (or even to build them, if they don't exist). In some cases this cost can be very small; however, network equipment can become very expensive, especially in large-scale experiments, or when it is necessary to build it from scratch. One issue to note in this context is that if a tool can be reused for making experiments, then it can be considered as a fixed cost that gets amortized over the years. Another aspect related to cost is the time required to prepare for, and effectively make, the experiments. Time can be translated into financial cost if needed, for instance by considering the necessary man-hours to accomplish a task.

A second issue to consider is *execution time*. We use this aspect to evaluate how efficient an experiment technique is from the point of view of execution time. This refers essentially to whether the act of effectively running the experiment happens in real time or not. However, even when execution doesn't happen in real time, but the decrease or increase in execution speed when compared to real time is constant, one still has good control over time; hence, such a technique's performance can be considered equivalent to the real-time case.

Another issue to take into account is *flexibility*. Given a set of tools, how much control does the user have over the experiment when employing a certain technique? This is particularly important with respect to experiment conditions. Ideally, one wishes to have full control over experimental conditions, so that many scenarios can be studied, and undesired interferences can be avoided. Therefore good control translates into the possibility to explore a wide range of scenarios.

A fourth issue related to judging experiment techniques is *reliability*. Assuming that a certain experiment was performed, how much can we trust the correctness of the results? Do they represent only a possible trend, or are they data we can use to make practical decisions about the system? In this context the realism of the results is probably the most important point.

One more issue to bear in mind is *usability*. This helps us evaluate how easy it is to use an experiment technique, meaning how straightforward are all the preparations and changes needed before and during the experiment. However, we do not include here the usability of the experiment tools by themselves, although we agree that the learning curve associated with a certain tool has a strong influence on its adoption, due to obvious human psychology reasons.

On the basis of the discussion above, we propose the following criteria for evaluating experiment techniques and for comparing them to each other:

- *Experimentation cost*, meaning the cost of practically conducting experiments with a certain technique, from the point of view of both finance and time, but excluding the fixed cost of acquiring tools that can be used repetitively over multiple experiments
- *Real-time execution*, meaning whether the experiment done by a certain method is effectively executed in real time or not[4]
- *Control over experimental conditions*, meaning how well the experiment conditions can be controlled for a particular technique and how wide is the range of experiment conditions that can be studied
- *Result reliability*, meaning what is the realism of the experimental results obtained with a particular method, and how much trust can one put in them for making practical decisions about the system
- *Ease of use*, meaning how easy it is to make experiments when employing a particular approach, but excluding the usability aspects referring to experiment tools by themselves

---

[4]By extension this can be applied to experiment techniques in which time is controlled, even though the execution time is not the same as wall-clock time.

Using these criteria, network emulation can be evaluated as follows:

Experimentation cost Although the cost of running emulated components can be viewed as low, network emulation does require physical equipment to be included in the experiment. A related issue is how expensive it is to make any changes to the emulation testbed, for example in order to test new conditions. For the emulated components, this cost is that of the model alteration, but for the physical ones, the cost may be higher. Therefore we consider the experimentation cost of this approach to be medium.

Real-time execution Emulation experiments are typically executed in real time, although this is not a definite requirement, since — as we already mentioned — some researchers consider time as just another parameter that can be emulated [32]. As long as the lapse of time is made slower or faster in a controlled manner for the entire system, emulation using real applications is still possible. We shall actually show an example of how to apply this approach in practice in Section 13.2.

Control over experimental conditions Network emulation can be said to provide full control over the experiment conditions, but this only extends to those components that are modeled; the real components that are part of the experiment cannot be interfered with more than one could do so in a real-world trial. Although the range of conditions that can be tested through emulation may seem infinite for the modeled components of an emulation experiment, the fact that the emulated components have to interact with real elements during the experiment makes that the emulation technique is subjected to the physical constraints of the real world. For instance, zero end-to-end delays are impossible to obtain in an emulation testbed, and the largest delays that can be introduced are practically limited by different physical parameters of the execution platform, such as the size of the buffers used to store the real traffic packets while in transit through the emulated components of the system.

Result reliability   Result reliability is difficult to evaluate in general, since it depends on a significant number of factors, but we claim that the best-case realism level is at least medium for the case of emulation, and this is owing to the real components being included in the experiment. Their use also makes the results of the experiment very intuitive, since they are obtained by really using the equipment under test, albeit in an emulated environment. Still, if the models based on which the emulated components run are too simplistic, then the final results of the experiment may very well lack realism.

Ease of use   When making emulation experiments, one has to control and configure several real systems and devices. However, the use of computer models, and the ability to easily reproduce some aspects such as mobility, significantly improve usability. Therefore the ease of use can be evaluated as medium at worst.

2.2 What is Emulation Good For?

Before diving into more details regarding network emulation and the other experiment techniques, let us first clarify what are the potential applications of emulation experiments. The main purpose of such experiments is to assess the performance of a network system, and depending on what is being evaluated one can distinguish several types of emulation experiments. One could, for example, use emulation experiments to assess

- network equipment
- network applications
- network protocols

2.2.1 *Equipment Assessment*

Let us assume that a company has manufactured a new generation of network equipment, or that the IT division of an enterprise wants to assess the performance of several network equipment produced by different manufacturers in order to decide which of them should be acquired. Both for basic network devices, such as NICs (network interface cards), and for more advanced equipment, such as switches and routers, a realistic environment needs to be created in order to make possible a thorough evaluation.

At this point network emulation can play an essential role. By using the technique of emulation, IT specialists can build a network environment in which the communication conditions and traffic load are similar to those in the production network for which the new equipment is intended. By inserting the equipment under test into such an environment, its properties can be thoroughly assessed. Since the environment is dedicated to testing, and it's not the production network itself, extreme situations can be reproduced without worrying about the influence on uninvolved users or customers.

This methodology is very similar to the idea of a network testbed. However, instead of using only the equipment at hand, emulation contributes at least one main enhancement. By emulation, network conditions are controlled so as to reproduce desired scenarios instead of the freely changing conditions of a standard testbed not using emulation. In addition, network traffic could also be recreated in a controlled way, so as to reproduce the load created by several human users, without effectively requiring the presence of the human users. This is usually done by using tools called *traffic generators*, which are typically part of most emulation testbeds.

A (non-exhaustive) list of network equipment that can be tested by emulation is given below:

- wired and wireless NICs
- wireless network access points
- switches and routers
- hardware firewalls and other network security devices
- IP telephony products
- videoconferencing equipment

We show in Fig. 2.5 an example of how IP phones could be tested by using network emulation. The two IP phones are connected through an emulated network using a "ΔQ controller" that will introduce artificial packet loss and jitter so that their effect on voice

Figure 2.5. Equipment assessment: evaluating IP phones by using network emulation.

quality can be assessed.[5] The assessment can be done by users in a subjective way, or objective metrics such as the PESQ (Perceptual Evaluation of Speech Quality) score could be used [45].

2.2.2 *Application Assessment*

Network application developers often face the following challenge: once an application is implemented and ready to be released, how can they make sure that it performs well? More specifically, developers ideally wish to be able to assess the performance of the application in a wide range of network conditions, so that they can detect potential problem before shipping the software to customers.

As an example let us consider the case of a Voice over Internet Protocol (VoIP) application. Although the application was tested on the local network and seemed to behave well, how can one guarantee that the application would have good performance when used on the Internet as well, where larger delays and packet loss as well as bandwidth limitations will occur?

Doing some real-world testing with the application may not be so difficult, but one can never make sure that the entire range of possible network conditions that can be met in a real deployment are explored in this way. Emulation can help exactly at this point: by enabling application testing in a wide range of conditions, network emulation will help developers understand the behavior of their application under various circumstances and will also help them determine the breaking points of the application, if any.

---

[5]Note that this setup is actually simplified for clarity purposes. Typically, access to a SIP server is required in order for IP phones to function; hence, such a server needs to be placed in the same network with the IP phones for being able to effectively run such an experiment.

In case any problems were detected, once they are fixed, the reproducibility property of network emulation ensures that re-testing the application in the same conditions that caused it to fail in the first place is possible. Thus emulation makes possible iterative development of network applications, as well as regression testing, which is an important component of modern software development (e.g., in extreme programming).

A significant aspect related to network application testing is the requirement to be able to test the application itself, and not a model or simplified version of it. This is where network emulation comes into play. Note that a prerequisite for such kind of experiments is the possibility to run the application under test on a host that is as similar as possible to the computing platform of the intended customers (e.g., in terms of CPU frequency, amount of memory).

As a side note, a desirable feature when assessing an application is to be able to evaluate quantitatively its behavior in different experiments, so that judgments about differences can be easily made. At this point the so-called quality of experience (QoE), also known as user-perceived quality (UPQ), plays an essential role. By associating a metric, be it subjective or objective, to the quality delivered by an application from the point of view of users, it becomes easy to compare performance between different scenarios. The issue of UPQ for file transfer and VoIP was studied, for example, in [13].

Basically, for any network/distributed application one can benefit from employing emulation for testing, in order to evaluate its end-to-end performance in realistic scenarios, and to determine its behavior in extreme conditions, as well as its breaking points. We provide below a few instances of network application testing scenarios for which the advantages of emulation should be obvious for any reader:

- Determine the end-to-end quality of VoIP and videoconferencing systems.
- Study the responsiveness of remote access and control applications.
- Study the behavior of content sharing and other kinds of peer-to-peer applications.

Figure 2.6. Application assessment: evaluating streaming video playback software by using network emulation.

Figure 2.6 illustrates an example of how streaming video playback client software could be evaluated by using network emulation. The video playback client is connected to the streaming server by means of an emulated network, in this case the "ΔQ controller" that will introduce artificial packet loss and jitter so that their effect on video quality can be assessed. This assessment can be done subjectively by human users, or it can be performed by employing an objective metric such as PEVQ (Perceptual Evaluation of Video Quality) [81].

2.2.3 *Protocol Assessment*

Network protocol assessment refers to experiments for evaluating the performance characteristics of a network protocol, such as a data transfer protocol, or a routing protocol.

If the network protocol under test is end-to-end, such as TCP, (a data transfer protocol), then the testing procedure is very similar to that described in the previous section, since such a protocol is almost always run as part of an application. For instance, in the case of file transfer, FTP is the typical application and high-level protocol running on top of TCP to transfer a file between two PCs.

However, network protocols, such as those for routing, are not part of any specific application, and their role is only to make sure that the network as a whole is operating properly. Since a network with no traffic is close to meaningless, protocol assessment is usually done by injecting application traffic into the network. Application traffic can be produced by one or more instances of real applications, or it can come from traffic generators that will produce traffic with the same characteristics as that of real applications, as it was already discussed in Section 2.2.1. Such an approach is often used for Web traffic generation, when a single software or hardware system is used to reproduce the traffic pattern of thousands of Web clients.

Network protocol performance assessment can be done either directly or indirectly. In this context, direct assessment refers to gathering data related to the behavior of the protocol during the experiment, such as the time needed to update routing tables in the case of routing protocols. Or, if we go back to the case of file transfer, one could measure the goodput for the transfer, or the time needed to finish the transfer (for a discussion of UPQ metrics for file transfer see [13]).

Perhaps a more important kind of assessment for routing protocols is the indirect one, in which the experimenter will gather data about the performance of the applications running over the network managed by the routing protocol under test. Such results will make it possible to evaluate whether the protocol under test performs better or not than other similar protocols, determine parameter values that give optimal performance, etc.

At first sight, network protocol testing may seem to be related more to researchers and developers, whereas network equipment and application testing may seem more oriented toward regular users and IT engineers. However, in many cases the protocols are part of more complex systems, such as videoconferencing appliances. In this context even a regular user or IT engineer may wish to evaluate the differences between several distinct transport protocols that can be used. For videoconferencing, UDP provides lower latency, but may not give good performance in lossy networks; on the other hand, TCP has higher latency, but supports well small levels of loss. Nevertheless, the best choice may depend on the actual circumstances and network conditions in which the application will be used. Therefore practical testing is usually necessary.

Below, you may find some examples of network protocols that can be tested by emulation:

- data transfer protocols
- VoIP

Figure 2.7. Protocol assessment: evaluating a data transfer protocol using network emulation.

- routing protocols
- peer-to-peer protocols
- distributed computing protocols and middleware

Figure 2.7 depicts an example of how a data transfer protocol could be evaluated by using network emulation. We assume in this example that data transfer performance is evaluated by using on top of the data transfer protocol a Web application using a high-level protocol such as HTTP. The Web client is connected to the Web server by means of an emulated network, in this case the "ΔQ controller" that will introduce artificial packet loss and jitter so that their effect on the data transfer protocol, and indirectly on the Web application performance, can be assessed.

2.2.4 *Complex Scenarios*

Although in the preceding sections we already gave several basic examples of what emulation could be used for, the real scenarios related to network testing are usually more complex and may imply the need to simultaneously test two or all of the elements that were mentioned so far (equipment, applications, and protocols).

Moreover, even though in some cases basic network degradation such as artificial packet loss or jitter may suffice, a realistic scenario usually includes a larger emulated network, similar to that shown in Fig. 2.4. In this case, the end-to-end network degradation is not controlled directly by the user, for instance by varying packet loss rates in a certain range of interest, but is the result of the interaction between the virtual network elements and the real network traffic passing through them.

To get a clearer understanding of how complex networking scenarios could benefit from using emulation as an experiment technique, let us look at several situations in which some major IT decisions must be made. Note that the scenarios presented below are not completely fictional, as they are loosely based on several real use cases made public by Anue Systems [4].

Operating systems   Let us imagine that a certain company is considering to upgrade their server operating system (e.g., from Microsoft Windows Server 2003 to Microsoft Windows Server 2008), as well as the operating system of client PCs (e.g., from Microsoft Windows XP to Microsoft Windows 7). Before doing this operation in the production network, IT engineers could use an emulated network that reproduces the bandwidth, delay, and loss characteristics of the company's network. By thoroughly testing the various operating system combinations in that controlled environment, IT engineers can determine which of those combinations provides the best cost/performance trade-off.

Data centers   Establishing a remote data center or relocating an existing one is a major challenge for any organization. Using an emulation testbed to reproduce the network conditions between user PCs and the remote location can help IT engineers answer questions such as the following: Which solution meets the business-critical storage needs of the organization? What are the performance parameters that need to be guaranteed by the network service provider[6] in order for the data center to operate satisfactorily?

Recovery from failure   Suppose that an enterprise wishes to implement a network failure recovery solution, so that its critical IT systems continue to operate satisfactorily in the event a major network failure occurs. Usually this involves setting up a backup system at a remote location that will provide the necessary services starting at the moment when the main system fails and until its recovery is completed. To validate a certain solution, instead of waiting for the worst to happen, IT engineers should attempt to test in advance how the backup system will perform by emulating

---

[6]Such guarantees may include basic metrics, such as minimum guaranteed bandwidth, maximum packet loss, maximum delay, or composite ones, such as the error-free seconds (EFS) figure.

both the network failure, and the network conditions at the remote location on an emulation testbed.

Network performance In order to verify correct and adequate functioning of its network, an operator or ISP may want to test what is the impact of delays and impairments across its own network on customer application traffic. This is particularly important as new services or equipment are deployed, but can also be used to evaluate the network performance in both normal utilization conditions, as well as in disaster scenarios. The operator can achieve this goal by reproducing in an emulated network the topology of its production network, and recreating in it those conditions that need to be tested. Thus the network operator may be confident about the behavior of its network in various hypothetical scenarios and is able to design, implement, and validate robust protection and service restoration mechanisms.

2.3 Emulation vs. the Others

In order to fully understand the particular aspects of emulation as a network experiment technique, and what differentiates it from the other approaches, such as analytical modeling, simulation, and real-world testing, we need to define those as well, and to evaluate them using the same criteria, i.e., those presented in the Section 2.1.3. At the end of this section we shall then compare network emulation to the other network experiment techniques.

2.3.1 *Analytical Modeling*

Although analytical modeling is only fit for *thought experiments*, and hence is not a genuine experimental technique *per se*, we do include it here for the sake of completeness and also because we find that it is a very useful starting point for any network evaluation. Moreover, modeling itself is actually an essential component of network emulation and it is *sine qua non* for network simulation.

Definition 2.6. *Analytical modeling* is a thought experiment technique, and hence a network experiment technique in a wider sense, that *exclusively* employs analytical equations to predict the behavior of network systems, applications, and protocols.

2.3.1.1 Methodology

Analytical modeling has always played an important role in understanding phenomena and systems, and also for system and protocol design. The mathematical models involved are usually built by making several assumptions to simplify reality and then by creating analytical equations that describe this simplified reality.

In connection with networks, the most used analytical models are those of queues, which can then be put together to build models of switches. A related class of models are those concerning network traffic, which closely interact with the queue models. One can model many other things, such as network protocols and applications, for example.

Although modeling cannot be used directly to verify whether a system works as designed, it does play a significant role in understanding the properties of the system and in making predictions related to its behavior. Modeling, be it very simple or more complex, is done (or should be done!) before proceeding with the implementation of any network system. This modeling activity can then become the basis for the next development and testing phase, which is experimental in nature. For instance, the developed analytical model could be integrated into a network simulator or emulator to reproduce the behavior of the modeled system.

2.3.1.2 Possible points of failure

The most important *caveat* related to analytical modeling is the following: since for creating most mathematical models a simplification of reality is necessary, one must always be aware that the analytical model can — at best — accurately predict the behavior of the *simplified* system, and only approximates, better or worse, that of the real system. In some cases this difference may not be so important, but one must always keep in mind this aspect and consider its influence when drawing conclusions.

2.3.1.3 Evaluation

Using the criteria introduced in Section 2.1.3, analytical modeling can be evaluated as follows:

Experimentation cost   Experimentation cost is very low for analytical modeling,[7] since at most computational processing is needed if numerical models are used.

Real-time execution   This is not available for analytical modeling, since a mathematical model cannot be executed directly, but only computed.

Control over experimental conditions   Analytical modeling provides full control over the conditions and characteristics of the system to be evaluated, since no restrictions whatsoever apply to the model. The range of conditions that can be studied is large, one could say practically infinite, since even physically impossible assumptions can be made.

Result reliability   Prediction realism can be low for analytical modeling, depending on the quality of the assumptions that were made in order to derive the models. Moreover, real systems always have a certain amount of *variability*,[8] which may be difficult or impossible to include in the mathematical model. Such restrictive assumptions (for instance, in modeling queues, particular distributions for arrival and service times are often used) do impact result reliability.

Ease of use   Analytical models typically have a high ease of use, since this requires, at most, for the model to be evaluated in order to obtain numerical results. Note that interpreting the results may not be so easy though, as the relationship between the mathematical models and reality needs to be established.

---

[7]Note that we don't consider here the creation of the model itself, which requires significant expertise and may be expensive, nor the potential implementation in view of numerical calculations.

[8]Variability is a property of systems referring to the changes that occur in them. This variations can be predictable, if it is known in advance when they will happen, or unpredictable, if it is not possible to tell in advance what these changes are (such as the variation of the arrival intervals of packets).

2.3.2 *Network Simulation*

Anybody who has been involved in the design and implementation of a network system has probably used simulation at one point or another. Network simulation is a widely spread experimental technique, and this is mainly because of the convenience with which some experiments can be done by simulation.

Definition 2.7. *Network simulation* is a network experiment technique that employs an experimental setup consisting *entirely* of computer models of network systems, applications, and protocols.

Network simulation experiments can be done even on a single PC, and therefore the infrastructure costs are minimum. The cost of the simulation software itself can vary between very low or free, for the open-source simulators, to very high, for the commercial ones.

Even though a thorough comparison from the point of view of realism between different simulators is yet to be done, we can probably say without worrying too much of being wrong that the main differences in cost between various simulator software tools don't necessarily derive from the realism of the results. The higher price of commercial simulators is usually paid for indirect features such as increased usability, customer support, and execution speed. Commercial simulators may sometime include a larger number of models, especially for military applications, in which the details of the corresponding technologies cannot be made public, and are only provided under non-disclosure agreements. This leads to the fact that the USA Department of Defense is one of the biggest markets for commercial network simulators.

In Fig. 2.8 we show a typical simulation setup. Both the nodes of interest and all the other nodes in the test scenario are virtual, and all their properties are represented by computer models.

2.3.2.1 Methodology

Network simulation is usually done using a technique called *discrete-event simulation.*[9] Discrete-event simulation is a general

---

[9] An alternative to discrete-event simulation is to use a probabilistic representation of the system, for example, by means of finite-state machines, but this approach is by far less used than discrete-event simulation.

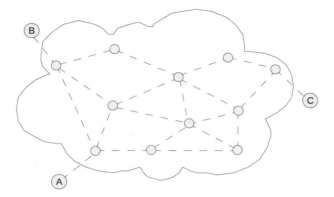

Figure 2.8. Typical simulation setup: all network components are virtual.

simulation method by which the operation of a system is represented as a chronological sequence of events. Each simulated event occurs at an instant in time and marks a change of state in the system [95]. It is usually said that simulations run in "logical time," because the discrete time of simulations is completely decoupled from the continuous real time (also known as the "wall-clock time").

Execution in discrete time is only one aspect of simulation, though. In order to be able to imitate a system through simulation, its behavior must be modeled, and this model transformed into computer-executable code. One way to accomplish this is to simply write programming code that can be directly compiled and executed on a PC. An alternative is to use a higher-level script language, which is interpreted and then executed on a PC.

To summarize, network simulation implies modeling *all* the components of a communication system, including both physical aspects (transmission media, queues, etc.) and logical elements (communication and routing protocols, applications, etc.). These computer models are then run in logical time on one or more (in the case of distributed execution) PCs. The results and observations of the experiment are then associated with the network system that was modeled.

2.3.2.2 Possible points of failure

One significant difference between reality and simulation is the use of logical time, which was discussed above. This makes simulated systems very predictable, but at the same time the simulation experiment results may not be very accurate when compared to reality.

For components that are functionally described very thoroughly by specifications (e.g., IETF RFCs), such as network protocols, accurate simulation models can be created. However, real protocol implementations may differ from standards, for example in order to improve performance compared to that of the standard protocol. Because of this, the usefulness of simulation results may suffer: the experiment may very well closely predict the performance of an ideal protocol, but may be more or less wrong when compared to the real implementations.

One more potential weakness, and perhaps the most important, is related to the necessity to model elements that enter the network scenario but for which no specification exists. The most obvious examples of this kind are radio propagation and node mobility. To model radio propagation and its components (attenuation, shadowing, etc.) one is limited to approximating the corresponding physical phenomena. The quality of this approximation depends on a series of assumptions about propagation, which may or may not hold in real cases. Similarly, to recreate node mobility one has to make several assumptions about how people and vehicles move in reality, which may or may not be relevant to all real situations. The realism of the assumptions as well as of the models themselves has a direct impact on the reliability of the results obtained.

2.3.2.3 Evaluation

Using the criteria presented in Section 2.1.3, we can evaluate network simulation as follows:

Experimentation cost One PC is sufficient to run simulation experiments, and any required changes can be introduced simply by implementing the necessary computer model modifications. Therefore, we consider experimentation cost to be low.[10]

---

[10] Simulation software itself may be quite expensive, though, and so too the expertise needed to analyze the network system under study and to create the computer models that represent it with sufficient accuracy.

Real-time execution Since simulation uses logical time, real-time execution doesn't take place.[11] For very simple scenarios, simulation execution will be much faster than real time, but for realistic large-scale scenarios, simulation is usually much slower than real time. Essentially, execution speed of simulation is not controlled, but depends on the complexity of the scenario and the processing power of the computing platform on which experiments are run.

Control over experimental conditions Simulation has absolute control over experiment conditions, since everything is virtual in a simulated environment, and hence no practical restrictions exist. The range of conditions that can be studied through network simulation is very large, since even physically impossible assumptions can be used, as in analytical modeling.

Result reliability Given the exclusive use of models in network simulation, the realism of the experimental results can be low, especially if very complex scenarios are simulated. Result quality also depends on how detailed the computer models are, but the trade-off between level of detail and execution speed implies that, more often than not, simulation uses simplified models of reality. The validity conditions of the underlying models, simplifications, and assumptions should always be considered when interpreting the experimental results of network simulations.

Ease of use Although the learning curve for network simulators is usually quite long, the ease of use when making the experiment itself is high, since all a user has to do is write the simulation scenario and execute it. The results obtained may be intuitive enough, since they are associated with virtual representations of real devices.

2.3.3 *Real-World Testing*

Real-world testing is used to verify that the characteristics of a network system, application, and protocol conform to design requirements or specifications. This is often done using prototypes

---

[11]Some network simulators do have a real-time scheduler as well, but this is used in the "emulation mode" of the simulator, so in this situation the simulator actually acts as an emulator.

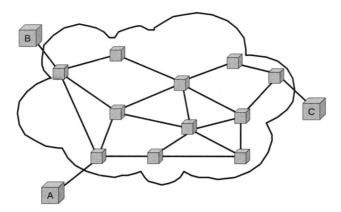

Figure 2.9. Typical real-world testing setup: all network components are real.

of the system that is to be manufactured, or early releases of the software, and — especially in the case of prototypes — happens toward the end of the development cycle.

Definition 2.8. *Real-world testing* (or *real-world trial*) is a network experiment technique that employs an experimental setup consisting *entirely* of real network systems, applications, and protocols.

In Fig. 2.9 we show a typical real-world testing setup. Both the PCs of interest and all the other network equipment involved in the experiment are real and physically available.

2.3.3.1 Methodology

The procedure for real-world testing consists in placing the real system, application, or protocol under test in a real environment (both physically and from network point of view) which is the same or very similar to that for which the corresponding system is intended. For most experiments, some kind of measurement equipment is also used, so that various parameters of the system can be quantified, and system performance can be assessed. The results of these experiments are often considered to be a definitive evaluation of the system under test, and if no problem occurs one can proceed to large-scale manufacturing of the system, or to public release in the case of software.

2.3.3.2 Possible points of failure

Even though a real environment is used in such trials, because of the intrinsic lack of control over the environment, influences that are beyond the control of the experimenter may perturb the results. If possible, all the potential influencing factors need to be measured, and their effect on the experimental results need to be estimated. Moreover, the lack of control implies that the tested conditions are limited to what the real environment provides at the time and place where the experiment is performed. The only alternative is to repeat the tests in different circumstances, aiming to obtain a statistically sound range of results. For network experiments it is customary to run the same test at different times of day and on different days of the week, since network state is tightly related to human activities. Typically one can expect a larger network utilization during business hours and on working days than during night hours and holidays. However, considering global scenarios wherein network components may be physically located in different areas of the world, planning the hours and days of an experiment so that the results are relevant may prove to be rather difficult.

To compensate for the lack of control, one may try to regulate the environment, by isolating it from external influences. This can mean using an isolated network segment, so that there is no influence from other traffic sources than those involved in the experiment. Or, for wireless communication, it can mean using a radio anechoic room, to keep out the potential interferences. Of course, one may argue that such an alteration of the real environment may actually influence the validity of the results, since the results obtained in a controlled environment may be completely different than the ones that would have been obtained in the unrestricted environment for which the network system is intended.

2.3.3.3 Evaluation

Using the criteria discussed in Section 2.1.3, real-world testing can be evaluated as follows:

Experimentation cost   Experimentation cost is high for real-world testing because of several reasons: real equipment needs to be used and configured, human users need to be involved in the experiment, etc. If the real systems don't exist yet and need to be built for the purpose of making experiments, then cost may become prohibitive. This is also true for the case when the system is already in use. Interrupting day-to-day operation of a computer network may be costly. The same can be said regarding customer dissatisfaction whenever there is a risk of worsening the system operation during the testing period.

Real-time execution   Real-world testing always implies real-time execution, since all the elements in the experiment exist physically. Although this is mostly regarded as an advantage, we have to mention that if the behavior of the system needs to be evaluated over a long duration, real-time execution may prove to be a disadvantage, and a (controlled) increase in execution speed may be preferable in such a situation.

Control over experimental conditions   In typical real-world testing, control over the global experiment conditions is low, and sometimes missing completely, since most factors may be independent of the experimenters. Trying to introduce such control may actually decrease the realism of the experiment. In real-world testing the conditions that can be studied are those of the environment in which the experiment takes place. Therefore the range of conditions that can be tested is low. One more aspect is that the behavior of potential human users participating in the experiment cannot be completely controlled (e.g., walking speed), and hence reproducibility of experiments may be low.

Result reliability   Since everything is "for real," result realism is implicitly high for real-world testing, although the results of a certain experiment may not necessarily be representative of all the possible cases. One issue to note is that when human users are involved in an experiment, one has to be aware of issues such as the "observer-expectancy effect," by which the behavior of a person involved in an experiment changes because of the explicit expectations the experimenter has from that person. Such a change may affect experimental results.

Ease of use Working with real equipment is usually very hard, especially as the scale of an experiment grows, and therefore the ease of use for real-world testing is generally low. That being said, for IT engineers it may be easier to configure a real network device — basically their daily job anyway — than to learn how to configure the equivalent virtual element that would appear in a simulation experiment.

2.3.4 *Comparison*

We claimed that network emulation is a hybrid experimentation technique that bridges the gap between network simulation and real-world testing. So far we evaluated each experiment technique, including analytical modeling, by several criteria. Readers are probably interested at this point in seeing the big picture and in knowing how exactly emulation compares to the other experimental techniques.

Let us use the same criteria as before to make an overall evaluation based on the individual ones made in the previous sections and to indicate for each criterion the strong and weak points of network emulation.

Experimentation cost Although emulation cost is typically higher than that of simulation and analytical modeling, it is still lower than that of real-world testing. Hence emulation can be regarded as an advantageous trade-off between those two experiment techniques from this point of view.

Real-time execution Network emulation is usually done in real time, and therefore it is comparable to real-world testing from this point of view, and superior to simulation and analytical modeling. Moreover, the ability to control time in emulation may actually prove as an advantage compared with real-time testing in some cases.

Control over experimental conditions Network emulation offers good control over experiment conditions, an advantage inherited from simulation and derived from the use of computer models. This makes it superior to real-world testing whenever it is desired to eliminate unwanted interferences. The ability to have reproducible experiments is a strong requirement. The range of conditions that can be studied by network emulation is large, an advantage it shares with simulation and analytical modeling, and this makes it superior to real-time testing whenever a wide range of scenarios needs to be tested.

Result reliability   Given the medium realism of network emulation experiment results, we can say that from this point of view emulation can do at least as well as simulation, if not better, and is certainly better than analytical modeling. The inclusion of real components makes emulation more fitted than simulation for scenarios in which real equipment or applications/protocols must be tested, and from this point of view it is only inferior to real-world testing.

Ease of use   Given its medium ease of use, emulation is superior to real-world testing, as it requires the use of less physical network devices. However, it is inferior to simulation and analytical modeling, since real network hardware is needed, and its configuration may become difficult for large-scale experiments. This reason may explain why simulation is actually the preferred experiment technique for most current network research. Note that in order to successfully conduct an emulation experiment one requires *both* knowledge about how to emulate the networks and skills related to setting up the real equipment. Therefore one may conceive emulation as a more challenging task, from this point of view, than doing only simulation or only real-world testing.

In Table 2.1 we summarize the above considerations so as to provide an easy-to-read qualitative view of the differences between network emulation and the other experiment techniques.

We would like to conclude this section with a remark intended to make users judge by themselves what is the best choice of an experiment technique for a particular situation. Although we believe that emulation does indeed borrow the best aspects of simulation and real-world testing, by no means do we suggest that the other experiment techniques can be disregarded. Each of them

Table 2.1. Comparison of network emulation with analytical modeling, simulation, and real-world testing

	Analytical modeling	Simulation	Real-world testing	Emulation
Experimentation cost	Very low	Low	High	Medium
Real-time execution	N/A	no	Yes	Typically yes
Control over experimental conditions	Very high	High	Low	High
Result reliability	Very Low	Low	High	Medium
Ease of use	Very high	High	Low	Medium

has its own advantages and disadvantages and may be more or less appropriate for a certain stage in the research and development process. Therefore, the technique that is the most appropriate for a particular situation should always be chosen by the involved persons after a careful and thorough deliberation.

Chapter 3

Emulators in the Wild

In the previous chapter, we discussed the concept of network emulation in general, and how it is different from other experiment techniques. Now let us give an overview of the network emulation tools that are available for use. You will see that there are almost 30 such relatively well-known tools and environments. Following the overview, we shall provide several criteria and use them to classify the presented emulators. This should help our readers put some order in the emulator world and make it an easier task for them if the need to choose and use a network emulator appears at some point in their career.

3.1 What is Out There?

The number of network emulators that exist is quite large; hence, we cannot mention all of them in this book. We have chosen some of the most important ones that are in use today in various fields of activity: research, education, commercial applications, etc. The list that we give below will briefly introduce, in alphabetic order, these tools so as to offer our readers an image of the diversity that exists "in the wild." The list will also be useful in providing examples as we

Introduction to Network Emulation
Razvan Beuran
Copyright © 2013 Pan Stanford Publishing Pte. Ltd.
ISBN 978-981-4310-91-8 (Hardcover), 978-981-4364-09-6 (eBook)
www.panstanford.com

shall proceed to classify emulation tools. Note that in Chapters 4 to 7, we shall make an in-depth analysis of several of the most frequently used emulators in several categories.

CORE   The Common Open Research Emulator, a framework that allows emulating entire networks on one or more hosts [2]. The emulated networks can be connected to live networks or other emulated networks. CORE uses virtualized networks stacks in a patched FreeBSD kernel (based on IMUNES, see below), or Linux virtual machines.

Dummynet   A software tool that can enforce queue and bandwidth limitations, delays, packet loss, and multi-path effects [94] for the outgoing and/or incoming traffic of a PC. The main execution platform for Dummynet is FreeBSD, but recently it has become possible to use it on Linux, Mac OS X and Windows. This emulator will be detailed in Section 4.1.

EMPOWER   A distributed network emulation system for both wired and wireless networks that uses virtual routers to emulate the target network topology [118]. EMPOWER can generate user-defined network conditions and traffic dynamics at packet level. EMPOWER is highly scalable in that each emulator node can be configured to emulate multiple network nodes.

Emulab   A network testbed, giving researchers a wide range of environments in which to develop, debug, and evaluate their systems [108]. Emulab provides integrated access to several experimental environments, such as a wired network testbed, a wireless IEEE 802.11a/b/g testbed deployed on multiple floors of an office building, and a sensor network testbed. This system will be described in more detail in Section 7.1.

Hurricane   A family of IP network hardware emulators developed by PacketStorm Communications, Inc., that provides WAN emulation and network simulation features [82]. Hurricane products can introduce various kinds of impairments so as to reproduce various network conditions in a repeatable and controllable lab setting. This series of emulators will be described in more detail in Section 5.2.2.

IMUNES The Integrated Multi-protocol Network Emulator/ Simulator, a network topology emulation/simulation framework based on the FreeBSD operating system kernel [117]. IMUNES uses multiple lightweight virtual nodes that can be interconnected via kernel-level links to form arbitrarily complex network topologies. Each virtual node offers a set of capabilities identical to the standard FreeBSD kernel. This enables each virtual node to run a private copy of any unmodified user-level application, including routing protocol daemons, traffic generators, analyzers, or application servers.

INE The iTrinegy Network Emulator, a family of emulation products by iTrinegy, Ltd. [44]. INE products enable users to recreate a variety of network conditions, such as latency, jitter, packet loss/error/reordering, and bandwidth restrictions. Therefore INE can be used to emulate environments such as WANs, WLANs, GPRS, 3G, satellite, and MPLS networks. Although most of the INE variants are hardware, a software solution is available as well, called "INE for Windows."

LANforge-ICE A software emulator from Candela Technologies capable of emulating networks of various latency, throughput, and packet degradation characteristics for speeds up to 1 Gbps [19]. LANforge-ICE applies these characteristics to flows defined by source and destination IP addresses (or sub-nets) and MAC addresses.

Linktropy A family of WAN emulation products from Apposite Technologies [5]. Linktropy WAN Emulators simulate wide-area network bandwidth, delay, jitter, packet loss, congestion, and other important link impairments to test the performance of applications in the lab under a spectrum of realistic conditions. The Linktropy Player/Recorder captures and replays the conditions of a live link, and the Linktropy Scheduler makes it easy to emulate even dynamically changing network conditions. This series of emulators will be described in more detail in Section 5.4.1.

Maxwell The Maxwell network emulator aims to help network managers, software developers, and testers learn how their products will perform in real-world production networks (satellite networks) and the Internet [41]. The emulator captures and changes network flows, so as to induce the conditions that cause network congestion, slow links, time outs, and many other adverse network conditions.

ModelNet A scalable Internet emulation environment that enables researchers to deploy unmodified software prototypes in a configurable Internet-like environment and subject them to faults and varying network conditions [109]. In ModelNet, edge nodes running a user-specified operating system and application software are configured to route their packets through a set of core nodes, which cooperate to subject the traffic to the bandwidth, congestion constraints, latency, and loss profile of a target network topology.

NCTUns An extensible network simulator and emulator capable of simulating various protocols used in both wired and wireless IP networks [111]. Its core technology is based on a kernel re-entering methodology, so that NCTUns can easily be used as an emulator. An external host in the real world can exchange packets with nodes in a network simulated by NCTUns. Two external hosts in the real world can also exchange their packets via a network simulated by NCTUns. NCTUns uses the real-life Linux TCP/IP protocol stack to generate the simulation results. Thus, any real-life UNIX application program can be run on a simulated node without any modification. Application programs developed during simulation studies can be subsequently deployed and run on real-world UNIX machines. This simulator will be described in more detail in Section 6.4.

NetDisturb An IP network emulator software developed by Omnicor [78]. NetDisturb can reproduce impairments (latency, delay, jitter, limited bandwidth, and lost packets) over IP networks. NetDisturb is inserted between two Ethernet segments (either on the same IP network or in two different IP networks) and operates bi-directional packet transfer on Ethernet, Fast Ethernet, and Gigabit Ethernet network interface cards.

NetEm A software tool that provides network emulation functionality for testing protocols by emulating the properties of wide area networks, such as variable delay, loss, packet duplication, and re-ordering [37]. NetEm is included in most Linux distributions with 2.6 kernels and is controlled by the command line tool "tc," which is part of the "iproute2" package of tools. The following effects can be introduced using NetEm: delay effects (including correlation and predefined distributions), packet effects (loss, duplication, corruption, re-ordering), and rate control by means of several queuing disciplines. This emulator will be detailed in Section 4.3.

Netropy A family of WAN emulation products from Apposite Technologies [5]. Netropy WAN Emulators simulate wide-area network bandwidth, delay, jitter, packet loss, congestion, and other important link impairments to test the performance of applications in the lab under a spectrum of realistic conditions. Netropy products can emulate terrestrial, wireless, satellite, Internet, and other type of wide area networks. This emulator series will be described in more detail in Section 5.4.2.

NIST Net The NIST (National Institute of Standards and Technology) Network Emulation Tool, a software package that allows a single Linux PC to emulate a wide variety of network conditions [22]. NIST Net is intended for reproducing performance dynamics in IP networks and can emulate the critical end-to-end performance characteristics imposed by various wide area network situations (e.g., congestion loss) or by various underlying sub-network technologies (e.g., asymmetric bandwidth situations of xDSL and cable modems). NIST Net is implemented as a kernel module extension to the Linux operating system. Some of its features include tunable packet delay distributions, packet loss, bandwidth limitation, and packet reordering or duplication. NIST Net can also be driven by traces produced from measurements of actual network conditions. This emulator will be detailed in Section 4.2.

Ns-2 A discrete event simulator targeted at networking research [105]. Ns-2 provides substantial support for simulation of TCP, routing, and multicast protocols over wired and wireless (local and satellite) networks. Ns-2 development began in 1989, and this tool has substantially evolved over the years.[1] Although Ns-2 is not a network emulator *per se*, it does offer emulation capabilities by allowing to introduce the simulator into a live network. Special objects within Ns-2 are capable of introducing live traffic into the simulator and injecting traffic from the simulator into the live network. Live traffic can pass through the simulator (transparently to the endpoints) and can be affected by objects within the simulation or by other traffic on the live network. Ns-2 can also include traffic sources or sinks that communicate with real-world entities. This simulator will be described in more detail in Section 6.1.

OMNeT++ An extensible C++ simulation framework for building network simulators for wired and wireless communication networks, on-chip networks, queueing networks, etc. [88]. OMNeT++ has a modular architecture, and support for new features can be added through custom extensions. Currently such extensions have been developed for real-time simulation, network emulation, database integration, and so on.

OPNET Modeler/SITL A network simulation suite developed by OPNET Technologies, Inc. [80]. OPNET Modeler can be used for analyzing and designing communication networks, devices, protocols, and applications. Users can analyze simulated networks to compare the impact of different technology designs on end-to-end behavior. OPNET Modeler incorporates a broad suite of protocols and technologies and includes a development environment to enable modeling of many network types and technologies. OPNET Modeler can perform network emulation when using the optional System-in-the-Loop (SITL) tool, so as to interface simulations with live systems. This simulator will be described in more detail in Section 6.2.

ORBIT A wireless network testbed project at Rutgers University, the United States [115]. The objective of the project is to develop a large-scale open-access wireless networking testbed for use by the research community working on next-generation wireless

---

[1]Note that a successor for Ns-2, called Ns-3, has started being developed in 2006.

network protocols, middleware, and applications. This testbed will be described in more detail in Section 7.3.

PacketStorm A family of IP network hardware emulators developed by PacketStorm Communications, Inc., that provide WAN emulation and simulation capabilities [82]. PacketStorm emulators can impair IP and non-IP traffic through various dynamic impairments. The data generation feature of PacketStorm products makes network emulation possible without utilizing additional network resources or equipment. These emulators will be described in more detail in Section 5.2.1.

PlanetLab A globally distributed network testbed with more than 1000 nodes at over 500 sites [84]. These nodes form a research network testbed that is used for the evaluation of network services over the Internet, in particular for the research and development of new technologies for various applications of networks, such as distributed storage and peer-to-peer systems. This testbed will be described in more detail in Section 7.2.

QOMB A wireless network emulation testbed developed by the National Institute of Information and Communications Technology, Japan [15]. QOMB is used to perform large-scale wireless network emulation experiments by dynamically reconfiguring a link-level emulator such as Dummynet to recreate in the wired network the wireless communications conditions corresponding to a user-defined scenario. This testbed will be described in more detail in the third part of this book, more precisely in Chapters 9 to 12.

QualNet Developer/EXata A simulation tool developed by Scalable Network Technologies [96]. QualNet Developer is intended for the analysis of alternatives, network design, and development. It is a network evaluation software that predicts wireless, wired, and mixed-platform network and networking device performance. Initially, QualNet used to support emulation via a tool named IPNE. Scalable Network Technologies now markets a separate product that combines the functionality of QualNet and IPNE, called EXata. EXata is intended for network testing, training, and operation activities. EXata makes it possible to evaluate on-the-move communication networks by creating a digital network replica that interfaces with real networks in real time, using real applications. These tools will be described in more detail in Section 6.3.

Shunra VE A family of WAN emulation products developed by Shunra, Inc. [99]. The Shunra VE (Virtual Enterprise) network emulators can create a replica of a network and incorporate a variety of network attributes into their emulation models, including the round-trip time across the network (latency), the amount of available bandwidth, a given degree of packet loss, duplication of packets, reordering packets, and network jitter. These tools will be described in more detail in Section 5.1.

Simena NE A family of hardware and software solutions for network emulation from Simena, Inc. [100]. The NE series of emulators reproduces bandwidth limitations, latency, and congestion by transparently capturing and processing the data packets. This series of emulators will be described in more detail in Section 5.3.3.

Simena PTC A hardware solution for network emulation from Simena, Inc. [101]. This appliance can be used for network protocols such as IP, IPX, and AppleTalk. Since it operates at Ethernet layer (true wire speed), it does not require any configuration change on networks or servers. This emulator will be described in more detail in Section 5.3.2.

StarBED A large-scale network experiment environment at the National Institute of Information and Communications Technology, Hokuriku Research Center, Ishikawa, Japan [64]. StarBED currently provides more than 1000 PCs for experiments; the PCs are all interconnected by means of several switches. The experiment-support software tools SpringOS and RUNE are available so as to facilitate large-scale experiments. This testbed will be described in more detail in Chapter 11.

Tornado A WAN emulation software developed by PacketStorm Communications, Inc. that transforms a PC into a wide area network [82]. This allows IT network professionals to perform pre-deployment testing in a lab environment for applications such as ERP, storage, VoIP, videoconferencing, e-commerce, data center consolidation, disaster recovery, and Web services. This emulator will be described in more detail in Section 5.2.3.

WISER   The Wireless IP Scalable Network Emulator, a network emulation software jointly developed by Telcordia Technologies and Candela Technologies for evaluating network system end-to-end performance in a large-scale environment [107]. WISER enables the development and testing of real-world software applications, middleware, and advanced networking features in connection with mobile wireless networks.

XGEM/GEM   A family of hardware Ethernet network emulation products by Anue Systems, Inc. [3]. GEM products are intended for emulating 10/100/Gigabit Ethernet or IP-based networks in a lab environment. XGEM products also support 10 Gigabit Ethernet. The XGEM/GEM emulators can reproduce the delay and impairments experienced by Ethernet frames across MANs and WANs regardless of the underlying transport mechanism. These emulators will be described in more detail in Section 5.5.1 and Section 5.5.2.

3.2 Emulator Classification

The definitions of network simulation and real-world testing place these two methodologies at two extremes: simulation uses exclusively logical models, whereas real-world testing uses exclusively real systems. Network emulation is situated in-between and uses, to various extents, modeling and real elements. How much is modeled and how much is real in an emulation influences the results obtained and is also related to other aspects such as execution speed. Execution speed is also determined by characteristics such as whether the implementation is done in software or hardware and whether execution is centralized or distributed.

The network emulation approach that is most suited for a particular case depends on the specific requirements of that case. To be able to judge quickly whether a solution is appropriate for a particular problem, we provide here a classification system that can be used for characterizing a network emulation solution to help readers easily determine whether that solution is fit for their problem.

The criteria we propose for classifying network emulation techniques and the corresponding classes of emulators are as follows:

(1) based on the availability of an emulation tool

    (a) free emulators
    (b) research emulators
    (c) commercial emulators

(2) based on the manner in which functionality is implemented

    (a) software implementation
    (b) hardware implementation (i.e., appliance)
    (c) network testbed

(3) based on the level at which the network is emulated

    (a) link-level emulation
    (b) topology-level emulation

(4) based on the complexity of the network model used

    (a) low-complexity modeling
    (b) medium-complexity modeling
    (c) high-complexity modeling

Let us now detail each of these classification criteria and emphasize the strengths and weaknesses of each class of emulators. As we shall provide a few examples in each category, please refer to Section 3.1 for a brief description of each of these emulators. Also note that Part 2 of the book contains a detailed discussion of the most important emulators and should be consulted for gaining an in-depth understanding of those network emulators.

3.2.1 *Availability*

Although availability is not an intrinsic characteristic of emulators, we believe that it is an important factor when deciding what emulation tool to choose for a certain purpose, and it does provide an insight into the expectations one may have from a certain emulator. Using this criterion, we distinguish the following types of emulators:

Free emulators This class includes those network emulators that are free to use and that have wide availability, being included in standard operating systems or very easy to install. In many cases, such emulators are open source and, hence, can be extended by users if the default functionality is insufficient. Support for free emulators is limited or may be lacking completely.

Research emulators   We consider a network emulator to fall into this category if its availability is limited to the research community, it may be difficult to obtain, and it requires moderate to high level of computer and networking skills to install and use. Note that such emulators may be free for use or may require licenses for use in commercial environments. Technical support may be available for research emulators, but is limited to the human resources that the teams involved in their development can spare.

Commercial emulators   This type of network emulator refers to all the emulation solutions that are provided on a commercial basis. Typically they are easy to use and install, and there is professional documentation and technical support available. The source code is usually not provided; therefore, they are not extensible by end users but could be extended by the company that markets them on a contract basis.

3.2.2 *Implementation Manner*

The manner in which emulation functionality is implemented is an important criterion in choosing a tool when one wishes to perform emulation experiments. On the one hand, software emulators are attractive from the point of pricing but may lack in performance and accuracy, especially at high operating rates. On the other hand, hardware emulators are usually expensive and may be bulky, but the performance they offer is often at line-rate level even for 10 Gbps ports.

3.2.2.1 Software emulators

Definition 3.1. A *software network emulator* is a network emulator that exists only in electronic form and requires additional hardware for execution, typically a PC or an equivalent execution platform.

   The functionality of software emulators is implemented as a computer program to be executed on a PC. Sometimes software emulator manufacturers also make available a customized laptop PC with the emulator being pre-installed, thus providing an out-of-the-box solution. However, most of the time, the computer platform for running the software emulator must be provided by the user.

Software emulators are the most often used type of emulators, especially in research environments, since they are usually cheap or even free. Their performance is, nevertheless, limited by the characteristics of the host on which they are executed. Still, since many instances of a software emulator can be deployed in the same environment, one can potentially use a distributed emulation approach, so as to spread the computing complexity to many hosts. Of course, this may introduce an overhead of communication between the emulator instances should such communication become necessary.

Software emulators are easy to deploy, since they can be run on off-the-shelf computer hosts. Most free software emulators are usually integrated with typical operating systems in research environments, such as Dummynet running on FreeBSD (see Section 4.1) and NetEm running on Linux (see Section 4.3). Others, such as the now-unmaintained NIST Net running on Linux (see Section 4.2) can be easily added to a running platform by following the installation procedure.

Free software emulators usually only have very basic emulation capabilities. This is when commercial software emulators come into play, offering a larger set of features and configuration options. Examples in this category are Shunra VE Desktop (see Section 5.1.3), Tornado from PacketStorm Communications (see Section 5.2.3), and LANforge-ICE from Candela Technologies [19]. Since they are intended for typical business environments, commercial emulators usually target Windows as execution platform and can be installed as any other Windows application.

3.2.2.2 Hardware emulators

Definition 3.2. A *hardware network emulator* is a network emulator that is supplied as a hardware appliance that provides the emulation functionality in a stand-alone manner.

It is important to note from the beginning that although a hardware emulator is an appliance, inside the "box" may very well be a PC on which a software emulation program is installed. The difference with respect to the typical software emulators is that the PC is dedicated to this task, and its operating system may be optimized for this purpose.

Another possibility is that the execution platform of a hardware emulator is FPGA based or uses an equivalent form of dedicated hardware. Such a solution typically offers higher execution speed and higher accuracy of the effects being introduced. These emulators are used mainly in commercial environments, since the high cost per unit makes deploying many of them prohibitive. Typically only one such emulator is deployed, and it is delegated the task to emulate the entire network.

Although it may be difficult to know which approach is used by a certain hardware emulator, carefully reading the documentation provided by the manufacturer should at least provide hints regarding this issue. As a rule of thumb, when line-rate execution is claimed for operating rates of up to 10 Gbps, the network emulation appliance is genuinely hardware based, since such execution rates are not yet achievable on PCs. When in doubt, do not hesitate to contact the manufacturer directly, who should provide this information.

If accuracy is an issue, understanding clearly whether a network emulation appliance is actually "hiding" a software emulator is an essential aspect. Readers should also distinguish here the hardware implementation from the all-in-one solution that some manufacturers provide, and that is only a customized laptop PC running a software network emulation implementation. The expectations from such an all-in-one solution are similar to those from software emulators, and they only bring the convenience of not having to install the software by oneself, at the cost of paying for the PC, and potentially for the customized operating system.

Hardware emulators may have more features than software emulators, especially when compared with the free ones. However, the main characteristic that make hardware solutions preferable to software ones under some circumstances is the fact that genuine hardware emulators are able to operate at line rate for each of their ports, even at 10 Gbps speeds.

Some examples of hardware network emulators are Shunra VE Appliance from Shunra (see Section 5.1.1), Hurricane series from PacketStorm Communications (see Section 5.2.2), PTC3000 from Simena (see Section 5.3.2), Netropy 10G from Apposite Technologies (see Section 5.4.2), and GEM from Anue Systems (see Section 5.5.2).

Note that many times the same company will sell both software and hardware versions of the same emulator. The two versions usually share some functionality, with the hardware version being the solution of choice for the case when high speed and high accuracy are needed. Considering the case of Shunra, for instance, Shunra VE Desktop is the software network emulator, and Shunra VE Appliance is the hardware-based network emulation solution (cf. Section 5.1). In the same way, Tornado is the software solution, and Hurricane is the hardware solution of PacketStorm Communications (cf. Section 5.2).

3.2.2.3 Network testbeds

Definition 3.3. A *testbed-based network emulator* is a network emulator that is built on top of a network testbed that is used as the experiment execution platform.

A network testbed is a cluster of computers and the related networking hardware (e.g., switches and routers). A testbed differs from a typical network by the fact that it is dedicated to testing purposes, and it is often isolated from production networks. Some testbeds do include nodes that are connected to production networks, and despite the complications that arise, related to security and the necessity to control the traffic that leaves the testbed, such a solution may be chosen for two reasons:

- A connection to an external network allows injecting outside traffic into the testbed.
- The external network connection makes it possible to include in the testbed nodes that are physically remote locations and thus use the Internet as part of the environment in which the experiment is performed.

Testbeds are certainly hardware based; however, they differ from the hardware emulators since they are a *collection* of hardware devices that can be used for network testing purposes, including network emulation. Testbeds are a convenient solution for network testing in general, and network emulation in particular, for several reasons:

- The testbed hardware can be reused for several experiments, without the need to set up and interconnect the hardware devices each time.
- Custom software can be written for a particular testbed to simplify the tasks of managing the experiment done on that testbed (see also Section 3.3.3.2).
- Testbeds allow conducting large-scale experiments at a cheaper cost than it would be typically possible by purchasing the necessary hardware, or by reallocating existing hardware for testing purposes.

Although testbeds are mainly used for research purposes and in connection with not-for-profit activities, some testbeds can also be used by commercial companies. Moreover, large corporations may be able to build their own testbeds if network experiments need to be done on a repeated basis.

Several examples of large-scale network testbeds are Emulab, which was created at the University of Utah in the United States (see Section 7.1), PlanetLab, a globally distributed testbed (see Section 7.2), and StarBED, run by the National Institute of Information and Communications Technology in Japan (see Chapter 11).

3.2.3 *Emulation Level*

In its simplest form, network emulation can be done at link level. This means that the emulator is in charge of emulating the network effects that occur on a network link: bandwidth limitation, packet loss, and delay. However, to obtain more realistic results, one may wish to use an emulator to reproduce an entire network topology, defined either node by node and link by link, or — in a more abstract manner — at sub-network level.

3.2.3.1 Link-level emulators

Definition 3.4. A *link-level network emulator* is a network emulator that creates in an unmediated manner the end-to-end characteristics (network quality degradation) of the connection between two network devices.

Given the simplicity of this approach, link-level emulators can be regarded as an "entry-level approach" to network emulation. While this alternative is supported by all emulators, do bear in mind that it may be the only feature of free or cheap software network emulators. Note that most modern network emulators, even when doing exclusively link-level emulation, will attempt to reproduce a realistic end-to-end connection through a complex network. This is done by introducing a variation of network parameters, so that the effect of varying conditions in a real network is reproduced.

Consider the case of packet loss. A basic link-level emulator allows the user to set a fixed packet loss rate, which is perhaps the most appropriate choice when loss is an effect of physical errors. A more complex link-level emulator would permit additional settings, such as parameters describing burst loss, which occurs in a real network due to the interaction between concurrent traffic flows.

Now let us look at delay. A basic link-level emulator permits to configure a fixed end-to-end delay. This is typical for reproducing constant parameters such as propagation delay and transmission delay.[2] A more complex link-level emulator would allow to configure a variable delay (e.g., by using a normal distribution with a certain mean and variance). Such a model is intended to reproduce the delay variation in a real network, where queue occupancy in the network devices between the two endpoints changes in time depending on traffic load.

In summary, we shall refer to a network emulator as a "link-level emulator" whenever the parameters it reproduces directly represent an end-to-end connection, no matter whether this is done using fixed end-to-end parameters, or the intermediate links are abstracted through statistical models into individual values of

---

[2] Note that transmission delay is only constant for constant packet size but will vary among packets with different sizes.

Figure 3.1.   Typical link-level emulation setup.

bandwidth, packet loss, delay, and jitter. A typical setup for link-level emulation is shown in Fig. 3.1. The block tagged "Link-Level Emulator" controls the network ΔQ between the two computers A and B according to a user-configured link model.

Examples of link-level emulators are Dummynet (see Section 4.1), NIST Net (see Section 4.2), and NetEm (see Section 4.3) for the free ones and Shunra VE Cloud (see Section 5.1.2), Simena NE100 (see Section 5.3.3), and Linktropy Mini2 from Apposite Technologies (see Section 5.4.1) for the commercial ones.

3.2.3.2 Topology-level emulators

Definition 3.5. A *topology-level network emulator* is a network emulator that reproduces fully or partially the network topology through which end points can connect to each other and the network quality degradation at link level within the reproduced topology.

Topology-level emulators use a more advanced approach to network emulation compared with the link-level ones. The idea in this case is to create in the emulation environment virtual representations of network devices, such as switches and routers, so that the network topology is built and emulated element by element. The resulting end-to-end network degradation is not the output of an overall statistical model but is the cumulative effect of the emulated virtual network devices on network traffic. The topology-level approach is supported by most commercial emulators, whether they are software or hardware. The fidelity with which the network topology is reproduced depends on how the process is actually implemented and, may vary in practice between different solutions.

For topology-level emulation, typically the user specifies on a hop-by-hop basis the topology of the network that has to be emulated. The properties of the links between hops are configured

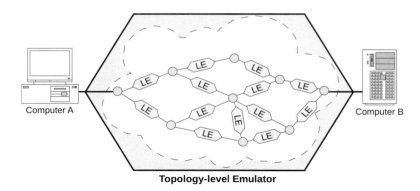

Topology-level Emulator

Figure 3.2. Typical topology-level emulation setup.

individually. Such links can represent either physical network connections, such as a 100 Mbps Ethernet connection, or can stand for physical sub-networks, such as a Transatlantic connection. Therefore, we can say that — conceptually — the network degradation on the links between the virtual network devices in a topology-level emulator is reproduced using individual link-level emulators. Of course, in terms of practical implementation, the design may be optimized so as to improve performance, and one may not necessarily find several instances of link-level emulators running in parallel within a topology-level emulator.

To summarize, we shall refer to a network emulator as a "topology-level emulator" whenever it allows the user to define the topology of the network to be emulated and the properties of its links. A typical setup for topology-level emulation is shown in Fig. 3.2. The blocks tagged "LE" are the conceptual link-level emulators that control the network ΔQ of each link in the virtual network defined within the topology-level emulator according to a user-configured link model. The end-to-end degradation between the two computers A and B is the cumulative effective of the network degradation in the virtual network devices and links on the virtual path between the two computers.

The approach of topology-level emulation is particularly useful when one wishes to reproduce a known network topology with minimal cost. This may be the case, for example, when one wishes to test *before deployment* the performance of an application on a corporation's global network. Such a corporation may have the headquarters in the United States and branches in Europe and Japan. By creating a virtual network containing the most important network devices in this global network (routers, gateways, and firewalls) that are of interest for the intended test, an IT engineer can run the application over this virtual network in a lab setting in a reproducible manner, while watching the interaction between the application and the virtual network elements.

Examples of topology-level emulators are Shunra VE Appliance from Shunra (see Section 5.1.1), Hurricane series from PacketStorm Communications (see Section 5.2.2), and NE3000 or NE2000 from Simena (see Section 5.3.3).

As a final remark, note that although link-level emulation may seem a simplistic approach when compared with topology-level emulation, it is actually useful and important in several testing scenarios and cannot be always replaced by the latter. Consider, for instance, the case of routing protocol assessment that we presented in Section 2.2.3. In such a case, it is imperative that the full topology is recreated by using real hosts, so that on each of them an instance of the new routing protocol that needs to be evaluated can be deployed. If one would use a topology-level emulator, the new routing protocol would have to be integrated with the network emulator. This may be a difficult task in itself and is actually against the goal of the experiment: testing the *real implementation* of the routing protocol. The right approach in this case would be to employ link-level emulators to reproduce the characteristics of the communication links between routers and use them in a distributed fashion running in real time on the physical network testbed on which the routing protocol is executed.

3.2.4 *Model Complexity*

The complexity of the network model used by an emulator has two consequences on emulation experiments: one related to the realism of the emulation and the other related to execution performance.

From the point of view of the realism of the network conditions that are being reproduced, too low a model complexity leads to recreating conditions that are very abstract and that never occur in practice. Although such conditions may very well be used to do some basic testing, their lack of realism may shed doubts on the results obtained in such tests.

Given the above, one may assume that higher model complexity is always better. Unfortunately, higher complexity translates into slower execution speed and, hence, into lower performance and into a lower scale of the experiments that can be performed. Therefore, in practice, there is always a trade-off to be done between the complexity of the model used for emulation and the scale and speed of emulation execution.

3.2.4.1 Low-complexity emulators

Definition 3.6. A *low-complexity network emulator* is a network emulator that only allows fixed-value configurations for the network degradation at link level.

In this category are included the emulators that only permit setting a fixed loss rate, or a fixed delay, and cannot account for more complex network phenomena such as congestion. Among the currently used emulators, we believe that only Dummynet, which is the oldest of them all, belongs to this class (see Section 4.1).

Readers should note that despite their simplicity, such emulators can, nevertheless, be successfully used in distributed emulation scenarios, a technique that will be described in Section 3.3.1.2. Moreover, extensions of Dummynet to allow specifying distributions for packet loss and delay do exist, such as the one created by the Internet Automobility Laboratory in Japan [42].

3.2.4.2 Medium-complexity emulators

Definition 3.7. A *medium-complexity network emulator* is a network emulator that allows specifying variable network parameters, either in a statistic manner, as distributions, or by using rules of variation.

When conducting experiments, it is important to choose the statistical distribution or rule of variation that is known and proved to represent the network to be emulated. Otherwise the results obtained with such an emulator may not be representative for real cases.

Most freely available network emulators, as well as most commercial emulators, such as NetEm (see Section 4.3) and Shunra VE product lines (see Section 5.1), fall into the category of medium-complexity emulators. Note that even though model complexity is increased, this does not necessarily imply that the emulated conditions are fully realistic. However, given their widely-spread use, we can infer that the level of realism of medium-complexity emulators is sufficient for most commercial applications. In other words, we can say that such emulators seem to provide currently the best trade-off between complexity (both for models and ease of use) and execution speed.

We also include in the class of medium-complexity emulators those tools that instead of, or in addition to, using models allow to "playback" a network trace that has been captured previously. Although this mechanism is certainly useful, it does assume that the captured traces include representative cases and that they fully characterize the possible conditions to be met in the real network of interest.

3.2.4.3 High-complexity emulators

Definition 3.8. A *high-complexity network emulator* is a network emulator that goes beyond simple modeling of network devices and link parameters and attempts to closely mimic reality.

Additional features that differentiate high-complexity emulators from lower-complexity one are

(1) detailed modeling of network protocols, communication channels, etc.
(2) using instances of real devices for the network topology instead of virtual ones

Table 3.1. Comparison of network emulation tools

Name	Availability	Type	Level	Complexity	Execution
CORE	Research	Software	Topology	Medium	Distributed
Dummynet	Free	Software	Link	Low	Centralized
EMPOWER	Research	Software	Topology	Medium	Distributed
Emulab	Research	Testbed	Topology	High	Distributed
Hurricane	Commercial	Hardware	Topology	Medium	Centralized
IMUNES	Research	Software	Topology	Medium	Distributed
INE for Windows	Commercial	Software	Link	Medium	Centralized
INE (others)	Commercial	Hardware	Topology	Medium	Centralized
LANforge-ICE	Commercial	Software	Topology	Medium	Centralized
Linktropy	Commercial	Hardware	Link	Medium	Centralized
Maxwell	Commercial	Hardware	Link	Medium	Centralized
ModelNet	Free	Software	Topology	High	Distributed
NCTUns	Free/commercial	Software	Topology	High	Centralized/ distributed
NetDisturb	Commercial	Software	Link	Medium	Centralized
NetEm	Free	Software	Link	Medium	Centralized
Netropy	Commercial	Hardware	Topology	Medium	Centralized
NIST Net	Free	Software	Link	Medium	Centralized/ distributed
Ns-2 (emulation mode)	Free	Software	Topology	High	Centralized
OMNeT++	Free	Software	Topology	High	Centralized
OPNET Modeler/ SITL	Commercial	Software	Topology	High	Centralized/ distributed
ORBIT	Research	Testbed	Topology	High	Distributed
PacketStorm	Commercial	Hardware	Topology	Medium	Centralized
PlanetLab	Research	Testbed	Topology	High	Distributed
QOMB	Research	Testbed	Topology	High	Distributed
QualNet Developer/ EXata	Commercial	Software	Topology	High	Centralized/ distributed
Shunra VE Appliance	Commercial	Hardware	Topology	Medium	Centralized
Shunra VE Cloud	Commercial	Software	Link	Medium	Centralized
Shunra VE Desktop	Commercial	Software	Link	Medium	Centralized/ distributed
Simena NE	Commercial	Hardware	Link/topology	Medium	Centralized
Simena PTC	Commercial	Hardware	Topology	Medium	Centralized
StarBED	Research	Testbed	Topology	High	Distributed
Tornado	Commercial	Software	Link	Medium	Centralized
WISER	Commercial	Hardware	Topology	High	Centralized
XGEM/GEM	Commercial	Hardware	Topology	Medium	Centralized

In the first category enter the simulation-based emulators, which by their nature reproduce in detail the network with all its components. Examples of simulators that have network emulation features are Ns-2 (see Section 6.1), OPNET Modeler (see Section 6.2), QualNet Developer (see Section 6.3), and NCTUns (see Section 6.4).

In the second category, we include the testbed-based emulation frameworks, in which the emulation experiment is performed on a large-scale testbed with tens and hundreds of PCs. Examples of testbed-based network emulators are Emulab (see Section 7.1), PlanetLab (see Section 7.2), ORBIT (see Section 7.3), and QOMB (see Chapter 9).

Such approaches are not so straightforward to use in a typical commercial environment; therefore, they are predominantly employed by researchers and sometimes by large companies.

3.2.5 *Summary*

Our readers may feel lost in the network emulator "ecosystem" that we have presented so far. To provide an overview of the most important emulators that are currently in use (as presented in Section 3.1), for each of these emulators we indicate in Table 3.1 the way in which we classify them according to the criteria we proposed in the current section. We add an additional criterion for this presentation, although the issue will only be detailed next in Section 3.3.1, namely the way in which emulation is executed. From this point of view, we distinguish two classes: (i) centralized execution, when the emulation functionality is exclusively provided by execution on a single system and (ii) distributed execution, when the emulation functionality is provided by execution on multiple systems.

3.3 Carrying Out Emulations

The following issues have to be considered in the context of effectively making emulation experiments:

- emulation execution, i.e., how to execute the emulation tool itself
- application execution, i.e., how to run the necessary applications
- experiment execution, i.e., how to perform the emulation experiment as a whole, including all of the above elements

3.3.1 *Emulation Execution*

The possibilities of emulation execution can be classified into the following categories and sub-categories:

- centralized emulation
- distributed emulation
  - — fully distributed emulation
  - — partially distributed emulation

When executing an emulation tool, one has several constraints related to the execution platform, since emulation tools can be run on one computer, using some specialized hardware, or using a testbed, depending on the implementation manner (see Section 3.2.2). Therefore, not all of the above categories may be usable in connection with a certain tool.

3.3.1.1 Centralized emulation

In centralized emulation execution, the emulation is effectively performed on a single piece of hardware, be it a computer when using a software network emulator or a dedicated device when using hardware emulation. A typical setup for centralized emulation is presented in Fig. 3.3.

The central emulation unit in Fig. 3.3 acts as a bridge through which all the network traffic passes. The application hosts are connected to the emulation unit and communicate through it. The simplest scenario one can imagine is that in which the application hosts (end nodes) are connected directly to the network interfaces of the emulation unit. This scenario eliminates any other source of network degradation, but the possibilities are limited by the number of ports on the emulation unit.

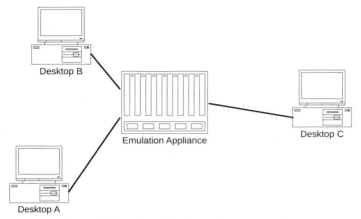

Figure 3.3. Centralized emulation execution.

If the unit does not have enough ports available to accommodate all the end nodes in the experiment, some kind of network switching equipment must be employed. Thus, an arbitrary number of end nodes can use the emulation unit. The drawback in this case is that the network equipment may introduce some additional degradation to that of the emulation unit. However, if the additional degradation can be considered negligible when compared with that of the emulation unit, this solution does not pose a significant problem.

In the example shown in Fig. 3.3, we consider that there are three clients, the desktops A, B, and C running an application, such as videoconferencing, or a routing protocol. The network traffic between all of the clients goes through the "emulation appliance," as all the PCs are connected directly to the ports of the appliance. Although this figure only shows a particular small-scale case, it is easy to generalize the setup for other situations, such as the following:

- The PCs involved in the experiment can have different characteristics, such as low specifications for clients and high specifications for servers, and the resulting setup can be used to test a Web-based application.
- Instead of the emulation appliance it is possible to use a computer running a software network emulator. In this case

a network switch is probably needed to connect the end nodes to the emulation host, since the number of NICs that are available on typical PCs is limited.

With the centralized approach, if the emulation unit does only link emulation, then system performance will depend solely on the load injected by the application hosts. However, if the emulation unit does topology emulation as well, then the complexity of the emulated network has an important influence on system performance and one must be careful to check in advance what the limits on the size of the emulated network are.

3.3.1.2 Distributed execution

In the distributed-execution approach, the emulation task is distributed to all or several of the hosts participating in the experiment. In this way the computational power needed per host is reduced. The disadvantage of this approach is that, if the emulation execution on a host cannot be done independently from that on the other hosts, then a communication mechanism between the hosts needs to be introduced. Such a requirement does not appear in the centralized-emulation approach, since all the processes are executed on the same host in that case.

Note that distributed emulation execution uses link-level emulators to reproduce the communication conditions between a node and all the other nodes with which it can communicate. The way in which link emulation is done is, nevertheless, implementation specific.

Within the class of distributed-execution approaches, we distinguish the following two categories, depending on whether all of the hosts in an experiment or only several of them participate to emulation execution:

- fully distributed execution
- partially distributed execution

Fully distributed execution　The straightforward way to distribute the execution of emulation is to assign the task of emulating the communication of one node to one host. Usually the host

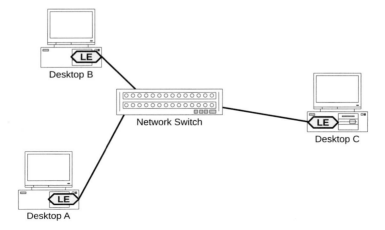

Figure 3.4. Fully distributed execution: Both applications and emulation run on the same host.

representing the network node will also run the emulation task that reproduces the communication conditions between that network node and the other nodes in the scenario. The disadvantage of this approach is that some restrictions are imposed on the operating system used for the application. For example, if one uses Dummynet as link emulator, then the application must also run on the same operating system as Dummynet, which is FreeBSD.

This type of approach is illustrated in Fig. 3.4. Note the module labeled "LE" that is running on each of the desktops involved in the experiment. This module is the link-level emulator that we discussed previously, and its role is to ensure that the communication conditions between a node and all the others recreate the conditions in the virtual network that is being emulated, which may very well be the global network that we showed in Fig. 2.3. Please bear in mind that for larger-scale experiments a single network switch may be insufficient; if that is the case, a switch cluster must be used instead for interconnecting all the participating nodes.

To eliminate the restriction on operating system mentioned previously, a possibility that was proposed by the authors of SWOON which is an emulation-based testbed created for security-related experiments, is to group hosts in pairs [39]. One of the hosts in a

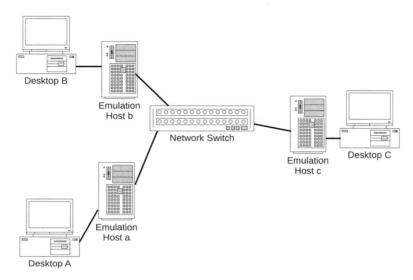

Figure 3.5. Fully distributed execution: Applications and emulation run on different hosts.

pair will be the application host, with an arbitrary operating system, and the other will be the emulation host (called "shadow node" by the authors of SWOON). The application node is connected only to the shadow node, which acts as a bridge and forwards the traffic to and from the application host to the other shadow nodes that correspond to the communication peer node of the application node. While such an approach allows using custom operating systems for emulation and arbitrary operating systems for applications, it does have the disadvantage of doubling the number of hosts effectively required to perform an experiment.

This second approach for fully distributed emulation is illustrated in Fig. 3.5. In addition to the three desktops, three additional PCs are needed for the emulation hosts, and are denoted by the lower-case letters a, b, and c in the figure. All the traffic exchanged between desktops passes through the emulation hosts that are in charge of reproducing the conditions of the emulated virtual network.

One can also imagine a hybrid approach between the two mentioned here, in which a hardware virtualization technology is

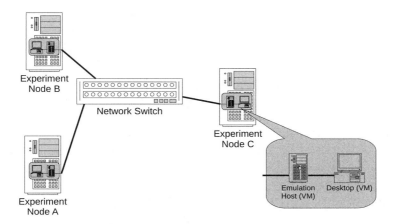

Figure 3.6. Fully distributed execution: Applications and emulation run on different virtual machines executed on the same host.

used to make it possible to run two operating systems on the same physical host, one for applications and the another for emulation. This solution eliminates the need to have double the number of hosts that was proposed for SWOON, while keeping the flexibility advantage for the application execution. Of course, this method has the performance penalty induced by hardware virtualization, and high-specification computers, possibly having hardware-assisted virtualization mechanisms, become mandatory for the experiment hosts.

This third approach for fully distributed emulation is illustrated in Fig. 3.6. Our example shows a scenario using three experiment nodes. On each of these hosts, hardware virtualization software such as VMWare, Xen or VirtualBox is used to create two virtual machines. One of these virtual machines will play the role of the desktop running the network application of interest. The other virtual machine will play the role of the emulation host, handling all the network traffic between the desktop virtual machine on the same host and the other virtual machines running on the other experiments nodes.

Partially distributed execution   Another approach, which is effectively at midway between the centralized emulation execution and the second type of fully distributed execution approach, is the following, as proposed by the authors of ModelNet [109]. In their system, application execution and emulation execution are done on separate hosts, but the number of hosts dedicated to emulation is smaller than that dedicated to application execution. Thus, there is a pool of emulation servers, and each of these servers is in charge of reproducing the communication conditions in an area of the virtual network connecting the application hosts. When such an emulation server receives traffic from an application host in its sub-network, the server will decide whether the destination is within the same sub-network. If this is the case, then it will apply the necessary network degradation and then it will forward the traffic to the destination. On the other hand, if the traffic is intended for a node in a sub-network assigned to a different emulation server, then the emulation servers will collaborate to apply the required network degradation equivalent to transiting the two sub-networks as well as all the intermediate sub-networks that may exist. Once the process of applying network degradation is fully completed, the traffic will be forwarded to the destination host.

The partially distributed execution approach is illustrated in Fig. 3.7. Three desktop PCs, A, B, and C in our example, are connected by a typical network switch. Let us assume that A sends a packet intended for C. The routing tables of the application hosts are configured to forward all traffic to the emulation servers. Therefore, the traffic from A will not go directly to desktop C. Instead, it is forwarded by the network switch dedicated to application hosts to the high-performance network switch in charge of connecting the emulation hosts, typically through trunking, and finally arrives at one of the emulation hosts M or N, specifically the one that is assigned to handle the traffic from the sub-network to which A belongs. Let us say that the emulation host handling node A is the one labeled M. Emulation host M will then consult the virtual network topology for the current time and will decide what are the communication conditions between A and C in the virtual network. These communication conditions may be very good or poor, and the nodes could even be disconnected from each other. Host M will then forward the packet after applying the corresponding network degradation for the sub-network it is in charge of, or it may even

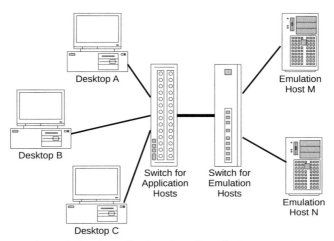

Figure 3.7. Partially distributed emulation execution.

drop it to recreate the conditions in the virtual network. The emulation hosts are connected to each other by high-speed links, so that they can quickly exchange packets if, let us say, the emulation host handling the sub-network of destination (node C) is different from the one handling the traffic source (node A).

The high-speed links (10 Gbps, or at least 1 Gbps) used in the emulation-side network are intended to minimize the undesired network degradation that is related only to the specificity of this experimental approach and does not originate from the virtual network that is emulated. Moreover, for making sure that traffic from the application hosts does not exceed the capacity of the servers, the network operating rate between the application hosts is lower, e.g., 100 Mbps. This ensures that the overhead induced by emulation when forwarding traffic, applying the network degradation, and possibly exchanging the necessary messages in order to maintain a common view of the virtual network they emulate does not interfere with the network degradation.

3.3.2 *Running Applications*

One of the specific features of emulation is that real network devices, applications, and protocols can be included in emulation experiments.

Network devices For the case of network systems, let us say a network device such as a switch or a router, powering the device, configuring and connecting it to the network, is sufficient for including it in an experiment. For this reason, we consider that for most network systems there are no significant difficulties from the point of view of emulation when conducting an experiment.[3] Two issues that one may have with emulation experiments targeted at validating network systems are as follows:

- starting and stopping the device at precise moments of time, including starting and stopping any embedded applications, such as the VoIP application in an IP phone
- logging data on the device and retrieving such logs once the experiment is finished

Both of these issues are related to the hardware nature of the network devices that we refer to. In some cases these tasks can be achieved on the device itself; however, more often than not an external device such as a network analyzer must be used to capture and record the traffic of interest. Such solutions are very specific to the devices being tested; therefore, they do not fall under the scope of this book.

Applications and protocols Network applications and protocols are software executed by a computer. This means that for application and protocol testing, the corresponding hardware infrastructure for running them must be available and their execution on the hardware platform must be initiated in a controlled way. The computer-based execution ensures that both initiation and logging can be done more easily than for network devices; however other specific issues appear.

The following sections will investigate the possibilities that exist for running applications in an emulation experiment. Most of the time our remarks also apply to network protocols, which can be seen in this context as a specific type of network application.

---

[3]We do not take into account the difficulties in configuring the network systems, which represents a different class of issues by itself.

Depending on what is being tested and the goal of the experiment, one can distinguish several alternatives when running applications, that will be detailed next:

- one application instance per host
- multiple application instances per host
- multiple applications per host
- application traffic generation

3.3.2.1 One application instance per host

The case in which each experiment host runs only one instance of an application is perhaps the most realistic scenario. This is because one human user is seldom running more instances of the same application at one time. One notable exception is that of file transfers, for which users tend to start several downloads simultaneously.

However, in a testing environment there may be scalability problems with this approach, since the number of hosts made available for the experiment must be equal to the number of application instances that need to be tested.

In Fig. 3.8 we show an example in which three desktops play the roles of Web clients and access a Web server. Emulation is done using a centralized approach by means of an emulation appliance. The number of hosts necessary to run the Web clients is three, and a total of four hosts are required.

3.3.2.2 Multiple application instances per host

To improve scalability given a limited set of hardware resources, it is possible to run several instances of one application on the same host. This mimics the case when more real users run the same network application. However, there are several reasons why such an approach may lack in accuracy:

- The total amount of traffic generated by all application instances may approach the link capacity for the connection between the host and the network.

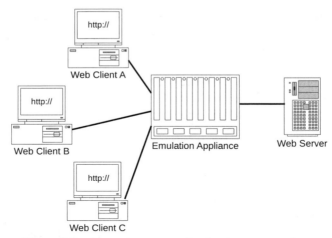

Figure 3.8. Executing one application instance per host.

- The total processing and memory requirements of all application instances may exceed the limitations of the host.
- Undesired interactions between application instances may perturb the experimental results. For instance, videoconferencing applications are probably not designed to run as multiple instances on the same host; hence, these instances may not function properly (e.g., when accessing the video card of the host).

Nevertheless, if these issues are properly handled, this method improves scalability, since the number of hosts required to run an experiment decreases proportionally with the number of application instances that are run on the same host. For the last issue that we mentioned here, a possible solution is to use hardware virtualization software and let that software handle the interactions between application instances and the physical resources of the host.

In Fig. 3.9 we show an example in which one desktop play the roles of three Web clients by running multiple instances of a Web application. Emulation is done using a centralized approach by means of an emulation appliance. Since only one host is necessary

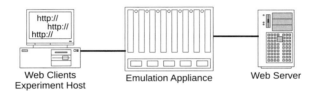

Web Clients
Experiment Host

Emulation Appliance

Web Server

Figure 3.9. Executing multiple application instances per host.

to run the three Web clients, a reduction by a factor of 3 could be achieved if using this approach compared to the previous one.

3.3.2.3 Multiple applications per host

So far we have only considered the case of instances of the *same* network application. Nevertheless, for some experiments, it may be important to see how applications interact with each other. For example, one may wish to see what is the performance of a videoconferencing or VoIP application while downloading files on the same host. For this purpose, most of the considerations made in the previous section hold. Virtualization is, however, not a solution in this case, because having multiple applications on exactly the *same* host is important for this type of experiment.

In Fig. 3.10 we show an example in which on three desktops several applications are run concurrently, such as a Web-based application, a VoIP software, and a file transfer application. Again, we consider that emulation is done using a centralized approach by means of an emulation appliance. Note that although the applications in this type of experiment can be real network applications, they could very well be application traffic generators, which produce network traffic with the same properties as real network applications; this possibility will be discussed in the next section.

3.3.2.4 Application traffic generation

In the previous sections, we have discussed general issues regarding how to conduct experiments with real network applications, done

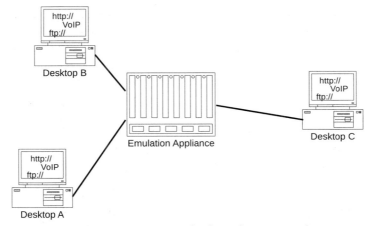

Figure 3.10. Executing multiple applications per host.

usually in order to evaluate their behavior in typical network conditions.

Nevertheless, under some circumstances, only one of the running applications is of interest and the other ones are just used to recreate the network traffic that corresponds to a realistic situation. This is the case for the file transfer traffic, whose influence on a VoIP application was being analyzed in the scenario presented in the preceding section. However, this kind of network traffic is not important *per se*, but only through the influence it has over the application of interest. Such network traffic that needs to be present in order to recreate realistic network conditions is called *background traffic*.

Background traffic generation is a method by which traffic that is *similar* to the traffic of a real application is produced in an artificial manner. For example, it is possible to reproduce traffic with the same characteristics as a sequence of file transfers (including parallel sessions), without actually transferring any useful data. A software tool such as iperf [43] and netperf [70] could be used for this purpose. In other cases, it may be important to generate traffic that is similar to one or more VoIP streams. This can be achieved by modeling features such as silence detection in VoIP software and the length of speech spurts in typical human speech. A software tool such as D-ITG (Distributed Internet Traffic Generator) [26] provides the necessary functionality in this case.

There are also several commercial tools that can be used for this purpose, both as software and hardware solutions. Products such as SmartBits from Spirent Communications [104] and the family of tools provided by Ixia [47] offer high-speed traffic generation solutions for many compliance testing purposes.

While traffic generation is certainly convenient, it may not be appropriate for all situations, such as for reasons of lack of accuracy, especially for custom applications that generate unusual traffic patterns. Moreover, if it is necessary to measure the UPQ for the application used, not only the traffic pattern but also the traffic content is important. In this case, real application content (or an equivalent) must necessarily be sent so that quality degradation from the user's point of view can be evaluated. Fortunately, most recent commercial tools include this feature for typical applications such as VoIP and video streaming.

3.3.3 *Performing Experiments*

In this section, we shall discuss all the other aspects that are relevant for putting everything together so as to perform an emulation experiment.

3.3.3.1 Experiment management

Let us assume that all the equipment and software needed for both executing the emulation and running the network systems, applications, or protocols are available, physically set up and ready to use. So what needs still to be done? Let us see in chronological order what the necessary steps for carrying out an emulation experiment are.

Configure experiment components Experiment configuration includes several or all of the following tasks:

- Configure the hardware used in the experiment, such as IP addresses for network devices and VLAN tags for switches.

- Configure the software used in the experiment, such as IP addresses for clients and servers and application or protocol-specific parameters.
- Configure the emulation software/hardware used in the experiment, such as the topology or scenario for the virtual network to be emulated and the emulated link parameters.

Manage experiment execution Managing the execution of an emulation experiment includes several or all of the following steps:

- Start the execution of the emulation software or hardware. The moment when this happens is considered to be the starting time of the emulated scenario.
- Start background traffic generation should such traffic be required for the experiment.
- Initiate the execution of the network system under test. For instance, one may need to power on the network equipment that is being evaluated, start executing the application or protocol that are being tested, etc. The order in which the experiment components are started depends on the experiment and does not necessarily happen at the beginning of the experiment. One may imagine a case in which many Web clients are started sequentially to reproduce a situation in which more and more users join the system and to help determine the breaking point of the Web server.
- End the execution of all the components involved in the experiment when the system under test has finished running or after a specified amount of time or number of events.

Collect the results Although collecting the results may not seem to be a significant part of experiment management, we believe it is important to stress that such a phase exists as well, as it may be not so trivial a task for large-scale experiments.

3.3.3.2 Management tools

Depending on how an emulation experiment is conducted, the aforementioned tasks can be more or less complicated to perform. For simple experiments, such as two end nodes communicating through an emulation host, it may be easy enough to do all the configurations by hand for all the three computers involved.

However, in order to be able to run large-scale experiments repeatedly — for instance, in order to explore the behavior of an application with hundreds of users in a wide range of network conditions — it is preferable to have a way to automate experiment execution as much as possible.

We shall now discuss two alternatives for automating experiment execution in the increasing order of their complexity.

Scripting   Scripts, such as shell scripts in Unix-based systems and batch files in Windows, are perhaps the easiest way of configuring devices, starting software, and collecting experimental results without human intervention. Here are some insights on scripting possibilities for different aspects of experiment management:

- Many emulation tools allow script-based configuration or even provide some kind of scripting language for configuration. For instance, Shunra VE Appliance includes an XML-based open API that makes it possible both to automatically manage other third-party lab resources and to be managed by them (see Section 5.1.1).
- Network devices such as switches also offer the possibility of being configured via scripting languages, such as Cisco IOS.
- On computers it is possible to use shell scripts to execute commands automatically.[4] Some applications, however, may not have good support for command-line execution; hence, we advise our readers to try to use or build applications that support configuration and operation without human intervention.
- Experimental results can be collected by using scripts, for example, by copying remotely log files from the PCs involved in the experiment to a centralized location for further analysis and study.

---

[4]A *caveat* applies when the execution of a software program needs to be started in a synchronized way on a large number of computers. In this case scripting and sequential execution of commands may not be accurate and/or fast enough for large sets of hosts.

Experiment-support software A more advanced method of performing experiments, especially for the experiment management phase, is to use special software tools that are dedicated to this a task. This solution is employed in particular in the case of network testbeds. In such a case, the investment in an experiment-support tool pays off quickly, since the same management software can be used many times on the testbed. Moreover, having a standard way of running experiments limits the trial-and-error phase that usually accompanies ad hoc scripting solutions. In addition, the experiment-support tools can be optimized for the testbed they are used on and can thus provide better performance characteristics compared with simple scripting approaches, for instance, in what concerns the time synchronization between commands. Examples of experiment-support software tools and the corresponding testbed they were designed for are

- Emulab software for managing the Emulab testbed (see Section 7.1)
- PLC (PlanetLab Central) on the PlanetLab distributed testbed (see Section 7.2)
- OMF/OML (ORBIT Management Framework/ORBIT Measurement Library) on the ORBIT wireless network testbed (see Section 7.3)
- SpringOS and RUNE experiment-support tools for StarBED (see Chapter 11)

PART II

NETWORK EMULATORS TO REMEMBER

Chapter 4

Free Network Emulators

At present, the user community widely employs three main free software network emulators:

- Dummynet
- NIST Net
- NetEm

All of these three emulators are of production quality. They are available in operating systems that are extensively used for research, such as Linux and FreeBSD. In addition to being used directly, these emulators are also integrated into testbed-based network emulators. For example, Emulab reportedly uses Dummynet on its FreeBSD nodes and NetEm on its Linux nodes [108].

4.1 Dummynet

Dummynet was developed in the second half of the 1990s by Luigi Rizzo at the University of Pisa, Italy, as a tool for testing network protocols. Dummynet can enforce queue and bandwidth limitations, delays, packet loss, and multi-path effects. The legacy Dummynet implements a weighted-fair queueing algorithm called WF^2Q+

Introduction to Network Emulation
Razvan Beuran
Copyright © 2013 Pan Stanford Publishing Pte. Ltd.
ISBN 978-981-4310-91-8 (Hardcover), 978-981-4364-09-6 (eBook)
www.panstanford.com

(improved worst-case weighted-fair queueing algorithm). Other queueing algorithms were added in recent versions. Dummynet can be used both on user workstations, to control the traffic to and from workstations, and on machines acting as routers or bridges, to control the traffic going *through* those routers and bridges.

Dummynet was initially developed for the FreeBSD operating system, with which it was integrated in 1998. Later, Dummynet was ported to Mac OS X (2006), and more recently to Linux (2009) and even Windows (2010). Despite its age, Dummynet is still actively used in many projects, such as Emulab [108] and OneLab [85].

The description we provide in this section is based on the seminal paper by Rizzo [94], as well as on a more recent technical report regarding the latest development efforts pertaining to Dummynet [21].

4.1.1 *Implementation*

Dummynet works by intercepting packets as they make their way through the protocol stack of the host. On FreeBSD, Dummynet is integrated with the tool called IPFW (IP Firewall), which is one of the FreeBSD firewall systems. IPFW *rules* are the filtering mechanism used to select which packets are passed through Dummynet and which are not.

Internally, Dummynet has a structure of objects called *pipes* and *queues*, which are used to practically enforce the network degradation effects. The pipes represent fixed-bandwidth communication channels and hence are used to enforce bandwidth limitations, but also delay and packet loss, thus reproducing data communication. The queues represent the queues of packets in network devices, which delay or drop packets when congestion occurs. The queues must to be connected to pipes; all queues that are connected to the same pipe share its bandwidth. A scheduling algorithm such as WF^2Q+ is used to determine the proportion of bandwidth that is available for serving each of these queues, depending on their allocated weights. Basically, in Dummynet the pipes are used to emulate the transmission, propagation, and reception of packets over communication networks, and the queue objects are used to reproduce the queueing effects in the network devices on the way.

Dummynet has very little overhead, as all the processing is done within the operating system kernel. There is no data copying involved to move packets through pipes, as these operations are handled using pointers. The implementation is designed to be able to handle thousands of pipes with $O(logN)$ cost, where N is the number of active pipes. The implemented weighted-fair queueing algorithm, WF^2Q+, has a complexity which is $O(logN)$ in the number of active flows, and hence it is also able to efficiently handle thousands of flows.

4.1.2 *Configuration*

Pipes and queues in Dummynet can be configured through the command-line interface provided by IPFW, and a set of operating system-specific control variables. Interested readers should consult the user manual for practical details about how to perform these configurations. We shall only conceptually discuss the possible settings in order to give an insight into the power and capabilities of Dummynet. In this subsection we use the information in the Dummynet command-line manual available on FreeBSD 5.4.

The following parameters can be configured for Dummynet pipes, but not for queues:

Bandwidth Set the amount of bandwidth allocated for the pipe, expressed either in bits or bytes per second. A value of 0, which is the default value, signifies that unlimited bandwidth will be provided for that pipe.[1]

Delay Configure the propagation delay, measured in milliseconds, through the pipe that is introduced by Dummynet. The value is

---

[1]This refers only to Dummynet-related settings; bandwidth will nevertheless be bounded by the host computer network interface data transmission rate, and possibly by operating system resources and host capabilities.

rounded to the next multiple of the operating system's internal clock tick. A clock tick on FreeBSD typically has 10 ms, but it is recommended to reduce the granularity to 1 ms or less in order to increase delay accuracy in Dummynet.[2] The default value for delay is 0, meaning that no artificial delay is introduced by Dummynet.[3]

The following parameters can be configured for Dummynet queues, but not for pipes:

Pipe number Specify the number of the pipe to which the queue should be connected. Multiple queues, having the same or different weights, can be connected to the same pipe, which computes the aggregate rate for the set of queues.

Weight Configure the weight to be used for the flows matching this queue. The weight must be in the range from 1 to 100, and defaults to the value 1.

Finally, the most important parameters that can be configured for *both* pipes and queues are as follows:

Packet loss rate Set the packet loss probability for the corresponding queue or pipe. The value must be a floating-point number in the range [0, 1], with "0" meaning no loss, and "1" representing 100% loss.

Queue size Specify the amount of storage allocated to the queue, expressed either in slots (i.e., packets) or in kilobytes. The default value is 50 slots, which is the typical queue size for Ethernet devices. Queueing delay is directly proportional to the queue size, and therefore its value must be thoroughly considered, especially when the bandwidth limit is set to low values, as the maximum queueing delay for the default queue size may be of the order of seconds in this case.

---

[2] On FreeBSD this can be done by configuring a kernel parameter named "HZ," which indicates the frequency in Hertz of the OS internal clock. For setting the frequency to 1000 Hz (hence the tick duration to 1 ms), one should use the kernel configuration instruction "options HZ=1000," and then recompile the kernel.

[3] This refers only to the intentionally introduced delays. Dummynet may actually create an unintended small amount of delay due to the processing that it performs.

RED parameters   Various parameters of the Random Early Detection (RED) queue management algorithm, which is intended to prevent congestion by dropping packets before congestion builds up. The meaning of RED parameter values depends on whether the queue size has been defined in bytes or in slots. Dummynet also supports the gentle RED (GRED) algorithm.

The following are a few other significant features of Dummynet:

- It supports dynamic queues and pipes associated with a statically defined "parent" queue or pipe. These dynamic objects are created automatically by Dummynet as needed by using flow identifiers that are constructed by masking the IP addresses, ports, and protocol types as specified by the user. For each different flow identifier, a new pipe or queue is created with the same parameters as the parent object, and matching packets are sent to it. When dynamic pipes are used, each flow will get the same bandwidth as defined by the parent pipe, whereas when dynamic queues are used, each flow will share evenly the bandwidth of the parent pipe with the other flows generated by the same queue. Queues with different weights may be connected to the same pipe. The total number of such dynamic objects is limited by a parameter called "hash table size," which has the default value 64, and the allowed range 16 to 65536. These dynamic structures are useful when it is necessary to differentiate between traffic flows that are difficult or impossible to define beforehand.
- It supports simulating loss or congestion at a remote router, by allowing the user to specify whether Dummynet packet drops are reported to the caller routine in the kernel, the normal behavior when a device queue fills up, or instead the packet is falsely reported as successfully delivered, thus mimicking a remote loss that the sender is not directly aware of.
- It allows for a packet to pass through several queues and pipes, thus reproducing the situation when a packet traverses a network made of a certain number of network devices. By default, a packet will only go through the first

matching queue and pipe pair, but this behavior can be changed by modifying the corresponding system setting.[4]

4.1.3 *Discussion*

Dummynet can be used in both classes of scenarios that were presented in Section 3.3.1, i.e., for both centralized and distributed emulation.

In the case of centralized emulation, the host on which Dummynet runs needs to be configured to behave as a bridge and must have at least two network interfaces. This means that the host will act as a sort of router and will pass the packets arriving at one of its network interfaces to the other one.[5]

For distributed execution, each host involved in the experiment must run Dummynet in order to control the traffic that it sends and receives. Note that the authors of Dummynet call this emulation manner "in-node emulation."

Let us go over the classification done in Table 3.1. As Dummynet is included by default in a standard operating system such as FreeBSD, and is also open source, we classified it as "Free" from the point of view of availability and of the "Software" type. Dummynet has no knowledge about network topology, and therefore it does emulation at the "Link" level. Since the amount of possible settings is not very high, we consider it to have a "Low" complexity.

Note that this section discusses the legacy version of Dummynet, which has been available for more than a decade. In recent years, new features were added to Dummynet, including support for more widely spread operating systems such as Linux, Mac OS X, and Windows. Moreover, the recent versions have additional

---

[4]On FreeBSD, the setting is named "net.inet.ip.fw.one_pass." The default value of "1" needs to be changed to "0" to enable multiple passes through firewall rules, and hence through Dummynet queues and pipes.

[5]On FreeBSD, in order to enable bridging, one has to assign the value "1" to the system setting "net.link.ether.bridge." Moreover, in order to also enable the firewall filtering for the traffic passing through the bridge, the setting "net.link.ether.bridge_ipfw" must also be assigned the value "1."

features such as *delay profiles* and *varying links*, which extend the emulation capabilities of Dummynet to wireless networks. Delay profiles allow users to reproduce wireless MAC overheads (such as contention, framing, retransmissions) through empirical profiles; the transmission time is thus extended by a random amount, computed by Dummynet according to a user-provided distribution. Varying links can be used to model the variability of wireless channels (including loss rates and bandwidth) over time due to factors such as external interference or mobility. A pipe corresponding to such an emulated wireless link can be in several states, each with its own set of parameters. For each state it is possible to specify, once again using empirical distribution curves, the amount of time spent in the state before moving to a new one, and the probability associated with each of the transitions. Dummynet will then randomly switch between states in a way that yields the same distribution as that programmed by the user. If we consider all these new features, then the "modern" version of Dummynet can be classified as a medium complexity network emulator.

4.2 NIST Net

NIST Net is a network emulation package that runs on Linux [22]. The first (beta) version was released in 1998, just one year after Dummynet, and several stable releases appeared in the following years. However, the project is not active anymore, and the last version was released in 2005. A reason for this is probably the emergence of another network emulator for Linux, called NetEm, that we shall discuss in Section 4.3.

The NIST Net network emulator is a general-purpose tool for emulating performance dynamics in IP networks in a wide variety of network conditions. The tool is designed to allow controlled, reproducible experiments with applications and protocols that are sensitive or adaptive to network performance in a simple laboratory setting. By operating at the IP level, NIST Net can emulate the critical end-to-end performance characteristics imposed by various wide area network situations, such as loss due to congestion, or by various underlying sub-network technologies, such as the asymmetric bandwidth provided by the various types of DSL modems.

From the NIST Net perspective, the word emulation refers to testing an application or protocol implementation inserted into a live scenario that imitates the performance characteristics of other networks. As opposed to this, simulation is a totally synthetic test environment, without a live component. Readers will notice that these definitions are in complete agreement with the ones we use in this book.

Our presentation in this section follows a paper written by Carson and Santay, who are NIST Net authors [22], as well as the web page of NIST Net [73].

4.2.1 *Implementation*

The core functionality of NIST Net is implemented as a kernel module extension to the Linux operating system. There is also an X Window System-based graphical user interface application that facilitates configuring NIST Net. The GUI allows the user to select and monitor specific traffic streams passing through the router and to apply selected performance degradation characteristics to the IP packets of each stream. Note that this functionality can also be achieved through the command line.

NIST Net allows an inexpensive PC-based router to emulate numerous complex network performance scenarios, such as

- tunable packet delay distributions
- congestion and background loss
- bandwidth limitations
- packet reordering and duplication

Two additional features are

- the possibility to drive NIST Net with traces produced from measurements of actual network conditions. This effectively allows to "play back" a recorded scenario, for instance in order to debug an application that failed in that network scenario

- support for extensions through user-defined packet handlers. Examples of uses for such packet handlers include
  - time stamping of packets
  - data collection by capturing the packets of interest
  - interception and diversion of selected flows
  - generation of protocol responses from the emulated clients

4.2.2 *Configuration*

NIST Net allows users to defines rules for pairs of source and destination IP addresses. The following parameters can be configured for each rule:

Delay Set the propagation delay introduced by NIST Net, expressed in milliseconds. NIST Net makes it possible to vary the delay in more realistic ways than the typical uniform distribution by letting users specify optional parameters, such as the variance of a Gaussian delay distribution, and the correlation of successive delay values.

Packet drop Configure the percentage of packets to be dropped by NIST Net. One can also specify the correlation between successive drop events. This also contributes to creating more realistic loss effects, since often in real networks, loss is caused by congestion and takes place as burst loss, i.e., when several packets are lost in a row.

Packet duplication Specify the percentage of packets to be duplicated by NIST Net. As for packet loss, it is possible to specify the correlation between successive duplication events.

Bandwidth Limit the throughput of the flow to a certain value expressed in bytes per second.

Congestion-dependent packet dropping mechanism NIST Net implements the queue management mechanism called DRD (derivative random drop) so as to emulate the behavior of a router in congestion conditions. NIST Net allows users to configure the minimum and maximum queue length parameters in DRD, measured in number of packets. When the number of packets in a queue reaches the configured minimum queue length, DRD starts dropping 10% of packets, and the loss percentage increases linearly until the actual queue occupancy reaches the configured maximum queue length. At the configured maximum queue length, DRD drops 95% of packets. This mechanism makes it possible to control downstream congestion. It is also possible to specify an intermediate congestion threshold between the minimum and maximum queue lengths, which are used in connection with ECN (explicit congestion notification). Thus, ECN-enabled packets that are to be dropped will only be marked with the ECN congestion flag if queue occupancy is between the minimum threshold and the congestion threshold and will be dropped if queue size exceeds the congestion threshold.

4.2.3 *Discussion*

Typically, NIST Net is installed on a computer that has two Ethernet cards dedicated to emulation. The computer is set up as a router between the two sub-networks, so that it can handle all the traffic flowing between them. This is equivalent to what we called the centralized approach. There is no restriction on the interface type, and, in addition to Ethernet, NIST Net can also operate on loopback, token ring, and PPP interfaces.

According to its developer, the computing requirements of NIST Net are reasonably low. Thus, it is reported that NIST Net has been run successfully on a 50 MHz 486 PC with 16 MB of memory doing emulation on 10 Mbps Ethernet, and also on a 200 MHz Pentium PC with 32 MB of memory doing emulation on 100 Mbps Ethernet. The measured per-packet overhead for the first configuration was around 28 microseconds, and for the second, around 5–7 microseconds. Since both these values are under the minimum inter-packet times on these networks, it is considered that NIST Net running on those platforms should have no intrinsic adverse effect on packet handling. Given that modern PC specifications largely exceed the above characteristics, it is realistic to assume that these claims should also hold for current computers. Note that NIST Net uses its own timer for operation and therefore does not depend on kernel configurations, as opposed to Dummynet and NetEm.

Regarding the second type of approach that we mentioned, that of distributed emulation, one issue to note is that the network degradation introduced by NIST Net only affects the *incoming* traffic, and not the *outgoing* one. When NIST Net is used on a router intercepting packets at receive time, this approach suffices to affect all traffic. However, this isn't true on an end node. Therefore, if NIST Net is set up on an end node, it will only process traffic going *into* that node. Although this doesn't prevent distributed emulation, it does limit the potential scenarios in which NIST Net can be used.

One more issue to note in connection with NIST Net is that, although it does not support direct configuration of packet reordering, this effect will occur if the jitter specified through a delay distribution is large enough compared with the inter-packet arrival time of a certain flow. While this can be a useful feature, at times it is something one wishes to avoid, since packet reordering may have an important effect on application performance. Whether reordering may occur naturally in the target scenario (such as through multi-path routing effects) or not is up to the user to decide. Once the decision is made, care should be taken when configuring NIST Net so as to allow or prevent the reordering effects.

If we go back to the classification done in Table 3.1, the following remarks apply to NIST Net. Since it is a tool that can be easily included in a standard operating system such as Linux, and it is also open source, we classified it as "Free" from the point of view of availability, and of the "Software" type. Since NIST Net has no knowledge about network topology, it only performs emulation at "Link" level. The range of possible configuration settings is relatively large, and therefore we consider it to have a "Medium" complexity.

4.3 NetEm

NetEm is a module providing network emulation functionality on Linux for testing protocols by emulating the properties of wide area networks [37]. The current version emulates effects such as variable delay, loss, duplication, and re-ordering. The NetEm module is enabled by default in recent Linux distribution with 2.6 kernel versions, such as Fedora, OpenSuse, Gentoo, Debian, Mandriva, or Ubuntu. NetEm is included in the collection of utilities for controlling networking and traffic in Linux called "iproute2."

Our description in this section uses the information in the paper written by the author of NetEm, Hemminger [37], as well as that on the web page of NetEm [68].

4.3.1 *Implementation*

NetEm is implemented as one of the components of the traffic controller in Linux and can be configured through the command called "tc," which is used to show and manipulate the traffic control settings of a Linux PC.

Traffic control can be used for tasks such as given below:

Shaping Control the transmission rate of a flow. Shaping doesn't refer only to lowering the available bandwidth. It can also be used to smooth out bursts in traffic for a better network behavior, since this reduces downstream congestion probability. Shaping occurs on egress.

Scheduling Plan the time for transmission of packets so as to improve interactivity for real-time traffic that needs this characteristic, while still guaranteeing bandwidth to bulk transfers. Reordering packets for transmission is also called "prioritizing" and happens only on egress.

Policing Control the properties of the arriving traffic, similar to the way in which shaping controls the properties of the outgoing traffic. Policing thus occurs on ingress.

Dropping Discard the traffic that exceeds a configured bandwidth limit. Dropping can take place both on ingress and on egress.

Traffic processing is controlled by three kinds of objects, called in this context *qdiscs*, *classes*, and *filters*. In particular, the type of object used in connection with NetEm is "qdisc," whose name is short for "queueing discipline." Qdisc is one of the elementary instruments of traffic control. Whenever the Linux kernel needs to send a packet to an interface, that packet is enqueued to the queue configured for that interface. The kernel also tries to get as many packets as possible from the queue, and provides them to the network adapter driver for being sent into the network. The simplest queueing discipline is FIFO (first-in, first-out). The FIFO queuing discipline does no processing at all, but does store traffic when the network interface cannot handle it immediately.

NetEm works by modifying the way in which queuing disciplines function and introduces additional delay or packet loss than those resulting from the normal operation of the networking interface.

4.3.2 *Configuration*

NetEm configuration is usually done via command line, using the "tc" command with the "qdisc" option followed by the "netem" modifier. Please consult the relevant documentation for specific details. Below, we shall only conceptually describe the parameters that can be configured in this way:

Delay Configure the WAN-emulated delay introduced by NetEm. The delay can be specified in several ways as follows:

- Fixed delay: This represents propagation and transmission delay (e.g., 100 ms).
- Delays uniformly distributed in a certain interval (e.g., 100 ± 10 ms): This is closer to real WANs, in which delay variation around an average occurs.
- Delays following a statistical distribution other than the uniform one, for more realistic emulation: By default NetEm supports the following distributions: normal, Pareto, and Pareto normal. However, it can also load tables specifying user-defined distributions.
- Correlated successive delay values, which try to mimic the effects of congestion: In this case a random delay value will depend on the previous one by a certain amount[6] (e.g., a 10% correlation means that there will be a 10% dependency on the previous delay value).

---

[6]The correlation in NetEm is not a true statistical correlation, but only an approximation of it.

Packet loss   Set the random packet loss introduced by NetEm, specified in percent. A value of 1%, for example, will cause approximately 1 out of 100 packets to be randomly dropped. An optional correlation between losses can also be configured. This causes the random number generator to be less random and is useful for emulating burst losses.

Packet duplication   Specify the amount of packet duplication introduced by NetEm, in percent. The syntax is the same as that used for packet loss. This feature is useful when trying to recreate a situation in which both the original packet and a retransmitted instance arrive at destination. This can happen in the case of an adaptive protocol, such as TCP, if the original packet is delayed long enough to make the protocol think that the packet was lost and retransmit it. It is important to verify how an adaptive protocol or application handles such duplication.

Packet corruption   Configure the packet corruption introduced by NetEm. Starting with Linux kernel 2.6.16, the "corrupt" option can be used to emulate the packet errors caused by noise in the transmission media. This option introduces a single bit error at a random offset in the packet. Although the bit error probability in wired and optical networks is very low (e.g., a maximum of 10^{-10} in Fast Ethernet), such errors have a considerably higher probability in wireless networks; hence, this option is particularly useful for emulating wireless networks, but can also be used to verify the robustness of the receiving end in coping with errored packets.

Packet reordering   Specify the amount of packet reordering intro-duced by NetEm. This is done to reproduce the effects that occur in networks where there are several disjoint routes between source and destination, which can cause packets to arrive at the destination in a different order than that in which they were sent. There are two different ways to effectively specify reordering in NetEm:

(1) Configure N, the index of the packet that will be sent out of order. This method uses a fixed packet indexing sequence and sends immediately every N^{th} packet, while delaying all the other packets by the amount of time configured for that queue. This is

a predictable reordering method, useful particularly for testing basic protocol aspects such as reassembly.

(2) Configure the percentage of the packets that will be sent out of order. This second method is more realistic, since in real life one cannot control precisely the fashion in which packets are reordered. A correlation between events can be specified for packet reordering, too.

Note that for any of these two reordering methods to function, a certain amount of delay must be specified for the corresponding NetEm queue. Moreover, if the configured delay is less than the inter-packet arrival time, then no reordering will take place.

Rate control   Although there is no rate control built into NetEm, one of the other disciplines in "tc" that controls bandwidth can be used for the purpose of limiting output, such as TBF (Token Bucket Filter).

4.3.3 *Discussion*

Several remarks need to be made regarding NetEm-based emulation:

- When NetEm is used to control the traffic of the host on which it is run (distributed emulation), it is important to note that loss introduced by NetEm will be reported to upper-level protocols. This may cause, for instance, TCP to quickly resend the packet; this behavior is different compared with the case when loss actually occurs in the network, is detected by TCP by the lack of the corresponding acknowledgment packet, and triggers the typical TCP retransmission mechanism and adaptation. Therefore, to test protocol response to network loss, it is necessary to use NetEm on a bridge or router (the centralized emulation approach).
- In addition to following the specific reordering configuration, NetEm will also reorder packets if the random delay values that it computes are out of order, because the default queueing discipline in NetEm keeps packets in order until they are sent. One should be aware of this potential effect

when specifying large delay variation values. Since some protocols may have very poor performance with reordering, and reordering mainly occurs in networks with multiple routes between source and destination, this "accidental" reordering may need to be avoided in some scenarios. For this purpose it is necessary to replace the internal queueing discipline of NetEm (called TFIFO) with a pure packet FIFO such as PFIFO.

- Although we have discussed only FIFO-based queueing so far, NetEm does support several other queuing disciplines that can be used for congestion control or prioritizing traffic, such as GRED and CBQ (Class-Based Queueing).

Similar to Dummynet on FreeBSD, NetEm on Linux uses the kernel tick, configured by means of the parameter named *HZ*. This configurable parameter takes values of either 100 (the default), 250, or 1000 Hz, corresponding to maximum delay resolutions of 10, 4, and 1 ms, respectively. For NetEm it is most beneficial to set HZ to 1000, which will allow for emulating delays in increments of 1 ms. In recent Linux kernel versions (2.6.22 or later), NetEm will use a feature called "high-resolution timers," if this feature is enabled. Thus NetEm can achieve a finer time granularity than when using kernel ticks.

An important thing to note is that although so far we have said that NetEm can be used only for outgoing traffic, there is actually a workaround for using NetEm with incoming traffic as well. For this purpose one needs to use a so-called Intermediate Functional Block pseudo-device (IFB). Such a virtual network device allows for attaching queuing disciplines to incoming packets and thereby enables the use of NetEm to control the network degradation of the incoming traffic. This possibility makes NetEm superior to NIST Net from this point of view and enables unrestricted distributed emulation with NetEm. We should also mention that when using NetEm on a network bridge (centralized emulation) and configuring it for both NICs of the bridge, no special workaround is needed for controlling traffic in both directions.

Concerning the classification we showed in Table 3.1, the following can be said regarding NetEm. Since it is included by default in a standard operating system such as Linux, and it is also open source, we classified NetEm as "Free" from the point of view of availability, and as a "Software" type emulator. Given that NetEm has no knowledge about network topology, it introduces network degradation only at the "Link" level. The range of possible configuration settings of NetEm is relatively large, and therefore we consider it to have a "Medium" complexity.

4.4 Comparison

After going through the detailed description of the three free network emulators Dummynet, NIST Net, and NetEm, the readers should have an understanding about the characteristics of each of them. Nevertheless, we believe that a direct comparison will help emphasize their respective strengths and weaknesses (see Table 4.1). For those who would like to have an in-depth comparison of these emulators, we recommend the paper by Nussbaum and Richard [75], from which the following table is derived.

Table 4.1 emphasizes first of all that out of these three free network emulators, only two are still being actively developed and maintained. The execution platform is different for Dummynet compared with NIST Net and NetEm. Moreover, regarding timer resolution, Dummynet is able to push the kernel clock up to 10 kHz, whereas the Linux emulators can only go up to 1 kHz or have to use different timers. Regarding the emulation direction, only Dummynet and NetEm (with a workaround) are able to introduce network degradation for both incoming and outgoing traffic. Constant bandwidth limitation is enforced by all three emulators. As for delay, only NIST Net and NetEm make it possible to use variable delay (jitter) and delay distributions. Moreover, only constant packet loss rate can be used with Dummynet, whereas the other two emulators allow specifying correlation for loss events. NIST Net and NetEm also make it possible to introduce other packet effects, such as duplication and reordering, features that are unavailable with Dummynet. As for additional network degradation support, both NIST Net and NetEm focus on reproducing congestion

Table 4.1.   Comparison of free network emulators: Dummynet, NIST Net, and NetEm

	Dummynet[a]	NIST Net	NetEm
Development status	Active (reactivated in 2006)	Inactive since 2005	Active
Platform	FreeBSD	Linux (patches required for new kernels)	Linux
Timer resolution	System clock, up to 10 kHz	Internal real-time clock	System clock, up to 1 kHz, or high-resolution timers
Emulation direction	Both incoming and outgoing	Incoming only	Outgoing only[b]
Bandwidth limitation	Constant	Constant	Constant (enforced indirectly)
Delay	Constant	Constant or variable (following a distribution, with optional correlation)	Constant or variable (following a distribution, with optional correlation)
Packet loss	Constant rate	Constant rate with optional correlation	Constant rate with optional correlation
Other packet effects	None	Duplication and reordering (indirectly)	Duplication, corruption, and reordering
Additional features	WF^2Q+ scheduling	Congestion-dependent packet dropping, traffic playback, user-defined packet handlers	Several queuing disciplines for congestion control and traffic prioritizing

[a] We discuss here the legacy Dummynet version; for the improvements starting from 2006, please refer to the discussion in the text.
[b] A workaround exists to enable network emulation for the incoming traffic, as mentioned at the end of Section 4.3.

effects. NIST Net has two features that are not available in any of the other two network emulators, namely network traffic playback and user-defined packet handlers.

Note that the modern version of Dummynet, released in March 2010, extends significantly the legacy version through features such as support for Mac OS X, Linux and Windows, delay profiles and distributions, and so forth. Therefore, while until recently it would have been easy to conclude that NetEm is currently the most feature-rich emulator and the most obvious choice for users in terms of capabilities, at this moment it is in a very tight race with the modern Dummynet, and a decision over which of them is the best becomes difficult. At least from the point of view of portability, Dummynet has the lead, and we guess that in the future more projects will exploit this flexibility.

Chapter 5

Commercial Network Emulators

The free network emulators that we have presented in the previous chapter are probably the most appropriate solution for individuals and for research environments. However, companies that have the necessary financial resources may prefer a commercial solution, and benefit of the possibility to use potentially very accurate hardware network emulators, as well as the provided customer support.

We would like to warn our readers that several of the features that we shall discuss in this chapter, such as the supported protocols and technologies, or the maximum supported bandwidth, are valid at the time of writing for the product versions that we present, and may change in the future. Therefore, their discussion should be taken only as an example of how differences between several solutions should be analyzed in order to determine which is the most appropriate alternative for a certain task.

5.1 Shunra

Shunra [99] is one of the first companies providing both hardware and software network emulation products that address the needs of IT groups throughout the application development lifecycle.

Introduction to Network Emulation
Razvan Beuran
Copyright © 2013 Pan Stanford Publishing Pte. Ltd.
ISBN 978-981-4310-91-8 (Hardcover), 978-981-4364-09-6 (eBook)
www.panstanford.com

Shunra solutions emulate production network environments in pre-deployment labs. They represent a flexible and easy way to test the performance of applications or network equipment under a wide variety of network impairments that mimic real production environments. Through this process users can understand the impact that the network and applications have on each other and on end-users, and become able to deal with potential problems before deployment.

According to the company, the three specific goals of the Shunra network emulation solutions are the following:

- Provide customers with a practical way to experience networked applications before deployment.
- Help customers mitigate the risk and cost that are associated with network-sensitive projects by addressing performance objectives before making important changes.
- Enable customers to apply software engineering practices in the early stages or even during the entire project life cycle.

Shunra was one of the pioneers of WAN emulation that lays emphasis on empirical measurements rather than mathematical modeling, a shift that focuses on the impact of the network on an application. Being able to quantify application performance not only in local development networks, but also in virtual geographically dispersed real-world-like environments helps customers handle the differences between these two.

In what follows, we shall look at the network emulation solutions provided by Shunra, generically called Shunra Virtual Enterprise (VE), starting with the hardware one, named, Shunra VE Appliance, and followed by the software solutions Shunra VE Cloud, and Shunra VE Desktop.

Our description in this section is based on the information provided on the website of Shunra regarding its Virtual Enterprise line of products [99].

5.1.1 *Shunra VE Appliance*

Shunra VE Appliance is the flagship of Shunra's network emulation solutions. Shunra VE Appliance makes it possible to construct a virtual network environment in a network lab. Thus it provides a way to test the performance of applications and network equipment under a wide variety of network impairments. However, Shunra products not only assist empirical experiments, but also provide report and analysis capabilities that can help users isolate and resolve the causes of network and application performance issues. Thus Shunra VE Appliance delivers the knowledge necessary to make informed decisions about the potential modifications of the application, network or infrastructure that may be necessary.

Shunra identified the following uses for its network emulation products, that we summarize below:

- Understand how new applications or network services will perform for remote end-users throughout the product development life cycle.
- Avoid production-related network or application problems.
- Help ensure an optimal end-user experience for remote users.
- Prevent the necessity of deploying fixes to remote end-users after deployment.
- Make informed investment decisions without the need for complex field trials.
- Troubleshoot post-production problems and verify their resolution.

5.1.1.1 Implementation

Shunra VE Appliance itself is a hardware-based network emulator. Shunra offers appliances with interfaces that range from 10/100 Mbps up to 10 Gbps, and a total switching capacity of up to 24 Gbps. Shunra's network emulation appliances have an architecture that supports flexible network topology emulation providing switching and routing capabilities between any two ports. Basically, Shunra VE Appliance functions as a bridge or router which changes on purpose the way in which network traffic travels across the local area network, by exposing data packets to network impairments similar to those on a wide area network. Shunra VE Appliance also includes packet capture buffers that enable a detailed application analysis.

Shunra VE Appliance supports a Web-based GUI for testing needs. This makes it possible for several teams to share a single appliance, and to run independent emulations in parallel. The appliances can also be controlled by a PC software program, that provides network modeling, test automation, and application performance analysis features.

5.1.1.2 Configuration

The network emulation capabilities of Shunra VE Appliance include the following:

- Various network impairments
  - delay and jitter
  - bandwidth limitation
  - congestion effects
  - packet loss
  - bit error rate
  - packet fragmentation
  - packet duplication
  - link disconnection
  - packet reordering
  - data corruption and modification
- Several types of network topologies
  - client-server scenarios
  - multiple branch offices with distributed data centers
  - full-mesh networks
  - n-tier network topologies
  - Internet-like structures
  - e-commerce-like topologies
- A wide range of network technologies
  - MPLS
  - ethernet
  - quality of service (QoS) mechanisms
  - frame relay
  - wireless and cellular networks
  - satellite networks
  - IPv4 and IPv6

- Capture and replay of production network conditions — can be used to create a "copy" of the production network in the emulator

This list of capabilities should give our readers an idea about the potential they may expect from a commercial network emulator, and emphasizes its advantages over the free network emulators described in the previous chapter. The disadvantages may be the cost, which is significantly higher, and potentially the lack of freedom to modify the emulator features as desired.

Amongst the network impairments supported by Shunra VE Appliance, there is an item which didn't appear for the free network emulators, namely *link disconnection*. Although at application level link disconnection can be emulated through a period in which packet loss reaches 100%, the "correct" way to create link disconnection is to produce the loss of signal conditions that lead to link disconnection at physical layer. Such an effect exceeds the capabilities of software network emulators, and can only be recreated on hardware platforms.

The other two elements that make the list of emulation capabilities of Shunra VE Appliance significantly longer than those for the other emulators we discussed so far are

- support for network topologies, i.e., making possible for the user to define more complex network structures than a simple end-to-end link
- support for network technologies, i.e., providing features that facilitate the emulation of other network types than those over which the emulator is running (typically Ethernet), such as wireless and satellite networks

Capture and replay is another important capability of Shunra VE Appliance that was not present in the free network emulators. This feature allows both to record production network conditions, such as latency, jitter and packet loss, and to import them into the network emulator. By replaying these recordings, Shunra VE Appliance recreates the same conditions that were seen on the production network, so that the user can test applications under conditions as close as possible to real-world ones.

Additional features of Shunra VE Appliance that are not directly related to the emulation process include

- a Microsoft Visio–based console that facilitates network modeling
- integration with load generation tools, such as LoadRunner from Hewlett-Packard, and with other traffic generators, such as the VoIP call generators, etc.
- reporting various performance metrics to facilitate the analysis of network-related troubles
- an open XML-based API for seamless integration with any lab automation tool

With the Microsoft Visio-based modeler software, users can create the desired network topology and experiment scenario. The activation of the scenario triggers the execution of the model on the appliance. From this point on, the network applications, services and infrastructures connected to the appliance will be subjected to the conditions defined in the model. This makes it possible to have a first-hand experience of how remote end-users will experience the application or server in a production environment.

Note that the experiment defined using the modeler software is not static, and users can edit any network parameter at any time, to create various scenarios (worst case, "what if," etc.). These scenarios can be replayed or modified repeatedly in order to try out alternative solutions, verify problem resolution, and compare performance between different versions or technologies.

As Shunra VE Appliance includes an XML-based open API, it is possible both to automatically manage other third party lab resources, and to be managed by them. These resources include PCs running batch scripts, FTP clients and servers, custom developed or off-the-shelf testing tools, traffic generators, network sniffers, network management systems, etc.

5.1.1.3 Discussion

Shunra provides a list of possible applications of the Shunra VE Appliance, that can be classified under two main categories:

(1) projects related to infrastructure

- data center or server consolidation
- disaster recovery and business continuity
- network capacity planning
- network design and WAN optimization
- VoIP and video conference planning
- infrastructure change management
- tasks related to the migration to IPv6
- deployment of network management tools
- deployment of network applications
- post-deployment troubleshooting of network problems

(2) projects related to performance testing

- storage-area network (SAN) testing
- pre-deployment testing for enterprise applications
- vendor equipment evaluation
- user-acceptance testing
- post-deployment troubleshooting
- wireless, cellular and satellite network testing
- e-commerce and Internet testing
- remote-application deployment
- network performance management

Let us discuss in more details two applications of Shunra VE Appliance, one from each of the two categories mentioned above:

Post-deployment troubleshooting   Shunra VE Appliance can be used to troubleshoot production network problems that occurred in the past, for instance following the deployment of a new application. The appliance stores network conditions for the last 30 days, therefore the user can "rewind" the recording to the time when the problem occurred, and determine the network state at that time. This information can help identify the source of performance problems, whether they occur in the application or in the network. Moreover, it is possible to verify whether the problem was indeed resolved after performing the required changes by replaying the network conditions that caused it in the first place.

Pre-deployment application testing Distributed applications are intended to be used by tens, hundreds or even thousands of remote end-users. The user-generated load impacts both application performance, and the performance of the network itself. Shunra VE Predictor and VE Profiler provide integration of the emulator with load testing tools, such as LoadRunner from Hewlett-Packard and SilkPerformer from Borland. These specific solutions automate the process of assessing application performance under remote end-user load and network conditions. Other third-party test tools, such as HP QuickTest Pro, IBM Rational Robot, Automated QA Test Complete, can be used as well, this time through the use of the VE Application Performance Analysis Package.

Defining a valid environment for load testing is a complex task. If the environment does not reflect real-world WAN conditions, it is possible that the results obtained and the decisions made are not valid. Examples of such potentia issues for the hypothetical case of a data center are given below:

- *Effects of WAN delay*: The larger latencies observed in WANs cause the transactions and sessions to stay open longer than they would do on a LAN. Without incorporating the WAN delay into a load testing scenario, memory usage, thread usage, and other critical server resources can be significantly underestimated.
- *Effects of WAN bandwidth limitation*: The available bandwidth for a WAN is typically lower than for a LAN, even by an order of magnitude. This limitation affects data transfers and transactions crossing the network by causing them to take longer, thus impacting on important server resources.
- *Complex effects*: The totality of the potentially increased network degradation in a WAN, induced not only by delay and bandwidth limitations, but also by the packet loss and jitter caused by congestion and interaction with other traffic, has complex effects on application performance. For instance, if specific response times are being targeted, it is important to incorporate the WAN degradation into testing so as to examine its impact on the total response time of the application under test. Shunra VE Appliance

makes it possible to quantify the total response time for remote end-users prior to deployment, and to analyze the breakdown of total response time into the client, network, and server components. Thus it assists users in diagnosing and resolving transactions that do not meet the response time requirements.

Reporting and analysis are important features of Shunra VE Appliance. For every test, the appliance provides a low-level analysis, and graphical diagnostics reports on application and network performance. This information indicates the network performance problems, and helps identify their cause. Reports and analysis are available for the following aspects:

- application performance over the network
- application availability over the network
- application performance thresholds against a range and combination of network conditions
- individual transaction performance measurements and de-tailed information (through VE Analyzer)

All the reports provided by Shunra VE Appliance can be exported to Microsoft Office documents or published in HTML format. An executive summary report in Microsoft Word is also provided. Additionally, all Shunra VE Appliance test results are stored in a central repository for easy version comparison, change control, and future reference.

5.1.2 *Shunra VE Cloud*

Shunra VE Cloud is a network emulation software product that is designed for small-to-medium sized businesses that cannot afford purchasing the appliance version.

Similarly to the appliance version, Shunra VE Cloud can be used for tasks such as

- simulating network conditions at a remote site
- exposing network problems during pre-deployment testing
- determining network capacity needs of applications and protocols

5.1.2.1 Implementation

Shunra VE Cloud is a software network emulation solution that simulates a point-to-point network link. This procedure enables testing, comparisons and predictions of application performance under a wide variety of network conditions including latency, packet loss, jitter, and bandwidth constraints up to 10 Mbps. Tests are customizable, and can be automated and easily repeated, making it possible to perform "what-if" scenarios, and to predict end-user experience, all this without requiring the costs, complexity and risks associated to testing over the production WAN.

5.1.2.2 Configuration

Shunra VE Cloud supports multiple ways to emulate network links, thus providing flexibility in creating the desired network scenarios. The parameters that can be controlled using Shunra VE Cloud are

- delay (maximum 8 s) and jitter
- bandwidth limitation

  — symmetric or asymmetric links
  — any bandwidth from 2.4 Kbps to 10 Mbps, or unlimited
  — physical layer protocol overhead

- packet loss (maximum 90%)
- queue management

  — queue size limit
  — byte mode and packet mode
  — tail drop or random early detection mechanisms

There are two manners in which the delay and loss parameters presented above can be used with Shunra VE Cloud, as follows:

- *Fully customizable mode*: The user has complete control over the testing process, and can fully customize the latency and packet loss parameters of any emulated link.
- *Pre-defined statistical latency and packet loss models*: The user can create statistical models of latency and packet loss, so as to simulate various WAN behaviors, including

worst-case scenarios. This capability is especially helpful in determining product and network limitations.

5.1.2.3 Discussion

Note that mechanisms such as queue management algorithms, which affect indirectly the loss and delay through the emulated WAN, are important for recreating realistic network conditions.

Although support for packet capture and replay are not built into Shunra VE Cloud, this can be done by using a companion software tool named Shunra VE Network Catcher. Using this tool one can capture and import real-life latency and packet loss values directly from the production network into the test environment. Shunra VE Cloud can replay these recordings, either in sequence or in random order, as well as multiply/divide them by a factor of 0–200%. This allows testing application performance and scalability in a wide range of realistic conditions representing the production network.

Similar to the appliance version, Shunra VE Cloud has reporting capabilities, albeit more limited. In particular, Shunra VE Cloud can measure and report throughput (total throughput per direction, and throughput per IP). Throughput reports and graphs help with analyzing and determining the root causes of application performance degradation. In addition, Shunra VE Cloud can also save packet traces, for a more in-depth analysis of network behavior.

5.1.3 *Shunra VE Desktop*

Shunra VE Desktop is another network emulation software solution, that comes in two versions: VE Desktop Standard and VE Desktop Professional.

5.1.3.1 Shunra VE Desktop Standard

Shunra VE Desktop Standard is a Windows-based software that emulates a network link so that application performance over a WAN can be assessed from a desktop PC. Shunra VE Desktop Standard is the entry-level version in this series, and allows the user to configure the network impairments (latency, packet loss and bandwidth) by using preconfigured drop-down menus, or by specifying fixed values through a GUI.

Shunra VE Desktop Standard is intended mainly as a simple tool for application developers that transforms the local network into a virtual WAN link. This makes the application behave as if it were being used by a remote end-user under the specified network conditions. As a result, the user can "see and feel" how the application would perform in the real world. However, no reporting and analysis support, nor the possibility to record and replay network conditions are provided.

5.1.3.2 Shunra VE Desktop Professional

Shunra VE Desktop Professional is an improved version compared to the standard software. First of all, the professional version has a client/server architecture that enables its use on multiple PCs by multiple users. Thus, Shunra VE Desktop Professional is in fact a distributed emulation tool that will transform a LAN-based testing environment to include realistic WAN-like conditions similar to those of the production environment.

Compared to the standard version, Shunra VE Desktop Professional allows users to select not only basic impairments but also complex network scenarios, thus offering more realistic emulation capabilities. Shunra VE Desktop Professional contains several pre-configured typical network topologies, and this library can be extended with user-defined ones.

Other enhancements included in the latest version of Shunra VE Desktop Professional include

- automatic delivery of post-test analysis, making it more convenient to review test results
- integration with the analysis tool called Shunra VE Analyzer for automated extraction of information from the results
- extension capabilities through an open API

5.1.3.3 Discussion

Because of the software nature of the Shunra VE Desktop solutions, they are mainly intended to be used in conjunction with application development and testing in order to verify the Quality of Experience (QoE) and performance when operating over a WAN. This makes it possible to address early potential design and implementation problems. Thus developers can save time, reduce the overall development expenses, and guarantee a satisfactory experience for end-users.

5.1.4 *Discussion*

Table 5.1 shows a comparison between the Shunra VE family products based on the presentation in [99]. The most important aspects readers that are interested in Shunra VE products should be aware of are the following:

- The VE Desktop series is intended for use on a small number of PCs by a small number of users, whereas the VE Cloud and VE Appliance versions are aimed at larger network labs and groups of users.
- The VE Desktop Standard version, as an entry level solution, is limited to very simple scenarios involving fixed parameters, and the VE Desktop Professional or VE Cloud solutions are required for investigating more complex network situations that include, for instance, congestion effects. Moreover, only the VE Appliance version allows to change network degradation while the experiment is running, or to program such changes.
- An important difference between the VE Desktop series and the other solutions is that it only allows emulating a point-to-point link originating *on* the PC on which the software is installed (distributed emulation). VE Cloud can also used on a computer bridging two networks and acting as a router, to do what we call "centralized emulation." Nevertheless, VE Appliance is the most advanced centralized emulation solution, by reproducing internally a large number of topologies.
- Regarding protocols and technologies, it is important to note that VE Cloud is only able to use the IPv4 protocol. As for network technologies such as MPLS, QoS or VLAN, they are only supported by VE Appliance.

Table 5.1.   Comparison of Shunra network emulation products

	VE Desktop Standard	VE Desktop Professional	VE Cloud	VE Appliance
Implementation platform	Software	Software	Software	Hardware
Intended use	Single desktop	Multiple desktops	Single lab user	Multiple lab users
Network impairments	Fixed latency, packet loss, bandwidth	Latency & jitter, packet loss, fixed bandwidth	Latency & jitter, packet loss, fixed bandwidth, queue management	Latency & jitter, packet loss, bandwidth, congestion effects; changes can be done in real time or programmed in advance
Network topologies	Single point-to-point link	Single point-to-point link	Single point-to-point link (can operate on a router)	Point-to-point links, hub and spoke, N-Tier, fully meshed networks
Protocols and technologies	IPv4, IPv6	IPv4, IPv6	IPv4	IPv4, IPv6, QoS, MPLS, Frame Relay, OSPF, VLAN
Reporting and analysis	None	Response time per transaction, transaction analysis breakdown, throughput per session, packet traces	Throughput reports, packet traces	Response time per transaction, transaction analysis breakdown, throughput per session, video and VoIP quality, application profiling, service level prediction
Record & replay of network conditions	No	Yes	Yes	Yes
Maximum bandwidth	1 Mbps	45 Mbps	10 Mbps	10 Gbps

- If reporting and analysis are important, the reader should consider that this feature is not available on VE Desktop Standard, and that VE Cloud has only basic reporting capabilities. For more advanced features, one should look at VE Desktop Professional or VE Appliance. The latter offers not only network-level information, but also transaction and application-level metrics, allowing, for instance, to determine the perceived quality for voice and video applications.
- Recording and replaying of network conditions is not available on VE Desktop Standard, but can be used with any of the other solutions.
- The maximum bandwidth that a user requires during experiments should also be considered when making a choice. VE Desktop Standard only supports rates up to 1 Mbps, which limits considerably the potential applications. VE Desktop Professional is usable up to 45 Mbps, which may be sufficient for most typical applications. VE Cloud restricts the maximum bandwidth utilization to 10 Mbps, probably due to the fact that in can operate in bridge mode, case in which it has to deal with the traffic flowing through two NICs. If bandwidth is a significant requirement, then VE Appliance, as a hardware implementation, is the most suited solution, allowing to go up to 10 Gbps (depending on configuration).

Note that there are several additional issues that should be taken into account when comparing network emulation products, and in particular the Shunra VE family of products. For instance, not only the maximum bandwidth is limited, but the maximum delay and jitter are also bounded to different values for each product model. The cost of the product is also an important factor in making a decision, but we did not consider this aspect in the present book.

5.2 PacketStorm Communications

PacketStorm Communications is another company with a relatively long activity in the field of network emulation [82]. PacketStorm Communications has a full family of network emulators, including both hardware versions, with PacketStorm 4XG being the top of the line, and software versions (Tornado). All the hardware-based network emulators have packet recording capabilities, and the PSCapture software can be used to provide this functionality on a PC. By capturing the network characteristics, a user can then transfer and replay them in a PacketStorm hardware emulator. The PSCapture software provides real-time graphs and histograms of the network characteristics that are being captured.

Each network emulator of the PacketStorm family is designed for a particular range of applications. The powerful PacketStorm 4XG can be used for links totaling up to 40 Gbps. The PacketStorm 2600E, PacketStorm 8400E, Hurricane, and Hurricane II are designed for Gigabit and/or many 10/100 Mbps port applications. The PacketStorm 1800E emulator targets multiple 10/100 Mbps port applications. In its turn, the Tornado software emulator addresses low bandwidth needs and simple network applications.

Our discussion in this section follows the documentation provided by PacketStorm Communication on its web site [82].

5.2.1 *PacketStorm Series*

The PacketStorm line of products is composed of PacketStorm 4XG, and also a family of lower performance products that we group under the name "E series."

5.2.1.1 PacketStorm 4XG

The PacketStorm 4XG network emulator is the flagship of the Packet-Storm Communications family of network emulation products, and provides WAN emulation for multiple 1 and 10 Gbps Ethernet ports. The most significant features of PacketStorm 4XG are the following:

- architecture supporting up to 40 Gbps and 64 million packets per second throughput[1]

---

[1] Providing the packet rate in addition to the data rate is necessary in order to indicate the performance of a network device when forwarding small-size packets, for which the packet rate corresponding to a certain data rate is much higher than for large packets.

- adaptable configuration, with up to 32 × 1 Gbps Ethernet or up to 4 × 10 Gbps Ethernet modules that can be installed in one chassis
- network and packet impairments, both for IP and non-IP traffic
- support for packet modifications and packet filtering
- collect and display traffic statistics
- capture and replay network conditions

Configuration The list of network impairments that can be introduced by PacketStorm 4XG is extensive and is as follows:

- delay and jitter
- packet drop, including decimation and burst drop
- packet duplication
- packet re-ordering
- bandwidth throttle, including packet accumulation and burst
- packet fragmentation
- packet sink
- bit error rate
- real-time packet modifications, such as changing fields, inserting and deleting data, etc.

For packet filtering, PacketStorm 4XG can use the following packet fields:

- source and destination IP addresses
- source and destination MAC addresses
- source and destination network protocol ports (UDP, TCP)
- network protocol identifier
- miscellaneous other fields, such as ToS, DiffServ, MPLS, VLAN
- a user-defined bit pattern

Discussion The PacketStorm 4XG emulator can be accessed remotely over any IP network through a browser control interface or a remote TCL command set. Such remote control provides the capability to monitor and modify if needed the emulated network scenario.

PacketStorm 4XG can do measurements and compute statistics for the following network parameters and metrics:

- bandwidth
- delay
- packet loss rate
- throughput (expressed in bytes or packets)
- media loss rate (i.e., loss rate at application level)
- QoE metrics (R-factor, MOS)

Given the high-speed processing capabilities of PacketStorm 4XG, PacketStorm Communications recommends it for network experiments in the following set of scenarios:

- network storage
- video applications
- defense industry
- network security
- network carriers
- network equipment manufacturers

5.2.1.2 PacketStorm E series

The family of products that we designated as "PacketStorm E series" includes the following products: PacketStorm 1800E, PacketStorm 2600E, and PacketStorm 8400E. The attributes that distinguish each member of the PacketStorm E series are the number and maximum data rate of interfaces they can use, as follows:

- PacketStorm 8400E has four 10/100/1000 ports and four SFP (Small Form-factor Pluggable) ports
- PacketStorm 2600E has five interface slots, which can take interfaces up to 1 Gbps
- PacketStorm 1800E has five interface slots, which can take interfaces up to 155 Mbps

The main features and capabilities of the PacketStorm E series are very similar to those of the Hurricane series, therefore the reader is referred to the previous section for details.

5.2.2 *Hurricane Series*

The Hurricane and Hurricane II network emulators create realistic network conditions in repeatable and controllable settings. This includes dynamic, time-varying impairments configured through an independent GUI, as well as data generation features.

The most important features of the Hurricane series of products are

- network and packet impairments, both for IP and non-IP traffic
- packet modifiers and packet filtering
- dynamic emulation support
- data generation capability
- statistics gathering
- support for multiple interfaces with rates up to 1 Gbps (five interface slots)
- network condition capture and replay

5.2.2.1 Configuration

When comparing in terms of network impairments, packet modifiers and filtering, the feature list of Hurricane products is similar to that of PacketStorm 4XG. The following are the two most important differences from this point of view:

(1) They support dynamic emulation, which allows users to change the degradation parameters of the emulated network as the experiment proceeds. This can be accomplished by defining the conditions that trigger changes. Each packet stream can have several different impairment profiles. In addition, impairment and modifier values can be changed on-the-fly by the user during an experiment.

(2) They support data generation, which makes it possible to inject traffic into the experiment network without the need for additional equipment.

Another difference regards the supported network interfaces. Thus, Hurricane series products can use in the five available slots only network interfaces with rates up to 1 Gbps, such as

- 10/100/1000 Ethernet
- T1/E1
- DS3
- X.21
- OC-3
- OC-12
- RS-232

5.2.2.2 Discussion

The Hurricane network emulators can decode over two hundred protocols, including IP, RTP, iSCSI, MPLS, SIP, VLAN, and WLAN. The packet analyzer tool can be used to monitor live or captured traffic. Network traffic can be filtered and displayed according to its protocol. Data is displayed in several formats: simple packet listing, with decoding of packet fields, or even in raw hexadecimal format.

The network testing fields envisaged by PacketStorm Communications for Hurricane and Hurricane II are

- enterprise networks (e.g., for intranet applications)
- application developers
- quality assurance
- network equipment manufacturers
- network carriers

5.2.3 *Tornado*

Tornado is a WAN emulation software developed by PacketStorm Communications that makes it possible to employ a PC to emulate a wide area network. This allows IT network professionals to perform pre-deployment testing for applications such as ERP, network storage, VoIP, video conferencing, e-commerce, data center consolidation, disaster recovery, and Web services.

The main features of Tornado are similar to those of the hardware emulators, albeit the number of options is reduced:

- several types of network impairments
- one-port and two-port WAN emulation
- possibility to define multiple IP networks
- traffic filtering

5.2.3.1 Configuration

The network impairments that can be reproduced with Tornado are as follows:

- delay and jitter (fixed delay, or delay following a statistical distribution)
- bandwidth/throughput limitation
- packet loss (random, including burst loss by dropping a group of packets)
- packet reordering
- packet duplication
- bit error insertion

5.2.3.2 Discussion

The number of applications for which PacketStorm Communications advises the use of Tornado is reduced compared to those for the hardware solutions. Thus, Tornado is recommended for tasks such as

- enterprise-level testing
- application performance evaluation
- remote location testing
- application development

5.2.4 *Discussion*

To conclude the presentation of the products of PacketStorm Communications, we shall first compare the network emulation solutions, and then present several other tools that are of use in this context.

5.2.4.1 Comparison

In Table 5.2 we compare the network emulation products of Packet-Storm Communications by using the corresponding documentation made available by the company on its website. The table shows that PacketStorm focuses mainly on hardware network emulation solutions, and only provides one software emulation product. The

Table 5.2. Comparison of PacketStorm Communications network emulation products

Model	Tornado	PacketStorm E Series	Hurricane and Hurricane II	PacketStorm 4XG
Type	Software	Hardware	Hardware	Hardware
Network impairments	Delay & jitter, packet loss, reordering and duplication, bandwidth limitation, bit error insertion	Same with Tornado plus packet fragmentation, packet modification, and packet sink	Same with Tornado plus packet fragmentation, packet modification, and packet sink	Same with Tornado plus packet fragmentation, packet modification, and packet sink
Number of ports	1 or 2 (multiple IP networks)	Multiple	Multiple	Multiple
Maximum data rate per interface	Not specified (host dependent)	155 Mbps for 1800E, and 1 Gbps for 2600E and 8400E	1 Gbps	10 Gbps
Filters	Advanced	Advanced	Advanced	Advanced
Dynamic emulation	Not possible	Possible	Possible	Not possible
Data generation	Not possible	Possible	Possible	Not possible
Traffic statistics	Not possible	Possible	Possible	Possible
Record & replay network conditions	Not possible	Possible	Possible	Possible
Impair IP and non-IP traffic	Not possible	Possible	Possible	Possible

hardware solutions are more or less equivalent from the point of view of network impairments they can introduce, whereas the software one, Tornado, lacks some of the advanced functions such as packet modification. Regarding the number of available ports, hardware solutions have again an advantage with a large number of ports (for instance, PacketStorm 4XG can take up to 32 1 Gbps interface). Tornado can be used with only 1 or 2 ports (including in bridge mode), however multiple IP networks can be defined. Similarly, the maximum supported rate goes from up to 10 Gbps for PacketStorm 4XG to an unspecified value for Tornado; in practice, the maximum throughput that can be handled by Tornado will depend on the specifications of the PC it is installed on, and possibly on the properties of the traffic (size of packets, lengths of bursts, etc.).

As far as the more advanced features are concerned, namely dynamic emulation and data generation, only the hardware-based emulators provide such support. At the time of writing, PacketStorm 4XG could not handle dynamic emulation nor data generation, which are supported by the other hardware emulators, but this will probably change in the future. One more thing to note is that Tornado, which is a software solution, is limited to impairing IP traffic, whereas the hardware solutions also allow impairing non-IP traffic, hence can be used for lower-level network investigations.

5.2.4.2 Other tools

PacketStorm markets two software tools that are not network emulators in themselves, but can be used in the context of network emulation. Therefore we shall briefly present them in what follows.

PSCapture The PacketStorm PSCapture network monitor and recorder software provides the capability to transfer the characteristics of a production network into the test lab. The real network data gathered by PSCapture can be replayed in PacketStorm's hardware emulators for repeatable WAN emulation experiments. Thus PSCapture is effectively a companion of the network emulation family of products.

Some of the relevant features of PSCapture are given below:

- is compatible with PacketStorm emulators
- displays real-time graphs and histograms of the traffic
- performs up to 16 simultaneous captures
- can use different formats for saving and retrieving captured data

In addition to network emulation, other potential applications of PSCapture are

- network monitoring
- network characterization
- network security

Route Analyzer   The Route Analyzer is another companion software product of the PacketStorm family of network emulation products. The Route Analyzer provides OSPF analysis and recording capabilities for network management. It is designed to monitor traffic and provide fast diagnostics. The Route Analyzer includes intelligent error analysis and four settable alarm conditions. The supported interfaces are 1 Gbps and 10 Gbps Ethernet, and OC-192C.

Route Analyzer is basically a tool for monitoring routing protocols, and could be used in the context of emulation to analyze routing-related protocol behavior or network issues. The most important features of the Route Analyzer that can be used in the context of network emulation are

- real-time monitoring of routing information
- dynamic data graphs
- recording of OSPF data

According to PacketStorm Communications, possible areas for using the Route Analyzer are

- service providers
- financial institutions
- large enterprises
- network management
- router upgrades

5.3 Simena

Simena is a company that focuses on hardware network emulators, and markets an entire family of such products [100, 101]. These products are meant to enable software developers and network engineers to determine how their product or service would perform under various network conditions, such as bandwidth limitations, latency, congestion, etc.

The network emulator products from Simena are network impairment generators, which can emulate network conditions by transparently capturing and processing the data packets. These emulators can be used for a number of network protocols, such as IP, IPX, AppleTalk, etc.

The presentation we make in this section uses information provided by Simena on its web site dedicated to network emulation products [100, 101].

5.3.1 *Overview*

Simena network emulators are available in several different models that meet various user requirements and budgets. The high-end models are true wire-speed, multi-user, multi-port appliances, and one of them is even portable, namely PTC3000.

5.3.1.1 General features

Some of the key benefits of the Simena network emulation family of products according to the company are given below:

- Speed up testing of network applications, equipments or services.
- Help organizations deliver fully tested products and services.
- Minimize the development cost and time by making it easier to find and eliminate software bugs.
- Provide quality assurance mechanisms for network applications and network equipment.
- Minimize the bandwidth cost by accurately determining bandwidth requirements of applications.
- Allow determining VoIP and video conferencing performance characteristics in a laboratory environment.
- Allow multiple users to run independent emulation experiments simultaneously.
- Realistically evaluate emerging applications, products and standards.

The general features of the Simena network emulator family of products according to the company are as follows:

- Patent-pending wire-speed network emulation for all ports. As the emulators operate at Ethernet level, no IP network reconfiguration is required. The emulator will forward the traffic between its ports soon after it is powered on, and only minimum configuration is required. The portable emulators solutions make tool sharing and carrying easy.

- Support various network connection types: point-to-point, hub and spoke, partially or fully meshed. In mesh network emulation mode, users can create uni-directional virtual connections among all the available Ethernet interfaces of the network emulator. Each such connection has associated filters that determine which packets should be sent to which virtual connections. This extended flexibility makes it possible to create any type of connection topology, such as ring, mesh, star, or fully connected. Any combination of impairments can be assigned to virtual mesh connections, and network statistics can be collected separately for each individual virtual connection.

- Support standard network models for evaluating multimedia transmission performance, namely ITU-T G.1050/TIA-921. The G.1050 standard refers to performance over IP networks in terms of network conditions and impairments. Simena's network emulators provide an interface for defining, customizing, and running G.1050-based network emulations.

- Provide up to 16 simultaneous multiple-link emulations. Simena's patent-pending technology allows users to emulate up to 16 different network degradation characteristics simultaneously through one pair of Ethernet interfaces. Users can divide the traffic into several classes using filters, and apply different network impairments to each of these classes. This capability does not require any network reconfiguration, since all of the traffic goes through the same network interfaces.

- Support QoS mechanisms through the use of up to 64 DiffServ classes.

- Provide mechanisms for multiple, stacked MPLS and VLAN (IEEE 802.11QinQ) emulation experiments. The extensive MPLS support in Simena's network emulation products makes it possible for users to filter, impair, modify, and also inject MPLS and stacked MPLS packets.

- Support real-time packet modifications. Any protocol field can be modified with user data, with checksums being optionally recomputed. With custom packet modifications, it is even possible to modify data located anywhere inside the packet, such as payloads or certain fields in proprietary protocols. Packet modifications can be utilized together with filtering and other impairments.
- Provide real-time packet analysis with packet filters on every interface. Several types of packet filters are supported, including custom filters with up to 4-byte patterns.
- Display real-time throughput in bits and packets per second in tabular and graphical formats. The results are collected from the network emulator core, therefore statistics will be reliable even when conducting heavy emulation experiments. The statistics can be saved in CSV format for further analysis with user-defined sampling rate and number of samples.
- Do not require a dedicated host, and can be configured and used via a Web browser interface that allows access to the network emulator from anywhere in the network. The GUI provides a complete set of management functions, such as configuring networking parameters, Ethernet interface properties, and system settings (date and time, user password, etc.), as well as to remotely reboot the network emulator.
- In addition to the Web-based remote management, provide in-line management capabilities. In-line management signifies that any port of the appliance can be used for management, in-line with the test traffic. This allows users to connect to the network emulator directly from the workstations used in the experiment, without the need for additional network cables.
- Provide Command Line Interface (CLI) for controlling the network emulators and scripting.
- Make available an on-line user guide in hypertext format that facilitates navigation when attempting to perform complex experiments or administrative tasks.

- Enable users to perform detailed IPv6 emulation tests. IPv6-specific filters, such as "traffic class," "flow label," and "hop limit," allow selecting specific IPv6 packets. Filtering can also use source and destination addresses (single values or a ranges of addresses). The "next header" filter can be used to parse cascaded headers. In addition, the "fragmentation ID" filter can be used to identify all or some of the fragmented packets.

5.3.1.2 Configuration

Simena network emulators allow saving, loading, and deleting multiple configurations. This makes it easy to switch between different experiments, and increases overall product usability.

The possible configuration options of Simena products are listed below, split into four categories:

(1) emulated network types

- point-to-point links
- partially and fully meshed networks
- hub and spoke networks

(2) experiment types

- uni- and bi-directional emulations
- simultaneous emulations

(3) network degradation parameters

- delay
  - — fixed delay
  - — uniform and normal distributions
  - — jitter
- packet loss
  - — fixed packet loss
  - — dynamic packet loss
  - — burst packet loss, including accumulate and burst
- bandwidth
- additional packet effects
  - — fixed and dynamic packet duplication

- — random packet reordering
- — packet modifications
- — congestion emulation
- — bit error injection

(4) other features

- packet filtering
- carrier loss emulation
- VLAN emulation
- jumbo frame support
- packet fragmentation

As mentioned before, Simena products allow to use filters for selecting the traffic flows to which network degradation is applied. These filters are described in an XML-based language that allows users to define custom packet filters. Thus one can easily define filters for specific network protocols, such as IPTV, iSCSI, etc. The filters can be combined with logical operators to create more complex filter sets. In addition, filters can be even defined on the packet payload.

For example, Simena network emulators can be used for impairing MPEG-based video streams, such as those for IPTV. Since the network emulator dynamically examines every byte in packets, users can easily impair specific video packets, such as the MPEG-specific I, P and B frames. The impairments can be applied to video streams both uni- and bi-directionally, and are configurable through detailed packet filters.

The following list shows the available filter types for Simena network emulators, split into several categories:

- Ethernet level
  - — Ethernet source and destination addresses
  - — Ethernet payload type
  - — VLAN priority
  - — VLAN IDs
  - — stacked VLANs
  - — MPLS
- IP level
  - — IP source and destination addresses

- IP payload type
- DiffServ TOS (Type of Service)
- IPv6 traffic class
- IPv6 flow label
- IPv6 payload length
- IPv6 next header
- IPv6 hop limit
- IPv6 source and destination addresses
- IPv6 fragment ID

- Other filters

  - TCP source and destination port
  - TCP flags
  - UDP source and destination port
  - custom filters: up to 4-byte patterns can be used to match packets against data found at user-defined offsets

One of the important features of Simena network emulators is that the packets can be modified on-the-fly during an experiment. The following packet modifications are possible in this manner, by category:

- Ethernet level

  - Ethernet source and destination addresses
  - Ethernet payload type
  - VLAN priority
  - VLAN IDs
  - stacked VLANs
  - MPLS

- IP level

  - IP source and destination address
  - IP payload type
  - DiffServ TOS (Type of Service)

- other modifications

  - TCP source and destination ports
  - TCP flags
  - UDP source and destination ports
  - payload modifications

— custom modifications at arbitrary packet offsets
— optional CRC computation (required in order to preserve the correctness of the packet should any modifications be performed)

5.3.2 *PTC Series*

The Portable Test Center (PTC) line of products by Simena currently includes only one item. PTC3000 is Simena's portable, multi-user and multi-port network emulator and traffic generator model, with up to 10 Gbps Ethernet speeds [101]. Multiple users can run independent experiments concurrently.

PTC3000 supports up to 22 fiber and/or copper-based 1 Gbps and 10 Gbps Ethernet ports. As it is a portable stand-alone system, including LCD screen, keyboard and mouse, PTC3000 can be used directly and transported between locations.

In addition to network emulation, PTC3000 also provides traffic generation features such as traffic injection and capture & replay. This makes it possible to run all or most of the necessary tests for evaluating a system without the need of any other equipment.

PTC3000 can be used not only for emulation experiments, but also for network measurements, for instance in connection with network problem diagnosis. The system can measure latency, bandwidth, packet loss, and other network characteristics, thus assisting with investigating the root cause of network problems. The results are displayed in real-time, and can be saved for future analysis.

5.3.3 *NE Series*

The Network Emulator (NE) line of products by Simena includes several models, with a relatively wide range of features.

5.3.3.1 NE3000 and NE2000

NE3000 and NE2000 are Simena's rack-mountable, multi-user and multi-port network emulator and traffic generator models, with up to 10 Gbps Ethernet speeds [100]. Similarly to PTC3000, multiple users can run independent emulation tests and traffic generations simultaneously.

Both models support up to 22 fiber and/or copper-based 1 Gbps and 10 Gbps Ethernet ports. These emulators are 19" wide and 13" deep, so that one can mount them in racks, or use them as desktop units.

NE3000 is the higher-end model in the series, as it provides, in addition to network emulation, traffic generation features. Thus, the following two functions are only available on the NE3000 model and not on the NE2000 model:

- traffic capture and replay, with modification, filtering and impairments; traffic is still forwarded through the appliance, both while capturing and while replaying
- packet generation, both along with traffic replay and with traffic forwarding; multiple packet streams can be generated per port, currently limited to a number of 20 streams

As with PTC3000, these two product models can also be used for network measurements, such as latency, bandwidth, packet loss, as well as other network characteristics; the results are displayed in real-time.

Note that a network emulator from the same family, called NE1000, is now discontinued. NE1000 could support up to 6 fiber and/or copper-based 10/100/1000 Mbps Ethernet ports, and had 1U size. Obviously both current models exceed its specifications.

5.3.3.2 NE100

NE100 is the compact model of the Simena network emulator family [100]. It is marketed as "ideal for traveling technicians and sales engineers, as it can easily fit in a laptop bag and carried on the field." The chassis of NE100 is small, being about the same size with a book according to Simena. By using the in-line management feature, NE100 can be employed between a workstation and the network without requiring additional network cables for management. As with the other network emulators, NE100 can also be accessed remotely via its Web interface.

NE100 has two 10/100/1000 Mbps test ports which can introduce network impairments at wire speed in full-duplex mode up to OC-12 rates (622 Mbps). Given its traffic generation capability, NE100 can also be used as a portable packet generator.

5.3.4 *Discussion*

Although the possible applications of the Simena network emulators are similar, there are nevertheless differences between models that make them more or less suited to some of the applications. In what follows we shall compare the emulator models, and also present several other tools that Simena markets in this area.

5.3.4.1 Comparison

Table 5.3 shows a comparison of the current Simena network emulator family of products according to [100]. Note that we excluded the discontinued model NE1000 from this comparison. The first part of the table shows that all models are equivalent from the point of view of basic functionality; thus, all models support layer 2 and 3 emulation, uni and bi-directional emulation, multiple protocols, per flow and per direction statistics, emulation of DiffServ, VLAN and MPLS (including stacked ones), bit error rates, packet filters, and delay and loss distributions. Notable differences include: the maximum forwarding rate per port and direction (622 Mbps for NE100, 10 Gbps for the rest), appliance size and whether it is rack mountable or not, the maximum number of Gigabit Ethernet interfaces (2 for NE100, 22 for the other models), and the maximum number of multi-link emulations (2 for NE100, 16 for the rest).

The second part of the table focuses mainly on the advanced features that differentiate the network emulator models from each other. Thus, NE100 *does not* support packet modifications, network measurements, IPv6 and mesh network emulation, command line interface, multiple users, 10 Gbps interfaces, nor the G.1050 model and MPEG impairment optional features, all of which are supported by the other models. Furthermore, neither NE100 nor NE2000 support traffic capture and replay, nor packet generation, both features being present in the higher-end models NE3000 and

Table 5.3.   Comparison of Simena network emulation products

Feature	NE100	NE2000	NE3000	PTC3000
Maximum forwarding rate per port and per direction	622 Mbps	10 Gbps	10 Gbps	10 Gbps
Layer 2 and 3 emulation	Yes	Yes	Yes	Yes
Uni and bi-directional emulation	Yes	Yes	Yes	Yes
Ethernet, IP, TCP, and UDP packet filters	Yes	Yes	Yes	Yes
Per flow and per direction emulation and interface statistics	Yes	Yes	Yes	Yes
DiffServ emulation	Yes	Yes	Yes	Yes
VLAN, MPLS, stacked VLAN, stacked MPLS emulation	Yes	Yes	Yes	Yes
Bit Error Rate emulation	Yes	Yes	Yes	Yes
Rack mountable	No (book size)	Yes	Yes	No (portable)
Number of Gigabit Ethernet test interfaces	2	2-22	2-22	2-22
Multi-link emulation limit	2	16	16	16
Custom packet filters	Yes	Yes	Yes	Yes
Custom delay & packet loss distributions	Yes	Yes	Yes	Yes
Packet modifications	No	Yes	Yes	Yes
Network measurements	No	Yes	Yes	Yes
IPv6 emulation	No	Yes	Yes	Yes
Mesh network emulation	No	Yes	Yes	Yes
Command line interface	No	Yes	Yes	Yes
Multi-user support	No	Yes	Yes	Yes
10 Gbps interface support	No	Yes	Yes	Yes
G.1050 network model emulation (optional)	No	Yes	Yes	Yes
MPEG video frame impairments (optional)	No	Yes	Yes	Yes
Traffic capture and replay with modification, filtering, and impairments	No	No	Yes	Yes
Packet generation along with traffic replay and traffic flow	No	No	Yes	Yes
Forwarding traffic while capturing and replaying	No	No	Yes	Yes
Multiple packet generation streams per port	No	No	Up to 20	Up to 20
Portable unit with LCD and keyboard	No	No	No	Yes

PTC3000. Finally, the only stand-alone portable network emulator model from Simena is PTC3000.

5.3.4.2 Other tools

Simena markets several other tools that are not network emulators, but can be used in connection with emulation experiments. We shall present these tools in what follows.

Traffic generators They are one type of equipment that can be used very effectively in conjunction with network emulation. Simena traffic generators have two main functions:

(1) packet generation (the feature is called "Traffic Injector" by Simena)
(2) packet capture and replay (the feature is called "Capture and Replay" by Simena)

The key benefits of Simena's traffic generators according to the company are as follows:

- Allow testing the same scenarios at different locations and times by means of the packet capture and replay feature.
- Generate realistic high-speed background traffic with the packet-generation feature.
- Help deliver products and services that are fully tested in realistic conditions.
- Reduce costs by helping find and eliminate software bugs.
- Assist with the quality assurance analysis of network applications and equipment.

Note that the above traffic generation features are already included in the PTC3000 and NE3000 network emulator models; therefore a stand-alone traffic generator is only required in conjunction with the other lower-end models.

Packet Flow Switch Simena's Packet Flow Switch (PFS) allows users to aggregate traffic and collect packets from many sources during an emulation experiment, and send them to various devices, such as traffic analyzers, loggers or monitoring systems. Thus, PFS eliminates the need for equivalent mechanisms, such as network taps (devices that allow monitoring network links) or port mirroring (an option on certain network switches that allow sending traffic seen on one port to another port).

A packet filtering mechanisms allows users to pick and choose which packets are to be forwarded. PFS can use up to 22 ports, and up to 10 Gbps speeds with jumbo frame support. PFS is available both as a stand-alone product, and also as a feature on PTC3000 and NE3000 network emulator models, as well as on traffic generators.

According to Simena, the most important applications of the Packet Flow Switch include the following:

- Load balance heavy traffic to multiple monitoring tools.
- Allow sharing of expensive network tools.
- Multicast critical traffic to multiple security devices.
- Bridge traffic between 10 Gbps and multiple 1 Gbps ports.
- XML-based packet filtering and packet slicing[2] to reduce the amount of traffic, and the potential overload on monitoring tools.
- Dynamically create aggregating and regenerating tap-like functionality, including the possibility to perform media and speed conversion.

5.4 Apposite Technologies

Apposite Technologies network emulators are intended for testing the performance of applications over wide-area networks by reproducing bandwidth limitations, latency, jitter, loss, congestion, and other important link impairments similar to real-world conditions [5]. The Apposite Technologies product family currently includes the following two lines of network emulation products and their respective models:

Linktropy Devices in this product line emulate a *single* network link through each pair of interfaces, thus they are appropriate for

---

[2] Packet slicing refers to the possibility of forwarding partial packets by striping the entire payload or only a portion of it. Users can specify to slice packets to sizes from 64 to 4096 bytes.

recreating simple scenarios with a single set of conditions between two networks. The models in this line are

- *Linktropy 10G*: three links, up to 10 Gbps
- *Linktropy 7500 PRO*: four links, up to 1 Gbps
- *Linktropy 5500*: one link, up to 1 Gbps
- *Linktropy Mini2*: one link, up to 100 Mbps

Netropy Devices in this product line emulate *multiple* separate network links (up to 15), each with their own bandwidth, delay, and loss characteristics, through each possible pair of ports. This makes Netropy models suited for recreating complex network topologies, or for running multiple concurrent tests. The models in this line are

- *Netropy 10G*: six ports, up to 10 Gbps
- *Netropy N80*: eight ports, up to 1 Gbps
- *Netropy N60*: two ports, up to 1 Gbps

The presentation in this section is based on the information provided by Apposite Technologies on its product web site [5].

5.4.1 *Linktropy Series*

Let us look first in more detail at each model in the Linktropy product line, which focuses on emulating single links.

5.4.1.1 Linktropy 10G

The Linktropy 10G WAN emulator provides network emulation for high-speed links up to 10 Gbps. Linktropy 10G emulates wide-area network bandwidth, delay, jitter, packet loss, congestion, and other important network characteristics. The product can be installed as either a network bridge or router, thus providing easy integration with existing test configurations in a centralized emulation approach.

The Linktropy 10G model has the following main characteristics:

- supports link speeds up to 10 Gbps
- has three separate links: 2 × 10 Gbps, and 1 × 1 Gbps: each link is implemented through an independent pair of interfaces

- aggregate capacity of 20 Gbps and 12 million packets per second
- Supports jumbo frames up to 9 kB

Configuration The network impairments supported by Linktropy 10G include the following features:

- bandwidth limitation, from 300 bps to the maximum operating rate in 1 bps increments
- delay, from 0 ms up to 10 seconds (0.1 ms increments) in each direction, either as a constant value, or following a normal or uniform distribution
- packet errors, either as packet loss rate, bit error rate, or both of them; loss rate can be between 0 and 100% in increments of 0.0001%
- other packet effects, such as packet reordering and duplication
- reproduce congestion conditions by specifying the background link utilization, and its burstiness; the background traffic utilization can be between 0 and 100% in increments of 0.1%
- possibility to adjust frame overhead and maximum queue depth to match real link behavior
- dynamic condition emulation: the device scheduler allows any combination of emulation parameters to vary over time; this makes it possible to emulate conditions such as connection outages, variable bandwidth links, satellite fade, wireless interference, etc.

Other features of Linktropy 10G are given below:

- capture and replay live network conditions, so as to reproduce the varying characteristics of the production network in a repeatable test environment
- traffic monitoring by displaying statistics and graphs in real time or post-experiment; up to 24 hours of statistics can be retrieved for further analysis
- automated testing through the use of the device scheduler, or through the command line interface

- a dedicated Gigabit Ethernet interface for management, as well as an RS-232 serial console

Discussion   Below we provide a list of possible applications of Linktropy 10G, and the corresponding usage scenarios, as indicated by Apposite Technologies:

- *Application testing and troubleshooting*: When developing a client/server application, testing it only on a local network may not be enough. This is because one cannot know how well it will run when users are located far away from the server. The only way to find out is to recreate the end-user experience. Basically, Linktropy 10G can be used to ensure that an application works well under all conditions before deployment. Linktropy 10G can also be used to troubleshoot application problems, and validate the solutions without disrupting the production network.
- *Network equipment testing*: High-speed network equipment developers need a way to emulate customer networks for product development, quality assurance, and customer support. This can be achieved by using Linktropy 10G to reproduce customer network conditions. Similarly, when evaluating network products in view of a purchase, it is possible to use Linktropy 10G to determine whether the product effectively delivers the expected performance characteristics.
- *VoIP and video assessment*: The quality of voice and video systems degrades with latency, jitter, and packet loss. VoIP is delay sensitive, and IPTV or tele-presence applications are both bandwidth-hungry, and highly sensitive to link impairments. Before making a purchase it is advisable to evaluate the quality of a solution under real-world conditions, so as to verify that it meets the requirements.
- *Remote backup and storage*: Assume that data at some remote offices needs to be backed up to a central facility, or that centralized records have to be moved off-site for backup purposes. Linktropy 10G can help ensure that bandwidth limitations and link latency do not prevent these processes from being completed within the available time frame.

- *Network validation*: When a company has to choose between different carriers, that provide different latency, loss, and jitter guarantees, assessment may be difficult. In addition to the cost differences, it is important to quantify how the different link conditions affect performance for the applications the company plans to use remotely. Configuring Linktropy 10G with the different network conditions makes it possible to perform such objective evaluations before a choice is made.

5.4.1.2 Linktropy 7500 PRO

The Linktropy 7500 PRO network emulator recreates bandwidth, delay, jitter, packet loss, congestion, and other network impairments at speeds of up to 1 Gbps per link. Linktropy 7500 PRO can emulate a maximum of 4 individual links simultaneously, and provides separate pairs of interfaces for each link.[3] The unit has an aggregate throughput of 4 Gbps and up to 3 million packets per second, making it ideal for both multi-link configurations and multi-user labs. The compact 1U-sized appliance includes both copper Gigabit Ethernet interfaces, and modular fiber/copper ones. Jumbo frames up to 9 kB can be used with the device.

The network impairments that can be emulated using Linktropy 7500 PRO are similar to those for Linktropy 10G in terms of bandwidth and delay control, as well as in terms of possible packet effects. This includes the possibility to introduce dynamic impairment variations.

The non-emulation features of Linktropy 7500 PRO also are similar to those of the 10G model. Thus, it is possible to capture and replay live network conditions, to perform traffic monitoring, and to automate testing procedures.

The fact that Linktropy 7500 PRO offers the possibility to emulate four 1 Gbps links (instead of the mixed 10 Gbps and 1 Gbps capabilities of Linktropy 10G) is the most significant difference between the two models. Having a larger number of links of the same type leads to more possibilities of using the device, such as given below:

---

[3]The Linktropy 7500 model, which could only emulate one 1 Gbps link, was discontinued in 2010.

- Allow up to 4 individual developers to use the device simultaneously to test different products, or to demonstrate the performance of different products to potential customers.
- Make it possible to run up to 4 sets of different tests in parallel, by using multiple instances of the same product, thus saving time and resources.
- Allow testing up to 4 separate products in parallel through independent links, so as to provide a direct comparison between competing solutions for video, voice, and other network applications.

We can say that with Linktropy 7500 PRO the focus shifts from high-speed performance to flexibility. Using this network emulator it is possible to test several types of network technologies and scenarios, such as the ones given below:

Terrestrial networks   Linktropy 7500 PRO can be used to emulate the bandwidth, delay, and loss characteristics of T1, E1, T3, E3, OC-3, ATM, xDSL, Frame Relay, and dial-up modems. In this way one can determine the necessary conditions that provide satisfactory application performance.

WANs and Internet   One can use Linktropy 7500 PRO in order to determine what happens to applications, such as e-commerce or VoIP, when they are run over WANs or over the Internet, and to plan their deployment in advance.

Wireless networks   Since network degradation characteristics of mobile as well as fixed wireless networks differ from those of terrestrial networks, one may use Linktropy 7500 PRO to determine whether a wireless solution is appropriate for a certain task or not.

Satellite networks   Communication using satellite networks has to cope with two main issue: high latencies (sometimes in excess of 500 ms), and high bit error rates (potentially larger than 10^{-6}). These conditions have a strong impact on network protocols and applications, which needs to be evaluated in advance should the use of such networks be envisaged. For this purpose, Linktropy network emulators were designed to accommodate the long delays and high error rates of satellite networks.

5.4.1.3 Linktropy 5500

The Linktropy 5500 network emulator is basically identical from the point of view of network emulation features to Linktropy 7500 PRO, but has a reduced number of ports. The characteristics of Linktropy 5500 are summarized below:

- emulation of only one link
- link speeds up to 1 Gbps and up to 1 million packets per second
- copper Gigabit Ethernet interfaces or optional SFP ports
- compact, 1U-sized appliance

With features similar to Linktropy 7500 PRO, Linktropy 5500 is basically a scaled down, lighter version of the other model. Thus, Linktropy 5500 is particular useful for product demonstrations, since it is easier to carry around. One can use Linktropy 5500 to demonstrate a product to customers under their production network conditions by taking the appliance to the customer site, and recording and replaying the actual conditions there. This avoids the hassles of installing the equipment in the live production network, and the disturbance of the network that may occur. Linktropy 5500 can also be used at trade shows, to demonstrate the performance characteristics and features of a product.

5.4.1.4 Linktropy Mini2

Linktropy Mini2 is a portable network emulator designed to recreate basic network conditions for use in connection with application development, and for demonstrations of networking products.

Linktropy Mini2 emulates bandwidth limitation, delay, and packet loss separately in each direction for one link at rates of maximum 100 Mbps, and up to 80,000 packets per second. Its small size (6" × 6") and light weight make it easy to carry. Linktropy Mini2 is easily configured via a browser-based interface. The GUI allows the audience to view the test conditions, and even to adjust the emulation parameters. Linktropy Mini2 displays throughput graphs and statistics, revealing the effects of network conditions on application performance.

The following parameters can be configured for Linktropy Mini2:

- bandwidth limitation, between 300 bps and 100 Mbps in 1 bps increments
- delay, between 0 ms and 10 seconds in 0.1 ms increments; it can be specified as a constant value, or as having uniform or normal distributions
- packet loss rate, between 0 and 100% with increments of 0.0001%
- additional parameters include: bit error rate, queue depth, framing overhead

Given the low operating rates of Linktropy Mini2, and the fact that Apposite Technologies claims its accuracy is not as high as that of the other models, it may be that this appliance is actually a small form computer running a network emulation software. This would make us classify it as a software emulator not a hardware one, but as we can only speculate about this aspect, we shall leave this question open.

5.4.2 *Netropy Series*

The other line of products from Apposite Technologies, focusing on emulating multiple links, hence, by extension, on network topology, is Netropy.

5.4.2.1 Netropy 10G

The Netropy 10G network emulator makes it possible to benchmark, troubleshoot, and optimize the performance of critical applications over 10 Gbps networks. Netropy 10G includes two 10 Gbps, and one 1 Gbps emulation engines, each of which can emulate up to 15 separate WAN links. It has four 10 Gbps ports (XFP or CX4) and two 1 Gbps ports (copper); the total capacity is of 22 Gbps and 10 million packets per second. Thus, one can use Netropy 10G to model high-speed complex network topologies, or run multiple concurrent tests.

Netropy 10G can be configured and managed through a browser-based interface for the most basic tasks, or through a comprehensive command line interface for integration with test automation tools.

Configuration The network impairments supported by Netropy 10G are almost identical to those of Linktropy 10G, as the list below proves:

- bandwidth limitation, from 100 bps to the maximum operating rate in 1 bps increments
- delay, from 0 ms up to 10 seconds (0.1 ms increments) in each direction, either as a constant value, or following a normal or uniform distribution
- Packet errors, either as packet loss rate, bit error rate, or both of them; packet loss can be random (uniform distribution), in bursts, or periodic
- other packet effects, such as packet reordering and duplication
- packet filtering, using a combination of source and destination IP addresses, VLAN ID, and MPLS label
- reproduce congestion conditions by specifying the background link utilization and its burstiness; the background traffic can be between 0 and 100% in increments of 0.1%
- adjust framing overhead and maximum queue depth to match real link behavior; in addition to the default tail drop queueing, the RED management mechanism can also be used
- dynamic condition emulation through a scheduler that allows any combination of emulation parameters to vary over time; this makes it possible to emulate conditions such as connection outages, variable bandwidth links, satellite fade, wireless interference, etc.

Other non-emulation features of Netropy 10G include the following features:

- Traffic monitoring can be done through the display of throughput graphs and link statistics. Throughput graphs are available for a 24 hour period and are reviewable with pan and zoom controls. Moreover, up to 24 hours of statistics can be retrieved for further analysis.
- Automated testing can be done through the use of a comprehensive command line interface.

- It is a dedicated Gigabit Ethernet interface for management, as well as an RS-232 serial console.

Discussion   Given the ability of Netropy 10G to emulate up to 15 separate WAN links on each of the three emulation engines, several utilization patterns become possible according to Apposite Technologies, as follows:

- *Emulate multi-site networks*: The high-speed and complex emulation capabilities of Netropy 10G make it possible to model a full enterprise network, including headquarters, regional, branch, and local offices, etc. IT engineers can then use Netropy 10G to accomplish tasks such as
  — experience applications as they will be seen by different end-users from the various remote locations
  — verify the correct operation of application servers with a potentially large number of concurrent users
- *Side-by-side benchmarking*: Since Netropy 10G has multiple ports and emulation engines, one can run separate experiments side-by-side, for example in order to
  — determine the effects of different network conditions on the performance of the same application, and possibly tune application settings so as to maximize overall performance
  — compare similar products from different vendors using the same network conditions, and analyze their benefits for the company
- *Concurrent testing*: Related to the previous item, concurrent testing helps minimize the time needed to complete a series of independent experiments — such as when using a matrix of conditions to explore a parameter space — by running multiple experiments in parallel using several instances of the network application of device under test.
- *Impair individual applications*: The filtering capabilities of Netropy 10G make it possible to differentiate traffic from individual sources. Thus, one can apply impairments *only* to specific applications, or can even apply *different* levels of impairment to different applications.

5.4.2.2 Netropy N80

The Netropy N80 network emulator offers the same network emulation capabilities with Netropy 10G. The differences with respect to Netropy 10G are restricted to the number of available interfaces and number of emulation engines, as well as the maximum link rate. Thus, Netropy N80 has four 1 Gbps emulation engines that can each be used for the emulation of up to 15 separate WAN links between any of the ports of the appliance. Netropy N80 is a compact 1U-sized device, with eight 1 Gigabit Ethernet ports (4 copper and 4 SFP). The aggregate capacity is of 4 Gbps, and up to 3 million packets per second.

More interfaces compared to Netropy 10G means that there are even more opportunities to share the appliance across multiple experiments, while bearing in mind the reduced maximum link rate (1 Gbps instead of 10 Gbps). The potential applications for Netropy 80N are similar to those previously indicated for Netropy 10G.

5.4.2.3 Netropy N60

The Netropy N60 network emulator is a scaled-down version of Netropy N80 that has only *one* emulation engine. This engine can still be used to recreate up to 15 separate WAN links, but this can only take place on the single connection between the two ports of the appliance. Netropy N60 can emulate complex networks up to 1 Gbps, and its two ports are Gigabit Ethernet, with a choice between copper and SFP. The aggregate throughput is 2 Gbps, and up to 1 million packets per second.

Netropy N60 is a compact, 1U-sized appliance. Being lighter than Netropy N80, it is a more appropriate for temporary deployments to customer sites or trade shows.

5.4.3 *Discussion*

Apposite Technologies is the company with the most diversified range of models among those that we have reviewed. Readers may therefore be puzzled by what are the actual differences between all these models.

In order to make things more clear, let us first compare the models in the older line of models, Linktropy, by using the information provided on the company website. Table 5.4 shows this comparison. When analyzing the table, several aspects become obvious:

- Linktropy 10G is the model aimed at high speeds, whereas 7500 PRO and 5500 focus on typical 1 Gbps connections, although the maximum number of links that can be emulated is different; Linktropy Mini2 is a portable but in the same time lower rate solution, and it is not classified as "high precision" by the company.
- All emulators can recreate basic network impairments, however Linktropy Mini2 lacks all the advanced features, such as packet reordering and duplication, introduction of background traffic and dynamic scheduling. Moreover, Linktropy Mini2 does not support network traffic capture and replay, nor statistics download for further analysis.

Let us compare next the models of the newer line of models of Apposite Technologies, Netropy, using again the information on the company's website (see Table 5.5). Note that, since Netropy series emulators have the same network emulation capabilities, in this table we shall focus on the performance differences. Table 5.5 emphasizes the fact that performance characteristics basically increase from one end, the Netropy N60 model, which has only 2 Gigabit Ethernet ports, to Netropy N80, which has 8 Gigabit Ethernet ports, and finally to the top-of-the-line Netropy 10G which has even 10 Gbps interfaces, and a total of 6 ports.

At this point, the differences that exist between models within the same line of products should have become clear. To conclude this discussion, let us compare the model lines to each other (excluding the entry-level Linktropy model, Mini2). Table 5.6 presents the comparison, as outlined by Apposite Technologies. An analysis of the table reveals the following aspects:

- The main difference between the Linktropy and Netropy lines is that Linktropy only supports emulation of 1 link per port pair, whereas Netropy can go up to 15 links per port

Table 5.4. Comparison of Apposite Technologies Linktropy network emulation products

Linktropy model	Mini2	5500	7500 PRO	10G
Number of emulated links	1	1	4	3 (2 × 10 Gbps, 1 × 1 Gbps)
Number of emulation interfaces	2 × 10/100 Ethernet	2 Gigabit Ethernet	8 Gigabit Ethernet (4 copper, 4 SFP)	4 × 10 Gigabit Ethernet, 2 × 1 Gigabit Ethernet
Maximum link rate	100 Mbps	1 Gbps	1 Gbps (4 Gbps total)	10 Gbps (20 Gbps total)
Maximum packet rate	80,000 pps	1 million pps	3 million pps	Over 10 million pps
High precision	No	Yes	Yes	Yes
Bandwidth limitation	Yes	Yes	Yes	Yes
Delay (constant or variable) and jitter	Yes	Yes	Yes	Yes
Packet loss	Yes	Yes	Yes	Yes
Bit errors	Yes	Yes	Yes	Yes
Packet reordering	No	Yes	Yes	Yes
Packet duplication	No	Yes	Yes	Yes
Background traffic	No	Yes	Yes	Yes
Dynamic scheduling	No	Yes	Yes	Yes
Capture and replay	No	Yes	Yes	Yes
Statistics download	No	Yes	Yes	Yes
Install as bridge or router	Yes	Yes	Yes	Yes
Jumbo frame support	No	Yes (9 kB)	Yes (9 kB)	Yes (9kB)
Form factor	Portable	1U	1U	2U

Table 5.5. Comparison of Apposite Technologies Netropy network emulation products

Netropy model	N60	N80	10G
Number of emulation interfaces	2 Gigabit Ethernet (copper or SFP)	8 Gigabit Ethernet (4 copper, 4 SFP)	4 × 10 Gigabit Ethernet, 2 × 1 Gigabit Ethernet
Maximum rate per link direction	1 Gbps	1 Gbps	10 Gbps
Aggregate throughput	2 Gbps	4 Gbps	22 Gbps
Maximum packet rate	1 million pps	3 million pps	10 million pps
Form factor	1U	1U	2U

Table 5.6. Comparison of Apposite Technologies lines of network emulation products

Product line & models	Linktropy 5500/7500 PRO/10G	Netropy N60/N80/10G
Number of emulated links	1 link per port pair	15 links per port pair
Number of port pairs	1/4/3	1/4/3
Maximum rate per port	1/1/10 Gbps	1/1/10 Gbps
Bandwidth limitation	300 bps to maximum operating rate in 1 bps increments	
Delay & jitter	0–10 s in 0.1 ms increments (constant or distributions)	
Packet loss/error	Random, BER	Random, periodic, burst, BER
Other effects	Packet reordering, packet duplication	
Queue management	Tail drop	Tail drop, RED
Rate control direction	Outgoing only	Both incoming and outgoing
Background traffic	0–100% in increments of 0.1%	
Jumbo frames	Supported, maximum 9kB	
Capture and replay	Yes	No
Dynamic scheduler	Yes	No
Statistics download	Last 24 hours	
Throughput graphs	Last 10 minutes	Last 24 hours, reviewable
Command line interface	Supported	

pair, resulting in a corresponding increase of the complexity of the networks that can be emulated with the model of the latter series.

- It is possible to draw a "correspondence" between individual Linktropy and Netropy models, according to their number of ports and the maximum supported operating rate per port. Thus, Linktropy 5500 corresponds to Netropy N60, Linktropy 7500 PRO to Netropy N80, and Linktropy 10G to Netropy 10G.

- Regarding the network emulation features, models in both lines of products are identical, with the exception of the following aspects:

  — In addition to the packet loss and error features of the Linktropy line, Netropy models also support periodic packet loss, as well as burst loss.
  — In addition to the basic tail drop available for the Linktropy series, Netropy models also support RED as a queue management mechanism.
  — Control can be enforced both for incoming and outgoing traffic in Netropy models, but only for outgoing traffic in Linktropy models.

- Concerning non-emulation features, the following differences should be noted:

  — Netropy products do not support traffic capture and replay, which means that live network conditions cannot be reproduced with these products, as it could be done with Linktropy models, but only modeled through the use of the available impairments.
  — Moreover, Netropy products do not support dynamic scheduling either; this implies that advanced emulation scenarios that are possible with Linktropy models, such as wireless or satellite networks in which conditions change over time, cannot be recreated.
  — As a minor difference, the throughput graphs provided by Linktropy products only contain the last 10 minutes of operation, whereas Netropy models can show up to 24 hours of traffic statistics, and have zooming and panning capabilities to allow investigating the data in detail.

5.5 Anue Systems

Anue Systems markets a series of Ethernet network emulators that are intended to reproduce impairments similar to those exhibited on MANs and WANs [3]. Note that Anue Systems also offers fiber channel and SONET/SDH network emulators, but we shall focus only on the Ethernet ones, which are equivalent to those of the other manufacturers. There are two Anue Systems products that enter in this category, namely

- *XGEM*: 10 Gigabit Ethernet network emulator
- *GEM*: 10/100/Gigabit Ethernet network emulator

The main benefits indicated by Anue Systems for its network emulators are as follows:

- Identify network performance issues before deployment.
- Troubleshoot systems in a quantifiable and repeatable manner.
- Create and use real-world network profiles that represent different locations or usage patterns.

The general features of Anue Systems Ethernet network emulators are as follows:

- Each models runs at 100% line rate.
- Emulator operation can be done interactively, locally or remotely, and can also be automated:
  - Local control is done via a front panel LCD.
  - Remote control uses a dedicated Ethernet port and can be done either through a Graphical User Interface or through a TCL API, which allows for the automation of common tasks.
- It has high emulation accuracy, down to one-bit time increments.

Regarding the network emulation features, Anue Systems products support a large range of configurable impairments, such as bandwidth control, delay and jitter, packet loss, reordering, duplication, fragmentation, modification, corruption, and even signal loss conditions. Frames can be selected for impairment based on a variety of Ethernet (Layer 2) or IP (Layer 3) characteristics, such as VLAN tag, source or destination address, or any other data in an Ethernet frame.

This section is based on information available on the web site of Anue Systems dedicated to its network emulation products [3].

5.5.1 *XGEM*

XGEM Ethernet network emulators are intended for precisely emulating 10 Gigabit Ethernet networks in a lab environment. They can reproduce the delay and impairments experienced by Ethernet signals across MANs and WANs regardless of the underlying transport mechanism. This makes it possible to test the behavior of network applications, protocols, and devices in the presence of delay and packet jitter, to determine how well they detect and handle errored frames, and how they manage situations with frames that are dropped, fragmented, duplicated or out of sequence.

The main characteristics of XGEM network emulators according to Anue Systems are as follows:

- They run at 100% line rate at 10 Gbps.
- They support up to 64 different impairment profiles selected based on user-defined filters.
- They can be automated or operated interactively, both locally and remotely.
- They have an impairment accuracy down to one-bit time increments.
- They provide a maximum delay of 250 ms at all supported bit rates.[4]

The XGEM network emulator is available as a 2U rack-mount chassis that supports data rates up to 11.3 Gbps. The 10 Gigabit Ethernet interfaces can be either copper or optical. The unit has a front panel LCD control that allows for standalone operation. It is also possible to perform remotely configuration tasks via a dedicated Ethernet control port. The remote control can be

---

[4]Anue Systems states that this value can be increased upon customer request.

either interactive (browser-based GUI with save/load capability) or automated (using a TCL script library).

5.5.1.1 Configuration

The network emulation features of XGEM as indicated by Anue Systems are the following:

Network profiles Users can define up to 64 distinct network profiles that represent 64 distinct network clouds. Throughput, delay and other network impairments are specified independently for each profile.

Packet filtering In order to determine which type of impairment (profile) is applied to an incoming packet, up to 512 filtering rules can be used. There are two types of possible rules:

- *Data-based rules*: Use a variable-length mask of up to 32 bytes to match data anywhere within an Ethernet frame. For instance, a certain rule could test the MAC address, IP address, VLAN tag, and a fixed byte offset. This type of rule is appropriate for scenarios in which the network through which a packet goes is deterministically decided by its content: packets to destination $D1$ go through network $N1$, packets to destination $D2$ go through network $N2$, and so on.
- *Order-based rules*: Select packets at regular intervals (i.e., every N^{th} packet), or at randomly distributed intervals (with Poisson, Gaussian, or uniform distributions). This alternative makes it possible to emulate scenarios in which networks are not decided deterministically, for instance when there are multiple paths from a source to a destination. Thus, a packet to destination D may go either through the network $N1$ or through the network $N2$, depending on factors such as congestion on the path.

Bandwidth control XGEM can limit throughput down to a minimum of 0.005% of line rate (equivalent to 500 kbps for 10 Gigabit Ethernet). The emulator can optionally generate Pause Frames (XOFF & XON messages, used for "software flow control"). Appropriate bandwidth thresholds are specified by the user in terms of surplus and deficit of bytes.

Delay/jitter For each network profile, the user can define specific delay and delay variation characteristics. With the standard configuration, it is possible to insert packet delays between 50 μs and 250 ms in 26 ns increments. The maximum delay value can be increased through a mechanism tagged Delay Doubler and Quadrupler; greater delay amounts are said to be available upon request. Inter-packet delay variation (jitter) can also be specified.

Packet impairments Several packet-level impairment types can be configured for each network profile. The following packet effects are supported:

- packet drop
- packet reordering
- packet duplication
- packet fragmentation
- packet corruption (both for data and CRC)

Multiple impairments can be combined for the same packet, and the emulator can optionally recalculate the Ethernet CRC or IP checksum. XGEM can also reproduce a "Loss of Signal" effect, equivalent to network disconnection.

Bit error rate One can set error rates from 10^{-12} to 10^{-2} (i.e., up to 1%) at Layer 1 or MAC layer. Errors can be injected with a fixed rate (periodic errors), or randomly, following a uniform, Poisson or Gaussian distribution. The error can affect a single bit or 32 bits, in the latter case either as a contiguous area or following a user-defined bit pattern.

As the above description shows, the range of impairments that can be introduced using XGEM is large. Two additional remarks regarding XGEM apply:

- Network impairment configurations can be modified in real time, without interrupting the traffic flow, hence not requiring to restart ongoing experiments.

- The following standard-based network impairment models are supported by XGEM: MEF-18, ITU-T G.8261, and ITU-T G.1050/TIA-921.

A non-emulation feature of XGEM is the fact that it can operate either in transparent mode (i.e., as an "invisible" network device), or in router mode, that routes network traffic between its interfaces. For router mode operation, up to 16 virtual ports are supported per physical interface.

5.5.2 *GEM*

The GEM Ethernet network emulators are intended for simulating 10/100/Gigabit Ethernet networks in a lab environment. They are basically a lower-end version of XGEM with similar general characteristics, but only supporting lower operating rates. GEM network emulators run at 100% line rate speed from 10 Mbps to 1 Gbps at any frame size.

The GEM network emulators are available on two different hardware platforms. Both platforms have a 2U rack-mount chassis that supports either up to four blades (and data rates up to 2.6 Gbps), or up to two blades (and data rates up to 11.3Gbps). Each interface supports the Ethernet standard at 10 Mbps (copper), 100 Mbps (copper), and 1 Gbps (copper or fiber).

5.5.2.1 Configuration

The network emulation features of GEM follow closely those of XGEM, and the differences that appear are caused by the dissimilarity concerning supported line rates. GEM features can be summarized as follows (we emphasize the difference with respect XGEM when this applies):

- There is a possibility to define up to 64 distinct network profiles and use up to 512 filtering rules to identify those profiles. Rules can be either data based or order based.
- Bandwidth limitation is configurable to a minimum of 0.005% of line rate (50 kbps at 1 Gigabit Ethernet, hence lower than for XGEM).

- Delay/jitter values from 50 µs to 250 ms in 16 ns increments for Gigabit Ethernet in the standard configuration (the smallest increment is 26 ns for XGEM).
- Packet impairment and bit error capabilities are the same with those of XGEM.

5.5.3 *Discussion*

The two network emulator models from Anue Systems are very similar, but a side-by-side comparison will emphasize the differences between them. We shall also present in this subsection another tool from the same company that can be used in the network emulation context.

5.5.3.1 Comparison

Table 5.7 shows the comparison of the two Ethernet network emulation models by Anue Systems according to the information on the company's web site [5]. From the beginning one notes that XGEM is superior to GEM both in terms of number of interfaces (up to 8 for the first, versus only 2 for the latter), and in terms of maximum supported rates per interface (10 Gbps for XGEM, versus 1 Gbps for GEM). However, beside these characteristics, the two network emulators are identical in terms of emulation features. The

Table 5.7. Comparison of Anue Systems network emulation products

Model name	GEM	XGEM
Number of emulation interfaces	2	Up to 8 or 4
Supported rates per interface	10/100/1000 Mbps	10 Gbps
Bandwidth control	Yes	Yes
Delay & jitter	Yes	Yes
Packet loss	Yes	Yes
Bit errors	Yes	Yes
Packet reordering, duplication, etc.	Yes	Yes
Capture and replay	Yes	No
Statistics	Yes	Yes
Jumbo frame support	Yes	Yes
Form factor	2U	2U

only difference of importance is the lack of the capture and replay capability for XGEM, which is undoubtedly caused by the high rate at which this emulator operates, which makes it difficult to store a significant enough amount of captured traffic.

5.5.3.2 Other tools

Network emulators are often employed in complex network scenarios. In this context, issues such as network monitoring and tool control become important. The Anue 5200 Series Net Tool Optimizer is a solution for optimizing the network monitoring activity. According to Anue Systems, the Net Tool Optimizer can be used in conjunction not only with network emulators, but also with tools such as intrusion detection systems, application monitors, traffic sniffers, protocol analyzers, compliance monitors, VoIP analyzers, data recorders, etc.

The Net Tool Optimizer is available in two models, supporting up to 28 ports per system. Moreover, both models can be daisy-chained to increase port capacity. The possible configurations of the models are one of

- twenty 1G RJ-45, four SFP 1G, and four 10G XFP ports
- twenty 10G/1G SFP+, four 10G XFP, and four 1G RJ-45 ports

The Net Tool Optimizer links in a simple manner test and monitoring tools with the experiment network. The possible operating modes of the Net Tool Optimizer are as follows:

(1) *Any-to-any*: This directs data from any link in the network to any test and monitoring tool.
(2) *Any-to-many*: This multicasts the traffic from one network link to multiple test and monitoring tools, thus eliminating the need for switch mirroring ports and TAPs.
(3) *Many-to-any*: This aggregates traffic from multiple network links, and provide it to any test and monitoring tool as a whole.

The flexibility in selecting traffic is enhanced by the packet filtering capabilities of Net Tool Optimizer, which ensure that only the necessary data reaches each test and monitoring tool. Filtering can be done on Layers 2 to 4, using criteria such as MAC addresses,

VLANs, Ethernet frame types, IP addresses, and UDP/TCP ports. The rules can be combined using Boolean operations, such as "AND," "OR," and "DENY." Anue Systems claims that filters are even automatically adjusted, to cope with testbed changes in terms of connections, other filter settings, or tools.

5.6 Comparison

In this chapter we have presented commercial network emulators from five companies, namely Shunra, PacketStorm Communications, Simena, Apposite Technologies, and Anue Systems. As the marketing efforts of these companies are driven by commercial purposes, the description of their products is often focused on emphasizing what are perceived as differentiating characteristics. Such an approach makes it difficult sometimes to objectively compare two products, especially since certain identical features are tagged with different names that are specific to each company.

While comparing in an exhaustive manner the products of these companies is not an objective of our book, in what follows we attempt, for illustration purposes, a comparison that should reveal at least some of the similarities and differences between the products of these five companies. For this purpose, we have selected from each company what we perceived as the flagship model, which has the highest supported operating rate per interface. Since some features were not present in the flagship model, but did exist for other products of the same company, we indicate this fact in our comparison so as to allow readers have a better overall perception of product capabilities.

Thus, in Table 5.8 we compare the following products developed and marketed by the corresponding companies:

(1) Shunra VE Appliance
(2) PacketStorm Communications 4XG (labeled as "PacketStorm 4XG")
(3) Simena PTC3000
(4) Apposite Technologies Netropy 10G (labeled as "Apposite Netropy 10G")
(5) Anue Systems XGEM (labeled as "Anue XGEM")

Table 5.8. Comparison of commercial network emulators by Shunra, PacketStorm Communications, Simena, Apposite Technologies, and Anue Systems

	Shunra VE Appliance	PacketStorm 4XG	Simena PTC3000	Apposite Netropy 10G	Anue XGEM
Platform type	Hardware	Hardware	Hardware	Hardware	Hardware
Maximum rate	10 Gbps	10 Gbps	10 Gbps	10 Gbps	10 Gbps
Bandwidth control	Yes, with packet accumulation and burst	Yes, with packet accumulation and burst	Yes, with congestion emulation, packet accumulation and burst	Constant bandwidth; background link utilization; RED	Yes, including Pause Frames
Delay & jitter	Constant, or variable with predefined distributions	Constant, or variable with predefined distributions	Constant, or variable with predefined and custom distributions	Constant, or variable with predefined distributions	Constant, or variable with predefined distributions; limit extension mechanism
Packet loss	Yes, including decimation and burst loss	Yes, including decimation and burst loss	Yes, including burst loss	Yes, including periodic and burst loss	Yes, including periodic and burst loss
Other packet effects	Reordering, duplication, fragmentation, corruption, modification	Reordering, duplication, fragmentation, modification	Reordering, duplication, fragmentation, corruption, modification	Reordering, duplication, corruption	Reordering, duplication, fragmentation, corruption (with custom bit patterns)
Other impairments	N/A	N/A	Carrier loss emulation; ITU-T G.1050; MPEG impairments	N/A	Loss of signal emulation; ITU-T G.1050 and G.8261, MEF-18

(Contd.)

Table 5.8. *(Contd.)*

	Shunra VE Appliance	PacketStorm 4XG	Simena PTC3000	Apposite Netropy 10G	Anue XGEM
Packet filtering	Data-based filters (MAC and IP layers)	Data-based filters (MAC and IP layers)	Data-based filters (MAC and IP layers)	Data-based filters (IP layer only)	Data-based filters (MAC and IP layers); order-based filters
Dynamic impairments	Yes (can also be programmed to change)	No (available on Hurricane models)	Yes (only packet effects)	Yes (can also be programmed to change)	Yes (can also be programmed to change)
Network topologies	Point-to-point, hub and spoke, N-Tier and fully meshed	None predefined	Point-to-point, hub and spoke, partially and fully meshed; up to 16 multiple-link emulations	Up to 15 links per port pair	Up to 64 impairment profiles
Protocols & technologies	IPv6, QoS, MPLS, Frame Relay, OSPF, VLAN	QoS, MPLS, VLAN	IPv6, QoS, MPLS, VLAN (including stacked)	MPLS, VLAN	VLAN
Reporting & analysis	Traffic statistics; transactions, video and VoIP quality, application profiling; service level prediction	Traffic statistics at network and application level, QoE metrics	Traffic statistics per flow and per direction	Traffic statistics per link	Traffic statistics per network profile
Capture and replay	Yes	Yes	Yes (with modification, filtering and impairments)	No (available for Linktropy 10G)	No (available for GEM)
Command line interface	Yes	Yes	Yes	Yes	Yes
Other features	N/A	N/A (data generation on Hurricane models)	LCD; data generation; uni and bi-directional emulation	Incoming and outgoing emulation	N/A

The comparison starts by looking at the platform type, and the maximum supported rate per interface for each of the examined network emulation models. We conclude that all products are hardware-based solutions, and can support rates up to 10 Gbps.

Bandwidth control is an important network emulation feature that is supported by all five products. Particular features in addition to the basic bandwidth control support include the following:

- Shunra VE Appliance, PacketStorm 4XG, and Simena PTC3000 all support packet accumulation and bursts effects, with the latter also having congestion emulation capabilities.
- While Apposite Netropy 10G only supports constant bandwidth for direct configuration, it does include support for emulating congestion through the use of the background link utilization feature; this emulator also supports the RED queue management technique.
- Anue XGEM has a particular feature that is related to bandwidth control, namely the support for pause frames at Ethernet level.

Delay and jitter are another important set of network parameters, and their control is supported by all the analyzed models. We emphasize the fact that not only constant values, but also distributions can be used for this type of impairment. Note however that, while the other emulators only allow the use of predefined distributions, Simena PTC3000 also lets users configure their own custom distributions. The Anue XGEM emulator has a specific feature in this category: the maximum value of the delay that can be introduced (by default, 250 ms) can be increased by a doubling or quadrupling mechanism at the expense of accuracy (the 26 ns increments become 52 ns and 104 ns, respectively).

The third basic type of impairment is packet loss. In addition to the usual random loss, several emulators allow to configure burst loss effects. Four of them, namely Shunra VE Appliance, PacketStorm 4XG, Apposite Netropy 10G, and Anue XGEM have a supplementary common feature, which is essentially the same although it is called "decimation" in the first two cases, and "periodic loss" in the last two ones.

Regarding other packet effects, we note that all emulators support packet reordering and duplication, and only Apposite Netropy 10G *does not* support fragmentation. The following are other important features:

- Shunra VE Appliance, PacketStorm 4XG, and Simena PTC3000 all support packet modification.
- Shunra VE Appliance, Simena PTC3000, Apposite Netropy 10G, and Anue XGEM all support packet corruption. It is possible to say that Apposite Netropy 10G, which only supports packet corruption, has limited modification functionality, since corruption is equivalent to modifying the packet, albeit one does not have control over the modification.
- Although PacketStorm 4XG has no direct support for packet corruption, the effect can be achieved through the packet modification feature it has, which is more general.
- Anue XGEM has the most advanced packet corruption mechanism, which allows using custom bit patterns.

Two of the examined network emulators, Simena PTC3000 and Anue XGEM have several supplementary impairment functions:

- First of all, we note the possibility to emulate link disconnection, a feature termed "carrier loss emulation" for Simena PTC3000, and "loss of signal emulation" for Anue XGEM.
- The two emulators also have support for using standards for evaluating multimedia transmission performance, such as ITU-T G.1050, with Anue XGEM adding support for ITU-T G.8261 and MEF-18.
- Simena PTC3000 additionally makes it possible to impair specific packets in MPEG-based video streams.

Packet filtering is an essential feature of network emulators, since it makes possible to select the packets of interest, to split the traffic into streams, etc. All emulators support what we called data-based filters, i.e., using packet data (including both headers and payload) to define filtering rules. The following remarks can be made:

- While the other emulators allow filter definition using either MAC or IP level information, Apposite Netropy 10G can only use IP data for this purpose.
- Anue XGEM introduces a distinct feature compared to the other network emulators, named "order-based filtering," which selects packets at constant or variable intervals, to emulate real network conditions such as multi-path.

Complex network scenarios are rarely static, therefore dynamic impairments that change in time offer users an increased flexibility in terms of possible experiments. All the examined emulators except PacketStorm 4XG support such a control method. Some aspects to note about dynamic impairments are given below:

- Shunra VE Appliance, Apposite Netropy 10G, and Anue XGEM provide mechanisms that allow not only changing the impairments in real time, but also controlling their change in a programmatic mode, either directly through a specific interface or through scripting support.
- While PacketStorm 4XG does not support this feature, it is present in a lower rate model from the same manufacturer, namely Hurricane.
- For Simena PTC3000, dynamic effects are limited to packet effects such as loss and duplication.

Network topology is an aspect where we noticed that vendors have a wide range of approaches and can conclude the following:

- Shunra VE Appliance and Simena PTC3000, in addition to the basic point-to-point connections, offer the possibility to define more complex network topologies, such as hub and spoke, and fully meshed; Simena PTC3000 claims up to 16 simultaneous emulations of such topologies.
- PacketStorm 4XG on the other hand, does not provide any predefined network topologies, nor clear statements about the limitations in this respect.
- Apposite Netropy 10G and Anue XGEM do not predefine topologies other, but clearly claim to support up to 15 links per port pair for the first emulator, and up to 64 impairment profiles for the latter.

Regarding protocols and technologies, we note the following:

- All the emulators support the VLAN standard, and only Anue XGEM *does not* support the MPLS technology.
- Support for QoS is present for Shunra VE Appliance, PacketStorm 4XG, and Simena PTC3000.
- Only Shunra VE Appliance and Simena PTC3000 recognize the IPv6 protocol.
- Shunra VE Appliance has the largest range of supported protocols and technology: in addition to the ones already mentioned, it also features Frame Relay and OSPF support.

Reporting and analysis are important in order to quickly provide users with a detailed view of the experiment, as well as with higher level information. All network emulators in our comparison support reporting throughput statistics, at least in text form but many times also in graphical forms. Specific remarks concerning each model follow:

- Shunra VE Appliance has the richest set of reporting features, including higher-level statistics such as those for transactions. Moreover, it supports application-specific reporting & analysis, such as video and VoIP quality, profiling, and even service level prediction.
- PacketStorm 4XG too has application-level reporting features, and also allows the calculation of QoE metrics.
- Simena PTC3000 has only traffic level statistics, but they can be computed independently per flow and per direction, hence could be associated to applications by the user.
- Apposite Netropy 10G only provides per-link statistics, hence does not allow a detailed analysis of the traffic.
- Anue XGEM only provides statistics per network profile, therefore, as in the previous case, does not allow a detailed analysis of the traffic.

Capture and replay makes it possible to reproduce conditions that were recorded in a real network, thus enabling repeated experiments in the same conditions. Shunra VE Appliance, PacketStorm 4XG, and Simena PTC3000 all support this capability, with the latter also allowing the recorded traffic to be subjected to modification, filtering, and even impairments. The other two models we examined, Apposite Netropy 10G and Anue XGEM, do not have capture and replay capabilities, although they are present in other models from the same manufacturers, namely Linktropy 10G and GEM, respectively.

Command line interface support makes it possible to run complex experiments with less effort, hence it is important in particular for complex experiments, such as those involving dynamic condition variations. All the models we compared support the use of a command line interface. However, some of them use custom PC programs and interfaces to achieve this goal (e.g., Shunra VE Appliance), whereas other use standard languages, such as TCL (e.g., PacketStorm 4XG).

Other features that we did not discuss so far are present on some of the analyzed network emulators. While nothing significant can be said for Shunra VE Appliance, PacketStorm 4XG (which does not support data generation, differently from the Hurricane models), nor for Anue XGEM, the following aspects are to be noted about the other two products:

- Simena PTC3000 provides an LCD to allow direct control of the appliance; it also has data generation, eliminating the need of using additional equipment for this purpose.
- Both Simena PTC3000 and Apposite Netropy 10G allow to introduce network quality degradation in both traffic directions, a feature called "uni- and bi-directional emulation" for the first one, and "incoming and outgoing emulation" for the latter.

As a final remark, the relatively large number of models for each company we discussed made it difficult to analyze each of these products individually. We refer our readers to the "rough" classification in Table 3.1 for a summary view on all commercial emulators that we presented in this chapter. We briefly note here that most of these emulators are of hardware type (Hurricane, Linktropy, Netropy, PacketStorm, Shunra VE Appliance, Simena NE & PTC, and XGEM/GEM), and only a few of software type (Shunra VE

Cloud & Desktop, and Tornado).[5] While some commercial emulators can only emulate links (Shunra VE Cloud & Desktop, and Tornado — note they are the software ones), all the others can emulate complex network topologies. In general, the commercial emulators have a medium complexity, and almost all solutions are executed in a centralized manner; the exception is that of Shunra VE Desktop, which includes support for distributed execution.

---

[5]As we have mentioned before, some of the appliances actually contain dedicated computers running a software emulator. Since it is difficult in general to know when this is the case, we included all appliances in the "hardware" type of emulator.

Chapter 6

Emulation-Capable Network Simulators

Simulation is probably the most used experimental technique. While it has many advantages over other methodologies, it does have its disadvantages too. This is one reason why many network simulators, in addition to the pure simulation functionality, offer the possibility of network emulation, that is interaction with live traffic. Basically, this means creating special interfaces that allow bringing real network traffic into and out of the simulation engine. In this chapter we review several of the most important network simulators, with emphasis on their emulation features, and discuss how effective from the network emulation perspective is the approach they propose.

6.1 Ns-2 Network Simulator

Ns-2 is a discrete event simulator targeted at networking research [105]. Ns-2 development began in 1989, under the name Ns (or ns), as a variant of the REAL network simulator. Ns-2 has evolved substantially over the years, and the digit "2" actually indicates the second version of Ns. Starting from 1995 until 2005, Ns-2 development was supported by the USA Defense Advanced

Introduction to Network Emulation
Razvan Beuran
Copyright © 2013 Pan Stanford Publishing Pte. Ltd.
ISBN 978-981-4310-91-8 (Hardcover), 978-981-4364-09-6 (eBook)
www.panstanford.com

Research Projects Agency (DARPA) through various projects, and it is currently also supported by USA National Science Foundation (NSF).[1] Development is done as a collaboration between several universities and laboratories, and the project includes substantial contributions from different other researchers.

Ns-2 provides substantial support for the simulation of TCP, routing, and multicast protocols over wired and wireless networks. It is the most used simulator in research and academic environments, and because of this, as well as due to its open source nature, also one of the most "abused." In this context it is important to note the warning that welcomes visitors of the Ns-2 website even at present:

> While we have considerable confidence in ns, ns is not a polished and finished product, but the result of an on-going effort of research and development. In particular, bugs in the software are still being discovered and corrected. Users of ns are responsible for verifying for themselves that their simulations are not invalidated by bugs. We are working to help the user with this by significantly expanding and automating the validation tests and demos. Similarly, users are responsible for verifying for themselves that their simulations are not invalidated because the model implemented in the simulator is not the model that they were expecting. The ongoing ns manual should help in this process.

This warning does not mean that the Ns-2 network simulator is not reliable, but is intended to inform users about the need to validate both the models used in simulation, and the experiment results obtained. Note that the fact that other simulators do not explicitly provide such a warning doesn't signify that they are necessarily better than Ns-2, and care should be taken whenever models are used in an experimental setup.

The presentation we make in this section is based on the documentation from the web site dedicated to Ns-2 at the institution that maintains its, the University of Southern California [105].

---

[1]A new version of Ns, called Ns-3, started being developed, and its first release occurred in 2008. However, even as of 2010, this newer version has not reached a very large user base, and we shall not discuss it in this book, despite the fact that it does have network emulation features, just as Ns-2.

6.1.1 *Emulation Support*

According to its authors, in the case of Ns-2 emulation refers to the ability to introduce the simulator into a live network. For this purpose, special objects exist within the simulator that are capable of performing the following two tasks:

- Introduce traffic from a live network into the simulator.
- Inject traffic from the simulator into a live network.

There are two primary types of scenarios for Ns-2 based emulation, as follows:

(1) The simulator appears to the real end nodes in the experiment as a router, or even as a larger network, depending on the simulated models. In this case, the live traffic from the end nodes passes through the simulator (transparently to end nodes), and is affected by the objects within the simulation, or by other traffic in the live network.

(2) The simulator appears to the real end nodes as another end station. This alternative means that the simulator can include traffic sources or sinks that communicate with real-world entities.

Of course, one may imagine a scenario in which the nodes within the simulated network (as per the first kind of scenario) generate traffic that interacts with the end nodes sending their traffic through the simulator. Note however that the interaction between internally generated traffic and real end nodes is not a fully developed feature in Ns-2.

6.1.1.1 Architecture for emulation

Figure 6.1 shows the architecture used by Ns-2 for network emulation. The interface between the real world and the simulator is handled by modules that perform the capture of the live traffic, and the injection of the traffic that went through or was generated within the simulator into the live network. However, the data representation within Ns-2 is different than that in a real network. This is because in simulation environments several optimizations

Figure 6.1. Emulation architecture of Ns-2.

are made in order to speed up simulation, and a class of such optimizations refers to representing data in a more compact way than the actual network encoding. Obviously such optimizations are not compatible with the live network. For this reason, traffic capture is immediately followed by a conversion of the real packets to Ns-2 internal representation. Similarly, once data leaves the simulator, it has to be converted from the internal representation to the live network format before it can be injected into the real network.

One more issue when using the emulation capabilities of Ns-2 is the event scheduler. As a discrete event simulator, Ns-2 normally uses a scheduler that orders events by the logical time associated to them, and executes them in this order. For the purpose of emulation, real time (the so called "wall clock") must be used when executing events. This function is accomplished by a real-time scheduler that, while using the same underlying structure as the standard calendar-queue based scheduler, ties event execution to real time.

6.1.2 *Operation Modes*

There are two operation modes for network emulation with Ns-2, as follows:

- *Opaque mode*: Data packets originating from the live network are treated as "opaque," i.e., their content is ignored.
- *Protocol mode*: Live data packets are interpreted by Ns-2, and can even be generated within the simulator.

In opaque mode, Ns-2 treats live network data as uninterpreted packets. This means that real-world protocol fields are not directly manipulated by the simulator. Thus, live data packets may be dropped, delayed, re-ordered, or duplicated by the simulator; how-

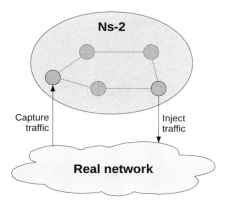

Figure 6.2. Ns-2 operation in "opaque mode."

ever, since no protocol processing is performed, protocol-specific traffic manipulation scenarios, such as dropping the TCP segment containing a certain sequence number, cannot be performed.

Figure 6.2 depicts a typical usage of Ns-2 based emulation in opaque mode. In this mode, the simulator acts as a router, allowing real-world traffic to be passed through without being manipulated. The internal representation of Ns-2 packets contains a pointer to the real network packet data. Simulator actions on Ns-2 packets are equivalent to actions on the real packets. For instance, when Ns-2 drops internally a packet, the corresponding real network packet will not be injected into the live network anymore, as if it would have been dropped in a real network. The opaque mode of operation is useful for evaluating the behavior of real-world network application and protocol implementations when subjected to adverse network conditions that are not protocol specific (packet loss, delay, packet reordering or duplication, etc.).

In protocol mode, Ns-2 interprets and/or generates live network traffic containing arbitrary data. This makes it possible to make more complex experiments, but puts a higher load on the simulator. This is because, as explained above, packet data (including headers) has to be dealt with in real time in the same encoding format with that of the live network. Moreover, simulator components that generate traffic have to do it using network packet representation and in real time. In protocol mode, the Ns-2 representation of a

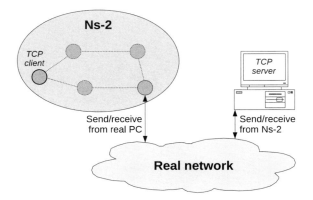

Figure 6.3. Ns-2 operation in "protocol mode."

packet will contain a pointer to the corresponding field within the real packet.

In Fig. 6.3 we present a typical example of using Ns-2 in protocol mode. In this example an emulated TCP client running in Ns-2 interacts transparently with a real-world TCP server that runs on a PC by generating and receiving real TCP traffic. At present, the emulation functionality of Ns-2 makes it possible to use in protocol mode ICMP, ARP, and TCP agents. Thus, Ns-2 based emulation can used for end-to-end application testing, protocol and conformance testing while applying in Ns-2 protocol-specific impairments to the traffic for these protocols.

6.1.3 *Emulation Components*

When running as an emulator, the interface between the Ns-2 simulator and the live network is provided by a set of objects, called *tap agents* and *network objects*. In addition, the aforementioned real-time scheduler must also be used when performing an emulation experiment with Ns-2. We shall describe next in more detail each of these components.

Tap agents Tap agents are software components that embed live network data into simulated packets, and create live network packets using the data from simulated packets. Tap agents can generate simulator packets containing arbitrarily assigned values within the Ns-2 packet representation. In particular, tap agents handle setting the packet size field and the type field[2] for the internal representations of the real packets injected into the simulator. Equivalent actions are taken for the packets than need to be injected by the simulator into the live network. One or more tap agents can be instantiated in a simulator, but each of these tap agents can have at most one associated network object.

Network objects   Network objects are components associated to tap agents, and provide an entry point for the sending and receiving of live data. They mediate the access to either a live network, or to a trace file of captured network packets. There are several classes of network objects, depending on the protocol layer used to access the underlying network. Generally, network objects provide an entry point into the live network at a particular protocol layer (e.g., Ethernet, IP, UDP, etc.), and with a particular access mode (read-only, write-only, or read-write). Some network objects provide specialized facilities, such as filtering or promiscuous access in the case of the Pcap/BPF network object, or group membership for the UDP/IP multicast function of the UDP/IP network object. Several types of network objects are currently supported by Ns-2, as follows:

- *Pcap/BPF network objects*: Provide an extended interface to the LBNL packet capture library called "libpcap." This library gives the ability to capture link-layer frames from network interface drivers. The library delivers a copy of the frames to those programs making use of it. Another function of the library is reading and writing packet trace files in the format of the "tcpdump" program. The interface provided by Ns-2 also allows for writing frames out to the network interface driver, provided the driver itself allows this action.

    An important issue related to capture is filtering. Ns-2 supports the Berkeley Packet Filter (BPF) mechanism, an implementation of which processes the filter rules, and applies the resulting pattern matching instructions to

---

[2]In the context of emulation, a specific value is used for the packet type field, called "PT_LIVE."

received frames. Only those frames that match the filter patterns are effectively "received" in Ns-2; the other frames are unaffected.

Although Pcap/BPF objects can be used directly to generate traffic, Ns-2 developers recommend using the raw IP network object for sending IP packets, as this will ensure that the system routing table is used to determine proper link-layer headers. Alternatively, one can use the Pcap/file network objects described below to generate traffic based on a trace file.

- *Pcap/file network objects*: Are similar to the Pcap/BPF objects, except that network data injected into the simulator is obtained from a previously captured trace file rather than from a live network. The opposite function, i.e., the ability to output data to trace files instead of injecting it into the real network, is said to be under development. This facility would make it possible to create with Ns-2 trace files that are compatible with tcpdump.

- *IP network objects*: Provide raw access to the IP protocol, and allow the complete specification of IP packets, including headers. This class of network objects can be used as a base for deriving network object implementations for higher-layer protocols.

- *UDP/IP network objects*: Provide access to the UDP implementation of the system on which Ns-2 is running. Another important function is the support for IP multicast group membership operations. However, this type of network objects is marked as "in progress" by Ns-2 developers, so one can only expect limited functionality.

Real-time scheduler   A software real-time scheduler that ties event execution within the simulator to real time. Provided sufficient CPU resources are available to keep up with arriving packets, the virtual time managed by Ns-2 should be close enough to the real time. However, if the simulator becomes too slow to keep up with real time elapse, a warning will be triggered. According to Ns-2 documentation, by default this warning will be generated if the clock skew exceeds 10 ms.

6.1.4 *Discussion*

The previous sections show that Ns-2 developers have put effort into making the simulator work as an emulator too. The fact that the required architectural changes are not so significant facilitated this task. Nevertheless, at this moment it is probably too early to claim the Ns-2 can be fully used as an emulator. The main reasons for saying this are given below:

- No guarantees whatsoever are given regarding execution speed. This is certainly first of all due to the fact that there is such a wide range of execution platforms and operating systems on which Ns-2 can be run. Moreover, as execution optimization for emulation is not necessarily a priority, we suspect that Ns-2 performance is lower when compared to tools designed on purpose for network emulation.
- The description of the supported network objects shows that the range of protocols for which interaction with real hosts is possible is still very limited; this restricts the range of possible applications of the Ns-2 based emulation.

Note that there are independent efforts in improving the accuracy and performance of Ns-2, such as the work in [62]. However, we believe that the new generation of the network simulator, Ns-3, will also address these concerns, and once the implementation is finalized, Ns-3 can become a strong competitor to the medium and high-complexity emulators that exist at present. This is because, if the entire range of existing models available in simulation mode in Ns-2 (or Ns-3) could also be put to use for emulation, experiments with complex scenarios could be performed.

Finally, let us justify the classification made in Table 3.1 regarding Ns-2. As an open-source software, Ns-2 is clearly part of the free network emulators, and of software type. Powered by a simulation engine, complex networks can be modeled with Ns-2, hence it is a topology level emulator. The same simulation engine ensures that the conditions that can be reproduced have a high complexity. As for emulation execution, it is centralized.[3]

---

[3] Note that extensions of Ns-2 that enable distributed execution do exist, such as the one called PDNS [93].

6.2 OPNET Modeler

OPNET Modeler is a network simulator developed by OPNET Technologies [80]. OPNET Modeler is intended for use in the R&D process for analyzing and designing communication networks, devices, protocols, and applications. Its users can employ simulated networks to compare the impact of different technology designs on the end-to-end behavior of applications and protocols. OPNET Modeler incorporates a broad suite of protocols and technologies, and includes a development environment to enable modeling several network types and technologies including

- network-layer protocols, such as IPv4 and IPv6
- transport-layer protocols, such as TCP and UDP
- traffic engineering techniques, such as MPLS
- routing protocols, such as AODV, OLSR, and OSPF
- network applications, such as VoIP

The description we provide in this section is mainly based on the information from the web site of OPNET Modeler [80].

6.2.1 *Feature Overview*

The key features of OPNET Modeler according to OPNET Technologies are the following:

- Fast simulation engine
- Large library of models for wired and wireless protocols, as well as for vendor devices, provided with source code to enable customization
- Object-oriented and hierarchical modeling environment
- Wireless simulation capabilities, including terrain, mobility, and multiple path loss models
- Multiple simulation approaches

    — *Discrete event simulation*: standard approach
    — *Analytical simulation*: less detail for faster execution
    — *Hybrid simulation*: combines discrete event and analytical simulation methods

- parallel simulation engine for 32-bit and 64-bit CPU architectures
- support for distributed simulation through grid computing
- possibility to interface simulations with live systems via the optional System-in-the-Loop (SITL) module
- open interface for integrating external libraries and other simulators
- integrated, GUI-based debugging and analysis

One of the strong selling points of OPNET Modeler is probably the extensive support for wireless networks through "Wireless Suite" and the "Wireless Suite for Defense" library suites. Wireless network professionals can use these libraries for analyzing the end-to-end behavior of applications, tuning network performance, planning networks services, and so on.

The OPNET Modeler Wireless Suite is a set of libraries that make possible the modeling, simulation, and analysis of a broad range of wireless networks. Researchers can use these libraries to design and optimize proprietary wireless protocols, such as access control and scheduling algorithms. Simulations for mobile networks are also possible, including ground, airborne, and satellite systems. OPNET Modeler Wireless Suite supports several types of wireless networks, such as

- cellular networks: GSM, CDMA, UMTS, WiMAX (IEEE 802.16), LTE, etc.
- wireless LAN (IEEE 802.11) and mobile ad hoc networks (MANET)
- personal area networks (PAN): bluetooth, ZigBee, etc.
- satellite networks

The OPNET Modeler Wireless Suite for Defense is a set of libraries containing implementations of military-specific protocols and architectures. In addition, it allows the three-dimensional display of network simulations, including network topology, node relationships, and performance statistics, all of them overlaid on a realistically rendered terrain.

6.2.2 *System-in-the-loop Module*

The OPNET System-in-the-Loop module provides an interface for connecting live network hardware or software applications to an OPNET Modeler discrete event simulation. This enables emulation experiments with OPNET Modeler for the evaluation of real implementations of network systems. Using this approach, the prototype hardware or software system can interact in real time with the simulated virtual devices within OPNET, potentially avoiding the need for an expensive test lab.

OPNET Technologies suggests the following use cases for the combination of OPNET Modeler with the SITL module:

- Test prototype hardware and software applications for R&D, interoperability, scalability, or conformance purposes.
- Create a virtual training facility for network devices or applications that run over a simulated network infrastructure.
- Assess the behavior and performance of prototype applications and protocols by deploying them on a simulated network topology into which real network traffic is injected.

In order to use the SITL functionality, the computer hosting OPNET Modeler must be connected to the live network. Multiple simultaneous connections to multiple live devices or network segments are possible through different network interfaces. For each of the connected live devices, the simulated model must contain a so-called "gateway," which transforms real packets into simulated packets and vice versa, as they flow between the real network and the simulated one.

When the OPNET simulation begins, packets will flow in real-time between the live devices and the simulated network. As live packets arrive, they are captured, filtered, and converted into simulated packets by the corresponding gateway, then passed to the simulation engine. This has to take place in real time in order to guarantee the synchronization of the packet conversion and the inward flow of traffic. Similar actions are carried out for the outgoing packets.

Conversion models are required to "translate" the traffic between live and simulated devices in both directions, hence to perform emulation experiments. Such OPNET models are available for the following protocols:

- Network-layer protocols: IPv4, IPv6, ICMP, and ICMPv6
- Transport-layer protocols: TCP and UDP
- Routing protocols: OSPF, RIPv1, and RIPv2
- Application-layer protocols: FTP

In addition to the built-in conversion models, users can develop their own custom models by using the OPNET modeling environment, thus extending the built-in capabilities of the simulator.

6.2.3 *Emulation Scenarios*

OPNET Modeler documentation distinguishes two types of usage of the OPNET emulation features, depending on the role of the simulator in the experimental setup, as follows:

(1) *Live-Sim-Live*: most suited for software application testing and training
(2) *Sim-Live-Sim*: mainly recommended for network hardware testing and training

Let us look in more detail at each of these two alternatives.

6.2.3.1 Live-Sim-Live

In the Live-Sim-Live scenario, a live prototype application operates through a virtual network created by OPNET Modeler, which plays the role of a "virtual lab." This usage scenario allows developers to thoroughly analyze network applications by subjecting them to various experiments and interoperability tests over the simulated network. Developers can also estimate the user-perceived performance of an application when subjected to network effects such as latency, errors, etc.

Figure 6.4 illustrates the Live-Sim-Live type of scenario. Although OPNET Technologies indicates "testing and training for software applications" as the primary use case for the Live-Sim-Live scenario, we note that it is actually suited for any kind of activity in which the end devices/applications are available, and only the network over

Figure 6.4. Emulation using OPNET Modeler & SITL in a Live-Sim-Live scenario.

which they communicate must be simulated. One could very well connect end devices such as IP phones through the OPNET Modeler running in emulation mode to determine how network conditions influence communication quality.

Some of the benefits of this approach when applied to live systems such as network applications, protocols, or devices are according to OPNET Technologies are given below:

- Experiment using models that are derived directly from operational network device configurations.
- Assess the holistic effects of a test network (albeit virtual) instead of only tuning end-to-end parameters such as packet delay and discard ratios.
- Study the interaction between users and the live systems over realistic networks.
- Train users on live systems that are subjected to realistic network effects.

6.2.3.2 Sim-Live-Sim

Hardware testing during R&D activities, for interoperability, or for scalability purposes, can be accomplished by creating first a small live network with a few prototype devices, and then expanding the testbed to larger scenarios by using virtual networks. Two typical setups using this approach are shown in Fig. 6.5. One possibility is to employ two instances of OPNET Modeler and SITL, as depicted in Fig. 6.5(a). However, if network complexity is not very high, two ports of the live system could be connected to two network interfaces of the computer on which OPNET Modeler is running; this scenario makes it possible to perform the experiment by using only one instance of the simulator, as shown in Fig. 6.5(b).

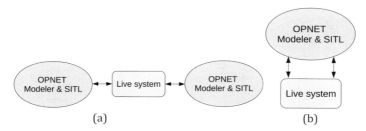

(a)   (b)

Figure 6.5. Emulation using OPNET Modeler & SITL in a Sim-Live-Sim scenario. (a) Using two simulator instances. (b) Using one simulator instance.

According to OPNET Technologies, integrating live systems into simulated network entities provides several advantages:

- Test prototype network devices with simulated control and data traffic.
- Scale-up testbeds beyond the number of prototype systems and other required network devices that are available for experimental purposes.
- Perform interoperability testing without the need to remove legacy systems from production networks.
- Train users on new production devices that are placed in realistic network conditions.

6.2.3.3 Complex scenarios

An important issue when using SITL is the real-time execution speed requirement. This can become a hindrance should one wish to emulate large networks. To cope with this, SITL provides a feature called "daisy chaining." This operation mode of SITL allows connecting together simulator instances, each running a portion of the overall simulation scenario. Reducing the complexity of the scenario executed by each simulator instance makes real-time operation possible even for large networks. Readers may recognize this operation mode as being similar to the approach we called "partially distributed emulation" in Section 3.3.1.

Another advantage of daisy chaining of OPNET Modelers is that it allows building more complex setups than the ones we discussed

Figure 6.6. Emulation using OPNET Modeler & SITL in a complex setup with multiple live and simulated components.

so far. A hypothetical "Live-Sim-Live-Sim-Live" scenario could be as follows:

(1) An end user runs a live application on a computer.
(2) The traffic is communicated via an emulated network to a real wireless station.
(3) The real wireless station sends the traffic via radio to another wireless station situated at a different location (e.g., by a satellite network).
(4) The wireless station at the other end communicates the traffic via a second emulated network to a central server.

OPNET Technologies suggests using such configurations for

- testing a live network application as it is transmitted over a set of live radios that are integrated with a more complex virtual network
- training on a network application during a live transmission over live radios that are integrated with a more complex virtual network
- testing live radio prototypes by driving real application traffic through them, and through virtual networks
- training on a live radio as live application traffic is being communicated through it

6.2.4 *Discussion*

OPNET Modeler is clearly a mature product, and its support for emulation through the use of the System-in-the-Loop (SITL) feature is good. Although OPNET Technologies indicates two types of scenarios in which simulator-based emulation can be used, we believe that the Live-Sim-Live approach, and the more complex scenarios that can be derived from it, are of most interest. The other scenario type, Sim-Live-Sim, is undoubtedly useful for some kind of tests, such as interoperability. However, the fact that OPNET Modeler is basically a software tool has a strong impact on the amount of traffic it can generate; therefore, it can never become a substitute for dedicated test equipment in situations when the load that must be injected into the device under test is significant, as is the case of switches/routers, for example.

A related issue that applies to all the alternatives of using OPNET Modeler is that there can be no guarantees on the real-time execution speed of the simulator for arbitrary-size networks. This means that success will vary depending on how complex the simulated networks are, how much traffic they are loaded with, and what is the processing power of the computer on which OPNET Modeler runs. While the support for distributed execution through grid computing should increase the size of the network that can be emulated, OPNET provides no figures regarding the performance level one may expect.

The list of protocols that are fully supported by OPNET Modeler in emulation mode is reasonably long (see Section 6.2.2). Nevertheless, we want to emphasize that this list is still far from being complete; for instance, none of the widely used protocols in ad hoc or mesh network, OLSR and AODV, are supported. For the unsupported protocols, the user has the choice to either implement the required conversion models, or use the simulator in what was called in the context of Ns-2 "opaque mode" (see Section 6.1.2). This means that the simulator will only let those packets flow through it, but will not be able to interact with them at protocol level.

Let us review now the classification presented in Table 3.1 regarding OPNET Modeler in an emulation context. As a software product of OPNET Technologies, OPNET Modeler is a commercial network emulator, and of software type. Emulation with OPNET Modeler and the SITL module makes use of the simulation engine and the associated libraries of network models; hence, complex networks can be modeled with it, making it a topology-level emulator with high scenario complexity. Both centralized and distributed execution are possible with OPNET Modeler, which also provides support for parallel execution.

6.3 QualNet Developer

QualNet Developer is a simulation tool developed by Scalable Network Technologies [96]. QualNet Developer is based on a wireless network simulator named GloMoSim that is still available freely for academic use. The simulation engine of QualNet Developer was however rewritten, and support for many additional protocols and technologies was added; hence, they cannot be currently regarded as equivalent solutions.

The QualNet Developer network simulator is intended for estimating wireless, wired and mixed network system performance, and runs on several versions of Windows, Mac OS X, and Linux operating systems. It was designed to take full advantage of the multi-threading capabilities of multi-core 64-bit processors; as such, it is said to support the simulation of thousands of network nodes. In addition, QualNet Developer permits distributed execution on computer clusters. It also features the required components for linking seamlessly with other modeling/simulation applications, as well as with live networks.

In addition to the included sets of libraries of models, QualNet Developer also allows users to develop and run custom network models. Using a visual development environment one can design the models, and efficiently code the required protocols. The same environment makes it possible to run the models, and presents to users real-time statistics for the experiment, as well as helpful packet-level information.

This section uses mainly information available on the web site of QualNet Developer [96].

6.3.1 *Components*

QualNet Developer is marketed as a suite of tools that complement each other when making simulation experiments. These tools are:

QualNet Scenario Designer   Modeling tool that allows users to set up the geographical distribution, the physical connections, and the functional parameters of the network nodes that are to be simulated. The tool uses a GUI in which the scenario can be built using a library of node types. The user can also define network layer protocols and traffic characteristics for each of the scenario nodes.

QualNet Animator Visualization and analysis tool that can be used to watch the traffic flows through the network, and view dynamic graphs of critical performance metrics while a simulation experiment is running. This visualizer can also be used to animate the results of a previous experiment.

QualNet 3D Visualizer QT-based tool for displaying rich-content 3D animations of network simulations. It can be used instead of QualNet Animator to visualize in a more realistic fashion the simulated scenarios.

QualNet Analyzer Statistics representation tool that displays the metrics of simulation experiments. One can use pre-designed reports in QualNet Analyzer, but also customize graphs with user-defined statistics. One can view the metrics in real time while a simulation is running. Other features include: multi-experiment reports, and graph export to spreadsheets.

QualNet Packet Tracer Packet-level visualization tool for viewing the contents of a packet as it goes through the network protocol stack. This tool is useful in particular for understanding low-level protocol behavior, and for debugging purposes.

6.3.2 *EXata Emulator*

Until recently, Scalable Network Technologies provided an optional library, called IPNE (IP Network Emulator), that added emulation capabilities to QualNet Developer. Nevertheless, since 2009 the functionality of IPNE was integrated with that of QualNet Developer, resulting in a standalone tool named EXata.

EXata is a wireless network emulator that creates a digital network replica that interfaces with real networks in real time, using real applications. This makes it possible to recreate realistic communication conditions at different layers of the network instead of the often-used "perfect communication."

Next generation communication system development lead to the concept of *net-centric systems*, which refers to those systems that use the network as an essential component, typically as the operating infrastructure that makes their operation possible. In a military context, net-centric systems aim at connecting all personnel, improve situational awareness, and provide a common operational picture. This makes that the network systems have gradually increased in importance, and are currently essential both in commercial and military applications, being often "mission critical."

All networks face impairments, such as bandwidth limitation, security attacks, scalability issues, traffic congestion, etc. Mobile networks present even more challenges, including terrain, weather and environmental conditions, mobility effects, and limited battery power. EXata is intended to help evaluate the effects of these conditions on network systems.

6.3.2.1 EXata features

The most important features of EXata according to Scalable Network Technologies are as follows:

- *Accuracy*: The digital representation of networks created by EXata is so accurate that a user or network system connected to the virtual network cannot differentiate between the digital representation and a real network.
- *Realism*: As EXata allows the digitally representation of network devices, software, transmitters, antennas, terrain effects, atmospheric effects, and human interaction effects, the virtual network created becomes a realistic alternative for the real network, as it includes the parameters that will affect the performance of network systems in reality.
- *Time and cost savings*: By using emulation instead of the typical network test equipment, evaluations that traditionally required a long time to complete can be performed faster by using EXata, and at a lower cost.
- *Scalability*: EXata is said to provide the same fidelity for networks between 50 and 5,000 nodes. This claim seems

to be based on the presence of multi-threading (parallel) and distributed execution features of QualNet Developer, as the following statement of Scalable Network Technologies indicates:

> Competitors' simulation programs, written with legacy sequential processing code, can only simulate a maximum of about 200 devices, and fidelity drops as you approach that number. With EXata, you get the same accurate representation of your network whether you're testing 50 nodes or 5,000.

Although QualNet Developer supports a large number of network protocols, those that can be used in an emulation experiment using EXata are limited. The current list of the supported protocols in EXata is given below:

- Network-layer protocols: IPv4, ICMP, ARP
- Transport-layer protocols: TCP, UDP
- Routing protocols: OSPFv2, RIPv2, OLSR
- Application-layer protocols: FTP, HTTP, Ping, SNMP, Telnet, Traceroute

6.3.2.2 EXata components

The components of EXata share many features with those of QualNet Developer, which is not surprising given that EXata is derived from QualNet Developer. The components are the following:

EXata Architect GUI intended for building network topologies. EXata Architect includes editors allowing detailed design of devices and networks; thus, the Device Model Editor can be used to build custom communication devices. Alternatively, one can use predefined devices models for routers, switches, hubs, wireless access points, base stations, and mobile users. As shown in the screenshot in Fig. 6.7, one can create complex and realistic 3D scenarios using EXata Architect. The visualization controls allow monitoring emulation progress, and event animation.

EXata Connection Manager In addition to the EXata emulation engine, that runs on a server and creates the virtual emu-

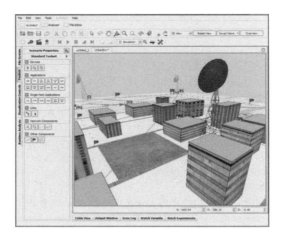

Figure 6.7. EXata Architect screenshot (from EXata web site).

lated network, using EXata requires the presence of Connection Managers that run on the end systems involved in the experiment. EXata Connection Manager ensures that the applications under test running on the end system communicate their traffic through the emulated virtual network. Note that applications require no modification or customization for being used with EXata.

An important feature of EXata Connection Manager is that it allows to "map" the computer on which it is running to *any* node in the emulated network. All traffic from that computer will be sent by EXata from the mapped node into the emulated network, and all traffic to the mapped node will be delivered by EXata to the associated computer.

EXata Analyzer An analysis and debugging tool that allows investigating network experiments as a complement to EXata Architect. With EXata Analyzer one can monitor the values of important parameters, and view dynamic graphs of critical performance indicators, such as received signal strength or throughput. EXata Analyzer also allows displaying customized performance metrics.

6.3.2.3 EXata/Cyber

EXata/Cyber is a specialized version of EXata that is intended for the analysis of cyber-security network issues. Network security is an increasing issue in computer networks, and affects wireless networks in particular. Such networks are vulnerable to radio jamming attacks that may be difficult to distinguish from phenomena such as interference, terrain and weather effects. Mobile ad-hoc networks (MANET) can also be subjected to other attack techniques, such as eavesdropping, network probes or port scanning, and denial of service attacks.

EXata/Cyber is a platform that builds on EXata, and adds features that allow users to create and modify network attacks and counter measures. The generated attacks can be targeted to both wired and wireless networks. Users can then analyze their impact on the network itself, on the applications, and on the end-users.

The two supplementary tools that makes such investigations possible with EXata/Cyber are:

Network Security Library A toolkit with models that encrypt, authenticate, manage key distribution and certificates, create wormhole attacks, route securely, and mimic adversaries. The library can be customized to include new attacks, network intrusion techniques, as well as counter measures.

Cyber Warfare Support EXata/Cyber includes features that allow users to dynamically launch cyber attacks on the virtual emulated network built in EXata. Such features include

- eavesdropping
- radio jamming attacks
- distributed denial of service (DDoS) attacks
- other specific attacks that can be detected using network intrusion detection software tools, such as "snort" [103]

6.3.3 *Discussion*

As OPNET Technologies did for the OPNET Modeler, Scalable Network Technologies too have added several years ago the capability of network emulation to their simulator product, QualNet

Developer. Nevertheless, Scalable Network Technologies decided to take emulation support even further, and market the emulator component as a standalone product, replacing the previously optional library for QualNet Developer. This shows that even large commercial companies realized the potential offered by network emulation for network system evaluation. We speculate that what may seem now as a niche market, will become larger and larger, and all companies developing network simulators, as well as all the free network simulator developers, will seriously consider emulation support in the near future, and will provide solutions targeted at this market.

One aspect that we believe needs more discussion regarding EXata is the claim regarding the network size that can be emulated (up to 5000 nodes without loss in fidelity). While this claim is certainly a strong selling point, we recommend that readers should take it "with a grain of salt." Although we agree that, given the right circumstances, such an exploit is possible, we warn about the fact that it cannot be accomplished on an ordinary PC, especially when the network throughput is high. Therefore, any user needs to determine empirically whether the scenario he/she intends to emulate, and the load that will be placed on the emulated network, do no exceed the capabilities of the execution platform. The parallel execution features of EXata should improve performance through a partially-distributed emulation approach, but Scalable Network Technologies doesn't provide any details about the conditions in which the said "5000 node network" was emulated. Nevertheless, the following related statement appears in QualNet Developer documentation:

> [...] a cluster of 16 dual 2 GHz Opteron systems connected by an Infiniband switch achieved real-time speed for 3,500 nodes (this scenario was designed for optimum performance in terms of traffic, mobility, and partitioning).

This statement shows that a 16 computer cluster was required to achieve real-time execution of 3500 nodes (hence, make emulation of that network possible). In addition, the scenario had to be designed in an *optimum* way to achieve this performance. We conclude that, given a sufficiently large cluster, one can probably emulate a 5000 node scenario. However, this may be a challenging task, especially since the scenario design methodology for such a purpose is not documented by the company. Moreover, as traffic details are not revealed for the cited experiment, network throughput may have been rather low. Achieving a higher throughput may require a significant increase in resources, or may very well be impossible at this time.

Nevertheless, Scalable Network Technology did provide more details about performance in an article about the parallel capabilities of its products [98]. The data shows the experiment duration when using QualNet Developer 4.0 running on three different multi-core platforms. The simulation experiment was an IEEE 802.11b wireless scenario running 700 nodes with terrain-based propagation, random mobility at a speed of 30 m/s, and AODV routing. The simulated time was 900 s. Traffic through the network consisted of 625 CBR sessions sending 512-byte packets at one second intervals.

Table 6.1 shows the results of these experiments based on the graphs presented in [98]. The data shows that all dual and quad-core trials ran faster than real time (about three times faster in the best case, the quad-core AMD CPU using all 4 cores). This means that such platforms could potentially be used for emulation experiments as well. We note however that, even though the network size is large, the total amount of traffic generated (approximately 625 512-byte packets per second, i.e., 2.56 Mbps) is not significant compared to the network capacity, in which the maximum operating rate of *each* wireless link is 11 Mbps. We suspect that a higher load on the

Table 6.1. Simulation experiment duration using QualNet 4.0 on three different multi-core platforms

CPU type	2 GHz Intel Core Duo		2.6 GHz AMD Quad			2 × 2.6 GHz AMD Dual Core		
Number of CPU cores	1	2	1	2	4	1	2	4
Experiment duration [s]	1247	806	982	620	334	963	610	352
Faster than real time	No	Yes	No	Yes	Yes	No	Yes	Yes

network may have changed the results significantly, and emulation of this scenario may have become impossible even on the fastest tested configuration. In such cases, distributed architectures such as computer clusters, which are supported both by QualNet Developer and EXata, may be the only alternative that is left for improving simulation speed.

Another issue that is worth noting regarding EXata is that, at this moment, it cannot be used to evaluate IPv6-related technologies. As such, related protocols, such as ICMPv6, are also not available. However, with the spread of IPv6, we expect that in the near future such capabilities will also be present in EXata.

As for the classification presented in Table 3.1, QualNet Developer, and more specifically EXata, were categorized as follows. Given the nature of the product, EXata is a commercial software network emulator. EXata is also a topology-level emulator, and it supports both centralized and distributed execution (as well as parallel one).

6.4 NCTUns

NCTUns is a different kind of tool compared to the ones presented so far in this chapter, as it is a *hybrid* between a network simulator and emulator [111]. As such, NCTUns is capable both of simulating and emulating various protocols used in wired and wireless IP networks. The core technology that makes this possible is a specific kernel re-entering methodology that provides several advantages when compared to typical network simulators, such as Ns-2 (see Section 6.4.2 for more details).

The NCTUns simulation engine is open source and has an open API, which can be used to implement new protocols and integrate them into the simulation engine. The settings and configurations of a simulation task are typically generated by a GUI, and are automatically transferred to the simulation engine for execution. However, these files can also be changed using a text editor, and distributed manually if needed.

Note that, although NCTUns is open source, it can only be used free of charge for non-commercial non-profit academic or education purposes. Use by commercial entities requires purchasing a commercial license.

Our presentation in this section is based on two papers related to NCTUns written by its authors [111, 112], as well as on the information available on the web site of NCTUns [67].

6.4.1 *Emulation Features*

NCTUns supports a wide range of network technologies, both wired and wireless. As for network protocols, NCTUns support the following ones:

- Network-layer protocols: IP, ICMP, Mobile IP
- Transport-layer protocols: TCP, UDP
- Routing protocols: OSPF, RIP, DSR, AODV, ADV, DSDV
- Application-layer protocols: FTP, HTTP, RTP/RTCP/SDP, Telnet, Traceroute, BitTorrent

The most important features of NCTUns, with focus on emulation, are given below following the description given by its developers:

- NCTUns can be used as an emulator, both to let a real-world host exchange packets with nodes in the network simulated by NCTUns, and to allow two real-world hosts to exchange packets through the network simulated by NCTUns. Thus, a seamless integration between real-life networks and simulated ones is achieved, with real-life network traffic passing through and interacting with simulated networks.
- NCTUns supports distributed emulation of large networks by employing multiple computers. For experiments that involve a large number of network applications and real-world devices, resulting in a significant amount of traffic, a single computer may not have enough CPU power and memory to run the emulation experiment in real time. In such situations, NCTUns can partition the emulated network into several smaller fragments, and have each such fragment emulated by a different computer. This distributed emulation mechanism is transparent for NCTUns users.

- NCTUns uses the Linux TCP/IP protocol stack to generate high-fidelity results. This is made possible by using a specific kernel re-entering simulation methodology that we shall discuss in the next section.
- NCTUns can run real-life Unix application programs on the simulated nodes without any modification. The real-life programs can be used to generate realistic network traffic. This capability also enables researchers to evaluate the functionality and performance of a real distributed application or system under various network conditions. Another important advantage of this feature is that application programs that are being developed during simulation studies can subsequently be directly deployed and run on real-world Unix machines. This eliminates the need to port the prototype implementation used for simulation to a real-world system, as required by traditional network simulators.
- Network setup and usage using NCTUns are the same as in real-life IP networks. For example, network interfaces in the NCTUns virtual network have an IP address automatically assigned to them, and application programs use these IP addresses to communicate with each other. Moreover, NCTUns employs real-life Unix network configuration and monitoring tools. For example, the Unix "route," "ifconfig," "netstat," "tcpdump," and "traceroute" commands can be run on the simulated nodes to configure and monitor the simulated network. For these reasons, any person who is familiar with real-life IP networks will easily learn how to use NCTUns. For the same reasons, NCTUns can be used as an educational tool to teach students how to configure and operate a real-life network.

6.4.2 *Basic Methodology*

The key difference between NCTUns and the other network simulators presented in this chapter is the technique called by its authors "kernel re-entering simulation methodology." We recommend the reference [112] to readers interested in obtaining more details

Figure 6.8. Target emulation scenario for NCTUns.

about this methodology, and how it is applied to enable network emulation using NCTUns; below we provide only a brief description.

The kernel re-entering simulation methodology uses a type of network interface called *tunnel network interface*. These interfaces are a pseudo network interfaces that are *not* attached to a physical network, but are associated to a real network interface. Tunnel interfaces are available on many Unix operating systems, and are treated in the same way as the real network interfaces by the operating system. A network application program can send or receive packets through a tunnel network interface, in the same way it would do through an Ethernet interface.

When using tunnel network interfaces, the communication between user applications and the operating system is done through special files. If an application program opens the special file of a tunnel interface, and writes a packet into it, the packet will enter the kernel. From the kernel perspective, the packet is like any other network packet, and will go up through the kernel network protocol stack. Similarly, when an application tries to read a packet from the special file associated to a tunnel interface, the first packet in the corresponding output queue maintained by the operating system kernel will be dequeued and copied to the application program. From the kernel point of view, it is as if the packet would have been transmitted on a real network interface.

Let us imagine that one would like the emulate the simple scenario depicted in Fig. 6.8, in which a TCP client wants to access a TCP server over a network link whose quality degradation is to be emulated.

The structure that NCTUns would build for such a scenario is shown in Fig. 6.9. The target scenario is completely created on one computer, on which the NCTUns simulation engine is also running, as follows:

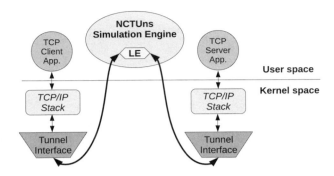

Figure 6.9. Emulation structure built by NCTUns for a target scenario.

- The two physical TCP client and server hosts are represented by equivalent application instances running on the same simulation host.
- The operating system routing table of the simulation host is configured so that packets originating from the TCP client are delivered to one tunnel interface, and packets coming from the TCP server are delivered to the other tunnel interface; the same interfaces are used to provide packets to the TCP client and server, respectively.
- Applications use the TCP/IP stack of the simulation host multiple times, but this has no adverse effect, and it doesn't require any specific processing from the point of view of the operating system.
- Both tunnel interfaces are attached to the NCTUns simulation engine, which ensure that the communication takes place as if it would over a network link. This is done as follows:

  — The simulation engine opens the two special files associated to the two tunnel interfaces and reads the outgoing packets produced by those interfaces.
  — Whenever the TCP client sends a packet, it is taken by the simulation engine, it is subjected to the network degradation for the emulated network link, including propagation delay, transmission time, possible packet

loss, etc., and then written to the special file of the tunnel interface associated to the TCP server.

— Similarly, packets from the TCP server are delivered to the TCP client via the emulated network link, possibly with different degradation characteristics.

The kernel re-entering methodology described makes that the emulated network is actually very similar to a real network from the protocol stack point of view, and only differs in the emulation of the network degradation that occurs in transit. Both the application and the simulation engine run in the user area of the operating system, but they communicate with each other by means of standard kernel mechanisms. This has the following effects:

- The TCP client and server programs, which run on top of the kernels, do not know about the network emulation process. Other existing real-world application programs can run on the emulated network as well, and network utility programs can be used on the emulated network in a straightforward manner.
- The kernel has no knowledge of the emulation process, since it occurs outside it, and is involved in a communication process no different compared to that taking place over a real network.
- Although Fig. 6.9 shows two TCP/IP stacks, they are actually a single one, the protocol stack of the computer on which the entire simulation process takes place. This makes that NCTUns doesn't have to model the protocol stack, which is a significant difference when compared to the other network simulators.

6.4.3 *Additional Features*

NCTUns has several other features that facilitate experiments, as follows:

- Despite the fact that NCTUns uses real implementations for some aspects of the simulation, as with other simulation tools, fixing the random number seed to a certain value for a simulation task will lead to obtaining the same results across different simulation runs, even though there may be other activities occurring on the simulation machine.

- NCTUns provides a GUI environment that helps users accomplish tasks such as

  — draw network topologies
  — configure the protocol modules used by the simulated nodes
  — specify the movement of mobile nodes
  — plot network performance graphs
  — replay the animation of a previous simulation experiment

- NCTUns supports remote and concurrent simulations by using a distributed architecture. The GUI and simulation engine are separately implemented, and use a client-server model to communicate with each other. Thus, one can submit from the GUI a simulation job to a server that runs the simulation engine. The server will execute the submitted simulation job, and return the results to the remote GUI when finished. This approach makes it possible to use cluster computing, and execute multiple simulation jobs in parallel on different servers to increase the simulation capacity.

- Unlike other free source programs, for which documentation is often lacking, NCTUns provides a rich documentation, including a user manual and a developer manual.

6.4.4 *Discussion*

A strong point that differentiates NCTUns from other simulators is that NCTUns uses the Linux TCP/IP stack for simulation/emulation, therefore it is in principle more accurate to real life compared to simulators that use specific TCP/IP model implementations. Readers should note however that, because NCTUns is limited to the Linux TCP/IP implementation, it is not possible to use it to build networks containing virtual Windows, FreeBSD, or Solaris computers. Such an approach would be possible with a typical simulator, since it would only require to implement a protocol model similar to that of the new operating system that needs to be emulated.

Although NCTUns has certain advantages over other network simulators, we have noticed that it is not so widely spread as Ns-2 in academic environments, or OPNET Modeler and QualNet Developer in commercial ones. However, it appears that the support for vehicular networks has received a wider recognition, and it represents one of its most appreciated features.

Table 3.1 includes the classification of NCTUns according to several categories, as follows. Regarding availability, NCTUns can be used both freely for non-commercial purposes, and also through a commercial license for purposes that do not fit the free use. As for implementation type, NCTUns is a software network simulator and emulator. Similar to the other emulation-capable simulators, NCTUns is a topology-level tool, and can reproduce scenarios with a high complexity. Moreover, NCTUns supports both centralized and distributed execution.

6.5 Comparison

In this section we shall compare the emulation-capable network simulators that we presented in this chapter. The comparison is summarized in Table 6.2.

If we look at the supported platforms, the clear "winner" appears to be Ns-2, which can be run basically on any modern operating system, and is followed closely by QualNet Developer. Readers should note that in the case of Ns-2 it is mainly the simulation engine that can run on all the supported platforms; however, for QualNet Developer most of the features are available on all the supported platforms, including the user-friendly GUI which lacks in Ns-2. OPNET Modeler supports mainly Windows, but also Linux. As for NCTUns, the only officially supported platform is Linux, which is understandable given the specific simulation methodology used (cf. Section 6.4.2).

Regarding the license type, Ns-2 is a purely free software, whereas NCTUns is only free for non-commercial uses. The other

Table 6.2. Comparison of emulation-capable network simulators: Ns-2, OPNET Modeler (SITL), QualNet Developer (EXata), and NCTUns

	Ns-2	OPNET Modeler (SITL)	QualNet Developer (EXata)	NCTUns
Supported platforms	Linux, FreeBSD, Mac OS X, Solaris, Windows	Linux, Windows	Linux, Windows, Mac OS X	Linux
License type	Free	Commercial	Commercial	Free for non-commercial use
Network-layer protocols	IPv4, ICMP, ARP	IPv4, IPv6, ICMP, ICMPv6, ARP	IPv4, ICMP, ARP	IPv4, ICMP, ARP, Mobile IP
Transport-layer protocols	TCP, UDP	TCP, UDP	TCP, UDP	TCP, UDP
Routing protocols	None	OSPF, RIP	OSPF, RIP, OLSR	OSPF, RIP, DSR, AODV, ADV, DSDV
Application-layer protocols	None	FTP	FTP, HTTP, Ping, SNMP, Telnet, Traceroute	FTP, HTTP, RTP/RTCP/SDP, Telnet, Traceroute, BitTorrent
Parallel and distributed execution	No	Yes	Yes	Yes
Facilitated emulation setup	No	No	Yes, using EXata Connection Manager	Yes, using the built-in GUI

two simulators, OPNET Modeler, and QualNet Developer are both commercial tools. We note that academic licenses at a significant discount are nevertheless available for these commercial tools.

The next rows of Table 6.2 refer to the emulation capabilities of the discussed simulators. Note that we focused only on those characteristics that are significant in the context of network emulation, and did not try to compare the features which are not directly relevant in this context, such as the types of wireless networks that each of them can simulate. The following remarks regarding the supported protocols can be made:

- All the presented simulators support the basic network-layer protocols for emulation experiments: IP, ICMP, and ARP. We note that OPNET Modeler does also provide support for the version 6 of IP and ICMP, unlike the other simulators. Another difference is the support of Mobile IP that is included with NCTUns.
- As expected, all the simulators make it possible to conduct emulations using both TCP and UDP at transport layer.
- A notable issue with Ns-2 is that *no* routing protocol is supported in emulation mode, which drastically reduces the area of potential applications. All the other simulators offer support for wired network routing protocols, such as OSPF and RIP. In addition, wireless routing protocols are also supported by some of them, as is the case of OLSR, supported by EXata, and DSR as well as several distance vector protocols, such as AODV, in the case of NCTUns.
- Ns-2 provides no support whatsoever for application layer either, and OPNET Modeler has only a minimal support for FTP. QualNet Developer and EXata, on the other hand, have an extensive support for emulating protocols such as HTTP, SNMP, and applications such as Ping, Telnet and Traceroute. NCTUns adds support for the RTP family of protocols, and for BitTorrent applications, pushed forward by the development of peer-to-peer network-related research.

One important issue related to all the emulation-capable network simulators is the size of the network that they can effectively emulate. Although it is not a direct indication of the supported network size, all the simulators except Ns-2 offer the possibility of distributed and parallel execution in a manner that is transparent to the user. Nevertheless, only QualNet Developer documentation provides clear figures about the performance one may expect in emulation mode (specifically, the 3500 node network emulated on a 16 dual-core 2 GHz Opteron computer cluster; see Section 6.3.3 for details).

We have mentioned in Chapter 2 that emulation experiments are more difficult to run than simulations, because of the increased configuration complexity. This is why our comparison also includes the facilitated emulation setup aspect. We observe that QualNet Developer (EXata) provides a tool called "EXata Connection Manager" that can be used to easily setup an emulation experiment. An equivalent task can be accomplished by using the GUI of NCTUns. The other two simulators do not provide such support.

If one had to make a global comparison by taking into account the emulation-related features that we emphasized in Table 6.2, we believe that the QualNet Developer-based emulation software EXata is the tool that totals the largest number of features, and could be the best choice, at least amongst the commercial tools. NCTUns appears as a strong contender as well, and its specific approach to simulation make it a good choice for emulation experiments; another advantage may be the fact that it can be freely used in academic environments. As for OPNET Modeler, despite its support for emulation through the System-in-the-Loop module, we believe that it does not reach the same feature and usability level with EXata. Despite the strong position that it has in the field of simulation, Ns-2 unfortunately seems to have only a very basic support for emulation, and we cannot recommend it for this purpose. Nevertheless, we hope that its successor, Ns-3, will improve the balance and provide a viable free software alternative to the other emulation-capable simulators.

Chapter 7

Network Emulation Testbeds

So far we have presented several network emulators, both freely available and commercial ones, that all share one common characteristic: they can be used as standalone systems. In this chapter we shall discuss a different class of network emulators, with a significantly increased complexity, namely the network emulation testbeds.

It is important to notice that a network testbed doesn't qualify automatically as a network *emulation* testbed. Network testbeds are widely used for making experiments. The element that differentiate a typical network testbed from a network emulation testbed is the fact that the emulation testbed has features that make possible experiments that could otherwise not be carried out using *only* that testbed's network hardware. Considering Def. 2.5, there has to be at least one component that is "reproduced virtually" on a testbed to qualify it as an emulation testbed. We only present in this chapter examples of those testbeds that meet this requirement.

7.1 Emulab

Emulab is probably the very first network emulation testbed, as its development started in 1999 [108]. The Emulab testbed was

Introduction to Network Emulation
Razvan Beuran
Copyright © 2013 Pan Stanford Publishing Pte. Ltd.
ISBN 978-981-4310-91-8 (Hardcover), 978-981-4364-09-6 (eBook)
www.panstanford.com

designed so as to provide researchers with a wide range of network environments in which to develop, debug, and evaluate their systems. Emulab is widely used by computer science researchers in the fields of networking and distributed systems. It is also designed to support education, and has reportedly been used to teach classes in those fields.

Note that the name "Emulab" is used by its developers to designate one of the following:

- a network facility, i.e., the testbed itself
- a software system, which is used to manage the network facility

The primary Emulab installation (testbed plus software) is run by the Flux Group, which is part of the School of Computing at the University of Utah. However, according to its developers, there are also installations of the Emulab software on other network testbeds at more than two dozen sites around the world, with up to hundreds of nodes. In what follows we shall refer exclusively to the main Emulab installation.

In this section we base our presentation on the information available on the web site of Emulab [108], as well as on the seminal paper regarding its design by White *et al.* [113].

7.1.1 *Overview*

Emulab is a public facility, and as such it is available without charge to most researchers worldwide. A policy document details the condition of use, which are very flexible. Basically any legitimate research/experimental use is allowed, including use by commercial companies. Emulab developers say however that the wide-area nodes can only be used for research purposes due to resource limitations, and educational and development use are not permitted.

The experimental environments to which researchers can currently have access through Emulab are the following:

Network emulation Users can specify arbitrary network topologies on Emulab. Moreover, the communication conditions between the nodes can be controlled in one of these three ways:

- using Dummynet on the FreeBSD nodes
- using NetEm on the Linux nodes
- using the emulation capabilities of Ns-2

Thus, users can create controllable, predictable, and repeatable settings for their network experiments.

Internet experimentation   Through its interface to a globally distributed testbed, namely PlanetLab (see Section 7.2), Emulab provides an environment for deploying, running, and controlling network applications at Internet scale.

To facilitate experiments, Emulab provides support for creating PlanetLab virtual nodes (called "slices"), automatic setup of these slices, slice visualization and control (including rebooting and termination), all through Emulab's user interface.

Wireless network testbeds   There are two types of general-purpose wireless network testbeds available on Emulab, as follows:

(1) An IEEE 802.11a/b/g (Wi-Fi) wireless network testbed, with fixed wireless nodes deployed on multiple floors of an office building. Users can configure them to act as access points, clients, or in ad hoc mode. All the nodes have two wireless interfaces, plus wired control network access. Although they are now discontinued Emulab used to also include several mobile nodes. These nodes were actual robots that carried wireless interfaces, and were able to move in a designated area of the lab. Robot motion could be controlled by the user in order to create the desired mobility scenarios.

(2) A testbed of software-defined radio devices called Universal Software Radio Peripheral (USRP) from the GNU Radio project [35]. These nodes give the user control over the physical layer of wireless networks, since everything is done in software, starting at the signal processing level. The GNU USRP hardware devices are connected via USB to Emulab nodes scattered in a building of the University of Utah campus. Each of these nodes also contains one or more Wi-Fi interfaces. The deployed USRP devices are said to have 900 MHz band transceiver boards and antennas.

It is important to note that Emulab unifies all of these environments under a common user interface, and integrates them into a common framework. This common framework provides the same type of abstractions for all the environments, and internally maps the abstractions into domain-specific mechanisms. Thus, Emulab masks much of the heterogeneity of the different resources, and simplifies the task of making experiments.

One interesting fact is that the Emulab team decided to use the same syntax with Ns-2 for defining experiments. This makes easier the transition from using simulation and Ns-2 to Emulab. Note that some extensions of Ns-2 were required to support on Emulab the emulation features that do not exist in Ns-2. Moreover, in addition to defining scenarios as text files, Emulab users have the possibility to employ a Java-based GUI to create their scenarios.

7.1.2 *Architecture*

Emulab architecture is composed of a number of control servers, the experiment hosts used to run experiments, and the network topology that interconnects all of these.

7.1.2.1 Control servers

Emulab uses a master computer, called "boss," that manages the entire testbed. This computer has several roles according to Emulab developers, such as given below:

- Control general testbed functionality.
- Store the database containing all the data related to the testbed.
- Allow node power cycling.
- Provide Web-based access to the testbed.
- Ensure name resolution functionality (Domain Name Server).
- Store disk images of the experiment nodes.

A second management component is the computer named "users," with the aliases "ops" and "fs." This is the main server machine for users of the testbed, and hosts the home directories and all project files. This server is intended to be used for those tasks that users cannot perform through the Web interface. The main functions of the "users" computer are

- file server
- interface for user login, low-level testbed control, and console access
- facilitate access to the debugging information that can be obtained from some of the Emulab nodes, such as the IXP network processors (see Section 7.1.2.4)

7.1.2.2 Experiment hosts

The most important elements of the testbed are undoubtedly the testbed nodes themselves. According to the Emulab website, there are currently 374 PCs available for experiments; some of them contain wireless NICs, and we counted a total of 72 wireless interfaces, 36 of them being installed in 18 PCs (two per PC), and the remaining 36 in other 36 PCs.

Testbed nodes run a variety of operating systems, including FreeBSD, Linux, and Windows XP. One can use the provided operating systems as they are, but also customize them, or even use other operating systems by loading the appropriate OS image. Although we shall not go into all the technical details, here is a brief description of the nodes, so as to give our readers an idea about what they can expect in terms of performance from a testbed such as Emulab:

- 20 hosts with

  - 2.4 GHz 64-bit Intel Core 2 Duo CPU
  - 2 GB RAM
  - built-in GbE NIC (the control interface)
  - dual-port GbE NIC (the one port in use is connected to the experimental network)
  - 250 GB SATA HDD

- 160 hosts with

  - 3.0 GHz 64-bit Intel Xeon CPU
  - 2 GB RAM

- — 6 GbE NICs (one being the control interface)
- — 2 × 146 GB SCSI HDD

- 18 hosts with[1]
  - — 3.0 GHz Intel Pentium IV processors
  - — 1 GB RAM
  - — 2 × Netgear WAG311 802.11a/b/g (Atheros) Wi-Fi cards
  - — built-in GbE NIC (the control interface)
  - — 10/100 Mbps Ethernet NIC
  - — 2 × 120 GB SATA HDD

- 8 hosts with
  - — 2.0 GHz Pentium IV processors
  - — 512 MB RAM
  - — 5 × 10/100 Mbps Ethernet NICs (one being the control interface)
  - — 2 × 20 GB IDE HDD

- 128 hosts with
  - — 850 MHz Intel Pentium III CPU
  - — 512 MB RAM
  - — 5 × 10/100 Mbps Ethernet NICs (one being the control interface)
  - — 40 GB IDE HDD

- 40 hosts with[2]
  - — 600 MHz Intel Pentium III CPU
  - — 256 MB RAM
  - — 5 × 10/100 Mbps Ethernet NICs (one being the control interface)
  - — D-Link DWL-AG530 802.11a/b/g wireless NIC with external antenna (only on 36 of these hosts)
  - — 13 GB IDE HDD

We note a broad range of specifications, from fast CPUs and large amounts of memory at the top of the list to slow CPUs and limited memory at the bottom. This is not necessarily a limitation, since not all emulation experiments require high-spec PCs. Moreover, such a

---

[1] Note that these hosts contain wireless network interfaces.
[2] Note that these hosts contain wireless network interfaces.

broad range of available hosts makes it possible to test the same software on different platforms, so as to recreate the experience of a wide range of end users.

7.1.2.3 Connectivity

A network testbed would not be complete without ensuring the connectivity between all its nodes. On Emulab this is done by using seven Cisco high-end switches. Five of these switches serve as the "programmable" backplane of the testbed, ensuring connectivity in the experiment network. The other two switches provide connectivity for the control network. One switch also has routing functionality, and operates as the core router for the testbed, regulating access to the testbed servers and the outside world.

Figure 7.1 shows the Emulab topology that corresponds to a simple scenario involving only 3 experiment hosts, named HOST 1, HOST 2, and HOST 3, that play the roles of a router, and of two computer nodes, respectively. The figure also includes the two Emulab servers mentioned before, namely, "boss" and "users." With thick lines we depicted the links between the host that are used for experiment traffic, and that are configured by the user. We used the convention we introduced in this book to denote by "LE" blocks the link-level emulators. In the case of Emulab, link-level emulators are managed directly by the testbed control software, and are called *delay nodes*. A delay node is essentially just another Emulab host that is loaded with an operating system such as FreeBSD, and uses a tool such as Dummynet to control the communication conditions between the other nodes in the experiment.[3] The thin lines in the figure represent the control network, used for all the management traffic, including the user access from anywhere in the Internet.

---

[3] Note that, despite their name, delay nodes can also be used to control bandwidth and packet loss, not only delay.

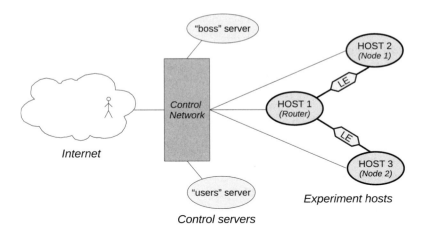

Figure 7.1. Emulab topology for a simple experiment.

7.1.2.4 Other components

In addition to the testbed components that we have mentioned so far, there are a few other elements that are part of the Emulab testbed, as follows:

NetFPGA Programmable network devices [69] that are available for remote experimentation in a similar manner to other Emulab resources. Thus, NetFPGA devices can be configured as part of an arbitrary topology with end nodes, links and LANs, traffic generators, etc. At the moment of writing, 6 NetFPGA devices were installed into 6 experiment hosts. Access to the devices is done via the computer that is hosting them.

ProtoGENI General control framework for networking testbeds that is developed by Emulab together with the NSF GENI project [90]. As part of this project, Emulab are deploying hardware at a number of sites around the USA, both on backbone networks and at edge sites (e.g., university campuses). Users can employ these nodes for experiments in the same way they do it with traditional Emulab nodes. Note that, since these nodes are not actually on the Emulab site, the communication conditions with them are not guaranteed. In this sense, the ProtoGENI nodes can be seen as some remote nodes integrated with Emulab to create a distributed testbed, similarly to the way in which PlanetLab nodes were also integrated with Emulab. Two NetFPGA cards are also available on two dedicated PCs in this class of hosts.

Network processors   Intel IXP1200 network processors are integrated into Emulab, and available to external researchers for remote experimentation. IXP nodes can be allocated through the usual Emulab mechanisms, and can be configured as part of an arbitrary topology of PCs, IXP nodes, etc. Control and debugging is done through the serial consoles of the IXP nodes. A number of 8 Emulab nodes host such network processors.

Although the following facilities are discontinued, and cannot be used anymore on Emulab, we present them here briefly in order to give readers a broader view on the testbed. In 2006, Emulab has opened to public external use for a limited period a mobile robotic wireless testbed [50]. The testbed used six remotely-controlled robots that could move in a designated area according to user instructions. Each robot was equipped with a sensor node (MICA2 mote, currently available from the company MEMSIC [63]). In addition, there were 25 static sensor nodes. The sensor nodes had a serial port for control and debugging purposes. The goal of this "mobile wireless testbed" was to give Emulab users an opportunity to conduct experiments with wireless nodes that are truly mobile, and that move in a controllable and repeatable manner. Such a testbed could be used, for example, to evaluate ad-hoc routing algorithms.

7.1.3 *Node Virtualization*

Despite the fact that Emulab has almost 400 hosts, there are times when users may wish to make bigger experiments that this. Alternatively, in busy periods, one may only be able to use a smaller number of hosts than necessary. In such cases, a solution to extend experiment scale given a limited number of hardware resources is to use the technique of *virtualization*. According to Emulab developers, if the CPU, memory, and network requirements of an application are modest, virtual nodes allow an experiment to use 10 to 20 times as many nodes as there are available physical machines.

7.1.3.1 Basic support

Conceptually speaking, virtual nodes fall somewhere between simulated nodes (for instance, using Ns-2) and real hosts in terms of accuracy of representing the real world. A virtual node in the default Emulab implementation is just a *lightweight* virtual machine running on top of a regular operating system. In particular, Emulab virtual nodes are based either on the "jail" mechanism in FreeBSD [52], or on the OpenVZ container-based virtualization in Linux [79]. Both methods allow groups of processes to be isolated from each other while running on the same physical machine.

Emulab virtual nodes provide isolation of the file system, processes, network, and accounts. This level of virtualization allows unmodified applications to run as though they were on a real machine. One can also introduce network impairments on the virtual network links connecting virtual nodes. These virtual links are multiplexed over physical links when used to connect to other physical hosts, and "exist" inside a single physical host when connecting virtual nodes within the same machine.

With some limitations, virtual nodes can have the same roles as normal Emulab hosts: end node, router, or traffic generator. They can be used in arbitrary topologies of links and LANs, including mixing virtual and real nodes. The number of virtual nodes that can be multiplexed on a single physical host depends on a variety of factors, such as

- resource requirements of the network applications that are run
- characteristics (CPU, memory, hard disk speed, etc.) of the underlying physical host
- throughput on the emulated virtual network links
- targeted emulation fidelity

Although the solution of virtualization may appeal to many users, readers should be aware of the limitations of the Emulab virtual node implementation. According to its developers, the most important such limitations of the Emulab virtualization technique are given below:

- *It is not a complete virtualization of a node*: The Emulab virtualization implementation does not create true virtual machines. The primary goal of Emulab developers was to provide functional transparency to applications. As a result, there are also security concerns, since virtual node separation is not complete, and they could spy on each other. This was not considered a problem in the case that all virtual nodes on a physical host are used for the same experiment.
- *It is not a complete virtualization of the network*: While each virtual nodes has its own virtual network interfaces and routing tables, much of the network stack of a physical host remains shared, in particular all the resources used by the higher-level protocols. Users should be aware of potential interactions and "interference" between nodes at that level.
- *There are no CPU and memory resource guarantees on the virtual nodes*: No performance isolation, and no specific CPU scheduling mechanisms exist. Processes running on the virtual nodes are just processes on the physical machine, and are scheduled according to the standard OS scheduler of the host. There are also no limits imposed on the memory consumption of virtual nodes.
- *Choice of operating systems is limited*: Due to the particularities of the Emulab implementation, both the experiment hosts on which virtual nodes are run, and the virtual nodes themselves, can only use a specific version of FreeBSD or Fedora Linux.
- *Maximum scale is only of about one thousand virtual nodes*: Due to several practical issues, it is not possible to use Emulab for experiments of more than about 1000–2000 nodes. These issues are related to: the algorithms used by Emulab for resource allocation; the characteristics of the physical nodes; the difficulty to visualize in a meaningful manner thousands of nodes.
- *Virtual nodes are not externally visible*: Virtual nodes are assigned addresses in the control network that are not

visible externally due to the limitation of the available IP address space. As virtual nodes cannot be accessed directly from outside Emulab, one must use a suitable proxy server, or access them through the Emulab "users" server.

- *Internal network bandwidth of experiment hosts is limited to about 400 Mbps*: This limitation comes from the performance characteristics of older hosts, which prevent running a significant number of virtual nodes or high-capacity virtual links.
- *Virtual nodes do not have a virtual console*: Users have to use login mechanisms such as "ssh" to access and control the virtual nodes.
- *Virtual node traffic is shaped on the host itself*: For virtual nodes, instead of using dedicated "delay nodes," network impairments are applied directly on the experiment host. This makes it possible to create a complete topology on a single node, and conserves testbed resources. The requirements and overhead of traffic shaping needs to be taken into account when designing an Emulab experiment that uses such features.

7.1.3.2 Xen-based virtualization

In addition to the basic support for virtualization using the default implementation presented above, one can also use the Xen virtualization technique on Emulab [108]. The main difference between Xen and the previous approach is that Xen does create a complete virtual machine on the experiment host. This makes it possible to use a wide range of operating systems on the virtual nodes, which can be different than the one of the physical host. Moreover, separation between the Xen-based virtual machines is complete from a logical point of view. Of course, the virtual nodes still share the resources (CPU, memory, network interfaces) of the host, so they may influence each other indirectly from a performance point of view. Hence, the expected fidelity of network emulation is still lower with Xen than when using physical links.

Support for Xen-based virtualization is present on Emulab, meaning that it is possible to create the Xen virtual nodes simply by selecting the appropriate node types. The nodes are created automatically, with predefined characteristics (amount of memory, etc.); shared file systems are also created. As with the virtual nodes created with the default method, the IP addresses of Xen-based virtual nodes are not directly accessible from outside Emulab.

Other limitations mentioned in the previous section also apply for Xen-based virtual nodes, as follows:

- no resource guarantees
- limited maximum scale
- limited internal network bandwidth
- traffic shaping is done on the host itself, etc.

7.1.4 *Wireless Network Testbed*

In addition to the wired network testbed, Emulab also provides wireless nodes to its users. As we have already mentioned in Section 7.1.1, there are 72 IEEE 802.11a/b/g Wi-Fi nodes in Emulab, which can be used through the same control system as the other nodes. The wireless NICs are split into two categories, distributed as follows:

- 36 NICs are installed in 18 PCs (3.0 GHz Intel Pentium 4 class) that are scattered at various locations in a large building. Emulab provides to registered users a floor map which indicates the location of these nodes, as well as their properties. These PCs also include one wired NIC that can be used for experiments.
- 36 NICs are concentrated in a machine room, and are installed in 36 PCs (600 MHz Intel Pentium III class). The external antennas of these wireless interfaces are deployed in a 6×6 grid on the back side of the racks housing the PCs, with all the antennas pointing down. The size of the grid is 300×224 cm. As the nodes are closely located to each other, and deployed in an unfriendly environment, signal interference is reported to be quite strong. These PCs also include four wired NICs for use in experiments.

Although the maker of the NICs in each of the two categories is different (Netgear for the first category, and D-Link for the second one), they all use the same Atheros 5212 chipset. The advantage of this chipset is that most of the 802.11 MAC layer functionality is handled in software, therefore it is highly configurable. Emulab uses the "madwifi" Atheros and derived drivers for the wireless NICs in the testbed.

7.1.4.1 Features

It is important to note that, although the wireless NICs in Emulab are dedicated to testing, they are not placed in an isolated environment. This means that both the traffic of the university wireless network, as well as the traffic of other users of the Emulab wireless nodes could interfere with any experiment. In this context, two policy items regarding wireless network transmission in Emulab should be considered according to web the site of the testbed [108]:

(1) Do not transmit on channels that another experiment on the testbed is using, unless it's your own. You can find out which channels are currently in use by looking at the top of the wireless floor map. Where possible, choose channels that have the least frequency overlap with other experiments.

(2) Do not flood a wireless network with non-responsive traffic for any significant period of time. The following channels are "production networks" used by others at this location, so are more restricted [table of channels provided]. You may not send "large" amounts of traffic on them, and may send only low rates of non-responsive traffic.

Such restrictions imply that, although certainly useful, the wireless Emulab testbed cannot actually be used for the full range of experiments one may wish to carry out.

To use wireless interfaces in an Emulab experiment, users must provide a few Emulab-specific Ns-2 commands in their scenario file. These commands also allow selecting which types of nodes are used from the two categories mentioned in the beginning of this section. Users can also control whether a wireless node behaves as a regular end station, or as an access point; networks without any access point can be configured to operate in ad hoc mode. Moreover, the standard used in the experiment can be selected from one of 802.11a, 802.11b, and 802.11g. Note that experiments using wireless nodes are not restricted to use only such nodes, and one can build topologies that mix wired and wireless links, as long as the number of links per node does not exceed the physically available number of network interfaces.

One limitation regarding the PCs hosting wireless interfaces is that users need to employ exclusively one of the two supported Linux distributions[4] if they want to be able to control the wireless interfaces.

Moreover, Emulab developers recommend to select the wireless nodes used in an experiment actively, instead of letting Emulab's mapping algorithm do it. This is because the algorithm does not take into account the connectivity of the nodes; as a consequence, automatic mapping may result in choosing nodes that cannot physically communicate with each other. Users should make sure by themselves that, for instance, at least the designated access point is in the communication range of all of the nodes in the wireless network topology they create. For ad hoc networks, users must make sure that none of the wireless nodes is completely isolated from the others.

7.1.4.2 Configuration

Emulab users can configure various wireless node settings using built-in mechanisms, either for the wireless LAN as a whole (e.g., communication channel), or for individual interfaces (e.g., transmit power). Most configurable parameters correspond to options that are available using the "iwconfig," "iwpriv," and "wlanconfig" commands in Linux. Below we give the list of the possible settings to emphasize the capabilities of the Emulab control system:

- *Operating mode*: Configure the LAN or interface to operate in one of the modes given below:

---

[4] Namely Fedora Core 4 or RedHat 9.0.

(1) "Master" — The interface behaves as an access point (not to be used for LANs).
(2) "Managed" — The interface behaves as an end station which connects to an access point (the access point needs to be configured separately).
(3) "Adhoc" — The interface or LAN operates in IEEE 802.11 ad hoc mode.
(4) "Monitor" — The interface or LAN are put in monitoring mode, useful in the context of network sniffing.

- *Operating channel/frequency*: Set the channel on which the interface or LAN operates to either a channel number or a frequency value. The channel is automatically selected for LANs that do not define it explicitly, but it is recommended to actively select the channel in order to prevent conflicts with other users.
- *Operating rate*: Change the operating bit rate of an interface. If not configured, interfaces use the "auto" mode, which performs rate adaptation, and varies the operating rate according to the communication conditions.
- *Transmit power*: Change the power used for transmission by an interface.
- *Receive sensitivity*: Change the sensitivity for receive operation of an interface.
- *RTS/CTS threshold*: Set the size of the smallest packet for which the interface will use the RTS/CTS mechanism. A value equal to the maximum packet size effectively disables the mechanism. The default on Emulab hardware is to turn off this mechanism.
- *Fragmentation threshold*: Configure the IP packet size above which the packet will be split into multiple fragments. Can also be set to "auto" or "off."

Although some of the above settings must necessarily be configured *before* performing an experiment, they can also be changed *on the fly*, while the experiment is running. Emulab provides functionality to assist with such dynamic operations, such as allowing settings to be "remembered" between operating mode changes.

7.1.5 *Discussion*

Emulab is perhaps the most widely used open network testbed, and a quick look at the long list of projects that have used Emulab reveals its popularity. Moreover, the wide range of features and capabilities make it the testbed of choice for a large class of applications. This has lead its developers to use the subtitle "total network testbed" for Emulab.

One thing to note about Emulab is the separation that exists between the control network and the experiment network. The main goal of this separation is to make sure there is no interference between the two networks, as follows:

- The traffic used for experiment control and management (including logging, etc.) does not perturb the experiment itself.
- The experiment traffic does not perturb the control network, thus avoiding potential influences to the experiments made by the same user and by others.

This separation is used by many other testbeds, and is a fundamental requirement in ensuring the accuracy of experiment results.

As we mentioned in the beginning of Section 7.1, Emulab is more than just a network testbed because it enables users to introduce controlled network impairments in a repeatable way. Therefore, the use of the word "emulation" agrees with the meaning we have given to this concept in the present book. However, this only applies to the wired network testbed in Emulab. The Wi-Fi testbed does not fit our definition. This is because there is no modeled component in the static Wi-Fi testbed currently available in Emulab (cf. Def. 2.5). However, the Mobile Emulab testbed that used to be available did agree with our definition for emulation, since it included the mobile robots, whose motion needed to be modeled and controlled by users. Consequently, we prefer to use the name "wireless network testbed" for the wireless component of Emulab, while we agree with the term "wired network emulation testbed" for the wired-network component of Emulab.

If we consider the classification in Table 3.1, Emulab is clearly a research emulation tool, and is of testbed type. As experiments are executed over a real network it means, experiments are done at topology level, and Emulab has a high complexity. A number of testbed hosts can be used to emulate network conditions, hence this is done in a distributed manner.

7.2 PlanetLab

PlanetLab is different type of network testbed that is globally distributed. At the moment of writing the PlanetLab website reports that there are 1087 nodes at 509 sites all over the world. These nodes form a research network testbed that is used for the evaluation of network services over the Internet [84]. PlanetLab started operating in 2003, and has been used by more than 1,000 teams for the research and development of new technologies for various applications of networks, such as distributed storage, peer-to-peer systems, etc. Note that, while PlanetLab use is free for academic institutions, use by for-profit companies requires paying a membership fee to support the running costs.

In this section we use mainly information provided on the web site of PlanetLab [86], complemented by two technical papers by its developers [7, 84].

7.2.1 *Overview*

According to its website, PlanetLab is composed of several elements, as follows:

(1) First of all, the testbed itself, as a collection of computers distributed over the globe. Most of these computers are hosted by various participating research and academic institutions, and some of them are placed in routing centers. All of the machines are connected to the Internet, forming a network that is distributed over the majority of regional and long-haul Internet backbones.

(2) Secondly, a software package that runs on all the computers in the testbed. This common software package includes the following components:

- a Linux-based operating system
- mechanisms for starting the nodes and distributing software updates
- a collection of management tools for tasks such as monitoring node health, auditing system activity, and controlling system parameters
- a facility for managing user accounts and for distributing access keys

The software package, called MyPLC, manages PlanetLab, but can also be used to deploy other PlanetLab-like testbeds, in a similar manner in which Emulab software can be used to create other Emulab-like testbeds.

(3) Thirdly, there is the PlanetLab Consortium, a group of academic, industrial, and government institutions cooperating to support and enhance PlanetLab. The consortium is responsible for

- overseeing the long-term growth of the PlanetLab hardware infrastructure
- designing and implementing the PlanetLab software architecture
- providing operational support to PlanetLab users
- defining policies that govern appropriate use of PlanetLab

7.2.2 *Features*

PlanetLab was designed mainly to serve as a testbed for overlay networks. For this purpose, researchers are given access to a distributed set of machines that are part of PlanetLab. To manage this access, PlanetLab uses an abstraction called *slice*. A slice is therefore a collection of resources distributed across multiple PlanetLab nodes. Slices are managed using a technique called "distributed virtualization." By reserving such a slice, researchers can experiment with planetary-scale services. Currently, PlanetLab reports over 600 active research projects in areas such as

- file sharing and network-embedded storage
- content distribution networks
- routing and multicast overlays
- network anomaly detection mechanisms
- scalable location systems
- network measurement tools

All the operations related to slice management are transparent to users and are handled by the MyPLC software package. This software performs the distributed virtualization task, i.e., allocate a "slice" of the network-wide hardware resources in PlanetLab to an application or service. The application or service will then run on some or even all of the PlanetLab computers that are distributed over the globe. The distributed virtualization also makes it possible to have multiple users and applications running simultaneously in different slices of PlanetLab, including the case when slices share the same physical machines.

The advantage of using PlanetLab compared to a network testbed with geographically co-located hosts is the opportunity to run experiments under real-world network conditions, and potentially at a larger scale. Services such as those mentioned above benefit from the distribution over the Internet, which according to PlanetLab developers provides benefits such as

- multiple points from which applications can observe and react to network conditions
- proximity to existing external data sources and data sinks
- communication across multiple administrative boundaries

To summarize, the value of using PlanetLab as a testbed derives from the following three points:

(1) a large set of geographically dispersed computers
(2) a realistic network infrastructure, including effects such as congestion, network failures, etc.
(3) a realistic client workload (given enough applications are running on the same PlanetLab host)

Note that its developers mention the fact that PlanetLab is not only a testbed, but also a deployment platform. This means that, in addition to short-term experiments, researchers can also deploy *long-running services* for client applications that are also running on PlanetLab. Thus, PlanetLab is envisaged as a platform supporting the entire life cycle of an application, from an early prototype, through design iterations, to an evolving live network service. Being able to deploy services on PlanetLab is part of a technology transfer view, allowing users to access the new services and potentially build upon them. According to PlanetLab developers, the following are some of the services currently running continuously on the testbed:

- *CoDeeN, Coral*: content distribution networks
- *ScriptRoute*: network measurement service
- *Chord, OpenDHT*: scalable object location services
- *PIER, Trumpet, CoMon*: network monitoring services

An important advantage of using PlanetLab for Internet-level experiments is that its virtualization mechanism allows to safely run applications and services that may perturb its functionality if run over the Internet itself. The PlanetLab team says the following about the difficulty to experiment on the Internet [86]:

> Unfortunately, the very commercial success that has fueled our increased dependency on the Internet has also reduced our ability to evolve its underlying architecture to meet new demands and correct emerging vulnerabilities.

We can say that Internet has become a sort of "production network" for the entire mankind, which makes it impossible to investigate new technologies through experiments that may perturb this "production network." The overlay network created by PlanetLab provides an opportunity to introduce disruptive technologies without risking an impact on other network systems. Thus, the overlay nodes can implement the new capability or feature, and use the conventional computers and networks they are run on to provide the underlying connectivity. After extensive testing and a long-term deployment, if the service deployed in the overlay network proves useful and secure, its developer may choose to migrate the functionality into the Internet itself, for instance, by adding it as a feature of commercial routers.

7.2.3 *Architecture*

At its core, PlanetLab functionality is provided through the technique of distributed virtualization, as mentioned previously. This means that each deployed application or service runs in a "slice" of the global resources in PlanetLab [7]. The concept of *slice* in this context refers to some amount of processing, memory, storage, and network resources that are provided to a user across a set of individual PlanetLab hosts that are distributed over the Internet. Thus, a PlanetLab slice is equivalent to a network of virtual machines, each providing a certain amount of local resources. A certain number of slices run concurrently on PlanetLab at any time, and act as network-wide containers that isolate services from each other.

7.2.3.1 Slices

Each PlanetLab host runs a Virtual Machine Monitor (VMM) software component that implements and isolates the virtual machines. Hence, all the remote services offered on PlanetLab are provided at host level by the VMM. This software component consists from the Linux kernel plus a set of kernel extensions that provide additional functionality.

All the virtual machines on one host are monitored and managed by a special, privileged virtual machine running on top of the VMM, which is called Node Manager (NM). The NM enforces policies on creating virtual machines and allocating resources to them. Local services interact with the NM to create new virtual machines. We emphasize the fact that *all* interactions with the NM are local, and only local services on a virtual machine can interact with the corresponding NM. Remote access to a specific NM is mediated by the VMM running on that node, thus creating a hierarchical relationship between these software components.

Figure 7.2 presents the software components that are running on each PlanetLab host. The base layer consists of the VMM, providing the interface with the physical host. On top of the VMM run all the virtual machines, including the privileged one, NM, and the ordinary ones, that are part of PlanetLab slices. Each of the virtual machines

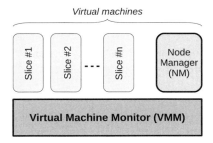

Figure 7.2. Software components running on each PlanetLab host.

runs a set of network applications and services that both provide the functionality related to the experiment, and also ensure the operation of PlanetLab itself.

The services that run on PlanetLab hosts can be divided into two classes, namely

- unprivileged services for PlanetLab end-users
- privileged services related to PlanetLab infrastructure

The unprivileged services run on normal slices, and don't require any special execution rights. As for the infrastructure services, there are three types of such services that are used to ensure the proper operation of PlanetLab:

- *Brokerage services*: Acquire PlanetLab resources and create slices linked to these resources.
- *Environment services*: Initialize and maintain the PlanetLab software components of each slice.
- *Monitoring services*: Discover the available resources on PlanetLab hosts and monitor the health of PlanetLab services.

The general policy in PlanetLab is to implement a service in a slice with the minimum required privileges that support the desired functionality. Thus, the implementation is done in unprivileged slices whenever possible, and in the privileged ones, NM and VMM (in this particular order), only when absolutely necessary.

7.2.3.2 Design challenges

The PlanetLab software package, MyPLC, is an implementation of various existing operating systems abstractions and techniques, applied to the context of a distributed testbed environment. In what follows we shall summarize the most important aspects of the design as reported in [7].

Node virtualization The first issue is the provision of a virtual machine abstraction for PlanetLab slices. While full hardware virtualization solutions such as VMWare are attractive by allowing to run multiple, unmodified operating systems, they have a major drawback: performance. Since each of these fully virtualized machines have large memory requirements, it is not possible to scale much the number of concurrent slices on a host by using this method.

Hence, PlanetLab adopted the system-call-level virtualization methodology, which is similar to the approach used in Emulab. In particular, PlanetLab uses the Linux virtualization mechanism called "VServer" [59]. Such a high-level virtualization proved to be adequate for supporting large numbers of overlay services on PlanetLab, while providing reasonable isolation mechanisms.

Resource allocation and isolation PlanetLab includes mechanisms for the distributed allocation and coordination of resources. As the testbed must support multiple approaches for creating and binding resources to slices, PlanetLab developers opted for implementing these mechanisms *on top of* the basic software platform. Currently available frameworks include, for instance, the Globus grid toolkit [31], and the account management system of Emulab [113].

Isolation mechanisms are an important requirement for Planet-Lab, given the resource sharing that takes place when using slices. The techniques used by PlanetLab for isolating service performance are said to be inspired by the contention management for shared resources proposed in Scout [65]. However, these mechanisms are controlled on PlanetLab in a different way than in a typical operating system, since each PlanetLab host runs multiple competing tasks that belong to a globally distributed slice, rather than a set of cooperating local tasks.

Network virtualization Another issue in PlanetLab design is network virtualization, i.e., how to provide to each of the slices running on a physical host the "illusion" of its own network connection. For this purpose, PlanetLab uses a modified version of the raw socket interface found in typical operating systems. The kernel of PlanetLab hosts is thus responsible for sharing raw access — reception and transmission of arbitrary packets — among multiple competing services in a controlled manner that complies with existing administrative policies. The kernel is also in charge of protecting the physical network from malicious or misbehaving services, an aspect that is typically ignored in normal network virtualization mechanisms.

Monitoring A challenge which is perhaps specific to PlanetLab, due to its testbed nature, is the support for the monitoring and management of the large distributed infrastructure of the testbed. This has to be done both on the network side, and for the PlanetLab hosts themselves. PlanetLab uses for this purpose a low-level sensor-like software interface that can export data regarding the underlying OS and network, as well as from individual services, in a uniform manner. Exported data may represent simple scalar values, such as the process load average on a host, or complex structures, such as the network topology obtained from the local BGP routing tables. Thus, the PlanetLab "sensors" encapsulate raw observations from different sources, and provide a shared interface through which this data can be access by the monitoring services.

7.2.4 *Discussion*

PlanetLab is a geographically distributed testbed, in which the experiment hosts are dispersed in the global Internet. This makes it possible to conduct planetary-scale experiments in realistic conditions. With more than 1000 hosts available for experiments, PlanetLab is indeed a large-scale testbed.

Despite the clear benefits of using PlanetLab, we would like our readers to note that the three most important features that we presented as PlanetLab advantages in Section 7.2.2 can also turn into disadvantages, depending on the perspective taken. The potential drawbacks of those three features are as follows:

(1) *A large set of geographically dispersed computers* It may be less effective to use thousands of computers managed by hundreds of organizations compared to the case of a testbed with geographically co-located hosts, since any physical issues may take longer to identify and fix in such a hierarchical distributed management scheme.

(2) *A realistic network infrastructure, including effects such as congestion, network failures, etc.* While realistic, the overlay network of PlanetLab offers no guarantees regarding the repeatability of the network conditions. This means that it is impossible to recreate a certain network state, for instance, in order to verify that a previously observed problem has been fixed, or to repeat an experiment in the same network conditions but with different parameters.

(3) *A realistic client workload (given enough applications are running on the same PlanetLab host)* Realistic workloads on the application clients are certainly important, however, the lack of control means that it is impossible to make reproducible experiments from this point of view as well.

As stated above, the same three properties can be regarded both as an advantage or as a disadvantage, depending on the point of view. For this reason, PlanetLab is perhaps the most appropriate for evaluating network applications and services that are mature enough from the point of view of the basic features, and which need to be tested in large-scale settings with realistic varying network conditions that don't necessarily need to be reproducible. In this sense, PlanetLab can act as a testbed platform for performing the final validation series of experiments. This means that it may be good to use a typical controllable network emulator in a first stage, to eliminate all the simple bugs, and proceed to PlanetLab usage only towards the end of the development process, for investigating in realistic network conditions issues such as scalability, parameter optimization, and so on.

One more issue to note regarding PlanetLab is that it is more difficult to use it for testing network hardware systems than for software systems. Applications and service implementations can be easily deployed using the built-in distributed virtualization mechanisms of PlanetLab. However, if one wishes to include hardware systems in the PlanetLab network, it has to be done at those network locations to which the user has direct physical access. Moreover, we are not aware about the policy of PlanetLab in this respect, since hardware systems cannot behave as typical PlanetLab hosts.

As a last remark, we would like to discuss the classification of PlanetLab as a network emulation testbed. It is obvious that network control and experiment repeatability in PlanetLab are low. This brings PlanetLab closer to a network testbed than to a network emulator. However, we claim that the virtualization technique employed by PlanetLab, which creates an isolation layer between the physical host and the virtual experiment nodes, and the overlay network which is constructed between these experiment nodes, are sufficient characteristics for including PlanetLab in a category of "virtual network" testbeds. Therefore, although PlanetLab is not a network emulation testbed in itself, the techniques it uses bring it very close to being one.

As for Table 3.1, PlanetLab is a research emulation tool of testbed type. Since experiments are executed over the Internet, it can reproduce network topologies, and it has a high complexity. Emulation is done in a distributed manner in the sense that the network conditions are determined by the totality of the network links used in an experiment.

7.3 ORBIT

ORBIT is a wireless network testbed project that was started in September 2003 under an USA NSF program [115]. The objective of the project is to develop a large-scale open-access wireless networking testbed for use by the research community working on next-generation wireless network protocols, middleware and applications. The project is a collaborative effort between several universities: Rutgers, Columbia, and Princeton, along with industrial partners Lucent Bell Labs, IBM Research and Thomson. ORBIT is being developed and operated by WINLAB, at Rutgers University. The ORBIT project is also related to the GENI (Global Environment for Network Innovation) program, as an experimental platform for the wireless aspects of GENI [30].

ORBIT development is motivated by the fact that large-scale experimental facilities for research in the area of wireless networking are scarce. Thus, most validation tests for new protocols are done using network simulation, or in small-scale environments. In the latter case, experiments are difficult to reproduce by independent researchers, due to variations in wireless equipment and radio environment. Among the advantages of a large-scale wireless network testbed compared to the other solutions, ORBIT developers include

- possibility to work with larger networks
- encourages result validation and extensions by other researchers
- platform for the trial deployment of new wireless services and software

The ORBIT testbed is available for remote or on-site access by researchers both nationally and internationally. According to the ORBIT website, the total number of registered users exceeds 250, with more than 12,000 experiments completed on the radio grid facility (data provided as of 2008).

The description in this section is mainly based on the information provided on the web page or ORBIT [115], with technical details obtained from two technical papers by ORBIT developers [53, 92].

7.3.1 *Overview*

The core of the ORBIT testbed is a 400-node two-dimensional radio grid providing facilities for reproducible networking experiments with hundreds of wireless nodes. While we shall not discuss it in this book, it is reported that the ORBIT testbed also includes an outdoor field trial setup, aimed at the real-world evaluation of the network protocols that have been already validated on the radio grid, as well as for application development involving mobile end-users. The field trial network is said to provide a configurable mix of both high-speed cellular (3G) and IEEE 802.11 wireless nodes in a real-world setting.

In addition to the radio grid and the outdoor setup, there are a number of hardware devices that facilitate the experiments, such as

- several "sandbox" units that can be used to get familiar with the testbed and prepare experiments before running them on the radio grid
- GNU radios (i.e., software-defined radios)
- noise generators that are intended to allow topology control on the radio grid

Construction of the 400-node ORBIT radio grid facility took place in one of the buildings of the Rutgers University, in New Jersey, USA. In October 2005 the testbed services were released to the public. Examples of some research topics for which ORBIT developers claim the testbed was used include

- mobile ad hoc networks (MANET)
- mesh network protocols for Wi-Fi access
- delay tolerant networks (DTN)
- future Internet architecture
- media streaming over wireless networks
- mobile content delivery
- wireless network security

Following the public release, ORBIT developers focused mainly on technology and service software improvements necessary to meet new research community needs. Such new features that were already or are being implemented include

- testbed enhancements
  — software-defined radio (SDR) nodes; reportedly, about 10 GNU/USRP (Universal Software Radio Peripheral) devices have been included in ORBIT and used for cognitive radio networking experiments; inclusion of the higher performance USRP2 radio is said to be in progress
  — improved topology and mobility control

— integration with wired-network testbeds, in particular, integration into the emerging GENI research infrastructure

- software development
  — enhanced user portal as well as software and operations support services; the ORBIT management framework (OMF) software includes support for grid virtualization and integrated experiments with PlanetLab
  — software kit for small-scale deployments at user sites and an open-source software repository; the design of the ORBIT kit has been completed, and a consortium has been established to enable other institutions to set up smaller ORBIT-like radio grids

ORBIT developers report that OMF was selected as one of the competing experimental network control architectures for the GENI Spiral 1 prototyping project in September 2009. The related GENI/OMF project is expected to lead to a broader availability of the ORBIT testbed resources integrated with wired-network components through the GENI experiment management framework.

7.3.2 *Architecture*

The ORBIT testbed is operated as a shared service that allows users to conduct wireless network experiments on-site or remotely. However, only one experiment can run on the testbed at a time. The use of the testbed is automated, so that to minimize lag in performing experiments, and the results are saved to a database for later analysis.

Its developers propose to view ORBIT as a set of services: users input experiment definitions and receive the experimental results as output. This concept is illustrated in Fig. 7.3.

The input of ORBIT, the experiment definition, is a script that manages ORBIT services through a control system. The control system supervises the radio grid and a configuration system in order to perform actions such as given below:

- Reboot the wireless nodes in the radio grid.
- Load the operating system, as well as other system and application software onto each node.

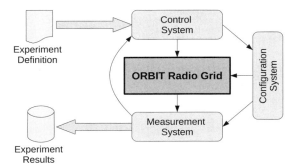

Figure 7.3. Architecture of the ORBIT testbed operation mechanism.

- Set the relevant parameters for the experiment both for the grid nodes, and for the additional ones that are used to introduce controlled interference, monitor traffic and interference, etc.
- Manage the measurement system by specifying the required parameters for the filtering and collection of the experiment results, and the database schema for storing the results.

The measurement system gets data from the radio grid, provides feedback to the control system, and also delivers the experiment results to users, which represent the output of ORBIT.

7.3.2.1 ORBIT hardware

The main component of the ORBIT testbed is the interconnected 20 × 20 grid of wireless nodes. The placement of the nodes is shown in Fig. 7.4, each of them represented by a small circle or filled square, depending on the type of adapter. The convention used in ORBIT when referring to nodes is to employ their coordinates, first the index on the horizontal axis, and then the one on the vertical axes, separated by a dash. Thus, the node in the bottom right corner is referred to as "node 20-1."

Each wireless node in ORBIT is a PC with a 1 GHz VIA processor, 512 MB of RAM, 20 GB of local disk, 2 × FastEthernet ports, 2 × IEEE 802.11 a/b/g cards, and a chassis manager. The two kinds of wireless cards in the main ORBIT radio grid are

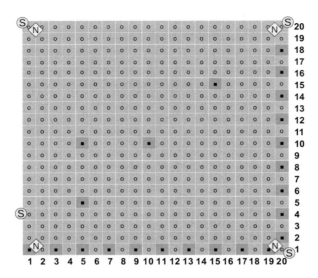

Figure 7.4. The radio grid of the ORBIT testbed.

- 377 × Atheros AR5212 (shown as circles on lighter background in Fig. 7.4)
- 23 × Intel IPW2915 (shown as filled squares on darker background in Fig. 7.4)

The chassis manager of ORBIT nodes is used to control them and has a 10 Mbps Ethernet port. The FastEthernet ports of the wireless nodes are dedicated one for control, to load and manage the ORBIT node and to collect measurements, and one for data communication for experiment purposes, as needed by the user. Readers may remember that a similar network separation was used by Emulab. Note that on ORBIT there is also a fundamental separation between the wireless experiment network, and the wired networks used for control and user data.

The other wireless devices that are represented in Fig. 7.4 are as follows:

- *Noise generation antennas*: A number of four, they are shown as a rhombus marked with the symbol "N," and are located between nodes 1-1 and 2-1, nodes 19-1 and 20-1, nodes 19-20 and 20-20, and finally between nodes 1-20 and 2-20. The electromagnetic noise produced using this antennas is used to emulate the effect of distance in wireless networks, as it will be explained in Section 7.3.3.

- *Traffic sniffers*: Also a number of four, they are depicted as circles marked with the symbol "S," and are located near the nodes 1-4, 20-1, 20-20, and 1-20. The sniffers, manufactured by Aruba, can be configured to sniff specific channels, and to report every sniffed packet to the ORBIT database. Thus, users can capture the experiment traffic in an independent manner, for further analysis, such as packet correlation, correctness checking, verifying experiment outcomes, etc. Note that the sniffers are reported to currently work *only* on IEEE 802.11b/g channels.

While we shall not go into details, readers should be aware that other hardware is available for experiments on ORBIT, which is as follows:

- IEEE 802.11 wireless cards used on the eight sandboxes, from manufacturers such as Atheros, Intel, Realtek, Intersil, and Zydas
- GNU radio hardware, installed into one of the sandboxes
- bluetooth cards, installed into 46 of the main radio grid nodes

7.3.2.2 ORBIT software

The software components of ORBIT are essential for facilitating experiments with the testbed. The functions of the ORBIT software, which is globally called "Experiment Management Service,"[5] are provided by several components that can be grouped into three categories given below:

(1) experiment control
(2) experiment execution
(3) measurement and result collection

Experiment control   The main component related to experiment control is the *Node Handler*. This software module sends commands

---

[5]More recently the software has been renamed to ORBIT Management Framework (OMF), which is the name in use currently.

to the radio nodes at the appropriate time, and keeps track of their execution. The peer of the Node Handler, which resides on each radio node, is called *Node Agent*. This software module listens for, and executes the commands from the Node Handler. Node Agents also report information back to the Node Handler.

The functionality provided by the combined execution of these two components is as follows:

- Give the user control over the testbed, by allowing actions such as controlling the power state of the wireless nodes, initializing the interfaces, launching applications simultaneously on the nodes involved in the experiment, etc.
- Enable the automated collection of experimental results. This function includes the creation of databases consistent with the measurements for that particular experiment. Occasional feedback may be required to fine tune the operation of the Node Handler, since it uses a rule-based approach for monitoring and controlling experiments.
- Load hard disk images onto the experiment nodes, and save the image of a hard disk into an archive for future use. This imaging process allows users to use customized OS images on experiment nodes.

All these actions can be performed through a single command-line interface, using the generic command "orbit,"[6] which is the interface for controlling the Node Handler, the experiment, and the nodes on the testbed.

The ORBIT management software also assists users in performing experiments. Thus, the ORBIT software includes several predefined scripts for performing experiment tasks such as

- starting applications, such as traffic generation
- defining active node placement

Starting applications is done in ORBIT via Ruby scripts, that are wrappers for the real applications to be executed. Such applications can be used for traffic capture (e.g., "tcpdump"), or for traffic generation. Regarding traffic generation, in addition to a specific

---

[6] In OMF, the command has been renamed to "omf."

tool developed for ORBIT, called ORBIT Traffic Generator (OTG), support is also included for commonly used software. Thus, tools such as Iperf and Distributed Internet Traffic Generator (D-ITG) were integrated with ORBIT, so that even when using these tools measurement collection is still done using ORBIT specific mechanisms, and the statistics are written to the experiment database.

By using specific ORBIT commands, users can select for experiments certain testbed nodes, thus creating networks with custom node placement (within the physical limits of the radio grid). More complex mechanisms are required should one wish to use, for instance, multi-hop network topologies, as it will be described in Section 7.3.3.1.

Measurement and result collection ORBIT uses for collecting experimental results a set of tools known as the ORBIT Measurement Framework & Library (OML). This framework has a client/server architecture as it will be explained next.

The Node Handler starts one instance of an OML Collection Server for each experiment run. The server will listen and collect experimental results from the various nodes involved in the experiment (see below). An SQL database is employed for archiving the results.

Each Node Agent on each experiment node controls one OML Collection Client that is associated with the applications used in the experiment. During experiment execution, the applications will forward any required outputs or measurement results to the OML Collection Client. After applying optional filtering/processing of the data, the OML Collection Client will send the results to the OML Collection Server mentioned above. The server collects the measurements sent by the clients, and inserts the data into the appropriate columns of the database.

While this client/server approach provide an easy-to-use high-level mechanism for conducting measurements, ORBIT also provides a low-level interface for such tasks, named "Libmac." According to ORBIT developers, Libmac is a library that allows users to perform low-level tasks such as

- inject and capture MAC layer frames
- manipulate wireless interface parameters, both at aggregate and per-frame levels

- communicate wireless interface parameters over the air on a per-frame level
- collect MAC layer measurements from experiments

7.3.3 *Emulation Features*

ORBIT is first of all a wireless network testbed. However, it is different from typical wireless network testbeds in that it has features that enable experiments that would not otherwise be possible by simply using the wireless hardware itself. The most important features in this category are

(1) network topology emulation
(2) mobility emulation

7.3.3.1 Network topology emulation

Users can select various nodes in the ORBIT testbed to create active node placements with different shapes. However, all these node configurations will be essentially located in the *same* communication range. This is because ORBIT developers report that even the lowest transmit power setting, 1 mW, still results in a communication range that is larger than 20 m, the length and width of the testbed. Moreover, using a low fixed transmit power setting prevents doing experiments with power control algorithms, thus reducing the usability of the testbed.

There are two solutions that can be used on ORBIT to create complex multi-hop network topologies, as it will be described next:

- MAC address filtering
- noise generation

MAC address filtering   ORBIT users can make use of standard MAC address filtering tools, such as "iptable," "ebtable," or "mackill," to force given nodes to ignore other ones. In this way it is possible to create virtual links between nodes, and thus emulate an arbitrary multi-hop connectivity.

Another lower-level approach is available in the MAC address filtering category. ORBIT developers have modified the driver of the wireless interfaces, called "madwifi" to allow a specific MAC filtering mechanism to be executed. Thus, the modified driver allows filtering incoming packets by the sending MAC address. The packets are not only filtered though; they can have a user-defined received signal strength indicator (RSSI) value assigned to them. Moreover, a specified percent of these incoming packets can be ignored, so as to simulate a poor radio environment in which packet loss occurs.

This driver modification is transparent to routing protocols and any other applications running on the wireless nodes. Hence, developers claim that this approach can be used to accomplish tasks such as

- emulate arbitrary static and mobile topologies
- emulate custom radio environments, including very noisy, low signal conditions
- real-time adjustment of the emulated topologies and radio environments

Note that this mechanism doesn't actually *create* those topologies and radio environments, but only *emulates* their effects. Therefore the following caveats should be noted:

- Packet filtering is only applied to correctly received packets, hence IEEE 802.11 MAC mechanisms such as frame retransmission have no effect on packet receive percentages as configured in the modified driver.
- Packets are still being sent and received at the hardware layer by all the wireless nodes involved, therefore the contention for the radio environment will still take place, even when configuring high packet loss rates in the modified driver.

Noise generation The noise generation subsystem in ORBIT, called Centralized Arbitrary Waveform Injection Subsystem (CAWIS), consists of an arbitrary waveform generator, namely Agilent ESG, that is connected through a distribution network to four multi-band antennas located in the four corners of the main ORBIT radio grid (cf. Fig. 7.4). Using CAWIS, users can inject additive white Gaussian noise signals into the main ORBIT grid, and thus control the radio environment of the nodes. Adding noise to the radio environment effectively changes the value of the signal-to-noise ratio (SNR) as seen by the wireless transceivers. This is because, while the signal level doesn't change, the noise level increases. In real wireless networks, low SNR values are typically related to increased distances between the transmitter and the receiver, which brings signal values closer to the noise level. Therefore, the effect of noise injection on SNR can be used to create the effects of distance in ORBIT, hence to create different network topologies. In a similar manner, noise injection can also be used to emulate mobility, as it will be explained in the next section.

By using an ORBIT experiment description script, users can define the noise generation antennas to be included in the experiment, along with the other experiment components. The configurable parameters for these antennas are

- *Operating channel*: any of the valid channels of the IEEE 802.11a/b/g standard
- *Noise power*: any value in the range from -95 to $+5$ dBm[7]

The distribution network that connects the waveform generator to the four antennas allows users to control the attenuation of each individual antenna feed. By default, this additional attenuation on all antennas is zero, which means that the injected noise power is equally distributed. To create unequal signal distributions, users specify an appropriate attenuation setting that will reduce the noise level in parts of the radio grid.

While the noise generation system makes it possible to control the radio environment, it doesn't by itself create the required multi-hop topologies unless it is appropriately configured. ORBIT developers proposed a method called Select Nodes with Fixed Interference (SNFI) to address this issue, and demonstrated that multi-hop topologies can be successfully created with only four noise sources [53]. Thus, SNFI could automatically select suitable nodes for a number of different 2 and 3-hop topologies. However, the long-term reproducibility of the results was reduced when nodes with marginal SNR were involved. We also note that those 2 or 3-hop

---

[7] Note that the noise floor in an interference-free environment (due to the so called "thermal noise") is around -100 dBm for the frequency band used by IEEE 802.11 networks.

topologies were actually relatively small when compared to the full 400-node size of ORBIT.

7.3.3.2 Mobility emulation

ORBIT is composed of a large number of fixed wireless nodes. Hence, real mobility is not possible on the main radio grid. However, ORBIT can emulate mobility by leveraging the tight grid topology of the radio antennas in the testbed through a technique called *spatial switching* [92]. Practically, ORBIT emulates mobility by switching a virtual mobile node to different radios and antennas as time progresses, thus changing physically the position of the transceiver that corresponds to the virtual mobile node. As a consequence, the path of the mobile node comprises a number of discrete steps, an approximation of the actual path a moving node would take. Although support for real-time control of the virtual trajectory of mobile node is planned, only predefined paths are possible for the moment.

Spatial switching is implemented by ORBIT developers in software, over the Gigabit Ethernet connections available on the ORBIT testbed. This method allows scaling up the setup to a large number of nodes at a much lower cost than by using hardware antenna switches. The software spatial switching system uses a split-stack architecture, meaning that the network stack of a single mobile node is split between a virtual mobile node and a real grid node. For every additional mobile node in the experiment, the emulator requires an additional pair of a virtual mobile node and a grid node.

The network layer of the virtual mobile node resides on the same physical computer throughout the experiment, and is connected to various grid nodes by means of network tunnels running on the wired Ethernet network available in ORBIT. As time progresses, the end point of the tunnel changes, so that the virtual mobile node effectively uses the link and physical layers of different grid nodes. The virtual mobile node can be either a dedicated grid node, or any computer that is on the same local area network as the grid nodes. On the virtual mobile node, the software components of the spatial switching system provide a virtual network interface, which is associated to a grid node radio interface. Therefore, network applications can be run over the virtual mobile network simply by changing the routing table of the virtual mobile node to point to the virtual interface.

Given that ORBIT testbed area has 20 × 20 m, and the fact that the nodes are separated by 1 m on both horizontal and vertical axes, it is possible to directly emulate motion with such bounds and movement accuracy. To emulate larger distances between the nodes, an experimenter needs to utilize the ORBIT noise generation system to raise the noise floor in the environment, which creates the effect of greater distances between transmitter and receiver, as it was described in the paragraph on noise generation in Section 7.3.3.1.

7.3.4 *Discussion*

ORBIT is definitely a great tool for making wireless network experiments. As an indoor wireless network testbed, it provides a large number of nodes that can be configured and used with ease by means of a specific management framework. However, the high density of the nodes prevents users from making certain types of realistic experiments. This is why ORBIT developers have added emulation mechanisms that extend functionality of the testbed itself with features such as mobility and network topology creation.

Readers should note that while these mechanisms are undoubtedly useful, they do not recreate the actual mobility patterns or target topologies, but only reproduce their effects. This may cause issues with experiments than employ such emulation techniques, as follows:

(1) Topology emulation through MAC filtering does not eliminate the contention that occurs when multiple nodes attempt to access the wireless media simultaneously. Therefore, only experiments with low amounts of traffic can be executed in this manner, since contention can only be ignored in such cases.

(2) Topology emulation through noise generation only allows creating a limited number of small topologies using a small percent of ORBIT nodes. Hence, this method leads to an

inefficient usage of resources, and seriously restricts the range of possible experiments.

(3) Mobility emulation through spatial switching, even with the addition of noise generation for large distance emulation, does not take into account the complex electromagnetic effects that occur in mobile networks, such as multi-path fading, shadowing, Doppler effects, etc. Hence, the mobility emulator can be used only for discrete small-scale mobility scenarios, such as laptop usage in an office or conference environments.

While the disadvantage mentioned at point (1) above cannot be easily eliminated, the issues described at points (2) and (3) are both related to the quality of the noise injection system. One can assume that a fine-grained variable noise control in many points of the radio grid (ideally near each node) would allow to faithfully reproduce a broad range of topologies with a high-utilization efficiency of the testbed, as well as more detailed and more accurate mobility effects.

When referring to Table 3.1, it is obvious that ORBIT was classified as a research emulation tool of testbed type. ORBIT experiments use real wireless network interfaces, and also control the topology, hence the testbed has topology emulation capabilities and a high complexity. Emulation is done by using several systems simultaneously, hence it is done in a distributed manner.

7.4 Comparison

In this section we shall compare the three network emulation testbeds presented in this chapter. Although these testbeds cannot be said equivalent from the point of view of their characteristics and intended usage, the comparison is intended to give our readers a quick overview on the features of each of them, and to emphasize the similarities and differences for those points that these testbeds do have in common.

Table 7.1 summarizes the main facilities provided by each testbed. Note that we did not include the aspects related to experiment preparation, such as the sandboxes on ORBIT, nor those features that were discontinued, such as the mobile robots on Emulab.

Table 7.1. Comparison of network emulation testbeds: Emulab, PlanetLab, and ORBIT

	Emulab	PlanetLab	ORBIT
Wired-node count	374	1087	None dedicated
Wireless-node count	72	None	400
Network features	Mbps Ethernet, NetFPGA, IPX network processors, GNU Radio, IEEE 802.11a/b/g	Virtual network interfaces only	IEEE 802.11a/b/g, GNU Radio, Bluetooth
Node virtualization	Possible	Used by default	Possible
Emulation features	Link degradation control, wired-network topology	Overlay network	Wireless-network topology, node mobility
External connectivity for experiments	Possible through PlanetLab	Used by default	Possible through PlanetLab (wired network)
Geographical distribution of nodes	Collocated	Globally dispersed	Collocated

The first criterion in Table 7.1 is the count of wired nodes. It is obvious the PlanetLab is the "winner" in this category, with over one thousand nodes. Note that those nodes are not owned by one institution, therefore the financial costs are divided among the PlanetLab members. Emulab, on the other hand, is the full owner of all the testbed nodes. While this implies higher costs, it also provides more freedom in using the nodes, upgrading them, better uniformity regarding the characteristics of the resources, and potentially a faster fixing of problems. The label "None dedicated" we used for ORBIT in this category means that, although the hosts for the wireless nodes are connected by wired networks, both for control and experiment purposes, these hosts are only intended to *support* the wireless network experiments, and are not meant to be used directly for wired network tests.

The second comparison criterion is the count of wireless nodes. ORBIT, which is the wireless network emulation testbed, has the lead, with 400 wireless nodes on the main radio grid. Emulab makes 76 nodes available for wireless experiments; however, they are hosted by some of the wired nodes in the testbed, so there is a resource sharing scheme that needs to be considered. Given that PlanetLab nodes connect over Internet, there are no wireless nodes available on that testbed, for the obvious reason that they could not connect in a wireless fashion with each other.

An analysis of the network features shows that Emulab offers the largest set of choices. While in terms of network interfaces Ethernet and IEEE 802.11 are definitely the most used, there are several other features that make possible a wider range of experiments on Emulab, such as the NetFPGA and the Intel IPX network processors, or the GNU Radio platforms. On the other hand, PlanetLab only provides virtual network interfaces for its overlay networks; this emphasizes the focus of PlanetLab not on low-level network issues, but rather on higher-level network protocol and application evaluations. The features of ORBIT are the most rich from the point of view of the available wireless network technologies; thus, ORBIT also provides Bluetooth interfaces in addition to the more "classic" IEEE 802.11 and GNU Radio platforms. Even though the hosts for the wireless nodes on ORBIT are interconnected by wired Ethernet too, as mentioned above, we did not include this feature, since it is not meant to be used exclusively for wired-network experiments.

Node virtualization is a technique that allows to logically increase the number of nodes available for experiments by running several virtual machines on the same physical host. This technique can be used on Emulab through a custom light-weight virtualization mechanism. PlanetLab uses node virtualization as a fundamental component in ensuring the separation of the overlay networks built by each user (the so-called *slices*). As for ORBIT, virtualization is indeed supported in the latest releases of the management software. Note that all node virtualization methods imply also the use of network virtualization, which boils down to having more virtual nodes use the same network interface. While it can be argued that when the network connection has very high speed, the effect of virtualization may be negligible, for high amounts of traffic, or for limited network capacities (such as the wireless networks), influences and interference cannot be ignored. Problems are most severe on a testbed such as ORBIT, in which the wireless nodes are closely located to each other, hence reducing the total network capacity that is useful. Such issues limit the usefulness of virtualization in the above cases to low-scale low-traffic experiments, or when doing experiment debugging and preparation work.

In addition to node virtualization, which can be regarded as an emulation mechanism in itself, each of the presented testbeds supports a series of features that effectively transform it into an emulation testbed. Thus, on Emulab, users can control the link conditions between the experiment nodes, and can build the desired topologies in the wired network. On PlanetLab, emulation is achieved by the use of overlay networks, which represent virtual networks spanning over the real underlying network, the Internet. As for ORBIT, the customizable wireless-network topologies, and the emulated mobility mechanism make possible a range of experiments that could otherwise not be conducted on the fixed wireless network testbed that the ORBIT radio grid is.

The external connectivity for experiments is an important aspect when considering the possibility to extend the capabilities of a testbed through connection to other testbeds or networks. Emulab includes such support, as it can be connected to PlanetLab. As for, PlanetLab external connectivity is intrinsic to the operation of the testbed, therefore it is included by design. Due to the wireless nature of ORBIT, no external connectivity exists for wireless network experiments. However, ORBIT is integrated with PlanetLab, and their combination can be used to run mixed experiments that include wireless nodes on ORBIT and wired nodes on PlanetLab.

The geographical distribution of the experiment nodes is an important characteristic of any testbed. Both in Emulab and ORBIT the nodes are located within the same area, in particular in university campuses. This ensures easy management, and — more importantly — the highest level of control over network conditions. On the downside, the observed network conditions are not necessarily representative of the wide range of possible situations that can occur over the Internet. PlanetLab gives up condition control to achieve the realistic, albeit not reproducible, network degradation observed in the Internet.

To conclude this comparison, we would like to indicate our view on what are the most appropriate applications for each of the wireless network emulation testbeds presented here:

- *Emulab*: As a testbed with a large number of wired and wireless nodes, that are all located in the same geographical area, Emulab is particularly suited for network experiments in which large scale, condition control, and reproducibility are the main requirements. Therefore, Emulab can be used to assess the performance of network applications and protocols starting from the early stages of the development process, and continuing to more advanced evaluation phases aimed at validation in view of public release.
- *PlanetLab*: Over one thousand physical hosts available for experiments, that are distributed at various locations in the Internet, recommend PlanetLab for situations in which network conditions realism is the main requirement. Thus, PlanetLab is mainly suited for real-life evaluation of network applications and protocols that are sufficiently stable for such environments.
- *ORBIT*: Focusing on wireless network experiments, ORBIT is obviously the best choice for the evaluation of network

applications over wireless networks, as well as for the assessment of wireless network protocols in realistic but controllable conditions.

Regarding wired-network experiments, we suggest that the combined testbed that can be created by combining Emulab and PlanetLab makes for a perfect evaluation platform, since users could potentially start on Emulab, and then "move" their experiments seamlessly to PlanetLab as the system they develop becomes more stable and more robust.

Chapter 8

More to Consider

In the first part of this book, "The Ins and Outs of Network Emulation," we have presented the fundamentals of network emulation. In the second part, entitled "Network Emulators to Remember," we have proceeded to analyze practical examples of network emulators. Building on this knowledge, we shall summarize in this chapter the main issues related to network emulation. Then we shall introduce several network emulators from the research community, so as to once more emphasize the challenges and requirements related to advanced network emulation characteristics.

8.1 Network Emulation Issues

We identify several issues that need to be considered in connection with network emulation:

- realism
- scalability
- flexibility

While this list is certainly not exhaustive, we believe it contains the most important factors that must be taken into account when

Introduction to Network Emulation
Razvan Beuran
Copyright © 2013 Pan Stanford Publishing Pte. Ltd.
ISBN 978-981-4310-91-8 (Hardcover), 978-981-4364-09-6 (eBook)
www.panstanford.com

analyzing a network emulator. Therefore, we shall discuss each of these issues in more detail in the following sections.

8.1.1 *Realism*

Realism is certainly the first issue that comes to mind when discussing network emulation, and network experiment techniques in general. In this context, realism refers to the accuracy with which a network emulation tool can reproduce reality.

For discussion purposes, we consider three classes of tools in this section:

- *Network testbeds*: all kinds of testbeds, including temporary experiment setups, that are employed for real-world trials
- *Network emulators*: all categories of network emulation tools, including network simulators used in emulation mode
- *Network simulators*: all types of network simulation tools

In Table 8.1 we make a generic comparison between the three classes of experiment tools mentioned before. To help judge the realism of each class of experiment tools, we use the following criteria:

- the nature of the network applications used
- the way in which time flow is considered
- the nature of the network protocols used
- the types of network interfaces employed
- the nature of the network conditions

Network applications are of course *real* in all the experiments performed using network testbeds, and are also *real* for network

Table 8.1.   Comparison of network experiment tools

	Network testbeds	Network emulators	Network simulators
Network applications	Real	Real	Simulated
Time flow	Real	Real/Emulated	Simulated
Network protocols	Real	Real/Emulated	Simulated
Network interfaces	Real	Real/Emulated	Simulated
Network conditions	Real	Real/Emulated	Simulated

emulators, as the ability of running such applications is one of the main goals of emulation. However, network applications are modeled, hence *simulated*, in network simulators.

Time flow is *real* in network testbeds but may be either *real* or *emulated* in network emulators. By emulated time flow, we understand the case when time flows in a controlled manner, even though it may be faster or slower than real time; this is a necessary property when dealing with real network applications. Network simulators use logical time during execution; hence we labeled time flow as *simulated* in their case.

Network protocols as well are *real* in all the experiments performed using network testbeds. As for network emulators, network protocols are also *real*, or at least equivalent to real in the case of network simulators running in emulation mode, since otherwise no interaction with real protocols could take place; we labeled this latter case as *emulated* network protocols. In pure network simulators though, network protocols are modeled, hence *simulated*.

Network interfaces too are *real* for network testbeds. In the case of network emulators, they can be either *real* or *emulated*. We categorize a network interface used in a network emulator as *real* when the physical interface effectively employed is of the same nature with that in the emulated network, and we categorize it as *emulated* when the physical network interface used is of a different nature than that in the emulated network. The first case corresponds to emulating wired networks over wired interfaces, whereas the second case represents, for instance, the emulation of wireless networks over wired interfaces. As an example in the second category, readers can refer to the cellular and satellite network emulation features of Shunra VE Appliance (see Section 5.1.1), or those of Apposite Technologies Linktropy and Netropy emulators (see Section 5.4.1 and Section 5.4.2, respectively). In the case of network simulators, network interfaces exist only logically, and are therefore *simulated*.

As for network conditions, they are naturally *real* in network testbeds and are typically *emulated* in the case of network emulators. However, some network emulators do use *real* network conditions; this is the case of PlanetLab, for instance. In network simulators, network conditions too are modeled, hence *simulated*.

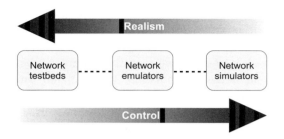

Figure 8.1. Realism versus control for network experiment tools.

Note that the nature of each of the network emulator differentiating criteria above, whether *real* or *emulated*, can be used to distinguish various classes of network emulators, such as the emulators using real network interfaces versus the ones using emulated interfaces, and so on. We shall return to this discussion with more details in Section 8.3.

Using Table 8.1 as a guideline, we represented in Fig. 8.1 the degree of realism that can be generally expected for each of the three classes of experiment tools. Note that in experimentation there is always a trade-off to be made between realism and control. Thus, the more realistic a setup is, the less control one has over that setup, and vice versa. To emphasize this trade-off, we also represented in Fig. 8.1, as a secondary characteristic, the degree of control that each class of tools provides.

Discussing the realism of a particular emulation tool compared with another is not our goal. This is because such an attempt is bound to provide conclusions that are only of limited use, given the large number of existing tools, and the fact that their features keep evolving in time. Instead we prefer to provide some guidelines that readers can use to determine how realistic an emulator is. Two key aspects in this respect are the following:

- *Models*: Emulators that contain models for networks and communication conditions that are close to reality will have an overall increased realism compared with those tools using simplified such models. As an example, let us consider delay emulation. While some emulators only allow configuring a fixed delay, others let users choose delay distributions, such as Gaussian or Poisson, and several emulators even make possible for users to define their own distributions.

- *Scenarios:*[1] Emulators that allow users to create scenarios that are close to reality (in terms of number of nodes, network topology, and so on) are more realistic than those that only make possible experiments in limited circumstances. In this context, some emulators only allow users to configure one end-to-end link, while others let users create a virtual network topology within the emulators, and some emulators allow to seamlessly mix real and emulated nodes to create arbitrary topologies.

Aspects such as those mentioned above must be thoroughly considered when making decisions about using or purchasing an emulation tool. Note that such criteria can also be used to differentiate between network emulators and network simulators, and also network simulators with respect to each other.

A related issue is that while network emulators do have the potential of a higher realism compared with simulators, it is obvious that a network emulator that uses low-fidelity models will be less realistic that a network simulator that uses high-fidelity ones. Hence, analyzing the realism of emulation tools and equivalent simulation tools may help users choose the best solution for a certain purpose, depending on the totality of their requirements.

8.1.2 *Scalability*

Scalability refers to the possibility of conducting experiments with a large number of nodes. It is obvious that in network testbeds scalability comes at a cost proportional to the number of nodes, which is potentially high. Given enough processing power to emulate more nodes on a single host, network emulators can achieve a reasonable scalability at a reasonable cost. Network simulators can push scalability to extremes and keep the cost at low values, since all the nodes are virtual. The relationship between scalability and cost for the three types of experiment tools is illustrated in Fig. 8.2.

---

[1]This issue is related also to the flexibility criterion that we discuss in Section 8.1.3.

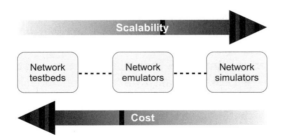

Figure 8.2. Scalability versus cost for network experiment tools.

A caveat regarding the discussion of scalability and cost is that there is a hidden factor, namely time. While network testbeds and emulators have a real flow of time, as discussed in the previous section, network simulators use logical time. This means that they can achieve extreme scalability, but only at the expense of time. This makes that, even though very large-scale experiments may be possible through simulation, they could be impractical to effectively carry out due to the potentially long time to complete. This aspect is important to bear in mind when comparing experiment techniques or equivalent experiment tools.

If comparing network emulators with each other, the size of the network that can be emulated is the most important feature related to scalability. In particular, emulators that use centralized execution are affected by scalability problems, which are generally more severe for software implementations than for hardware ones due to processing speed capabilities. We have thus seen that in centralized approaches the size of the emulated network is limited to tens of nodes and network profiles. To cope with this issue, the distributed emulation approach comes to rescue and allows making experiments with hundreds and even thousands of nodes.

8.1.3 *Flexibility*

Flexibility is another important feature when comparing experiment tools. There are several aspects related to flexibility, and in this context we mainly refer to the amount of freedom users have in doing the following things:

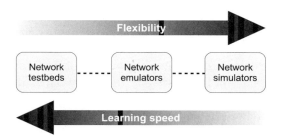

Figure 8.3. Flexibility versus learning speed for network experiment tools.

- Customize the tool and even improve its functionality according to their needs.
- Employ the tool in various manners and configurations.

With network testbeds, there is in general a reduced flexibility, since it is typically difficult to customize the hardware devices involved in the experiment or to change the configuration, topology, etc., unless one designs the testbed. At the other extreme, we place network simulators, which can, in principle, be customized as needed and used in many configurations. Network emulators fall in between due to that fact that they combine the use of real systems and that of modeled ones.

In Fig. 8.3, we represent graphically the flexibility for the three classes of experiment tools that we analyze. As flexibility usually comes at the cost of complexity, we show in the same figure how the learning speed changes for the same classes of tools. As network testbeds use real equipment mostly in static configurations, the time required to learn how to use that network equipment is usually low for engineers and researchers in the area, since they are similar to the systems they use in their daily activities. Network simulators typically have their own specific interfaces, description languages, etc. All these make learning slow, in particular if one wishes to be able to exploit the full capability of a flexible (hence complex) network simulator. Again, emulators fall somewhere in between network testbeds and network simulators, as users can employ well-known practices for the real equipment, but must learn new procedures for the emulated components.

The same way of thinking can be used to compare different network emulators with each other. Some emulators may have more restrictions, and thus less flexibility, than others. If we consider the issue of user customization, it is obvious that features such as user-defined models, and the possibility to modify the source code are key. This makes that many hardware-based emulators will fall in the low-flexibility category, although some of them do allow users to upload their own custom network models; source-level changes are nevertheless impossible. Open-source emulators are at the high end of the flexibility axis, since a user has absolute freedom in customizing such network emulators.

As for the possibility to employ a tool in many configurations, we note that many network emulators that used a centralized approach restrict the user to a single topology, with the emulated network being in the middle and the end nodes connected to each other through it.[2] However, such restrictions are not intrinsic to the centralized emulation approach, as we shall see next.

Let us consider the following two use cases: In Fig. 8.4, we show a typical emulation scenario that can be created by using, for instance, a hardware network emulator. Notice the difference that exists between the real nodes, denoted by A, B, and C that can only be placed at the edges of the emulated network, and the emulated network nodes that exist within the inner virtual network created by the emulator. Therefore, this topology only allows for simple end-to-end emulation experiments.

In Fig. 8.5 we show a more complex situation, in which the real nodes, again denoted by capital letters, are "immersed" into the emulated network. Such a topology can of course be created by using a testbed and many instances of a link-level emulator, hence a distributed approach. However, the same scenario can be create by using an advanced network emulator, such as the simulator-based ones, simply by a mechanism that allows to associate virtual nodes in the emulated network with real nodes. This mechanism is implemented, for instance, by EXata from Scalable Network Technologies, as we discussed in Section 6.3.2.2. Such flexibility

---

[2]Obviously, this restriction doesn't apply to distributed approaches, in which users have the freedom to build any desired network topology.

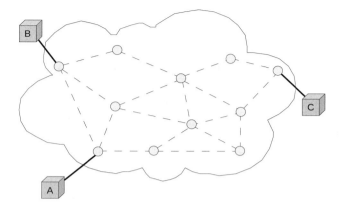

Figure 8.4. Simple emulation topology: the real nodes are at the edges of the emulated network.

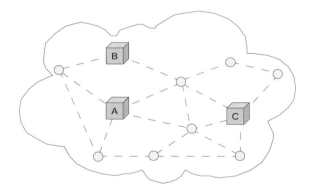

Figure 8.5. Complex emulation topology: the real nodes are "immersed" into the emulated network.

makes it possible to experiment with complex network topologies, in which the real nodes closely interact with each other and with the emulated ones.

8.1.4 *Other Issues*

In addition to the aforementioned issues, which concern all classes of experiment tools, and all types of network emulators, there are other aspects that are of particular importance for some categories of network emulators.

An issue that we have already partially discussed is that of open source, namely in the context of flexibility. However, the fact whether a software network emulator is open source or not has other effects as well. The user of an open-source emulator can not only make any desired modifications but also package the changed version and distribute it as a new tool. Depending on the copyright associated to the open-source tool, one could potentially even create commercial products in this way. We appreciate that code availability is important in order to increase the speed with which network emulators evolve and gain new features. We also note that these remarks could apply to some hardware emulators as well: If the source code would be available, the corresponding emulator could be improved by the developer community in the same way it is done for many hardware open-source projects, such as GNU Radio.

One other issue, mainly regarding large emulation deployments such as testbeds, is security. While this is not a problem that concerns only emulators, and is also critical for network testbeds in general, we would like to stress its importance. Network experiments can produce a lot of traffic and in some cases may involve malicious behavior, either intended (e.g., malware study) or unintended (not-yet-discovered program bugs). In such cases, it is important to properly isolate the traffic and prevent it from reaching production networks or even the Internet. Nevertheless, this requirement may conflict with the need to sometimes allow traffic from remote sources to flow through an emulator, hence external connectivity. Therefore security is an issue that needs to be carefully analyzed for any large-scale network deployments.

8.2 Network Emulator Research

In the previous chapters, we have discussed network emulation solutions that are well established and that have been in use for years or even tens of years. While such solutions are definitely the most important for an introduction to network emulation — the goal of our book — they do not totally encompass the wide range of ideas and concepts that have been put forward in recent years in the field of network emulation.

In this section, we shall briefly discuss some of the research projects focused on network emulation. Our presentation borrows some ideas from the survey in [32], which we recommend for a relatively exhaustive discussion on this issue. Another thorough survey, albeit dedicated to MANET emulators, is the one presented in [56].

We remind our readers that in Table 8.1 we emphasized the main characteristics of network emulators that differentiate them from other experiment techniques. While we said that applications are real for all network emulators, as a most distinctive characteristic that differentiates them from network simulators, all the other features of network emulators could be either real or emulated. Thus, we distinguished four aspects that network emulators must take into account in this respect:

(1) time flow
(2) network protocols
(3) network interfaces
(4) network conditions

In what follows, we shall discuss several examples of network emulators that we have selected and grouped to illustrate various approaches proposed for the four aspects that we enumerated above.

8.2.1 *Time Flow*

Most network emulators use real-time flow during execution, and in many ways this is regarded as a defining property of network emulators. However, as we have stated in several contexts, time flow is just another component of an emulator that can very well be emulated instead of being real.

While this is not true for most typical network systems, a particular case in this respect is represented by ubiquitous systems, such as sensor networks. For such systems, emulation faces additional challenges. Differently from typical networks, which are established between computers or equivalents, ubiquitous systems use special low-power processors and other specific hardware, such as sensors or actuators. These circumstances make impossible the direct emulation of ubiquitous systems on PC hardware.

As a consequence, all the hardware components of such an ubiquitous system need to be emulated, including the processor, so as to be able to run unmodified application programs (typically called firmware). ATEMU is such an emulation system which allows different hardware configurations [87]. Similarly, MEADOWS allows running multiple virtual motes per physical host participating in the emulation [60]. While mote applications can be run unmodified on such emulators, not only the hardware components (including sensors and actuators) but also the network communication between the devices, often done through a wireless medium, must be emulated in this approach. This makes that such systems can be seen as running in an emulated time that can flow slower or faster than real time, but also with the same speed as the real time. Nevertheless, in all cases time needs to be accounted for in some way, which constitutes a significant difference compared with the typical emulators, which do not specifically take time into account. An important requirement for systems that use emulated time, which differentiates them from simulators, is that time flow should be controlled in a deterministic manner, so that a direct correspondence can be established between such emulated devices and the real devices that are emulated.

8.2.2 *Network Protocols*

Network simulators use — by design — models of network protocols when conducting experiments. Many see this as an important drawback of network simulation and of the corresponding simulator-based network emulation. As a consequence, researchers have worked considerably on devising techniques that make more realistic experiments possible through the use of real protocol implementations. This is mainly achieved by integrating real protocol implementations from open-source operating systems with network emulators/simulators by creating suitable wrappers, so that those protocol implementations can be used for experiments from within network emulators/simulators.

The ENTRAPID system packed the FreeBSD network stack, allowing protocol developers to experiment with their own protocol implementations integrated into the stack [38]. For this purpose though, the processes running on the experiment nodes require modifications. The other characteristics of the network, i.e., the topology and the physical layer are nevertheless emulated.

IMUNES goes further than ENTRAPID regarding flexibility and modifies the protocol stack of FreeBSD in order to allow for *multiple* independent instances of the protocol stack to coexist in the kernel, connected via emulated links [117].

The project Network Simulation Cradle aims to integrate the protocol stacks of multiple operating systems with the Ns-2 network simulator [48]. This project packed network protocol stacks in the Linux, FreeBSD, and OpenBSD as shared libraries, and implemented an Ns-2 agent that allows researchers to use these stacks from within the simulator.

Another approach is used by the VINI project, which builds a virtual network infrastructure on top of PlanetLab's overlay network [8]. Network functions are provided by using open-source software implementations for routing, packet forwarding and network address translation, etc.

One can also use virtualization techniques in order to realistically reproduce the behavior of different operating systems and protocol implementations. The User Mode Linux (UML) project provides a virtual Linux kernel running in user mode. UML has been used for implementing virtual nodes that are then connected through a virtual network driver to an emulated network. Examples of UML-based systems include vBET [49], which targets wired networks, and the system developed by Guffens and Bastin [33], which targets MANETs. A similar technique is that of using micro-kernel based Linux systems, such as the work of Engel *et al.* [27], which targets wireless network emulation.

8.2.3 *Network Interfaces*

Using real network interfaces is the main advantage of many emulation systems, as this creates a behavior of the connected devices that is very close to reality. While this is possible without much difficulty for *wired networks*, a trade-off situation appears regarding *wireless networks*. Thus, one has two choices when wishing to perform wireless network emulation:

(1) Use real wireless network interfaces and take advantage of the realism they provide but lose in terms of control and sometimes risk undesired interferences.
(2) Emulate the wireless network interfaces, thus gaining full control over their behavior, at the cost of increased system complexity and a potential lack of realism.

The first approach is mainly used by wireless network emulation testbeds such as ORBIT. We have seen in Section 7.3 that achieving a high level of control is difficult on ORBIT and can only be accomplished partially through rather complex hardware and software solutions.

The second approach is taken by several other network emulators whenever they emulate networks of a different nature with that of the actual interfaces they are equipped with. We have seen many examples so far of such network emulators, for instance, the emulation of satellite, Wi-Fi and cell phone network using a hardware-based emulator such as Shunra VE Appliance, or Apposite Technologies Linktropy and Netropy emulators, as we have already mentioned in Section 8.1.1.

Note that in order to facilitate the control of network conditions, some researchers have chosen to use emulated network interfaces even for wired-network emulation. This functionality can be implemented through operating system specific drivers that are designed for creating user-defined tunneling mechanisms or virtual network interfaces. In addition to NCTUns, which we have already discussed, EmuNET [54] and NEMAN [91] also use this approach. Of the two, EmuNet has the advantage of distributed execution capabilities. In all of these systems, the protocol layers starting at IP level, as well as the network applications, are those of the experiment hosts, hence real.

8.2.4 *Network Conditions*

The most challenging task related to network emulation is definitely that of recreating the communication conditions between the experiment nodes in a realistic manner. This is true for all types of emulators, no matter how many of the other components are real and how many emulated. The possible approaches for recreating network conditions in an emulator are as follows:

- Use real network conditions between the nodes, which can be either controlled or uncontrolled.
- Use communication models to create the network conditions between nodes.

8.2.4.1 Uncontrolled real conditions

If realism of the experiment results is the most important, then alternatives that use as much as possible real components are the ideal solution. In addition to PlanetLab, which falls in this category and we have discussed already, we introduce below several other projects that focus on the use of uncontrolled network conditions.

Monarch is a system that attempts to recreate the communication conditions (in particular, delay) between two virtual nodes by using real values of this parameter [36]. Thus, Monarch uses the latency observed between the host on which both the virtual sender and the virtual receiver reside, and a remote host on the Internet that is "associated" to the virtual receiver. The implementation works as follows. Every packet transmitted by the virtual sender is captured by Monarch, which sends a probe packet of the same size to the remote host associated with the virtual receiver. Only when Monarch receives a reply from the remote host, it will deliver to the virtual receiver the packet destined to it. For the opposite direction, from the virtual receiver to the virtual sender, Monarch passes the packets without delay. This ensures that both the sender and the receiver observe the round-trip time experienced by the probe packet, albeit in an asymmetric manner.

The record and replay mechanisms that we have discussed for NIST Net as well as for several of the commercial network emulators can also be included in the category of "uncontrolled real conditions" approaches, since they reproduce in an emulated network conditions that were previously recorded in a real production network. Although the conditions are reproduced in a repeatable manner, they are nevertheless "raw" in the sense that the experimenter had no control over them when they were captured.

8.2.4.2 Controlled real conditions

Experiments with uncontrolled real conditions are limited to conditions they reproduce. To give users more power over the experiment, emulator designers attempted to exert a certain influence over the real conditions.

One example in this category is "replay with modifications," a feature that we have seen for the Simena PTC3000 and NE3000 network emulators that we have presented in Section 5.3.2 and Section 5.3.3, respectively.

Due to the nature of wired networks, the control one can exert over network conditions and still keep them real is limited. Things are, however, different for wireless networks. Wireless communication is by its nature open, which means that it is easy to exert an influence over it. Of course, this fact can be both negative and positive, depending on whether the influence is undesired, such as accidental interference, or desired, case in which it becomes an instrument of control.

Using controlled real conditions is of particular importance for wireless networks because such network communication is traditionally difficult to model. This makes that many researchers prefer to use field trials for wireless network evaluation, although their results can end up biased because of external influences. As a consequence, network emulator developers have paid significant attention to the possibility of controlling to a certain degree the wireless communication conditions, either directly or indirectly. An example in this category has already been provided through ORBIT, but other projects in this category exist as well.

Direct condition control This approach refers to exerting an unmediated influence over the wireless media used by the network interfaces. This can be done by using noise generators to create adverse communication conditions, as we have seen for ORBIT, or by using anechoic RF shielded rooms to isolate the experiment area from external influences, as we will see later for iWWT.

Another possibility in this class of methods, which enables controlled wireless network experiments with unmodified hardware, is to connect the communicating network interfaces through a wired media instead of the wireless one. The simplest solution is to use cables and configurable attenuators. A more powerful approach is used by Judd and Steenkiste under the name "physical emulation" [51]. Their proposal is to capture the radio signals at the antenna and to use an FPGA-based digital signal processor to attenuate signals between the transmitting and receiving stations in a controlled way. Thus, it becomes possible to accurately reproduce wireless physical layer effects in repeatable experiments, while still employing unmodified NICs.

Indirect condition control These methods work by managing in a reproducible manner various aspects of the experiment that indirectly influence the communication conditions between the experiment nodes. One typical example of such an aspect is node mobility. We have already mentioned that through Mobile Emulab researchers tried to recreate controlled mobility conditions for wireless network experiments by using robots. Another solution, the Ad hoc Protocol Evaluation testbed (APE) presented in [74], coordinates the movement of the human participants in the experiment through motion instructions displayed on their laptop screen as they move, thus controlling motion to a certain degree, and achieving reproducibility.

Combined condition control We include in this category the network emulators that mix direct and indirect control methods to achieve higher experiment flexibility. For direct control, the Illinois Wireless Wind Tunnel (iWWT) uses an anechoic chamber to prevent outside RF interferences and create an enclosure for experimentation [110]. This project also employs the following techniques for extending the range of possible experiments:

- Similar to ORBIT, network topology is controlled through the explicit introduction of background noise; transmit power level is also reduced for topology-control purposes.
- Similar to Mobile Emulab, iWWT employs small mobile robots to create reproducibility in connection with mobility experiments.

An equivalent approach from a functional point of view is used in MiNT (Miniaturized Wireless Network Testbed) [25]. Instead of noise generators, in MiNT signal power is reduced by attenuators attached to the wireless devices. MiNT nodes are mounted on small mobile robots that are remotely controlled to create control movement trajectories.

8.2.4.3 Modeled conditions

Another approach instead of using real conditions is to model the network communication and route the traffic of the experiment nodes, be they real or virtual, through a virtual network built on top of the real one. In addition to the solutions in this category that we have already discussed, such as the simulator-based emulation in Ns-2, or an emulation testbed such as Emulab, we provide a few more examples of such tools in what follows.

An important research direction in this class is related to emulators that are designed to be used in a distributed manner. For example, IP-TNE [102] uses the Critical Channel Traversing (CCT) algorithm for parallel discrete event simulation and employs real network interfaces for getting traffic into and out of the network emulator.

Another system that uses a discrete event simulator for network emulation purposes is RINSE [58]. RINSE uses a multi-resolution modeling approach to achieve the target performance level as follows. Background traffic is simulated in RINSE by using fluid models requiring less computation resources to simulate, whereas the traffic of interest is simulated at the packet level.

ModelNet distributes the emulation process by using two sets of hosts: core nodes and edge nodes [109]. The virtual network is modeled as a set of pipes, which are managed by the core nodes. These core nodes cooperate to subject the traffic to the impairments corresponding to the target network topology. The edge nodes are the real hosts in the emulation experiment, and their traffic is routed through the virtual network create by the core nodes. We recall that we named such an approach "partially distributed emulation" in Section 3.3.1.2.

While ModelNet is intended for wired IP networks, MobiNet is an extension of the same approach that targets mobile ad hoc networks [61]. MobiNet also introduces a virtualization mechanism on the edge nodes, allowing to scale up experiments to a node count that exceeds the number of physical edge nodes.

An often-used approach in network emulation is the use of link-level emulators to control the network conditions for each experiment node, thus achieving a fully distributed emulation solution. The link-level emulators are inserted in-between the protocol stack and the network device driver of an operating system. This approach makes it possible to use the existing protocol stack and programs running on a host, while emulating the rest of the network. EMPOWER, which targets the emulation of both wired and wireless IP networks is an example of a network emulator employing this technique [118]. As already mentioned in Section 3.3.1.2, the wireless network emulation testbed SWOON employs two experimental nodes to emulate one single wireless node in order to separate emulation execution from application execution [39].

8.3 Discussion

In Table 8.1, we have mentioned that several aspects can be either real or emulated in the case of network emulators. The order in which we listed these aspects corresponds to the order in which they can be conceptually ordered in real life when considering network communication. Thus, when starting from the bottom of the list, we see first "network conditions," which corresponds to the medium through which network communication takes place. Following that, "network interfaces" refers to the physical devices used to perform the network communication. Further up, "network protocols" contains those software components that are used to mediate the network communication that takes place at application level. The item "time flow" is a global issue that indicates whether the communication process takes place in real time or not. As we previously said, we placed "network applications" at the top because it is the component that is always real for at least some of the nodes involved in the emulation experiments, and that distinguishes

Table 8.2. Classes of network emulators

	Network testbeds	Class A	Class B	Class C	Class D	Network simulators
Network applications	Real	Real	Real	Real	Real	Simulated
Time flow	Real	Real	Real	Real	Emulated	Simulated
Network protocols	Real	Real	Real	Emulated	Emulated	Simulated
Network interfaces	Real	Real	Emulated	Emulated	Emulated	Simulated
Network conditions	Real	Emulated	Emulated	Emulated	Emulated	Simulated

emulators from simulators. Note, however, that applications should be viewed rather as a component of the experimentation process than as a building component of network emulators.

Existing network emulators can be grouped by how many components of the communication process they emulate and how many they use as real. While it may not be always true, we noticed that most network emulators will draw a line between real and emulated aspects somewhere in the list that we presented, while preserving their order. We illustrate this idea in Table 8.2, where we denoted the resulting classes of network emulators with alphabet letters from A to D. We indicated again the properties of network testbeds and network simulators at the left-hand and right-hand sides of the table for clarity purposes.

Note in Table 8.2 how some systems use mostly real components and emulate only the network conditions, placing themselves closest to network testbeds. Other systems will use mostly emulated components, thus being closest to network simulators. Yet some systems will use a different balance between the real and emulated components, and fall somewhere in the middle. In what follows we shall give a brief description and several examples for each network emulator class:

Class A Closest to network testbeds, the emulators in this class use real components for all experiment aspects except for network conditions, which are emulated. In this category, enter testbeds such as Emulab [108], using link-level emulation for recreating the network conditions of a target scenario, or like ORBIT [115], using various mechanisms to control the network conditions in a wireless network. The most important characteristic of this class of emulators is that their physical interfaces match those used in the emulated network (e.g., wired network emulated on wired interfaces, or wireless network emulated on wireless interfaces).

Class B   The emulators in this category introduce one more level of modeling, thus getting one step further away from network testbeds. In this class enter those emulators that use physical interfaces that are different in nature from those used in the emulated network (e.g., wireless network emulation over wired network interfaces). Examples include distributed emulation solutions such as MobiNet [61] or EMPOWER [118], which are dedicated to wireless network emulation on top of wired-network testbeds. Another group of emulators is represented by those that use centralized approaches, in which a software or hardware system is used to emulate a series of network elements; the constraint is that the network protocols used are real, as is the case of NCTUns [111], for example. PlanetLab [84] can also be included in this class if we consider that the network interfaces of the virtual nodes on PlanetLab are also virtual — hence emulated — even though the traffic finally flows through real network interfaces.

Class C   Network emulators of this type use models of network protocols that are compatible, but not necessarily identical with the real implementations. In this category, enter most centralized emulation solutions, which use a software or hardware system to emulate an entire network, and use models or re-implementations of network protocols for this purpose. Simulator-based network emulators are the most representative member of this class. Hence, typical examples include Ns-2 [105], OPNET Modeler/SITL [80], and QualNet Developer/EXata [96] network simulators when used in emulation mode.

Class D   Closest to network simulators, the network emulators in this class emulate all aspects, including time flow. The need for a time flow that is not real appears rarely for emulation applications targeting PC-based (or equivalent) network technologies. For ubiquitous systems, such as sensor networks, RFID tags, and so on, it may be necessary to emulate several hardware components, such as the processor, in order to allow emulation experiments to run on PCs. An example of such a system is the wireless network testbed QOMB [15], which we shall discuss in the third part of this book.[3] A related example is ATEMU [87]; note that ATEMU is, however, defined by its authors as a simulator, since time flow is not strictly controlled; hence, it should be treated only as a closest possible alternative, and not as an example *per se*.

We warn our readers that the above classification is not exhaustive, as some network emulators do not fit in any of these classes. This is because the layered view for real and emulated aspects is not a requirement. For example, systems such as PlanetLab or Monarch use real network conditions (i.e., the lowest layer in Table 8.2 is real), but they emulate the network interfaces and network hosts through virtualization techniques (the higher layers in Table 8.2).

Nevertheless, most existing network emulators can be included in this classification, since most researchers and developers are faced with the decision over which components to emulate and which to keep real in negotiating the trade-off between realism and control. Drawing the boundary between the layers that we presented provides an easy-to-understand such trade-off, since the layers above the boundary will provide the degree of realism, and those below the boundary will provide the desired degree of control.

Please note that the layered structure that we presented in Table 8.2 is not fortuitous, as this structure loosely corresponds to the ISO-OSI network layer model used in most current network implementations, as follows:

- The item "network conditions" parallels the network media below the physical network layer (PHY).
- "Network interfaces" is related to the physical (PHY) and data link (MAC) layers.

---

[3] Note that QOMB falls in Class D only when used in the context of ubiquitous systems. When used for other purposes, such as WLAN emulation, QOMB falls in Class B, since it emulated wireless networks over wired interfaces.

- The item "Network protocols" is equivalent mainly to the network (IP) and transport (TCP/UDP) network layers.
- "Network applications" refers to the layers above transport layer, such as session, presentation, and application layers (with focus on the latter).

The way in which we split the network layers into four aspects was determined by the separation of hardware and software components that exist on most network systems. When emulating a system though, one can make even more detailed separations. For instance, one may choose to emulate the network conditions and the physical layer of a system, but use real implementations for the MAC protocols and above, by creating the necessary interfaces between the real and emulated domains. Thus, one can effectively split the "network interfaces" category into its two components and deal with them separately.

Note that time flow is the only criterion in our classification that is unrelated to such a layered structure. Since most emulators do use real-time flow, we considered that we can safely place it at the top of the list just below network applications, as the most unlikely aspect that is going to be emulated.

Part III

A CASE STUDY: QOMB

Chapter 9

QOMB Overview

With this chapter starts the third part of our book, dedicated to the thorough presentation of QOMB, a wireless network emulation testbed to the development of which we participated and still contribute actively [15]. QOMB is a relatively new network emulation tool, hence not so widely known in the research community. Nevertheless, the issues that we encountered during its development also apply to other network emulators. We therefore think that reporting our hands-on experience with QOMB will help our readers in two possible ways:

- Those involved in developing network emulators should find helpful hints by reading the description of the components of QOMB, and their integration (Chapter 10, Chapter 11, and Chapter 12).
- Those interested only in using network emulators can focus on Chapter 12 for an outline and on Chapter 13 for finding practical information about how to run experiments.

In this chapter we shall provide first of all some background information about our work and the motivations that lead to the development of QOMB. Then we shall outline the architecture of

Introduction to Network Emulation
Razvan Beuran
Copyright © 2013 Pan Stanford Publishing Pte. Ltd.
ISBN 978-981-4310-91-8 (Hardcover), 978-981-4364-09-6 (eBook)
www.panstanford.com

QOMB and briefly introduce its two main components: StarBED and QOMET.

9.1 Motivation

The WLAN technology is currently widely deployed in corporations, universities, homes, and even public spaces. Terminals with a wide range of specifications and processing power, in both static and mobile settings, use this technology as an essential component to ensure that their users can freely accomplish various tasks that require Internet connection.

New wireless network technologies, such as ZigBee or WiMAX, have appeared in recent years to address the nascent needs that appear as users start to value more and more their connectivity. The new technologies also target the limitations of existing technologies, by providing lower power consumption, or higher throughput.

The realistic evaluation of network applications and protocols running over such wireless technologies plays a significant role in understanding their performance characteristics. While the range of possible applications of wireless network technologies is large, we shall focus below on two of them, namely Internet access and smart environments.

9.1.1 *Internet Access*

Network users rely more and more on the fact that they can connect to the Internet to accomplish their business-related or private tasks. Emailing, Internet browsing, photo sharing, are only a few examples of activities that necessitate an Internet connection.

The most used wireless network technology for Internet access is currently WLAN. Other technologies have also emerged as solutions for ensuring Internet connectivity from non-computer devices such as mobile phones. In this category enter the 3G generation of standards, which were more recently followed by so-called 4G standards, LTE (Long Term Evolution) and Mobile WiMAX.

Such technologies make it possible to connect wirelessly not only to the Internet but also with other users. Thus, one could use a

WLAN connection to make a VoIP call even from a mobile phone, thus making significant savings on call charges in those areas where WLAN connections are possible. These technologies could also be used in the case of disasters to connect rescue workers with each other and with the command center. In these contexts, the quality of voice communication and the performance of routing protocols are some of the issues that need to be fully understood before deployment.

Experiments with such technologies are nevertheless difficult, first of all because of the evanescent nature of the wireless communication, which makes it difficult to thoroughly observe and capture the traffic. This issue is amplified by factors such as mobility and the potential significant number of nodes distributed over a large geographical area. Moreover, the possibility of undesired and uncontrollable interferences further contributes to increasing the experimentation difficulty.

9.1.2 *Smart Environments*

A concept that seems very promising as a near-future application of wireless network technologies is that of smart environments, also known as Ambient Intelligence (AmI), or ubiquitous computing. Such intelligent environments combine a large number of small sensing and computing devices in order to "proactively, but sensibly, support people in their daily lives" [6]. Each of these devices has limited communication, computational and energy resources, but together they can be used to accomplish a wide range of tasks, such as people and asset localization and environment condition control.

AmI devices are typically embedded in homes or deployed in outdoor environments, which makes controlled experiments difficult. Development is further hindered by the small form factor of such devices and by the limited access to their internal state. Moreover, the usual organization issues related to large-scale experiments make it difficult, if not impossible, to exhaustively validate a system.

Ubiquitous systems often employ wireless networks to communicate with each other. This is because wireless interfaces provide significant advantages in terms of deployment facility if considering a large number of small-size devices. The performance of the algorithms and protocols that are implemented in the firmware of the ubiquitous network systems should be assessed as they communicate wirelessly, so as to validate their operation, and in order to decide the various parameter values that ensure optimum performance characteristics under specific circumstances.

9.2 Requirements

As we have mentioned in several places in this book, traditionally, most of the investigations related to network applications and protocols are done using network simulations, including for the case of wireless networks. The opposite alternative, real-world trials, suffers from disadvantages such as potential undesired interference, and difficulties in orchestrating mobility, all these resulting in low result reproducibility. The technique of network emulation, bridging the gap between simulation experiments and real-world trials, is a hybrid approach that is particularly suited for wireless network experiments.

9.2.1 *Background*

Our activity in the field of networks started in 2001, when we joined a team at CERN, the European Laboratory for Particle Physics, located in Geneva, Switzerland. The team was (and still is) involved in activities related to the design, implementation, and management of the network architecture used by ATLAS, one of the particle physics experiments on the LHC (Large Hadron Collider). LHC, which is being built at CERN, is at this moment the world's largest and highest-energy particle accelerator, and it started operation in March 2010.

Our work was related to the study of the relationship between network QoS, i.e., the conditions in a network, and application QoE, that is the user-perceived quality (UPQ) for the applications running over that network. While this activity was of significance for ATLAS-related network traffic, it is also of general interest for widely used network applications, such as VoIP and video streaming. This is because our work resulted in a methodology for answering two types of questions:

(1) Given a certain network, with its respective QoS, what is the QoE that one can expect to have for a certain application?
(2) Given some requirements regarding the QoE of an application, what is the minimum network QoS that is needed in order to achieve the desired QoE?

This work is presented in detail in our PhD thesis, "Measuring Quality in Computer Networks" [10]. One of the issues that became obvious during this activity was that in order to be able to conduct objectively a study on the relationship between network QoS and application QoE, one needs the ability to control network state, so as to perform repeatable experiments in a wide range of conditions. This fact basically emphasized the need for *network emulation*.

In our PhD thesis, we performed network emulation mostly in simple wired-network scenarios, and we employed for emulation purposes Dummynet, which we have already described in Section 4.1. Due to its limitations in terms of speed, accuracy, and realism, we started working with a colleague, Mihai Ivanovici, on implementing a hardware-based network emulator that operates at line-speed for 1 Gbps rates, has a high accuracy, and includes background traffic models. This work is described in his PhD thesis, "Network Quality Degradation Emulation — An FPGA-based Approach to Application Performance Assessment" [46].

9.2.2 *Large-Scale Wireless Emulation*

From a current perspective, our previous work had two main limitations:

(1) It only dealt with *wired-network emulation*.
(2) It only targeted *small-scale experiments*.

While high-speed wired networks are certainly the backbone of the Internet, one can notice a proliferation in recent years of the use of wireless networks. These networks have gained significant ground and may have become the access method of choice for typical users, especially in public places, but often at home too.

Moreover, since wireless network quality degradation is usually more severe than that in wired networks, even in mixed scenarios the wireless communication is the component that has a dominant effect on application QoE. Therefore, the possibility to emulate wireless networks appears as an important feature of modern network emulators.

Small-scale experiments are certainly useful do determine baselines for the operation of a network system. However, any real network, be it wired or wireless, will have a large number of users. Hence, the ability to perform large-scale experiments emerges as another significant requirement for modern network emulators.

In 2006 we joined the Hokuriku Research Center[1] of the National Institute of Information and Communications Technology, located in Ishikawa, Japan. Since then, our activity was dedicated to designing and implementing a wireless network emulation testbed that answers the aforementioned requirements, which can be summarized as follows:

(1) Make wireless network emulation experiments possible.
(2) Do this for large-scale scenarios, with a minimum of several tens of nodes.

The range of possible applications of such a testbed is broad, from experiments related to mobile networks and mesh networks, to research related to ubiquitous systems and sensor networks. As an example, we ask our readers to imagine the following scenario. In order to design and validate wireless network equipment that is to be used in mission-critical circumstances, such as the rescue operations following a disaster, one needs to perform a thorough validation of the equipment under test. While this can certainly — and should necessarily — be done up to a certain point by using the real equipment under evaluation, practical reasons may restrict the extent of the scenarios that can be explored in this manner. A wireless network emulation testbed can help the network engineers assess the performance and validate the equipment under test in a wide range of network conditions. This will help provide the required guarantees that at the time when rescue workers will

---

[1]Starting with 2011 the center was renamed to "Hokuriku StarBED Technology Center".

actually use the equipment in real circumstances, it will operate as intended and at the desired QoE level.

9.3 Design Outline

The process of designing the wireless network emulation testbed QOMB was driven by the two requirements presented in the previous section. To tackle those requirements we employ two elements:

- a software component named QOMET, which is a set of tools for wireless network emulation
- a hardware component named StarBED, which is a wired-network testbed, and the experiment-support software tools associated to it

The software tools provided by QOMET enable experiments with emulated wireless networks over physical wired networks. Our choice of using such an approach for our testbed design is motivated by two factors:

- As discussed in Section 8.2.3, emulating the wireless network interface gives more control over the experiment compared to the use of real wireless network interfaces (e.g., the approach used in ORBIT).
- Software tools allow more flexibility in designing the experiment platform, and in our case allow for a distributed-execution mechanism, that makes large-scale experiments possible.

StarBED is the large-scale network experiment environment that is managed by our research center. It was natural to leverage this resource in designing QOMB, so as to enhance its functionality with additional capabilities. Note that StarBED comes with a set of experiment-support software tools, namely SpringOS and RUNE, that make it easier to run experiments on this testbed.

The two components that we discussed so far will be presented in more details in the next chapters, QOMET in Chapter 10, and StarBED and its tools in Chapter 11, respectively. Note that while there is no strict dependency between these two QOMB components — in the sense that QOMET can be run on top of other testbeds as well — the integration between QOMET and StarBED makes it possible to conduct wireless network emulation experiments in a straightforward manner on the resulting testbed, QOMB, as it will be illustrated in Chapter 12. In fact, the name QOMB simply stands for "QOMET on StarBED."

Chapter 10

QOMET

In this chapter, we describe the wireless network emulation set of tools named QOMET. We present first the fundamentals behind QOMET and the libraries that provide the network emulation functionality, namely *deltaQ*, *wireconf*, and *chanel*. Then we outline the command-line tools used to effectively perform emulation experiments, namely "qomet" and "do_wireconf."

10.1 Overview

QOMET is a wireless network emulator that was initially dedicated to IEEE 802.11 networks (WLAN, also known as Wi-Fi) [17, 18] and was later extended to support other wireless network technologies, such as IEEE 802.15.4 and active RFID tag wireless communication. Support for IEEE 802.16 (WiMAX) is planned for the future.

Differently from ORBIT, QOMET does not rely on real wireless network cards. Instead, QOMET employs a scenario-driven architecture with two stages to reproduce the wireless network communication conditions in a *wired-network environment*. The

Introduction to Network Emulation
Razvan Beuran
Copyright © 2013 Pan Stanford Publishing Pte. Ltd.
ISBN 978-981-4310-91-8 (Hardcover), 978-981-4364-09-6 (eBook)
www.panstanford.com

Figure 10.1. The logical organization and processing flow of QOMET.

logical organization of QOMET is presented in Fig. 10.1. The processing flow is as follows:

(1) In the first stage, QOMET computes from a real-world scenario representation the network quality degradation (ΔQ) description that corresponds to the real-world events. This computation is done by the library called *deltaQ* (presented later in Section 10.2).

(2) In the second stage, the ΔQ description is applied into the wired network during the live experiment execution to recreate the wireless network communication conditions. This function is ensured by the libraries *wireconf* or *chanel*, depending on the type of experiment (more details about each of these libraries and their use will be provided in Section 10.3 and Section 10.4, respectively).

The main features of QOMET are summarized as follows:

- support for wireless communication emulation
  - wireless network technologies
    * IEEE 802.11a/b/g
    * active RFID tag communication
    * IEEE 802.15.4
  - 2D and 3D wireless network antennas
  - propagation models
    * free space path loss model
    * log-distance path loss model
- support for node mobility models
  - linear motion
  - circular and rotation motion

— random way point motion
— behavioral motion[1]

- support for synthetic environments[2]

  — 2D and 3D objects, such as buildings
  — 2D street topology

- support for routing protocols

  — Optimized Link State Routing (OLSR)

All of these feature sets except the last one are supported via the deltaQ library, and will be described in more details in the next section. Routing protocol support is only needed during live execution, and is implemented in the wireconf library (see Section 10.3).

10.2 DeltaQ Library

The role of the deltaQ library is to convert the scenario representation of the emulation experiment to a network degradation description as the first stage of the process presented in Fig. 10.1. The library is called to perform this computation process by the two executable programs in QOMET, namely "qomet" and "do_wireconf," as it will be detailed in Section 10.5.1 and Section 10.5.2, respectively.

The conversion process makes use of several models for handling the three main functions of the deltaQ library:

- wireless communication emulation
- node mobility emulation
- synthetic environment creation

---

[1] The behavioral motion model implemented in deltaQ is a mechanism for computing the trajectory of a mobile node given its start position and destination. We shall discuss this model more thoroughly in Section 10.2.3.

[2] QOMET can use real map data in JPGIS format for the definition of buildings and streets, so as to create a realistic virtual environment for the emulation experiments.

10.2.1 *Scenario Representation*

The scenario representation is the input of the deltaQ library. This representation is provided by the user as an XML-based description of the experiment conditions that must be emulated. The scenario representation will indicate, for example, the initial position of the wireless nodes, their motion pattern, the topology of the virtual environment which is being reproduced (such as streets and buildings), and so on. While the syntax of this representation is not within the scope of this book, readers can consult the user manual of QOMET for details [40].

As an experiment progresses, new information is added to the scenario representation, such as, for instance, the amount of traffic that is being sent during the actual emulation experiment.[3] Moreover, the initial XML-based scenario does not have to include all the information that is used during the experiment. For example, one can define only the initial position of mobile nodes but dynamically determine their trajectory *while* the experiment is running. This approach has been used in conjunction with the evaluation of robot motion-planning algorithms [76].

All the information in the scenario representation, both the one provided at the beginning of the experiment and any dynamic information gathered or provided during the experiment, is used by the deltaQ library to compute the communication conditions between any two given wireless nodes at each moment of time. This computation uses communication models that are specific to each supported wireless network technology.

10.2.2 *Wireless Communication*

The wireless communication emulation represents the core of the deltaQ library functionality. The three components that are necessary to provide this functionality are

- wireless network technology models
- wireless network antenna models
- electromagnetic wave propagation models

---

[3]These traffic statistics are employed to calculate the contention in the emulated wireless channel.

10.2.2.1 Wireless network technologies

As already mentioned, three wireless network technologies are currently supported by QOMET (with a fourth one, WiMAX, being planned for the future):

- IEEE 802.11a/b/g
- active RFID tag communication
- IEEE 802.15.4

While there are certainly many differences between these network technologies, the approach used for all of them in deltaQ is to employ probabilistic models to compute the most important parameters that characterize wireless communication in the synthetic emulated environment, and then at different network levels.

Wireless communication is first of all influenced by the distance between the wireless nodes, a property of the synthetic environment in which the experiment takes place. Wave propagation through the wireless medium depends on the properties of the communication environment, such as attenuation. These parameters represent the input of the wireless propagation models (see Section 10.2.2.3) that are used to compute the receive power which characterizes communication at the physical network layer (ISO OSI Layer 1). Other parameters influencing communication at this level are the transmit power of the wireless adapters and the properties of the antennas (see Section 10.2.2.2), which are all Layer 1 parameters.

Receive power, together with other properties of the physical network layer, namely receive power sensitivity, noise power, and technology characteristics (encoding, etc.), represents the input of the error model that is used to compute the frame error rate, a parameter of the data link network layer (ISO OSI Layer 2). For some transceivers, error models are provided by manufacturers, typically as a dependency between bit error rate and signal-to-noise ratio. Given that such information is difficult to obtain for all wireless devices, we used the fact that this dependency is almost exponential to create an equivalent generic error model. Our error model has, as the main parameter, the receive sensitivity of the wireless transceiver, which is specified in the regular documentation of most wireless devices, and it computes the frame error rate given a certain received power level.

Frame error rate, together with technology-specific parameters such as operating rate, can first of all be used to compute other Layer 2 parameters, such as frame delay and jitter, or L2 bandwidth. They also represent the input of the data link network layer model, which is employed to compute network layer parameters (ISO OSI Layer 3). These L3 parameters are packet delay and jitter, packet loss, and bandwidth. Our readers will probably observe that the above are exactly the network quality degradation parameters (see Def. 2.2) that we labeled as ΔQ parameters.

The parameters used at each level of the overall multi-layer model that we presented, as well as the individual models used to convert one layer characteristics to next layer ones, are presented in Table 10.1. We emphasize with italic font those parameters that are actually computed by the deltaQ library; the non-italicized parameters are provided by the user or are derived from the characteristics of the specific wireless network technology used.

Note that not all of the above levels must necessarily be implemented for each modeled wireless network technology, depending on its properties. For instance, the active RFID tag communication

Table 10.1. Generic multi-level characterization of wireless network technologies

Level at which characterization is performed	Parameters characterizing the level	Models for conversion to the next-higher level
Synthetic environment	*Distance*, environment properties (attenuation, shadowing)	Propagation model
Physical layer (ISO OSI Layer 1)	Transmit power, antenna properties, *receive power*, receive sensitivity, noise power, wireless network technology characteristics	Frame error rate model
Data link layer (ISO OSI Layer 2)	*Frame error rate*, wireless network technology characteristics, *frame delay and jitter*, *bandwidth* (L2)	Data link layer models
Network layer (ISO OSI Layer 3)	*Packet delay and jitter*, *packet loss rate*, *bandwidth* (L3)	

supported in QOMET uses no data link layer protocol model, as no such protocol exists. As a consequence, computation is only done up to data link layer parameters, which represent the ΔQ description for this case. Similarly, for IEEE 802.15.4 emulation we execute a Layer 2 implementation to account for the corresponding functionality; therefore, again no Layer 2 model is required, and computation is only done up to data link layer parameters.

Table 10.1 emphasizes the fact that our modeling stops at Layer 2 in all cases, which allows us to use the Layer 3 and above protocol implementations that are available on the experiment hosts. This increases the emulation realism compared with the case of a typical simulator-based emulation, for example.

10.2.2.2 Wireless network antennas

One factor that characterizes antennas is *antenna gain*, which represents how much an antenna amplifies a signal. This parameter refers to both the transmitting side and the receiving one; hence, it can appear twice in the electromagnetic wave propagation model.

Another issue related to antennas is directionality. An idealized version of an antenna will send the same signal power in all directions (or receive with equal gain from all directions). This type of antenna is called *omni-directional*. Note that for a 2D antenna this corresponds to a disc around the antenna, while for 3D antennas it corresponds to a sphere centered at the antenna. Other antennas will focus the energy in certain areas of the space, thus allowing to increase the communication range and to control the area in which an antenna induces interference. This type of antenna is typically called *directional*. For the receiving side, a directional antenna will provide better gain for certain directions, and high attenuation for the remaining portion of space.

While an omni-directional antenna is fully characterized by its gain, for directional antennas other parameters are needed to specify directionality properties. In our models we focus on how wide the signal beam of the antenna is. The parameter that characterizes this property is called *beamwidth* and represents the angle around the direction on which the transmitted signal has maximum power at which the power attenuation reaches 3 dB. The deltaQ library supports both omni-directional and directional antennas, characterized by gain and beamwidth, in both 2D and 3D environments.

Note that other factors may attenuate the signal on the path between the sender and the receiver in a wireless communication scenario. One of them are the losses in the transceiver circuits; this aspect in not specifically modeled in deltaQ but can be taken into account by subtracting this attenuation from the antenna gain. The other reason for attenuation is the propagation of the electromagnetic waves through space that will be discussed next.

10.2.2.3 Propagation models

As electromagnetic waves travel through space, their signal strength is attenuated. While there are several models that describe this attenuation, deltaQ implements the following two ones:[4]

- free space path loss model
- log-distance path loss model

Free space propagation assumes that the wireless communication medium is ideal, and the sender and receiver are located on a line-of-sight path without any surrounding obstacles. According to this model, path loss is proportional to the square of the distance between transmitter and receiver.

The log-distance propagation characterizes more realistic environments, both indoors and outdoors, with buildings and other obstacles. The parameters used in this model are given below:

- *Attenuation coefficient*, α: exponent of the proportionality between path loss and distance
- *Shadowing parameter*, σ: standard deviation of the normally distributed random variation of signal strength, expressed in dB
- *Wall attenuation*, W: signal attenuation induced by important obstacles such as building walls, expressed in dB

We note that the values $\alpha = 2$, $\sigma = 0$ dB, and $W = 0$ dB, transform the log-distance model into the free space one. Actually, this is how the free space path loss model is implemented in deltaQ.

---

[4]The Ricean and Rayleigh fading models are currently being implemented as well.

10.2.3 *Node Mobility*

The possibility of node mobility is one of the main features that makes an approach such as that used by QOMET preferable to wireless emulation testbeds such as ORBIT. Providing mobility emulation features requires offering users support for different mobility models that can be used to create node trajectories in the synthetic environment created within the emulator.

The types of node motion currently supported by deltaQ are as follows:

- *Linear motion*: The node moves in a straight line, either with constant velocity or in accelerated manner.
- *Circular motion*: The node moves on a circle around a certain motion center.
- *Rotation motion*: The node turns around its own axis; used especially in relation with directional antennas, for which node orientation becomes important.
- *Random walk motion*: Each node selects randomly and independently a speed and direction and then moves into that direction for a predefined amount of time; movement is followed by a waiting period, then the process is repeated.
- *Behavioral motion*: The node moves autonomously between a specified start position and a destination, while taking into account the buildings and street topology in the synthetic environment in which motion takes place. The behavioral motion model that we implemented is based and extends an idea proposed in [57].

10.2.4 *Synthetic Environments*

Synthetic environments allow creating a virtual world in which the wireless nodes are located, move, and communicate with each other. In order to allow realistic emulation experiments, deltaQ includes support for defining 2D and 3D synthetic environments.

In 2D, users can define objects with polygonal shape that can represent communication obstacles, buildings, etc. DeltaQ also supports the use of real map data to create representations of roads and buildings that correspond to real locations. Only the JPGIS format is supported at present, which is a Japanese version of the standard GIS format for map representation. Note that map data has been available free of charge in Japan for the entire country starting April 2008.

Synthetic 3D environments in deltaQ are an extension of the 2D ones and use height information as an additional parameter to create 3D objects that correspond to 2D polygons. This feature makes it possible to create realistic 3D buildings that correspond to locations in real cities (when using map information to generate the 2D building contours).

10.2.5 ΔQ Description

The ΔQ description is the output of the deltaQ library and contains the network degradation parameters that correspond to the emulated scenario representation at each moment of time.

Note that the deltaQ library itself only produces this ΔQ description in the memory of the computer on which the library is called. However, the description corresponding to the entire experiment duration can also be saved in the form of a file, both in text and in binary formats, by using the command "qomet" that is included in the QOMET set of emulation tools. These files can be used to initialize the scenario representation in an emulation experiment and also in order to draw graphical representations of the evolution of ΔQ parameters in time, for instance for scenario verification purposes.

10.3 Wireconf Library

The wireconf library is one of the options for the second stage of the process presented in Fig. 10.1. We remind our readers that the goal of this second stage is to configure the wired network on top of which the emulation experiment is performed based on the ΔQ description computed by the deltaQ library.

10.3.1 Overview

The wireconf library is intended for the emulation of computer-based wireless network technologies, such as Wi-Fi. The main characteristic of these networks is that the corresponding network interface is designed for being included in computer platforms. Hence, the network applications and protocols used over the emulated wireless network are also running on computer platforms, and use IP addressing mechanisms.

If these conditions are met, network conditions can be configured using a link-level network emulator running on a computer, that is driven by the ΔQ description. In particular, wireconf uses Dummynet [94] for this purpose, and continuously updates at regular time intervals the network degradation induced by Dummynet during the experiment.[5] Support for an alternative link-level emulator, NetEm [37], is currently being added to wireconf.

Note that the wireconf library itself is just an interface to control the link-level emulator, and in order to perform an experiment the command-line tool called "do_wireconf" must be used, as it will be discussed in Section 10.5.2.

10.3.2 *Network Configuration*

To facilitate the understanding of the mechanism through which the wireconf library controls the network conditions, we present the conceptual architecture of the network configuration process in Fig. 10.2. While there may be implementation differences for different platforms, we consider that the architecture we present, which is based on the case when wireconf uses Dummynet, is still sufficiently general.

10.3.2.1 Link-layer emulator actions

A link-layer software network emulator intercepts packets as they go through the protocol stack of the computer host on which the emulator is running. However, not all the packets are intercepted, but usually only those that meet certain conditions, typically using a built-in filter mechanism of the operating system, such as the firewall. In Fig. 10.2 we show the case when the filtering is done

---

[5]The interval between updates was 0.5 s for most of the experiments that we have performed so far.

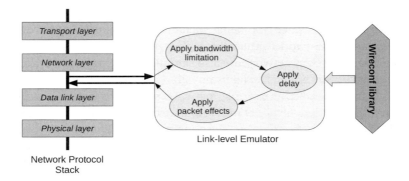

Figure 10.2. Conceptual architecture of the network configuration process in wireconf.

between the data link and the network layer, but in principle it could be also done at a lower level.

For each packet that the emulator has to handle, the emulator can perform the following actions (if configured to do so, and if the necessary support is implemented):

- Apply bandwidth limitation: Make sure that the throughput of the traffic flow to which the packet belongs does not exceed a configured limit.
- Apply delay: Keep the packet in the system (network emulator queue) until the configured delay has elapsed.
- Apply packet effects: Perform any necessary additional actions on the packet. Although packet drop (discarding the packet on purpose) is supported by all emulators, other effects such as packet reordering or packet erroring may be implemented as well.

The packets that have underwent all the emulation actions are reinserted into the protocol stack and continue their course towards upper or lower levels, depending whether the traffic flow it belonged to was incoming or outgoing.

Note that the order of the three actions that we show in Fig. 10.2 is that followed by Dummynet. The following remarks concerning this order are to be considered:

(1) The order in which the link-layer emulator actions take place is important, because changing the order will also change the network degradation observed. Let us imagine that the user wants to apply a 1 Mbps bandwidth limit and a 10% packet loss. Assuming an input stream of 2 Mbps, applying bandwidth limitation first and packet loss second will lead to having a 0.9 Mbps output stream. However, if packet loss is applied first and bandwidth limitation second, then the output stream will have 1 Mbps. The remark about the importance of order also holds as far as delay is concerned. Since delaying packets in a queue will lead to packet loss if the queue becomes full, applying delay before loss will lead to a potentially larger overall delay and higher packet loss than in the opposite case.

(2) Not only the link-emulator actions are non-commutative, but also they must be executed in a predefined order in order to realistically reproduce the network degradation in a communication network. Thus, delay represents mainly packet transmission (which takes place at the sender) and propagation delay, therefore it must necessarily be applied before packet loss, which represents the loss in the network. As for bandwidth limitations, it should be applied before delay if it represents the limitations at the sending network adapter (for instance a IEEE 802.11b WLAN link at 11 Mbps emulated over a 100 Mbps Ethernet adapter). Given that the combination mentioned here above may not accurately emulate all situations one may encounter (such as bandwidth limitations on bottleneck links instead of those at the sender), ideally one may wish to use a chain of degradation elements that closely follow the target network path taken by the traffic.

10.3.2.2 Wireconf actions

A look at Fig. 10.2 makes clear the fact that most of the hard work regarding network configuration is done by the link-level emulator on top of which the wireconf library runs.

The only function that must be performed by wireconf itself is to change, at regular time intervals, the configuration of the link-level emulator (bandwidth, delay, packet effects) following the variation of the ΔQ parameters. This causes the network degradation introduced by the link-level emulator to vary in time according to the user scenario describing the emulation experiment.

Note that in connection with multi-hop routing protocols such as OLSR, special steps have to be taken in order to ensure that the ΔQ parameters used correspond to the nodes that effectively communicate with each other (e.g., next-hop nodes), not the IP-level source and destination of the traffic. For this purpose, a routing information module is used to retrieve the next-hop information from the routing table on the PC on which the wireconf library is called. The next-hop information is then employed to select the appropriate ΔQ parameters that correspond to the next hop.

10.4 Chanel Library

Not all wireless network systems are computer based. Hence, some of them will not meet the requirements stated in the previous section. In particular, the general class of ubiquitous network systems is typically represented by embedded systems, such as active RFID tags, sensors, actuators, etc. Their network interfaces are specifically designed for these systems, and the network applications and protocols used over the wireless network are running on low-cost, low-energy, and typically low-performance processors that are specific to each type of embedded system. Moreover, such ubiquitous network systems often do not use IP addressing for communication.

As a consequence, the wireconf library and the link-level emulator solution used on computer systems cannot be employed for the emulation of ubiquitous network systems. For their case we created an alternative library called *chanel* that plays the role of the link-level emulator for ubiquitous system emulation. Thus, the chanel library is used to recreate the scenario-specific communication conditions between the ubiquitous network systems by using the ΔQ description computed by the deltaQ library.

To achieve this goal, the chanel library is inserted between the node that the library is in charge of, and the other wireless nodes in the experiment. As with wireconf, the chanel library too is not intended for standalone use. In particular, chanel is integrated with the ubiquitous network system emulation environment called RUNE (see Section 11.4), as it will be described in Section 12.4.

The main functionality of chanel is ensured by two independent threads, as follows:

- *Receiving thread*: This thread adds the incoming packets from the node the current chanel library instance is in charge of to the internal queue of the library.
- *Sending thread*: The packet at the head of the internal queue is removed and forwarded to the other wireless nodes after the corresponding ΔQ description is applied for each link; note that if packet loss criteria are met, the packet may be dropped instead of being forwarded.

10.5 Command-Line Tools

While the libraries described so far provide the core functionality of QOMET, they are in principle not intended for direct (standalone) use by those who perform experiments. Instead, users should employ the command-line tools that are also part of QOMET and that are described below. In addition, users can also integrate these libraries with their own source code so as to have more flexibility in their usage. Note that, as mentioned before, the chanel library is not included in any QOMET command-line tool but integrated with RUNE (see Section 12.4).

10.5.1 *Qomet Executable*

The command "qomet" integrates with the deltaQ library to provide the following functions:

- Read an XML-based scenario representation that describes the emulation experiment.
- Use the scenario description to calculate the motion of the wireless nodes (if motion occurs) and to compute the ΔQ description that corresponds to the emulated scenario.[6]

---

[6]Since the experiment is not yet running at this point, during processing with qomet, deltaQ assumes contention-free communication between the wireless nodes.

```
initialize scenario representation and deltaQ
parameters do for the entire experiment duration
adjust deltaQ parameters based on contention
information wait for next time step
apply adjusted deltaQ parameters
```

Figure 10.3. Pseudo-code of the algorithm implemented by do_wireconf.

- Output the ΔQ description to a file that can be used to graphically represent the data, and also to initialize an effective emulation experiment.

In summary, qomet is used to validate the scenario of the emulation experiment, to compute off-line those aspects of the scenario which are known in advance (such as motion trajectories), and to create the file that is used to initialize the effective emulation experiment.

10.5.2 *Do_wireconf Executable*

The command "do_wireconf" integrates with the wireconf and deltaQ libraries to provide the following functions:

- Initialize the emulation experiment using the ΔQ description file produced by the qomet command.
- Adjust the current ΔQ parameters by taking into account the contention of the emulated wireless media.[7]
- Configure at regular intervals the underlying link-level emulator (Dummynet) using the ΔQ parameters corresponding to the current moment of time.

The algorithm followed by do_wireconf is given in Fig. 10.3 as pseudo-code.

Note that in addition to the two libraries already mentioned, one other important module is included in do_wireconf in order to be able to provide the above functionality. In particular, a traffic statistics collection module is used on each node to determine the

---

[7]An extension of the data-link layer model in deltaQ was required to perform this contention-dependent adjustment.

contention of the emulated wireless channel. Thus, each node will compute the statistics for its own traffic and send the information to all the other nodes using multicast messages in the management network. Every node uses this information to calculate a global view of the network utilization, hence channel contention, during the experiment. This information is then used to adjust the ΔQ parameters based on real-time network conditions before providing them to the wireconf library, which uses the adjusted parameters to configure the underlying link-level emulator.

10.6 Discussion

QOMET is a set of tools for wireless network emulation that can be used to perform emulation experiments with wireless networks over a wired-network testbed. QOMET was designed in a distributed emulation paradigm; hence, it is not a standalone wireless network emulator. Although execution on one or a small number of PCs is certainly possible for small-scale scenarios, the full power of QOMET is only "unleashed" when using it on top of a large testbed, such as StarBED. This is exactly the approach we have taken in creating the QOMB wireless network emulation testbed, as it will be detailed in Chapter 12.

One more aspect readers should note is the following. Due to the approach taken in QOMET, this emulator is mainly intended for network application and protocol evaluation at ISO OSI Layer 3 and above. This is because — at least for Wi-Fi — the lower network layers, namely the data link and physical layers, are modeled in QOMET in a probabilistic manner as it was explained in Section 10.2.2. Nevertheless, QOMET can also be used for MAC layer evaluations if employed in the following manner:

- The physical network layer is modeled using a probabilistic model similar to the ones in the current implementation.
- The MAC layer, or at least those aspects that need to be evaluated through emulation, is implemented in software and run during the emulation experiment like any other network protocol.

While this approach sounds promising, and we are currently using it in connection with IEEE 802.15.4 network system emulation, and also investigating it in connection with WiMAX data link layer scheduling algorithm evaluations, we have to warn potential users about two important difficulties that arise when using such an approach:

(1) The software MAC layer implementation needs to be integrated with QOMET and the network stack of the computer on which the experiment is running, for example by intercepting the traffic that flows through the normal network stack, by creating some virtual network interfaces, or possibly by other equivalent solutions. This requires OS support when running emulation directly on a computer but is easier to achieve when emulating ubiquitous systems, for which the device itself is emulated hence, under the direct control of the emulation framework.

(2) The expected performance of a software MAC implementation is not comparable to that of a hardware implementation. This limitation may restrict the operating rate and complexity of the software MAC implementation, depending on the characteristics of the computer on which the software is executed. Alternative solutions, such as an FPGA-based implementation may improve performance at the cost of increasing further the complexity of the system and its cost.

Chapter 11

StarBED

In this chapter, we describe the StarBED network testbed, its architecture, its hardware components, and the experiment-support tools developed for StarBED.

11.1 Overview

StarBED is a large-scale network experiment environment designed and managed by the Hokuriku Research Center of the National Institute of Information and Communications Technology (NICT), located in Ishikawa prefecture, Japan [64].

StarBED development started in 2002 with the goal of creating a testbed on which researchers can evaluate network technologies in realistic situations similar to those in the Internet. Thus, the main initial target was to enable scalability experiments for Internet technologies.

As new network technologies gained ground, the focus of StarBED changed during its second phase, which started in 2006. The coverage area of StarBED widened to include more network technologies, such as ad hoc networks, mobile networks, home networks, and sensor networks, all of them being included under

Introduction to Network Emulation
Razvan Beuran
Copyright © 2013 Pan Stanford Publishing Pte. Ltd.
ISBN 978-981-4310-91-8 (Hardcover), 978-981-4364-09-6 (eBook)
www.panstanford.com

the name of "ubiquitous networks." Another change is related to broadening the area of applications. Thus, in addition to scalability, experiments investigating dependability issues also became targets of StarBED development.

StarBED is composed of both hardware and software components that work together to help users achieve the above-mentioned goals, as follows:

- *Hardware*: More than 1000 PCs and more than a dozen switches make up the physical infrastructure of the testbed.
- *Software*: Two main sets of tools, called SpringOS and RUNE, were developed to enable experiments on the testbed.

The use of actual computers and network equipment makes large-scale realistic experiments possible. Similar to other testbeds, virtualization technologies can be used to increase experiment scale over the number of physically available hosts. The experiment-support software tools make the process of running experiments faster and more secure. Moreover, built-in support for link-level emulators, such as Dummynet and NetEm, allows users to do basic network emulation experiments on StarBED.

The main features of StarBED are summarized as follows:

- support for various operating systems (Linux, FreeBSD, Windows)
- support for virtualization technologies (VMWare, Xen)
- concurrent use and configurable topologies (based on VLANs)
- external connectivity to Japanese research networks (WIDE, JGN2)
- possibility of remote access (via VPN)
- powerful management and experiment-support software (SpringOS)
- ubiquitous systems emulation support software (RUNE)
- link-level network emulation capabilities (Dummynet, NetEm)

Note that for more complex experiments that include mobility and wireless communication, StarBED has been integrated with

QOMET (the set of network emulation tools presented in Chapter 10), resulting in QOMB, as it will be described in Chapter 12.

11.2 Infrastructure

The testbed hardware represents the experiment execution infrastructure for all network experiments, both using when and not using network emulation mechanisms. The architecture of StarBED is presented in Fig. 11.1.

The fundamental components of the StarBED infrastructure are the *experiment hosts*, consisting of more than 1000 commodity PCs. The hosts have each between three and five network interfaces, operating either at 100 Mbps or at 1 Gbps. This allows to have redundant full connectivity by means of two sets of switches, the *experiment switches* and the *management switches*. Thus, there are two separate networks in StarBED, the *experiment network* and the *management network* (see Fig. 11.1). Network separation ensures that the management traffic does not interfere with that of the experiments being run.

Experiment execution is controlled by a *management server*, which can be effectively any PC in the cluster that does not participate in the experiment. Specific switch configurations are used to

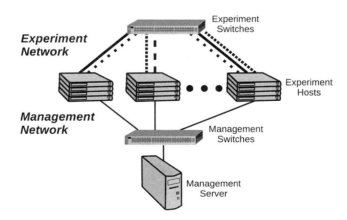

Figure 11.1. StarBED architecture.

produce logically separated experiment network topologies by using VLANs, so that several users can actively carry out experiments simultaneously. By means of the dedicated management network, experiment hosts can be loaded with the appropriate software, controlled and monitored, all without affecting running experiments.

The standard operating systems currently supported on StarBED are Linux, FreeBSD, and Windows. One can also deploy specialized installations, such as software router systems, or use link-level emulators, such as Dummynet on FreeBSD.

StarBED infrastructure can be extended in two ways. First of all, in a virtual manner as, users can employ machine virtualization techniques, such as VMWare, to logically increase the number of experiment hosts available for experiments. Second, the core network has several empty locations where users of the experiment environment can plug in their own devices and thus integrate them in the experiment network. Examples of such devices are products under test, commercial routers, measurement equipment, etc. One can also connect StarBED to external networks and the Internet, so that remote locations can be included in experiments.

To assist StarBED users, two experiment-support software tools are available: SpringOS and RUNE. Thus, by using StarBED as a network experiment platform assisted by these support tools, one benefits from the following general features:

- use of commodity PCs in a large-scale setup that makes it possible to emulate large network environments
- flexibility of the experiment environment that allows to easily switch between multiple different configurations, depending on the intended experiment
- powerful management and experiment-support software tools that enable easy control, quick reconfiguration, and concurrent use of the facility for independent experiments

11.2.1 *Experiment Hosts*

Experiment hosts in StarBED are divided into groups, and all the PCs in a group have the same specifications. Groups are denoted by capital letters that were assigned in the order in which hardware purchases were made. Therefore, the groups assigned letters at the beginning of the alphabet include the oldest and lowest-performance PCs (namely groups A to E).

The specifications of the experiment hosts are given next for each of the groups. We also indicate the number of hosts in each group. Note that the network interfaces mentioned in the list are those connecting the hosts to the experiment network. All the PCs have an additional NIC, either FastEthernet or Gigabit Ethernet, that connects them to the management network. The groups are as follows:

- Group A (208 PCs)
  — 1 GHz Intel Pentium 3 CPU
  — 512 MB RAM
  — 1 x Gigabit Ethernet NIC
  — ATA HDD
- Group B (64 PCs)
  — 1 GHz Intel Pentium 3 CPU
  — 512 MB RAM
  — 1 x ATM and 1 x FastEthernet NICs
  — ATA HDD
- Group C (32 PCs)
  — 1 GHz Intel Pentium 3 CPU
  — 512 MB RAM
  — 1 x ATM and 4 x FastEthernet NICs
  — SCSI HDD
- Group D (144 PCs)
  — 1 GHz Intel Pentium 3 CPU
  — 512 MB RAM
  — 1 x FastEthernet NIC
  — ATA HDD
- Group E (64 PCs)
  — 1 GHz Intel Pentium 3 CPU
  — 512 MB RAM
  — 4 x FastEthernet NICs
  — ATA HDD

- Group F (168 PCs)
  - 3.2 GHz Intel Pentium 4 CPU
  - 2 GB RAM
  - 4 x Gigabit Ethernet NICs
  - SATA HDD
- Groups G (150 PCs)
  - 2 GHz AMD Opteron CPU
  - 4 or 8 GB RAM
  - 1 x Gigabit Ethernet NICs
  - SATA HDD
- Group H (240 PCs)
  - 2.66 GHz Intel QuadCore Xeon CPU
  - 8 GB RAM
  - 2 x Gigabit Ethernet NICs
  - SATA HDD

11.2.2 *Switches*

Network switches interconnect all the experiment hosts in StarBED. They are divided into two classes:

- *Experiment switches*, which ensure the connectivity between hosts for experiment purposes and also make possible external connections when necessary.
- *Management switches*, which ensure both local and remote user access to experiment hosts through the management network; VPN technology is used in the case of remote access.

The experiment switches must have a large number of ports and good switching performance, in the range of terabits per second, so as to allow high-throughput experiments. The switches used in StarBED are the following:

- Brocade (formerly Foundry) BigIron
  - 1 x MG8
  - 4 x RX16
  - 1 x RX32

- Catalyst

  — 1 x 6009
  — 2 x 6509

The management switches do not need to support very large amounts of traffic, therefore can have lower performance specifications than the experiment switches. In particular, the models used in StarBED for this purpose are as follows:

- D-Link

  — 5 x DGS3427
  — 30 x DGS3450

11.3 SpringOS

SpringOS is an experiment-support software tool used to manage experiment execution on StarBED. SpringOS also makes it possible for multiple users to use the testbed simultaneously in terms of experiment hosts and switches. This is accomplished by access restrictions and mediation mechanisms for sharing such resources that are built into SpringOS by design.

The steps that a user must take in order to perform an experiment on StarBED are the following[1] (see next sections for detailed descriptions for each of them):

(1) Reserve a number of experiment hosts.
(2) Prepare one of the experiment hosts to act as management server.
(3) Set up the other hosts for experiment purposes.
(4) Write a SpringOS configuration file (scenario) that describes the experiment.
(5) Run the experiment.

---

[1] For explanation purposes we assume the user has already registered with StarBED and is therefore authorized to conduct experiments.

11.3.1 *Host Reservation*

Each time a user starts a new series of experiment, he/she needs to reserve a number of experiment hosts to which exclusive access is granted. While the procedure itself does not enter the scope of our book, we note that for making a reservation each user must decide details such as

- the group from which hosts will be requested, depending on desired host specifications for the intended experiments
- the number of hosts to be requested in the selected StarBED group depending on the scale of the intended experiments
- the number of VLAN tags that will be requested, depending on the complexity of the network topology of the intended experiments

11.3.2 *Management Server*

The current policy of StarBED is to let each user set up his/her own management server for performing experiments. While this introduces some overhead when doing experiments for the first time, it also helps ensure the good performance of the management server, since the user has full control and exclusive access to it. Of course, the alternative of sharing a management server with other users exists and can be employed if the experiment allows it.

Setting up a management server is a simple procedure that involves as its main step installing the SpringOS software, a straightforward process on the supported operating systems. Users can leave the default SpringOS configuration files unchanged if there are no special requirements, or can customize them if necessary.

Note that the possibility to set up a management server and to customize the configuration files makes it possible to use SpringOS on other testbeds than StarBED, or even in other types of environments, such as those using virtual machines.

11.3.3 *Experiment Hosts*

The experiment hosts on StarBED can be used with pre-configured operating systems, which are one of Fedora Linux, FreeBSD or Windows. In this case, no special configurations are needed, since the required SpringOS components are already installed and ready to use.

However, in many cases users need to install their own software in order to perform experiments. In addition, users may wish to use other versions of operating systems than the one provided by StarBED. Under such circumstances, in order to prepare the experiment hosts, a user has to take the following actions on one of the experiment hosts, which will play the role of a "template host":

(1) *Install and configure a custom OS*: Users who want to make experiments with a different OS than the default ones need to install and configure this OS on the template host.
(2) *Install and configure SpringOS*: An optional step that is only required when using custom OSes but not needed when using one of the default OSes.
(3) *Configure the network interfaces*: This is again an optional step only required for custom OSes; the DHCP protocol should be used so that the network interfaces are dynamically assigned predetermined IP addresses based on their MAC address.
(4) *Install and configure any required custom software*: Users must install and configure any custom software that may be required for their specific experiments.
(5) *Create a disk image*: In order to quickly create a large set of experiment hosts with the same software properties, the disk image of the template host is saved, and written to the other hosts that will be used in an experiment; this procedure is performed using two SpringOS tools, namely "pickup" for saving the image, and "wipeout" for writing it, respectively.

In summary, the above procedure makes it possible to create a large set of experiment hosts that have identical configurations in a simple and straightforward manner.

11.3.4 *Scenario File*

The scenario file contains all the information needed to perform an experiment on StarBED by using SpringOS. In particular, the scenario file must include information such as the following:

- *Global experiment settings*: parameters regarding the experiment as a whole, such as user and project names, the IP address of the master server, etc.
- *Experiment host settings*: information related to host-specific items, such as the path to the disk image file, and the identifier of the partition onto which the disk image should be written for an experiment host[2]
- *Node scenario*: actions to be executed by each experiment host, typically referring to specific application execution commands; note that more types (classes) of nodes can be defined, each with a different type of scenario
- *Node sets*: instructions to create sets of experiment hosts of a certain type by specifying the type and the number of hosts that are included in that class
- *Network topology*: definition of sub-networks and assignment of node sets to sub-networks; sub-networks are effectively created using VLAN mechanisms
- *Global scenario*: description of the main scenario that coordinates the actions of all classes of nodes through a message-passing mechanism

We emphasize the important role played in SpringOS by the message-based synchronization of scenario actions. Specific commands are available for sending messages, including sending to multiple destinations, and stopping execution until a specified message is received from one or more nodes. All these commands make it possible to coordinate the actions of the nodes for performing tasks such as given below:

- Delay the execution of a command until an initialization process is finalized on all nodes.

---

[2]This information is only required when disk images are effectively used in an experiment, since users can also make this configurations independently, by using the SpringOS commands pickup and wipeout.

- Synchronize the start of execution of a command on multiple nodes.
- Perform conditional execution of commands, for example by only executing a client application once the server application has reached a certain execution stage, etc.

A thorough description of the SpringOS language is not within the scope of this book. Hence, for more details about the SpringOS configuration file syntax, as well as regarding the effective operation of SpringOS, we refer our readers to [64]. However, in Section 12.3 we shall provide a sample SpringOS scenario for an example experiment. With that occasion we shall describe some of the SpringOS commands, so as to give our readers an idea about the capabilities of the SpringOS language.

We note that the SpringOS scenario file can be used to launch both end-user commands, such as network applications, but also daemons, such as routing protocol ones, or even link-level emulators, such as Dummynet. In this way, users can create scenarios of high complexity by combining the appropriate commands placed in the right order of execution.

11.3.5 *Experiment Execution*

Once users write the SpringOS configuration file that describes the experiment they intend to perform on StarBED, SpringOS takes over for effectively performing the experiment. This is done by means of the SpringOS "master" command that, in addition to several configuration parameters, takes as input the scenario file. Based on the instructions included in the scenario file, the SpringOS "master" command automatically performs the following tasks:

(1) Assign to the user the requested number of experiment hosts from the pool of reserved cluster PCs.
(2) Upload the appropriate operating system disk image to the assigned experiment hosts (when this applies).
(3) Configure the StarBED experiment switches to build the required network topology.

(4) Drive experiment execution according to the global scenario and the node scenarios described in the configuration file by executing the actions defined therein.

Note that SpringOS must necessarily be used to perform the steps (1) to (3) above in order to ensure that the experiment is properly configured in a multi-user environment. This is because at each of those steps a verification process takes place to ensure that the user has the required credentials for accessing the requested experiment hosts and switches. The execution itself, i.e., step (4), can only use the hosts for which verification was successful. Hence, experiment execution can be done either by using SpringOS, or by using an alternative solution, such as RUNE (see Section 11.4). Shell scripts are another possibility for experiment execution, but they are only appropriate for simple experiments, in which no synchronization is needed between the actions of the experiment hosts.

11.4 RUNE

RUNE (Real-time Ubiquitous Network Emulation environment) is another experiment-support software tool that is being developed for StarBED [66]. RUNE was designed specifically to support the emulation of large ubiquitous network systems. This is because SpringOS has a PC-oriented architecture, intended for controlling computer hosts that run IP network applications. This approach is not suited for ubiquitous network systems, such as active RFID tags or sensor networks, which do not run on computers, and do not necessarily use IP networking. As a consequence, RUNE was developed to allow the fine-grain control level needed for running ubiquitous network experiments.

The most significant features of RUNE that are particularly targeted at ubiquitous network system emulation are the following:

- *Support for the concurrent execution of numerous nodes*: A characteristic of ubiquitous network systems is that they are composed of a potentially large number of elements that need to be executed simultaneously in order to make emulation experiments possible.

- *Provision of multi-level emulation layers*: Given the complexity of ubiquitous systems, flexibility is necessary to allow experiments that contain the desired combination of modeled, emulated, and real components according to the goals and constraints of each experiment.
- *Ability to emulate the surrounding environment*: Ubiquitous network systems are usually immersed in a physical space and are often used to sense its properties, such as temperature, humidity, and luminosity; the properties of the surrounding environment must therefore be emulated as well in order to allow for realistic experiments.

11.4.1 *Scenario Elements*

In order to describe an experiment, RUNE users have to define first its components in logical terms. The basic elements of the logical structure used in RUNE are called *spaces*. A space is an entity that behaves as any of the emulated elements according to their function. Hence, spaces can represent any of the following:

- *Nodes*: physical ubiquitous network devices, such as sensors, actuators, and active RFID tags
- *Environments*: the characteristics of interest of the surrounding environment, such as the temperature in a room
- *Networks*: communication mechanisms between ubiquitous network devices

Information is sent and received between spaces by another class of RUNE elements called *conduits*. A conduit is an abstract error-free communication pipe between two spaces. Communication via conduits is transparent to the user, making it possible to execute spaces on the same experiment host, or on different hosts, without any modification. Thus, conduits play an essential role in the concurrent execution mechanisms of RUNE. Note that conduits are essentially unidirectional, and for bidirectional communication one has to define a pair of conduits going in opposite directions.

We use Fig. 11.2 to illustrate the two concepts, spaces and conduits, as used in an example RUNE-based experiment topology. The hypothetical scenario includes two ubiquitous computing

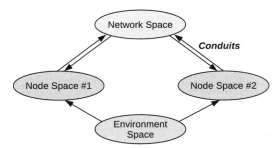

Figure 11.2.   RUNE experiment topology for a two node scenario.

devices placed in a certain environment and communicating with each other via a wireless network technology such as IEEE 802.15.4. The two devices are represented by the two spaces "node space #1" and "node space #2." The communication conditions between the two devices are reproduced by the "network space" pictured in the upper part of the figure. This space is in charge of recreating the network degradation effects, such as frame errors and packet loss, delay and jitter, and bandwidth limitations that would occur in the corresponding real-world scenario. Node spaces are connected to the network space by means of RUNE conduits, represented by arrows in the figure; one such conduit is needed for each communication direction. The "environment space" is introduced so as to reproduce the physical environment in which the nodes are placed, for instance by providing them with temperature values in a realistic fashion. Data is communicated to node spaces by means of conduits.

11.4.2 *Architecture*

The scenario elements presented in the previous section, spaces and conduits, are those RUNE components that are of relevance to end users. However, in order to effectively make large-scale experiments, the end-user spaces and conduits must be executed and supervised by RUNE in a unified manner.

Like SpringOS, RUNE achieves this goal by employing a master controller that manages the entire experiment, called *RUNE Master*. This module performs global functions, such as initiating and ending

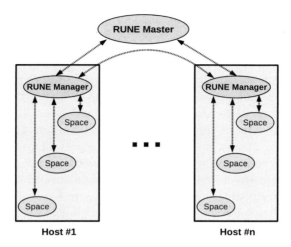

Figure 11.3. RUNE general architecture.

the execution of the experiment. Figure 11.3 shows the general architecture of RUNE, with RUNE Master in the top position.

As experiments usually involve more computers, RUNE uses another module, named *RUNE Manager*, which is executed on each experiment host to manage locally the emulation process. RUNE Manager is in charge of operations such as loading the space objects, calling interface functions in spaces (internally named "entry points"), and relaying the communication between spaces via conduits. Regarding communication we would like to emphasize the following aspect. Conceptually, from an end-user perspective, spaces are connected to each other by conduits, as it was illustrated in Fig. 11.2. However, practically, all the communication between spaces is being mediated by RUNE Manager, as follows:

- If two communicating spaces are located on the same computer, the RUNE Manager in charge of that computer will directly pass the messages between the sending and receiving spaces.
- If the two communicating spaces are located on different computers, the RUNE Manager in charge of the computer on which the sending space is executed will relay the

messages to the RUNE Manager on the computer on which the receiving space is executed; that RUNE Manager will finally pass the messages to the destination space.

While this mediation process is entirely transparent to the user, it is important to understand it, as it is the mechanism that makes possible the distributed execution of RUNE-based experiments without any direct user intervention. In this context note that the arrows in Fig. 11.3 do not represent conduits, but the internal communication channels between spaces and RUNE Manager, between RUNE Manager entities on several computers, and between RUNE Master and RUNE Managers. As a consequence, instead of the unidirectional thin continuous lines used previously for conduits, we employ bidirectional thick interrupted lines in this figure.

One more thing to note is that spaces are implemented as shared objects loaded by RUNE Manager using the operating system dynamic loading mechanism. In RUNE architecture, each space is required to have five entry points, one for each of the following five operations: initialization, execution step, finalization, read, and write. For more low-level details about RUNE, we recommend our readers to consult [66].

11.4.3 *Experiment Execution*

A RUNE-based experiment includes the following steps that are executed without any direct user intervention once the start of an experiment is triggered:

(1) Upon the "start" command issued by a user, experiment execution is initiated by RUNE Master, which informs the RUNE Managers on all experiment hosts.
(2) RUNE Managers load the objects corresponding to spaces and then notify RUNE Master of completion.
(3) RUNE Master commands the initialization process of all spaces to the RUNE Managers on each host.
(4) RUNE Managers initiate heap memory allocation for spaces; this area is permanently needed for emulation execution, and RUNE Managers store a pointer to the memory area for each space

they are in charge of.[3] Once initialization is complete, each RUNE Manager informs the RUNE Master.

(5) Following initialization, RUNE Master commands the iterated invocation of the execution step function.

(6) RUNE Managers proceed with the iterations until one of the spaces on the PC they control returns an exit status. This status is then communicated to the RUNE Master.

(7) Upon receiving the exit status notification, RUNE Master commands experiment finalization by notifying the end of experiment to all RUNE Managers.

(8) Under RUNE Managers' control, spaces release the work area allocated in the initialization process, and the experiment finishes.

The description above mentioned three of the entry points we discussed: initialization, execution step, and finalization. The other two, the I/O operations read and write, are performed by spaces as needed during the iterative execution step.

Note that RUNE is practically a stand-alone tool for ubiquitous network system emulation experiments, therefore its dependency on StarBED-specific mechanisms is minimal. Nevertheless, RUNE-based experiments on StarBED must also use SpringOS for experiment preparation steps, such as imaging the experiment hosts, configuring the network, authenticating users, and so on. Only the execution of the experiment itself is done by RUNE independently from SpringOS.

11.5 Discussion

StarBED is a large-scale general purpose testbed for network experiments. In this sense, StarBED is very close to Emulab from the point of view of functionality. SpringOS is used on StarBED as an experiment support and management tool, and is similar to the equivalent Emulab software and management architecture.

---

[3] RUNE spaces do not use stack memory for execution. Thus, each space object can emulate multiple instances of the same node on one host, while sharing the binary code. This approach also ensures that spaces are thread-safe, since they do not have any static data.

The second experiment-support tool that is being developed for StarBED, RUNE, has no equivalent on Emulab though. Thus, RUNE makes it possible to use the testbed's IP wired-network infrastructure even for non-IP network experiments, including those using wireless network emulation. RUNE also provides mechanisms to support various features that are necessary for ubiquitous device emulation, such as the processor emulation of those devices.

The feature-rich support tools of StarBED, combined with the versatility of the wireless network emulation set of tools provided by QOMET, made it possible for us to create the wireless network emulation testbed named QOMB, which can be used for both IP and non-IP wireless network systems, as it will be discussed in the next chapter.

Chapter 12

QOMET on StarBED

In this chapter, we describe the mechanisms that made it possible to integrate QOMET with StarBED to create the wireless network emulation testbed named QOMB. QOMB merges the realistic wireless network emulation capabilities of QOMET with the large-scale experiment support of StarBED into an emulation testbed that allows performing experiments reproducing large-scale realistic wireless network scenarios.

12.1 Experiment Features

The QOMET wireless network emulator makes it possible to emulate the wireless network communication between a node and its peers. In this sense, QOMET is a link-level emulator, similar to Dummynet, for instance. The main difference with respect to an emulator such as Dummynet comes from complexity and synchronized distributed execution. While Dummynet only allows users to configure link degradation to predefined values, QOMET has several features that make it possible to emulate complex wireless network scenarios in a realistic fashion, as follows:

Introduction to Network Emulation
Razvan Beuran
Copyright © 2013 Pan Stanford Publishing Pte. Ltd.
ISBN 978-981-4310-91-8 (Hardcover), 978-981-4364-09-6 (eBook)
www.panstanford.com

- Communication conditions between nodes are computed on the basis of scenarios that include descriptions of the wireless network nodes, their motion, the communication environment, and street and building topology.
- The communication models include properties of wireless network technologies, as well as of the wireless network media, including dynamic characteristic such as contention.
- Computations are done locally but with a global perspective, and the communication conditions are reproduced on the participating hosts in an unified manner; this distributed approach is key for making realistic large-scale scenario emulation possible.

StarBED is a large-scale network testbed that can be used to run various experiments on its large computer and switch infrastructure. The most important features of StarBED from the perspective of its integration with QOMET are as follows:

- rich infrastructure, with more than 1000 interconnected computers available for experiments
- experiment-support software tools that allow users to make experiments in a straightforward manner

While StarBED does make it possible to run large-scale network experiments, and does support link-level network emulation commands in SpringOS scenarios (e.g., Dummynet or NIST Net), StarBED has no built-in wireless network experimentation mechanisms. While oversimplifying to a certain extent, we could say that QOMET is a tool that cannot be used without an infrastructure, since it cannot be executed standalone, and StarBED is an infrastructure that cannot be used for wireless network experiments without QOMET, as only wired-network interfaces are provided on StarBED.

As a consequence, integrating the two systems appears as an obvious solution for enabling large-scale wireless network experiments. The resulting wireless network emulation testbed, QOMB, combines the features mentioned above for QOMET with those of StarBED in a synergistic manner. Hence, using QOMB, one can perform in a straightforward manner realistic wireless network emulation experiments with complex scenarios in dynamic communication conditions and at large scale.

12.2 QOMB Architecture

Neither StarBED and its support tools nor QOMET was specifically designed for each other. This is because StarBED is intended as a general-purpose testbed, for which emulation is only one of its possible uses. QOMET is also intended as a general-purpose wireless network emulator that could be executed on both small and large testbeds and was designed to be independent of the infrastructure on which it is run.

Creating QOMB required putting in place several integration mechanisms that allow users to make experiments on QOMB without having to spend time on making these tools work with each other. While the integration mechanisms that we shall describe next are definitely dependent on both QOMET and StarBED, we believe that they can be used to derive more generic design principles, so that QOMET can be integrated with other testbeds should the need arise.

Before going into more technical details, let us have first an overview look at the relationship between all the components at play. Figure 12.1 presents the logical hierarchy of the elements we discuss, as follows:

- The lowest level is represented by the infrastructure of StarBED, the hardware on which everything is executed.
- The next level is represented by SpringOS, which manages the access to hardware resources and can supervise experiment execution.
- RUNE is placed at a higher level in the hierarchy, adding support for ubiquitous network emulation.
- QOMET is the highest-level component of QOMB that performs the wireless network emulation. For some experiments, such as Wi-Fi emulation, QOMET tools are executed directly on top of SpringOS mechanisms, whereas

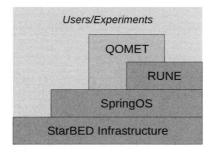

Figure 12.1.   Logical hierarchy of testbed components.

for ubiquitous network experiments, QOMET is used on top of RUNE.

- Users and experiments are represented above the testbed components to suggest the various possible ways to employ these components:

  — Experiments can use StarBED hardware infrastructure directly for certain purposes.
  — Most operations on StarBED are executed by means of the SpringOS commands.
  — RUNE can also be used independently for making experiments that do not involve wireless network communication.
  — Finally, users can employ QOMB for wireless network emulation experiments. QOMB is represented in our figures by the combination "QOMET on SpringOS on StarBED," or alternatively, "QOMET on RUNE on SpringOS on StarBED," depending on the nature of the experiment.

Note that the QOMET software, as any other software running on StarBED, is practically executed on the StarBED infrastructure of computers. However, logically, all the QOMET-specific commands and tools are run by means of either SpringOS or RUNE experiment-support mechanisms, as our figure suggests. Therefore, in what follows, we shall discuss in more detail the integration of QOMET with StarBED from the point of view of these two software tools.

12.3 Integration with SpringOS

QOMET was integrated with SpringOS for the experiments involving computer-based wireless networks, such as Wi-Fi. In this context, QOMET makes use of SpringOS features for the following purposes:

- Prepare the experiment:
  - Power the experiment hosts.[1]
  - Create and write disk images once the installation process on an experiment host template has been completed.
  - Configure the experiment network.[2]
- Run the experiment:
  - Configure and start the QOMET command do_wireconf.
  - Configure and start the applications and protocols required in the experiment.
  - End experiment execution.

12.3.1 *Alternatives*

While experiment preparation contains no QOMET-specific issues, running a wireless network experiment on QOMB requires writing a SpringOS scenario file that is customized for QOMET, in particular for the do_wireconf command. Moreover, there are two possible choices related to the integration of the execution of do_wireconf and other network applications and protocols via SpringOS:

(1) *Light-weight integration*: SpringOS is used for all the configuration tasks and launches a shell script that in its turn executes all the necessary commands.

(2) *Tight integration*: SpringOS is used both for all configuration tasks and for executing all the individual commands that are necessary in the experiment.

The first approach limits the flexibility of command execution, since the SpringOS-specific message passing mechanisms cannot be

---

[1]SpringOS can also be used to power off and reboot the experiment hosts if needed.
[2]Since no wired network topology is required in wireless network emulation experiments, all the experiment hosts are included in the same VLAN.

used to create complex execution patterns. However, it simplifies the SpringOS scenario, which can be then regarded as a template that does not change most of the time, since modifications are only made to the shell script that is launched by SpringOS.

The second approach makes full use of the power of SpringOS but increases the complexity of the SpringOS scenario and makes changes more difficult for beginners. Moreover, while shell script languages may already be familiar to users, SpringOS syntax needs to be learned from scratch the very first time.[3]

While none of the above solutions is perfect for all situations, we preferred solution (1) in the experiments we carried out so far. One reason is that the applications and protocols used in our experiments are mostly the same all the time, with only minor differences between experiment series. Moreover, no complex orchestration of command execution is required. In addition, we believe that the separation of the SpringOS-specific issues from those particular to running applications and protocols by means of shell scripts makes this method of carrying out experiments more easily understandable for new users. Note that we may use solution (2) at some point in the future, especially if the need for running complex experiments arises.

We would also like to share with our readers a fact that we learned from our experience with using SpringOS. While the disk image creation and writing mechanisms that are provided by SpringOS are undoubtedly useful for initially setting up the experiment hosts, we have found them of limited use for later phases of the experiments. This is because the changes done between series of experiments tend to be minor and hence do not justify the full process of image creation and writing, which is time consuming. As a consequence, we found it useful to use what one may call a "file distribution mechanism" that will only copy a limited set of files from an experiment host template to all the other hosts. This distribution mechanism simply makes use of commands such as "scp" or "rsync" to achieve this goal and has the advantage of a faster completion time

---

[3]While SpringOS scripting language is relatively simple, and contains instructions from other languages, such as "if," or "for," it does also contain specific instructions that are not found in typical languages, especially related to the message-passing mechanisms in SpringOS.

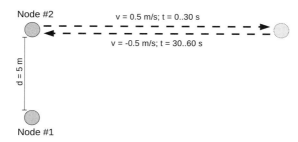

Figure 12.2. Example experiment with two nodes.

(depending of course on the magnitude of the changes that are being propagated to all the experiment hosts involved in the experiment).

12.3.2 *Example Experiment*

Let us consider the following experiment that we shall use to illustrate how to write the SpringOS scenario and shell scripts in a practical case. The example experiment contains two nodes, as shown in Fig. 12.2. Initially, the two nodes are placed at a distance of 5 m with respect to each other. The first node, labeled "Node #1," is fixed, and the second one, "Node #2," moves for 30 s towards right and then returns to the initial position during the next 30 s. The absolute value of the speed is 0.5 m/s for both movement directions.

In what follows, we shall present the various files necessary to describe this experiment on QOMB by using SpringOS and QOMET. Note that for each file lines will be numbered so as to make explanation easier, but the line numbers themselves are not part of the files that we discuss. Some long lines have been split for better readability, but this is only for display purposes, as line numbers indicate in each case the lines in the corresponding file.

12.3.2.1 QOMET scenario

To use QOMB, first of all one has to write the corresponding QOMET scenario, as shown in Fig. 12.3. The content of this file is the following:

- Define the global parameters of the scenario in the "qomet_scenario" XML element (line 1), namely experiment duration (60 s) and the time step used for computation of communication conditions (0.5 s).
- Specify the properties of the wireless nodes (lines 2 and 3), in particular the node internal names and ids ("node1" with id 0, and "node2" with id 1, respectively), their initial position (the coordinates $(0, 0, 0)$ and $(0, 5, 0)$, respectively), and the transmit power (20 dBm).
- Indicate the properties of the environment used for wireless communication (line 4), specifically the internal name ("env"), the parameters of the log-distance path loss model ($\alpha = 5.6$, $\sigma = 0$ dB, and $W = 0$ dB), and the strength of the environment noise (−100 dBm).
- Define the motion trajectory (lines 5 and 6). The definition specifies the internal name of the node to which motion description should be applied ("node2"), the movement speed (0.5 m/s on the horizontal axis, with positive sign for the first motion definition, and with negative sign for the second one), and the start and stop time (first motion description applies between 0 and 30 s, and the second one between 30 and 60 s).
- Provide the parameters of the connection between nodes (line 7). Thus, the file specifies the source ("node2") and destination ("node1") of the wireless connection, the communication environment ("env"), the wireless network standard used ("802.11b"), and the expected size of the communicated packets (1024 bytes).
- Close the XML element "qomet_scenario" that was previously opened on line 1 (line 8).

Note that this QOMET scenario is intended only as a simple example that demonstrates the basic capabilities of the wireless network emulator, and should not be taken as a complete reference to the features of QOMET. For more details readers are advised to consult the QOMET user manual [40]. When performing an actual experiment, the above scenario should be processed using the command "qomet" for validation purposes before proceeding to the next step.

```
1: <qomet_scenario duration="60" step="0.5">
2: <node name="node1" id="0" x="0" y="0" z="0"
       Pt="20"/>
3: <node name="node2" id="1" x="0" y="5" z="0"
       Pt="20"/>
4: <environment name="env" alpha="5.6" sigma="0" W="0"
       noise_power="-100"/>
5: <motion node_name="node2" speed_x="0.5" speed_y="0"
       speed_z="0" start_time="0" stop_time="30"/>
6: <motion node_name="node2" speed_x="-0.5" speed_y="0"
       speed_z="0" start_time="30" stop_time="60"/>
7: <connection from_node="node2" to_node="node1"
       through_environment="env" standard="802.11b"
       packet_size="1024"/>
8: </qomet_scenario>
```

Figure 12.3. QOMET scenario for the two-node example experiment.

12.3.2.2 SpringOS script

The SpringOS script that is required in order to run the above experiments on QOMB is shown in Fig. 12.4. Following is the detailed explanation:

- Assign the necessary number of experiment hosts (line 1), and export the variable for future use (line 2).
- Define a class of experiment hosts called "client_class" (lines 3 to 17), as follows:
  - Specify that the disk image does not have to be rewritten by specifying the "thru" keyword (line 4); thus, it is assumed that the appropriate disk image has already been written to the corresponding experiment hosts.
  - Indicate that the second partition will be used, and that the operating system installed on is FreeBSD (lines 5 and 6).
  - Describe the actions to be executed by each experiment host (lines 7 to 16):

```
 1: assure num_nodes=2
 2: export num_nodes
 3: nodeclass client_class {
 4:    method ''thru''
 5:    partition 2
 6:    ostype ''FreeBSD''
 7:    scenario {
 8:       test_name="two_node_test"
 9:       test_duration="60"
10:       packet_size="1024"
11:       offered_load="200k"
12:       recv my_id
13:       send "setup_done"
14:       recv start_msg
15:       callw "/bin/sh" "run_experiment_node.sh"
               test_name my_id offered_load test_duration
               packet_size > "/tmp/scenario.log"
16:    }
17: }
18: nodeset clients class client_class num num_nodes
19: for(i=0; i<num_nodes; i++) {
20:    clients[i].agent.ipaddr = "172.16.3."
         + tostring(10+i)
21:    clients[i].agent.port = "2345"
22: }
23: scenario {
24:    for(i=0; i<num_nodes; i++) {
25:       send clients[i] tostring(i)
26:    }
27:    sync {
28:       multimsgmatch clients "setup_done"
29:    }
30:    multisend clients "start"
31:    sleep 60
32: }
```

Figure 12.4. SpringOS script for the two-node example experiment.

* Assign values to several variables that will be used in the experiment, such as the name and duration of the experiment, and the packet size and offered load used during traffic generation (lines 8 to 11).
* Wait to receive the ID of the current node in the variable "my_id" (line 12); this ID is being sent by the experiment master using the instruction to be found at line 25 (see below for explanation).
* Send the "setup_done" message to master to indicate the end of the initialization phase (line 13).
* Wait to receive a message in the variable "start_msg" (line 14); this reception effectively triggers the execution of the body of the experiment.
* Call the shell script that executes the body of the experiment (line 15); the SpringOS keyword "callw" (i.e., call with wait) is used to specify that SpringOS processing should stop until the called script returns. Note how the above variables are passed to the shell script and that the output is redirected to a log file.

- Create the set of experiment hosts (line 18); the set is called "clients" and will use the class "client_class" for each member. The member count is equal to "num_nodes" (i.e., 2 in our example).
- Assign IP addresses to the experiment hosts that will be used by SpringOS, and the SpringOS-specific communication port (lines 19 to 22); the IP address assignment we use here is employed so as to control which of the PCs in the pool of available experiment hosts is effectively used during an experiment.
- Describe the actions to be executed by the SpringOS experiment master (lines 23 to 32), as follows:

  — Send to each of the experiment hosts their corresponding ID (lines 24 to 26); IDs are sent to each client as string Representations.
  — Wait for the "setup_done" message from all the hosts (lines 27 to 29); waiting is done in a "sync" block, which stops execution until the block terminates. In

particular, the block contains an instruction that matches a specified string ("setup_done") to those received from all the clients.

— Send the message "start" to all the clients to trigger the beginning of the execution of their main body (line 30). The SpringOS instruction "multisend" is used to accomplish this task simultaneously for all destinations; this mechanism is employed to ensure that all nodes start the execution of their body of actions in the same time.

— Pause the execution of the master until the experiment finishes on all clients (line 31).

12.3.2.3 Shell script

The body of actions to be executed by each QOMB experiment host in our example is described as a shell script with the following content (see Fig. 12.5):

- Assign command-line arguments values to internal variables (lines 1 to 5).
- Initialize a variable that will be used when calling the "do_wireconf" command (line 6), namely the IP address used for broadcast messages.
- Initialize the variables that will be used for controlling traffic generation (lines 7 and 8), specifically the node ID and the IP address of the first node.
- Launch the "do_wireconf" command in the background and with super-user execution rights (line 9); the necessary arguments are passed to the command, including the file "node_settings.txt" that will be described below.
- Launch the traffic generation command "iperf"[4] (lines 10 to 16); the execution mode differs on the two hosts, as follows:

  — If the script is executed on the first node, with ID 0, then the "iperf" command will be executed in server mode (line 11), that is as a traffic sink, and after the experiment duration period elapses (line 12), it is forcefully terminated (line 13).

---

[4]For the detailed use of this command, please see its user manual.

```
 1: test_name=$1
 2: node_id=$2
 3: offered_load=$3
 4: test_duration=$4
 5: packet_size=$5
 6: broadcast_IP=192.168.3.255
 7: first_node_id=0
 8: first_node_IP=192.168.3.10
 9: sudo -b ../wireconf/do_wireconf -q $test_name -i
        $node_id -s node_settings.txt -m 0.5 -b
        $broadcast_IP
10: if [ $node_id -eq $first_node_id ]; then
11:    iperf --server --udp --interval 0.5 --format k
           --len $packet_size &
12:    sleep $test_duration
13:    killall -INT iperf
14: else
15:    iperf --client $first_node_IP --udp --interval
           0.5 --format k --len $packet_size
           --bandwidth $offered_load --time
           $test_duration
16: fi
```

Figure 12.5. Shell script for the two-node example experiment.

— If the script is executed on the second node, then "iperf" is executed in client mode (line 15), that is, as a traffic generator; the duration of the generation action is included as one of the arguments.

The file "node_settings.txt" that was mentioned above is necessary to inform the "do_wireconf" command about the association between node IDs, which are a QOMET internal representation, and IP addresses, which are used on StarBED to identify experiment hosts. The content of the file is given in Fig. 12.6, the meaning of each line being the following:

```
1: 0 192.168.3.10
2: 1 192.168.3.11
```

Figure 12.6. The file "node_settings.txt" used to configure the command do_wireconf for the two-node example experiment.

- Associate QOMET node with ID "0" to StarBED host with the experiment network IP address "192.168.3.10" (line 1).
- Associate QOMET node with ID "1" to StarBED host with the experiment network IP address "192.168.3.11" (line 2).

12.4 Integration with RUNE

Computer-based network applications that use IP addressing can be easily integrated with SpringOS and QOMET for performing experiments on QOMB, as everything can be dealt with in terms of standalone processes running on a PC. However, ubiquitous network applications do not run on typical computers. Hence, they can only be executed on a computer by means of a processor emulator that reproduces the processor of the embedded devices composing the ubiquitous network system to be experimented with.

That is why the emulation of ubiquitous network systems requires a tight integration between the modules providing the various emulation functions, including those related to application execution and those related to communication. This tight integration is ensured by RUNE.

12.4.1 *Ubiquitous Network Devices*

In Fig. 12.7, we represent the components that logically form an instance of an ubiquitous network device in RUNE. Note that even though we consider for explanation purposes that these separate components form a single unit in practice they are only logically integrated through RUNE conduits.

The functions of an ubiquitous network device can be split into two main categories:

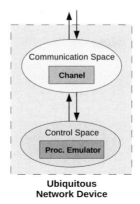

Figure 12.7. An instance of an ubiquitous network device as represented in RUNE.

- *Control*: These components control the behavior of the ubiquitous network device. In our implementation, this is achieved through a RUNE space called "Control Space," which has at its core the "Processor Emulator" that directly executes the firmware of the ubiquitous network device through processor emulation.
- *Communication*: These components perform the communication function of the ubiquitous network device. In our implementation this is accomplished through a RUNE space called "Communication Space," which wraps the QOMET chanel library into a RUNE-compatible form and interfaces the communication between the current ubiquitous network device and the other devices in the experiment.

Note that depending on the properties of an ubiquitous network system, other functions and the corresponding RUNE spaces may be required in order to perform experiments, such as spaces emulating the surrounding virtual environment (and providing temperature information, for instance). Such sensing spaces should be connected to the control space, providing it with sensor data that is used to make decisions or is reported to other systems. However, for clarity reasons, in what follows, we will focus our explanation on the above example, which can be considered a baseline.

12.4.1.1 Control space

The most important component of the control space is the processor emulator. This module runs the firmware of the ubiquitous network device in the same way the real processor would run it, but uses the resources of a PC to achieve this task. This means that the processor emulator must recognize the binary instructions in the firmware and must be able to deal with hardware properties such as memory and interrupts. All this has to be done while keeping a constant execution speed, similar to that dictated by the clock of a real device processor.

As each ubiquitous network device may use a different processor, the task of processor emulation is perhaps one of the most difficult in the context of ubiquitous network system emulation. During our research, we have already implemented a PIC processor emulator for active RFID tag experiments and also an OpenRISC processor emulator for IEEE 802.15.4 experiments.

12.4.1.2 Communication space

The communication space is the emulation component that is in charge of reproducing the wireless communication conditions for the communication between the ubiquitous network devices in an emulation experiment.

As shown in Fig. 12.7, the communication space mediates the sending and receiving of data from and to the control space of the ubiquitous network device. The core of the communication space is represented by the chanel library in QOMET. Thus, the communication space uses this library to forward the data from the current ubiquitous network device to all the other devices in its communication range by applying the appropriate ΔQ parameters. Note that since communication conditions are applied in the outgoing direction, in the incoming direction data can simply be delivered to the corresponding control space in a transparent manner; hence, the two conduits incoming into the communication space and control space of an ubiquitous network device can in practice be replaced by a single conduit reaching directly the control space. Nevertheless, there are cases when actions have to be taken for incoming packets, for instance in order to account for packet collision on a per packet basis at ingress, instead of the probabilistic model at egress.

Similar to the "do_wireconf" command described in Section 10.5.2, the communication space also includes a thread that periodically reconfigures the ΔQ parameters so as to reproduce the potentially changing conditions that correspond to the real-world scenario description.

12.4.2 *Example Experiment*

In order to make emulation experiments with large ubiquitous network systems, all the spaces composing the logical module shown in Fig. 12.7 — which represents a single ubiquitous network device — must be connected to the spaces corresponding to other equivalent devices. For illustrating the use of RUNE in QOMB, we shall use the same example scenario that was already presented in Fig. 12.2 of Section 12.3.2. Note that the QOMET scenario that corresponds to that example remains unchanged even when using RUNE and is detailed in Section 12.3.2.1. The additional configuration file that is required relates to RUNE itself.

12.4.2.1 RUNE definition file

RUNE uses a specific definition file called "runedefs.h," which must include all the information needed to perform the experiment. This file should be included with the source code of RUNE and compiled together with all the other source files that make up RUNE. The resulting executable commands, called "runemaster" and "runemanager," need to be executed on the experiment hosts involved in the experiment; this process will be detailed in the next subsection.

The information included in a RUNE definition file refers mainly to the following aspects that are particular to it:

- space information (for each space)
  - internal name of the space
  - IP address of the experiment host on which the space should be executed
  - name of the object file that should be loaded for the space
- conduit information (for each conduit)

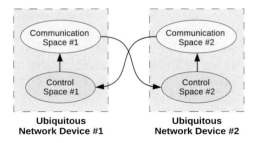

Figure 12.8. Logical view of the two ubiquitous network device example experiment.

> — internal name of the space representing the start point of the conduit
> — internal name of the space at the end point of the conduit

To make the following explanation easier to understand, let us first draw in Fig. 12.8 the logical view of the experiment scenario previously shown in Fig. 12.2, this time considering it an ubiquitous network system experiment. Basically, we used the architecture presented in Fig. 12.7 for each of the two ubiquitous network devices and interconnected them by conduits, taking into account the fact that communication conditions are applied only for outgoing messages and incoming messages for a certain device reach directly its control space, without passing through the communication space of that device.

The RUNE definition file "runedefs.h" that corresponds to the two device example experiment is shown in Fig. 12.9. The meaning of the information in the file is as follows:

- Include for compilation purposes the C header file "runebase.h" that is required in order to successfully parse "rundefs.h" (line 1); the header files includes among others the RUNE-specific keywords BGNSPACELIST, END-SPACELIST, BGNCONDUITLIST, ENDCONDUITLIST, SPACE, and CONDUIT that will be used next to define RUNE spaces and conduits.
- Describe the RUNE spaces used in the experiment (lines 2 to 7):

```
 1: #include "runebase.h"
 2: BGNSPACELIST
 3: SPACE(ctrl_space1, 192.168.3.10, control.so)
 4: SPACE(ctrl_space2, 192.168.3.11, control.so)
 5: SPACE(comm_space1, 192.168.3.10, communication.so)
 6: SPACE(comm_space2, 192.168.3.11, communication.so)
 7: ENDSPACELIST
 8: BGNCONDUITLIST
 9: CONDUIT(ctrl_space1, comm_space1)
10: CONDUIT(ctrl_space2, comm_space2)
11: CONDUIT(comm_space1, ctrl_space2)
12: CONDUIT(comm_space2, ctrl_space1)
13: ENDCONDUITLIST
```

Figure 12.9. RUNE definition file "runedefs.h."

— Define the control spaces named "ctrl_ space1" and "ctrl_space2" to be executed on the hosts with IP addresses "192.168.3.10" and "192.168.3.11," respectively (lines 3 and 4). Both control spaces will be executed by loading the object file "control.so".

— Define the two communication spaces named "comm_ space1" and "comm_space2" to be executed on the hosts with IP addresses "192.168.3.10" and "192.168.3.11," respectively (lines 5 and 6). Both communication spaces will be executed by loading the object file "communication.so".

• Specify the RUNE conduits used in the experiment (lines 8 to 13):

— Connect the control spaces named "ctrl_space1" and "ctrl_space2" to their counter part communication spaces "comm_space1" and "comm_space2," respectively (lines 9 and 10).

— Connect the two communication spaces named "comm_ space1" and "comm_space2" to the control spaces of their peer devices, "ctrl_space2" and "ctrl_space1," respectively (lines 11 and 12).

Note that the object files "control.so" and "communication.so"
depend on the actual functionality of the ubiquitous system that is
emulated. However this issue is outside the scope of this book; we
recommend for instance [16] for practical examples of such systems.

12.4.2.2 Experiment execution

For a better understanding of the internals of RUNE, we also present
in Fig. 12.10 the actual architecture that RUNE uses for the definition
file given previously. The following should be noted about this
architecture:

- RUNE Master is supervising the entire experiment by communicating with the RUNE Managers on the two experiment
  hosts in StarBED.
- The two RUNE Managers control locally the experiment
  under RUNE Master supervision and communicate with
  each other to exchange data that is created by the spaces on
  the host they manage.

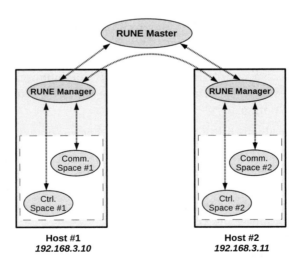

Figure 12.10. Actual RUNE architecture of the two-node example
experiment.

- The logical module on each host that is marked by dashed line emulates a ubiquitous network device via its communication and control functions, which are reproduced by the communication and control RUNE spaces.
- Communication between RUNE Master, RUNE Managers, and spaces is achieved by internal communication channels, marked by bidirectional thick lines.

Note that even when using RUNE, SpringOS is still employed, but mainly for experiment preparation tasks. This is because in a RUNE-based experiment the only required commands to be executed are "runemanager" on the experiment hosts and "runemaster" on the master host. This execution simplicity makes it possible to launch a RUNE experiment independently from SpringOS. Nevertheless, it is straightforward to start the RUNE experiment via a SpringOS script if desired.

One more thing to emphasize is that although in our example we have only two emulated devices and each of them is executed through emulation on a different experiment host, in practice it is possible to emulate more ubiquitous network devices on the same experiment host. This is achieved simply by specifying the same IP address in the RUNE definition file for several of the spaces in charge of control and communication. This effectively instructs RUNE to execute several logical modules representing ubiquitous network devices on the designated experiment host, hence increasing experiment scale.

12.5 Discussion

The QOMB wireless network emulation testbed was created by integrating QOMET with StarBED and its experiment-support tools, SpringOS and RUNE. While we have already discussed in this chapter in detail the mechanisms of this integration, we would like to stress now a few additional issues.

Integration between QOMET and SpringOS is *loose*. This is first of all because of the nature of the experiments that this integration aims at: computer network application and protocol performance evaluation over wireless networks such as IEEE 802.11a/b/g. Besides using SpringOS to perform all the experiment preparation tasks, QOMB also employs SpringOS to launch the QOMET-specific and experiment-specific commands by means of a SpringOS scenario script. In this sense, we view the scenario we presented in Section 12.3.2.2 as a QOMB configuration template that enables users to make use of the testbed only by minimal modifications of this script.

On the other hand, integration between QOMET and RUNE is *tight*. Again, this is mainly because of the nature of the experiments that are envisaged through this integration: ubiquitous network application and protocol performance evaluation over wireless networks such as active RFID tags or IEEE 802.15.4. The definition file presented in Section 12.4.2.1 can be used by potential users as a template for using QOMB in this context, or at least as a starting point for their own definition file.

One more issue that needs to be stressed is the following. The approach used in QOMB, which is to employ QOMET-based wireless network emulation over the wired-network testbed StarBED, makes possible a large range of experiments with network applications and protocols, including ubiquitous network systems. However, an area that cannot be tackled using QOMB is that of physical network layer research. Due to the fact that QOMET models cover the physical layer, and currently most of the data link layer, experiments with QOMB only allow investigations of higher layer protocols (starting at Layer 3) and, of course, network applications.

Finally, to position QOMB with respect to other wireless network experiment approaches, we go back to the discussion in Section 8.1.1. There we made a generic comparison between network testbeds, network emulators, and network simulators. Here we focus only on wireless-related tools, as follows:

- wireless network testbeds, which are pure testbeds without any emulation feature, such as those used for field trials
- several examples and classes of wireless network emulators

  — ORBIT, as a representative of wireless-network-hardware-based wireless network emulators
  — QOMB, as a representative of wired-network-hardware-based wireless network emulators

Table 12.1. Comparison of QOMB with other approaches for wireless network experiments

	Wireless network testbeds	ORBIT	QOMB	Simulator-based wireless network emulators	Wireless network simulators
Applications	Real	Real	Real	Real/Emulated	Simulated
Time flow	Real	Real	Real	Real	Simulated
Network protocols	Real	Real	Real	Emulated/Real	Simulated
Network interfaces	Real	Real	Emulated	Emulated	Simulated
Network conditions	Real	Emulated	Emulated	Emulated	Simulated

> — simulator-based wireless network emulators, such as Ns-2, QualNet, or OPNET when used in emulation mode

- wireless network simulators, such as Ns-2, QualNet, or OPNET

Table 12.1 summarizes the characteristics of each of these approaches from the point of view of the executed applications, time flow, network protocols, network interfaces, and network conditions, similar to the comparison made in Table 8.1. While we have already discussed the characteristics of wireless network testbeds and simulators from these points of view in Section 8.1.1 (albeit not for the particular case of wireless networks), let us see how the three types of wireless network emulators compare to each other:

- Executed applications are typically real for all three wireless network emulator classes, although the simulator-based solutions do sometimes emulate applications as well.
- Time flow also is real for all three emulator types, either naturally for ORBIT and QOMB or by synchronization of logical time with the wall clock for the simulation-based approaches.
- Network protocols are real for ORBIT and QOMB, since they use real PCs for node execution, and typically emulated for simulator-based solutions (an exception is, for instance, NCTUns, which uses real protocol stacks).

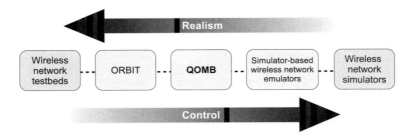

Figure 12.11. Realism versus control for QOMB and other wireless network experiment approaches.

- Network interfaces are real only for ORBIT, which uses real wireless network hardware, but are emulated over wired-network interfaces in the case of QOMB, and as logical interfaces for simulator-based emulators.
- Network conditions are emulated for all the three classes of emulators that we compare.

o provide a better insight into the differences between emulation approaches, we further extend Fig. 8.1 to include the three types of wireless network emulators that we discussed in this section. Thus, the realism of QOMB versus other approaches for wireless network experiments is shown in Fig. 12.11, based on the comparison done in Table 12.1. The figure suggests that QOMB is placed in the middle of the realism axis, allowing us to say that QOMB is a trade-off not only between the advantages and disadvantages of wireless network testbeds and wireless network simulators but also between those of wireless network emulation testbeds such as ORBIT, and simulator-based wireless network emulators.

While we shall not discuss other aspects here, such as scalability or flexibility, Fig. 12.11 can be used as an indication for positioning QOMB with respect to other approaches from those points of view as well, as we argued in the general case of emulation techniques in Section 8.1.2 and Section 8.1.3, respectively. Also regarding positioning, an inspection of Table 8.2 in Section 8.3 shows that QOMB can be included in the "Class B" of network emulators if we follow that classification and the corresponding discussion.

Chapter 13

QOMB Experiments

In this chapter, we shall present a series of experiments to demonstrate how QOMB can be used in practice. We shall focus on the procedure of making experiments and underline some of the advantages of using QOMB in each case when compared with other experiment techniques. For the scientific results of each experiment, we recommend consulting the references we shall provide for each experiment class.

13.1 WLAN Experiments

We start by reviewing several IEEE 802.11 (WLAN) experiments that we performed while developing QOMB. In particular, we shall present the following classes of experiments:

(1) *VoIP performance assessment*: a small-scale experiment done on QOMB that demonstrates the use of QoE metrics for the objective assessment of VoIP user-perceived quality
(2) *Motion planning for robots*: a large-scale experiment emphasizing the integration between an end-user application — the motion planning algorithm implementation — and the QOMET deltaQ library

Introduction to Network Emulation
Razvan Beuran
Copyright © 2013 Pan Stanford Publishing Pte. Ltd.
ISBN 978-981-4310-91-8 (Hardcover), 978-981-4364-09-6 (eBook)
www.panstanford.com

(3) *Routing protocol evaluation*: a medium-scale experiment under-lining the use of QOMB for the assessment of the performance of an ad hoc network routing protocol, OLSR, in a realistic scenario involving mobility

Note that since all these experiments refer to IP networks, we used the QOMB components QOMET, SpringOS, and StarBED to perform them.

13.1.1 *VoIP Performance Assessment*

When talking about real-time applications, voice and video com-munication are the most often used examples. This is because applications such as Voice over IP (VoIP) or Video Tele-Conferencing (VTC) impose more strict requirements on the network compared with other applications, such as Web browsing or file transfer.

Using QOMB for the evaluation of VoIP communication makes it possible to use real VoIP applications, and not abstract models, as it would be done by simulation. Moreover, since real network traffic flows through the emulator, users can experience by themselves the quality of the VoIP communication. When using QOMB, speech signals can also be recorded for later playback, or for comparisons against the input waveform to determine objectively the quality degradation through the network.

13.1.1.1 VoIP requirements

VoIP requires low packet loss conditions, because missing packets will lead to a poor voice quality at the receiver. Various methods exist for coping with packet loss, such as using redundant information in the VoIP packets, or reconstructing missing voice data from the samples that precede and follow the gap. Nevertheless, no matter whether any kind of packet loss concealment techniques are used or not, when packet loss exceeds a certain threshold, voice quality will suffer.

VoIP also has specific requirements regarding the one-way delay. Probably the most important aspect is jitter, or better said the lack thereof. This is because VoIP applications must play back the audio data at the receiver; however, they may not be able to do it properly if there is too much variation in the arrival time of the packets. Basically, if a packet arrives too late compared with the previous packet, the packet may not be in the system in time for its playback. Hence, even if the packet is not lost, it is still useless, and its late arrival contributes to lowering VoIP quality. VoIP applications use a buffer in which arriving packets are temporarily stored before playback. This helps coping with a certain amount of jitter, but the size of the buffer cannot be made indefinitely large. This is because VoIP has another requirement on delay, this time on the value of the one-way delay itself. Recall that VoIP is a communication tool, meaning that VoIP data flows in both directions between the conversation participants. As a consequence, if the time lapse between speaking at one end of the communication line and hearing the voice at the other end is too big, communication interactivity will suffer and the general call quality will degrade.

Regarding the bandwidth requirements of VoIP, we would like to stress that they are not significant, with most VoIP codecs topping at 64 kbps, while typical bandwidth requirements can be as low as 8 kbps, especially if mechanisms such as silence suppression are used. Nevertheless, even such low bandwidth requirements may pose problems in high-congestion periods.

13.1.1.2 User-perceived quality

While the general requirements for VoIP are clear, the problem that remains is how to estimate the quality of a VoIP call, so that the performance of a VoIP system can be evaluated over a certain network. One possibility is to use subjective scores, such as the mean opinion score (MOS) defined in the ITU-T Recommendation P.800. Another possibility is to use the E-model, defined in ITU-T Recommendation G.107, which is an objective metric calculated based on the values of the network degradation parameters for a given connection.

In our work, we preferred to use yet another objective metric, namely the perceptual evaluation of speech quality (PESQ) score, as defined in ITU-T Recommendation P.862. PESQ is a method for predicting the subjective quality of narrow-band telephony and speech codecs by using the original and degraded waveforms as the input of an algorithm that will calculate a quality score. This algorithm employs models of the human speech perception system to produce a score that corresponds to what human subjects would perceive as quality level for a certain communication.

As a side note, we refer our users to an exhaustive analysis that we have done on the relationship between network quality degradation parameters and user-perceived quality for several VoIP codecs [12]. That work provides guidelines regarding the requirements that the network must meet in order to achieve a certain speech quality level.

13.1.1.3 Experiment overview

The experiments we did with VoIP on QOMB demonstrate how the testbed can be used for the objective evaluation of VoIP quality in a realistic scenario. While we did several types of experiments in this context [11, 15, 17, 18], the key points regarding all these experiments are the following:

- Our experiments focused on ad hoc wireless networks such as MANET.
- We used both simple scenarios with up to 5 nodes and also more realistic scenarios with 13 nodes that take place in a virtual street environment using real map data from an area in Kawasaki, Japan.
- Some of the scenarios tried to reproduce situations related to the intervention of rescue workers after a disaster, when the quality of VoIP communication becomes essential for the accomplishment of their task.
- For the assessment of VoIP quality, we mostly used a PESQ implementation acquired from OPTICOM. In some cases, however, we simply used network metrics such as packet loss as indication of VoIP quality.
- The input data for the PESQ algorithm were sample speech files provided with the ITU-T Recommendation P.862 and their degraded versions as recorded after being sent through the emulated wireless network.

- The VoIP application used in our experiments was a modified version of SpeakFreely 7.6a [114].

The following steps were carried out in order to effectively perform the experiments:

(1) Define the appropriate QOMET scenario, specifying the number of nodes, their properties, motion trajectory, as well as the environment conditions.
(2) Define the appropriate SpringOS scenario file, indicating the number of experiment hosts used and their generic behavior.
(3) Define the actions of the nodes in a shell script file. In particular, the following commands are important[1]:

  - Launch the QOMET "do_wireconf" command, which reproduces the WLAN communication conditions in the emulated network.
  - Launch the VoIP application that sends and records the VoIP Traffic.

(4) Execute the experiment using SpringOS mechanisms.
(5) Compute VoIP communication quality off-line by using the PESQ algorithm implementation.

13.1.2 *Motion Planning for Robots*

The development of autonomous robots is an important step in making possible access to areas where humans cannot enter due to hazardous conditions, physical size of the environment, etc. An important component of the artificial intelligence embedded into such autonomous robots is the motion planning algorithm that decides the trajectory of the robot based on the environment properties (e.g., obstacles), other moving objects and robots, etc.

In order to evaluate a motion planning algorithm, experiments must be performed that re-create the environment and the communication conditions of the target area, as well as the intended number of robots. Emulation can play a significant role

---

[1]Some of the experiments did not use real VoIP traffic but a similar traffic stream sent using the "iperf" tool. Moreover, in some cases we used the "ping" command for round-trip delay measurements.

in this process, and QOMB, in particular, provides all the necessary functionality for accomplishing this task. We used this approach in several instances, as reported in [18, 76].

13.1.2.1 Robot assumptions

For the purposes of motion planning algorithms, robots do not have to be modeled in great detail (such as joints and so on). Instead, only the most basic features of the robots need to be taken into consideration, at least in a first stage.

Thus, we considered the robots to have a known size and movement speed. They are equipped with visual sensors that allow them to detect optically obstacles and other robots (it was assumed that once an object enters the visual range of a robot, it will be immediately detected). Robots also have a GPS system that makes it possible for them to know their absolute position. Finally, robots can communicate with each other using WLAN technology.

Of course, in later stages of the evaluation one could make more detailed models of the robots, including physical motion properties such as acceleration and inertia, and integrate a real object-detection algorithm with the system. Nevertheless, our simple model did allow the evaluation of the most important features of motion-planning algorithms in large-scale scenarios.

13.1.2.2 Evaluation methodology

In our scenarios, the robots depart from initial positions and head toward predefined destinations. The trajectory they follow was computed by the motion planning algorithm in real time as the experiment progressed. The objective of the algorithm was to lead a robot to its destination while avoiding collisions with obstacles and other robots.

Although there are several criteria for evaluating motion-planning algorithms, we focused on the time to reach the destination as the main performance indicator when comparing different motion-planning algorithms, or versions of the same algorithm that use different parameter values, or slightly different assumptions.

13.1.2.3 Experiment overview

The key points of the robot experiments for motion-planning performance evaluation are as follows:

- A large number of robots (from 10 and up to 400) are placed in virtual environments that include certain obstacles; the number of obstacles in an environment is proportional to that of robots so as to create equivalent conditions.
- The positions of the robots and obstacles, and robot destinations were defined by the user for some small-scale experiments, or selected randomly for the large-scale ones.
- The motion planning algorithm of the robots was integrated with the QOMET deltaQ and wireconf libraries.
- Log files were used after each experiment to compute the time needed for robots to reach their destination and to verify that no collisions occurred.

We would like to discuss in more detail the third point above, referring to the integration of the motion-planning algorithm with QOMET libraries. As mentioned in Section 10.2.3, the QOMET scenario file allows users to define the motion trajectory of the emulated nodes in advance. However, for robots that autonomously plan their motion, this is obviously not possible. As a consequence, the motion-planning algorithm has to be integrated with the deltaQ library, as follows:

- The robots first load a QOMET scenario that describes their initial position and all the other components of the virtual environment.
- Following initialization, whenever a robot decides its next-step position, it will also update the information in the virtual world scenario that it keeps in its memory.
- In order for all the robots to have the same information (hence have a unified view of the virtual world), robots also multicast their intended future position to all the other robots through the management network.[2]

---

[2]Note that this information is in principle only used for wireless communication condition computation and is not available to the motion-planning algorithm itself. However, a version of the algorithm that communicates through the experiment

- Each robot uses the deltaQ library to compute the communication conditions between itself and the other robots for the next step in the future.

The integration with the deltaQ library was necessary so that the robots can compute the communication conditions in the changing world representation by themselves, which would have been impossible using the standalone command "qomet." In a similar manner, since the robots compute by themselves the communication conditions, they cannot make use of the standalone command "do_wireconf" either. Instead, robots also integrated the QOMET wireconf library, which allows each robot to re-create the communication conditions with the other robots by itself.

The steps that we carried out for the robot motion planning algorithm evaluation are the following:

(1) Define the appropriate QOMET scenario, specifying the number of robots, their properties, and their initial position, as well as the obstacles; no mobility is defined for the robots at this point.

(2) Define the appropriate SpringOS scenario file, indicating the number of experiment hosts used and their generic behavior.

(3) Define the actions of the experiment hosts. In this particular case, since all the necessary functionality was integrated into one executable, the executable that represents the emulated robots and performs motion planning (including the related communications when necessary) and communication condition computation and re-creation, must be started.

(4) Execute the experiment using SpringOS mechanisms.

(5) Evaluate off-line experiment logs to compute the time needed by the robots to reach their destinations in the virtual environment and to check that no collisions with obstacles or other robots took place.

We would like to note that these robot experiments are the largest to date carried out using QOMB. In particular, we ran 100

---

network and uses announced the future position of the neighboring robots to optimize planning has also been implemented. This version of the algorithm showed an improvement in the time to completion over the agnostic version, which only uses optical sensors to detect neighboring robots and obstacles.

robot experiments using 100 StarBED hosts (one robot per host) and also 400 robot experiments using the same 100 StarBED hosts (four robots per host). We can mention that some limitation effects were noticed at such a large scale at the level of the shared file system (NFS) used for logging purposes, but no significant scalability problem occurred regarding QOMB itself.

13.1.3 *Routing Protocol Evaluation*

Routing protocols are an essential component of multi-hop wireless networks, since they decide which path the packets must take from source to destination. Ad hoc networks and their variant Mobile Ad hoc Networks (MANET) require such protocols in order to function. The same can be said about mesh networks, another type of wireless networks that gained ground in recent days.

The evaluation of the performance of routing protocols requires creating scenarios that are representative for the intended use of these protocols. By using QOMB, one can evaluate not models of routing protocols, as it would be done by simulation, but real implementations of such protocols. Moreover, users can run real network applications over the network managed by those protocols and evaluate firsthand the effects of the protocols on application performance (such as shortages cause by route reconfiguration when the network topology changes, for instance, due to the movement of mobile nodes).

13.1.3.1 OLSR protocol

The Optimized Link State Routing (OLSR) protocol is one of the main contenders in the area of ad hoc network routing protocols, next to its competitor, AODV. The OLSR protocol is part of the so-called "pro-active" class of routing protocols, since it actively maintains the topology of the network by a periodic message exchange between the wireless nodes.

Although there are several variations of the protocol that attempt optimizations under some circumstances, and there are several configurable parameters, one could say that the protocol in general is stable enough for everyday use. Nevertheless, an area that is actively researched at present is that of the routing metrics employed by the protocol.

A routing metric is a measure of the quality of network links and paths and is used by the routing protocol to determine the best path between a given source and a destination. Note that we use the terms "quality" and "best" in a generally accepted way, since each routing metric tends to define these concepts in specific ways. The hop count metric, for instance, uses the number of hops on a certain path as a measure of its quality, and the best path is that with a minimum number of hops.

While hop count is only the simplest routing metric, more advanced metrics have been developed by various researchers. The effect of different metrics on a routing protocol, and the effects of various system parameters on that protocol can all be evaluated by emulation on QOMB.

13.1.3.2 Experiment overview

The routing protocol evaluation experiments we have performed are characterized by the following key points [14, 15, 71]:

- We performed two classes of experiments, one in static conditions (mesh network) and another one including mobility (MANET):
  - For the static scenario, a number of wireless nodes (up to 50) were distributed randomly over a certain area; some of them were designated as gateways, i.e., the destinations of the traffic, and some of them as traffic sources.
  - For the scenario with mobility, a number of wireless nodes (up to 50) were placed in a virtual street environment that was defined using real map data for an area in Kawasaki, Japan; the mobility was defined using the behavioral model in QOMET, by specifying a (common) starting position and a destination for each node; the gateway was fixed in this case at the departure position, and all the other nodes could represent traffic sources.
- Each of the above classes of experiments had different goals:

— For the mesh network, the goal was to compare the performance of the routing protocol when using different routing metrics; the performance was evaluated from the point of view of the throughput and delay for the traffic sent by the designated sources.

— For the MANET, the goal was to evaluate the effect of wireless network parameters, such as transmit power, on the topology being built dynamically by OLSR (when using the same routing metric) as the mobile nodes moved from their starting position to their individual destinations.

- In all experiments we used the version 0.5.5 of the OLSR protocol as implemented by the olsr.org project [77].
- We logged the network topology created by OLSR in real time so that we can see how it evolves in time, useful in particular for the MANET experiments.

The necessary steps for carrying out the routing protocol evaluation experiments were the following:

(1) Define the appropriate QOMET scenario, specifying the number of static or mobile wireless nodes, their properties, and — for the MANET case — their motion; the street topology that constrained the motion of the mobile was also indicated.

(2) Define the appropriate SpringOS scenario file, specifying the number of experiment hosts used and their generic behavior.

(3) Define the actions of the nodes in a shell script file. In particular, the following commands are important[3]:
- Launch the QOMET "do_wireconf" command that reproduces the WLAN communication conditions in the emulated network.
- Launch the "iperf" traffic generation command that sends traffic between the designated traffic sources and the gateways.
- Launch the "ping" command that we used for round-trip delay measurements.

---

[3]Note that the OLSR daemons also have to be launched, but this was not done at each experiment execution, but only once for a series of experiments; hence, the daemon-launching command was not included in this shell script.

(4) Execute the experiment using SpringOS mechanisms.
(5) Evaluate off-line the experiment logs to compute the perfor-
    mance of the routing protocol, either in terms of network
    performance or from the point of view of the network topology
    produced.

13.2 Active RFID Tag Experiments

Active RFID tags have many applications in the area of location
tracking, mainly in relation to assets. However, they could also be
used for tracking the location of people, as Panasonic Corporation
is aiming to do by developing an active RFID tag-based pedestrian
localization system.

Active RFID tags are a perfect example of ubiquitous systems.
Real-world trials with such devices are difficult, especially in the
context of person localization system. This is because in addition
to the typical difficulties associated with ubiquitous systems (small
size, wireless communication), real-world trials must necessarily
include people wearing these devices that move according to known
scenarios.[4] QOMB played an essential role in evaluating the above-
mentioned pedestrian localization system, since it allowed using
the same firmware with the active RFID tag prototype system in
an emulated virtual environment, in which pedestrian mobility
could be accurately controlled and repeated for performing series
of experiments in the same mobility situations [16].

13.2.1 *Pedestrian Localization System*

To facilitate the understanding of the challenges related to the
emulation of the active RFID tag system, and the motivation behind
the various types of experiments that we performed, we proceed by
introducing first the pedestrian localization system.

---

[4]Known or pre-defined scenarios are essential in order to be able to evaluate how
accurate the localization provided by the system is and serve as a reference for this
evaluation.

13.2.1.1 Prototype system

The location tracking system prototype developed by Panasonic Corporation uses the AYID32305 active RFID tags manufactured by Ymatic Corporation [116]. The processing unit of the tags is the PIC16LF627A micro-controller, which has an operating frequency of 4 MHz. The active tag wireless transceiver works on the 303.2 MHz frequency, and communicates at an effective data rate of 2400 bps. According to Ymatic Corporation, the error-free communication range of these tags is between 3 and 5 meters, depending on the type of antenna being used.

The pedestrian localization system developed by Panasonic Corporation uses these active RFID tags to provide to a central software component, called localization engine, the information required for automatically computing the trajectory to date and the current location of the active tag wearer.

The communication protocol used by the active RFID tags was custom designed by Panasonic based on the time-division multiplexing paradigm. The protocol uses a pre-configured number of communication slots, one of which is selected at random before the effective transmission procedure. Communicated data contains the ID of the transmitting tag and current time information. Given the memory limitations of the active RFID tags, the received data items are not saved individually but merged into a unique record that indicates the IDs of the tags that were met during a certain time period. The duration of the period for which merging occurs is defined as a system configuration parameter.

13.2.1.2 Real-world trials

Several real-world trials were done by Panasonic with the prototype localization system. The most important ones orchestrated the movement of 16 pedestrians, each carrying an active RFID tag, in an area of approximately 100 m × 300 m that included several buildings. Each pedestrian received movement instructions indicating the time in minutes and the location at which the participant should be at that moment of time, including both indoors and outdoors trajectories. Timing the motion was done by participants on their own. Participants were also equipped with GPS devices, so that the robustness of the two tracking methods could be compared.

The experiment made it possible to validate the basic behavior of the prototype localization system. However, it also revealed several issues:

(1) *Organizing the real-world trials was time consuming*: A 15-minute 16-person experiment took several hours to prepare and could be repeated only two times during one day.

(2) *Movement variations prevented the reproducibility of the results*: The results of the two trials were not comparable because of the variable movement speed of the participants and the fact that they used sometimes other information than the movement instructions to decide when to move, such as the fact whether their active tags were communicating with each other or not.

(3) *Battery depletion was relatively fast*: This caused the wireless signal to weaken during and between trials and further amplified the lack of reproducibility.

(4) *Off-the-shelf GPS receivers could not be used for validation*: The GPS receivers had difficulties in providing a reliable location for small-scale movements and did not function inside buildings (as expected).

13.2.2 Emulation Framework

The issues related to real-world trials motivated the collaboration between NICT Hokuriku Research Center and Panasonic Corporation, which lead to the development of the emulation framework presented here. The goal of our research was to make possible reproducible experiments with the pedestrian localization system, by emulating the communication between active RFID tags while running the same firmware that was used in the prototype system, so that its performance characteristics could be more thoroughly assessed.

The emulation framework that we designed and implemented builds upon the RUNE-based ubiquitous system emulation mechanism that we developed for QOMB. In particular, creating the active RFID tag emulation framework required to implement specific functionality in the generic communication and control spaces that were shown in Fig. 12.7.

13.2.2.1 Communication space

The communication space uses the QOMET chanel library to apply the computed network degradation in the emulated network. This is a generic procedure that does not change for the case of active RFID tag emulation. However, computing the network degradation needs to be done using specific models that correspond to the communication of the active RFID tags that we emulated. This model was integrated with the QOMET deltaQ library.

The active RFID tags use a simple wireless communication technology and protocol when compared with IEEE 802.11. Therefore, we created a communication model that sufficiently approximates the real communication conditions between active RFID tags, while not being exceedingly accurate. This is because our focus was on the evaluation of the functionality implemented as the firmware of the active RFID tags.

As a consequence, for active tags we used a model that establishes the relationship between the distance that separates two active RFID tags and the average frame error rate (FER) that occurs during communication. This model is based on measurements made by Panasonic with the prototype system in an RF-shielded room while using a helical antenna, the same with the one used in the practical experiment. A second-degree equation was fitted on the measurement results to make computation possible in an easy manner.

In order to enable emulation experiments with the active RFID tag system in a wide range of network conditions, we further extended this model by introducing a parameter for scaling the communication range of the devices. This parameter makes it possible to evaluate the performance of the system by emulation experiments in situations when using a communication range of the active RFID tags different than the default one. In principle, range may also be changed in reality by varying the transmission power of the active tags.

As mentioned before, the deltaQ library of QOMET supports the definition of realistic virtual spaces, including buildings and streets. As buildings interfere with the active RFID tag communication, we had to take them into account when computing the wireless communication conditions. Given the low transmission power and short range of the emulated active tags, we could ignore complex propagation aspects such as multi-path fading and absorption and made the simplifying assumption that only line-of-sight communication is possible between two active tags. Line-of-sight calculations are done by taking into account the position of the tags, and the shape and position of the buildings present in the virtual environment that we emulated.

13.2.2.2 Control space

In order to be able to execute the active RFID tag firmware on our emulation framework without any modification or recompilation, we emulated the active RFID tag micro-controller, which is a PIC processor. The following aspects were taken into account and implemented:

- instruction execution for all 35 instructions of the PIC processor
- data I/O through the only method used by the active RFID tag application, USART (Universal Synchronous Asynchronous Receiver Transmitter)
- all the interrupts that were necessary for the active RFID tag application

We evaluated by experiments the time accuracy of the PIC processor emulator, and demonstrated that even on a low-spec platform such as 1 GHz PC (with FreeBSD 5.4 operating system), it is still possible to have 3 instances of the processor emulator running in parallel at the correct frequency of 4 MHz. Performance improved quickly with processor frequency, as the operating system overhead becomes less and less important when more processor emulator instances are run simultaneously. Thus, almost 40 instances of the PIC processor emulator could be run in parallel if experiments would be executed on a 3 GHz PC (with FreeBSD 7.1 operating system).

13.2.2.3 Time flow

We initially intended to use a time flow for experiments that is the same with the wall-clock time (i.e., 1 emulated second lasts 1 real-time second). However, the jitter in the StarBED wired network prevented us from doing that. The reason is that each of the communication slots of the real active RFID tags has a duration of 53 ms. This value is only one order of magnitude higher than latency and jitter values in a wired network, which are in the order of milliseconds. As a consequence, there was a risk that network latency and jitter would perturb experimental results. For instance, two packets sent simultaneously from logical point of view may have physically arrived in different communication slots during the emulation process.

The solution for countering this issue was to use time flow emulation. Thus, we decided to execute the experiment 10 times slower than wall-clock time (i.e., 1 emulated second lasts 10 real-time seconds). The actual duration of a communication slot in the emulation framework became 530 ms when following this approach (although logically it is still 53 ms). The 530 ms value is two orders of magnitude greater than the undesired network effects, thus eliminating the potential of interference with the communication protocol.

As discussed previously in this book, a constant slow-down factor of time flow compared with real time still allows for emulation experiments that are different in this respect from simulation. This is because simulation uses purely logical time, and the duration of an experiment always varies, depending on how many nodes are involved, the complexity of calculations, the amount of traffic, and so on.

13.2.3 *Experimental Results*

We used the QOMB-based active RFID tag emulation framework for several series of experiments, which will be summarized next. Note that for comparison purposes we have also performed several real-world trials with the prototype localization system developed by Panasonic.

The metric we used to evaluate the performance of the localization system is the average localization error, i.e., how well the system can identify the location of the pedestrians at each moment of time. For emulation experiments, the average localization error is computed as the mean of the distances at each moment of time between the position tracked by the pedestrian localization system, and the pedestrian position in the virtual emulation environment. For the real-world trials, the average localization error is computed as the mean of the distances at each moment of time between the position tracked by the pedestrian localization system, and the scenario-based (intended) position of the pedestrian in the real environment.

13.2.3.1 Emulation framework validation

First of all, we carried out a two-pedestrian real-world trial with the prototype localization system developed by Panasonic in an outdoor environment. The goal of the experiment was to validate our emulation platform by comparing the results obtained in the real-world trial with those of an emulation experiment that reproduced the said trial.

Comparing the mean localization error calculated for each pedestrian, in both the real-world experiment and the emulation experiment, showed a good agreement between the two experiment techniques. The confidence in the correctness of the emulation framework built in this manner allowed us to proceed toward using QOMB to investigate the properties of the localization system prototype.

13.2.3.2 Prototype system analysis

We performed several emulation experiments that reproduced the conditions of the 16-pedestrian experiment carried out by Panasonic. These emulation experiments were aimed at assessing the firmware running on the active RFID tags of the localization system.

We first analyzed how the localization error differs between the real-world trials done by Panasonic and the results on our emulation testbed. Our results showed that the localization error follows the same trend in both types of experiments, demonstrating again the correctness of the emulation framework. As expected, emulation results had better reproducibility, given the lack of uncertainty in the virtual environment.

Through the analysis of the experimental data, we were also able to identify two issues with the active RFID tag based system, as follows:

(1) The random number generation implementation was incorrect in the active RFID tag firmware, causing many tags to choose the same slot for communication. The negative effect of this firmware issue was an artificially induced high collision rate between tags that were in the same communication area. Following our observations, Panasonic has fixed this firmware problem.

(2) The time synchronization algorithm was causing a drift whenever two active RFID tags would be next to each other for a long period of time, as each of them would repeatedly try to speed up its internal clock to catch up with the other one. Panasonic has revised the algorithm so that this issue does not occur in the next version of the localization system.

13.2.3.3 Parameter selection

One important use of the emulation framework that we designed and implemented is for system parameter selection, such as determining the optimum values in specified circumstances. In particular, the parameters that we investigated through emulation on QOMB are the following:

Transmission range Transmission range is an important parameter of the localization system since it determines the average distance over which the active tags can communicate with each other. Transmission range mainly depends on the antenna and transmission power of the active RFID tags. However, it may be difficult to perform many experiments while changing such hardware parameters. Under such circumstances, the approach of emulation simplifies considerably the task of experimentally evaluating different conditions. Through our experiments we have identified for a certain emulated scenario the optimal transmission range that ensures best localization accuracy through a trade-off between the communication probability and interference conditions that correspond to a given transmission range.

Number of communication slots   The prototype localization system uses 9 slots for the time-multiplexed communication, preceded and followed by one guard slot. The advantage of using a smaller number of slots is that the active duration of the RFID tags is decreased, and therefore battery life potentially increases. The disadvantage is that when several tags want to communicate with each other, a smaller number of slots leads to a high collision rate and impedes information exchange. Our experimental results indicated that there is a performance gain when increasing the number of slots, especially for long-range communication (around 9 m), and an optimal value was determined.

ID record merging period   One other parameter of the localization system is the length of the period used when merging ID record information, as it was already mentioned in Section 13.2.1.1. The two-pedestrian experiment was used to illustrate how our emulation framework can be employed for analyzing this parameter. In this case as well, we identified the merging period that provides optimum performance in term of localization error and results stability.

13.2.3.4 Large-scale experiments

Perhaps one of the most important motivations for developing an emulation framework such as QOMB is running large-scale experiments that cannot be easily executed in the real world. For the pedestrian localization system, this corresponds to experiments with groups of several tens and even 100 pedestrians, which are difficult to organize in reality. To carry out such large-scale emulation experiments, the movement of the pedestrians in the virtual space was automatically generated by using the behavioral motion model in QOMET. The topology of the virtual space was based on real map data for a region in Kawasaki, Japan.

Although we have performed several series of 100-pedestrian experiments, due to an issue related to the active RFID tag communication protocol, we were not able to obtain the localization results in the same way we did for the other smaller-scale experiments. The issue was the following: In the 100-pedestrian experiment, the number of tags that reach the one or two destinations in our scenarios is large compared with the previous experiments. This leads to having many collisions as the active RFID tags try to upload their information to the localization system. As a result, many tags do not manage to upload enough information before the experiment ends. Panasonic Corporation is designing an enhanced communication protocol that includes collision avoidance, since our experiments have clearly shown that without such an algorithm the active tag localization system cannot function for relatively crowded areas. This is one of the important findings that were made possible by using our emulation framework for large-scale experiments.

A related problem we discovered is that the current version of the localization system software is not able to cope with the case when only incomplete information is available. This meant that although more than half of the tags did upload some information, no localization results were produced. This robustness issue with the software implementation of the localization algorithm is now being considered by Panasonic.

13.2.3.5 Experimentation procedure

In order to perform the active RFID tag experiments that we have described so far, the following steps need to be carried out:

(1) Define the appropriate QOMET scenario, specifying the number of emulated active RFID tags (corresponding to pedestrians), their initial position, as well as the destination of their movement.
(2) Create the RUNE definition file that describes the spaces and conduits that represent the emulated active RFID tags; when using a large number of emulated tags, we recommend generating the definition file in a programmatic manner in order

to avoid mistakes that may appear if writing the file by hand, for instance, in interconnecting the RUNE spaces by conduits.

(3) Execute the experiment on the allocated StarBED hosts.[5]

(4) Compute off-line the localization error by using the localization information provided by the localization engine and the known trajectories of the pedestrians.

Note that in these experiments, we did not use SpringOS mechanisms for the execution of the experiment but only for the preparation phase. However, SpringOS could have been used for experiment execution as well.

13.3 Discussion

The experiments presented in this chapter demonstrated the wide range of evaluation procedures that can be carried out by using QOMB, both for computer networks and for ubiquitous ones.

We are currently in the process of finalizing the support for IEEE 802.15.4-based ubiquitous network systems. For this purpose, we use an approach that is similar to the one presented for active RFID tags. Our preliminary results show that QOMB functionality can be easily extended to this new type of network and system.

We also envisage extending QOMB functionality to support WiMAX networks, and in this case we plan to use the same approach employed for WLAN networks. Although the work in this area is only in an initial phase, again we expect to be able to easily modify the framework of QOMB to allow carrying out WiMAX experiments as well.

---

[5]These hosts should be prepared for experiment in advance by using SpringOS mechanisms.

Chapter 14

Concluding Remarks

In this final chapter, we shall first summarize on a chapter-by-chapter basis the most important issues that we discussed in each part of this book. Then we shall use some of the information already presented in the book to provide a series of practical advices identifying and detailing the network emulation approach that is most suited for three real-world situations.

14.1 Summing It All Up

In this book we tried to cover a large varieties of issues related to network emulation, so as to provide our readers with a comprehensive background regarding this topic. We believe that summarizing the most important issues discussed in each chapter would help readers to better grasp the overall content of our book.

14.1.1 *The Ins and Outs of Network Emulation*

The first part of this book was intended as an introduction to the general concept of network emulation.

Introduction to Network Emulation
Razvan Beuran
Copyright © 2013 Pan Stanford Publishing Pte. Ltd.
ISBN 978-981-4310-91-8 (Hardcover), 978-981-4364-09-6 (eBook)
www.panstanford.com

In Chapter 2, we started by presenting the background and motivations that lead to the development of network emulation techniques. We then defined formally the concept of network emulation, as well as the other network experiment techniques. Following that, we discussed how network emulation can be put to use to accomplish tasks such as network equipment assessment, application assessment, protocol assessment, and finally some more complex scenarios. The chapter ended with a comparison of network emulation against the other network experiment techniques, namely analytical modeling, network simulation, and real-world testing.

In Chapter 3 we attempted to provide a quick overview on the wide range of network emulators that have been or are being developed. To facilitate understanding, we provided a classification methodology that used criteria such as availability, implementation manner, emulation level, and model complexity. We also gave a summary of the most important aspects related to the manner in which to effectively carry out experiments through emulation. In particular, we focused on how to execute the emulation tools how to run applications, and how to perform the overall experiments.

14.1.2 *Network Emulators to Remember*

Whereas the first part of the book was a general introduction, the second part plunges into more details regarding network emulation. We opted for a hands-on approach, in which we discuss particular cases of network emulators, grouped by several classes: free emulators, commercial emulators, emulation-capable simulators, and emulation testbeds. The discussion of each class and each network emulator belonging to that class provides a series of practical details that both facilitate the understanding of that particular tool and also help gaining a better insight into the general concept of network emulation.

In Chapter 4, we focused on free network emulators, which are most popular with regular users, as their source code is available for use, inspection, and modification without any financial costs. We started by introducing Dummynet, which is the oldest member of the network emulator family that is still currently in use. Then we discussed NIST Net, which was the initial equivalent of Dummynet for Linux, and further contributed to popularizing the concept of network emulation. NetEm followed as the modern incarnation of the concept on Linux, which has now become a popular operating system in research communities.[1] The chapter ended with a comparison of these three network emulators, emphasizing their most important properties.

In Chapter 5, we presented examples from the most used class of network emulators in business environments, namely the commercial emulators. Our discussion revealed the large number of companies that provide network emulation solutions and the variety of tools each company provides. Specifically, we discussed products of Shunra, PacketStorm Communications, Simena, Apposite Technologies, and Anue Systems. While the large amount of information available prevented us from being exhaustive, we tried to capture the most significant data related to each emulation product. The comparison section, which selected a representative product for each of the above companies, hopefully helped underline the most important features of each of these network emulators.

In Chapter 6 we moved to a different category of tools, the emulation-capable network simulators, which are most popular in the research or business environments that also embrace those network simulators. In that chapter, we discussed Ns-2, OPNET Modeler, QualNet Developer, and NCTUns, with focus on their emulation features. These four simulator-based network emulation solutions were compared in the final section of the chapter.

In Chapter 7, we presented yet another type of network emulators, the testbed-based ones. Network emulation testbeds are mainly used by researchers with affiliation to universities, research institutes, and sometimes commercial companies. Such affiliation represents the necessary credentials needed in order to obtain access to those testbeds. We presented in that chapter Emulab, PlanetLab, and ORBIT, as representative examples for the various alternatives of this category of network emulation tools. Although

---

[1] We noted that Dummynet was itself revived in recent years and ported to both Linux and Windows, thus becoming a strong contender for NetEm.

the three testbeds have largely different purposes, we tried to emphasize both their similarities and differences, as well as advantages and disadvantages in the comparison section of that chapter.

Chapter 8 concluded the second part of our book. In that chapter, we dealt first with several generic issues related to network emulation, which we discussed in the light of the details about various network emulators that had been presented that far. Thus, we analyzed the issues of realism, scalability, and control, as well as other aspects related to network emulation as an experiment technique (e.g., security). That chapter also included a more thorough discussion of various approaches in network emulation research, and solutions proposed for the different levels of the emulation process.

14.1.3 *A Case Study: QOMB*

The third and final part of this book went even more practical. To achieve this goal, we thoroughly discussed a system for which we have firsthand knowledge, since we actively participated to its design and development. This system is the wireless network emulation testbed named QOMB. QOMB is particularly suited for a detailed analysis in the context of network emulation because it addresses at least three factors that are important and challenging in this area: wireless network support, large-scale experiments, and distributed execution.

In Chapter 9, we presented the motivation behind the project that resulted in the design and development of QOMB, with focus on two issues: Internet access and smart environments. We also discussed the requirements that have driven the design of QOMB as a large-scale wireless network emulation testbed. The chapter ended with an outline of the design of QOMB that briefly introduced its components to readers, and explained their relationship to each other.

Chapter 10 presented QOMET, the set of tools for wireless network emulation that provide the corresponding capability on QOMB. After an overview of QOMET, we proceeded to presenting the library called deltaQ, which is in charge of computing the communication conditions between wireless nodes based on the characteristics of a user-defined scenario. The deltaQ library is also in charge of creating mobility patterns in the synthetic environment that constitutes the virtual world in which the wireless nodes communicate with each other. The two other libraries discussed, wireconf and chanel, are used during the effective emulation experiments to enforce the communication conditions computed by deltaQ in a wired network, thus effectively recreating the conditions corresponding to the user-defined scenario. Wireconf is used for IP-based communication between PC hosts, whereas chanel is dedicated to the case of non-IP communication between ubiquitous network devices. We also introduced in that chapter the command-line tools "qomet" and "do_wireconf" that users can employ to drive the above-mentioned libraries.

In Chapter 11, we presented StarBED, the large-scale wired network experiment testbed that represents the infrastructure of QOMB and on which QOMET is executed in a distributed manner. Following a discussion of the hardware components of StarBED, we introduced SpringOS, which is an experiment-support software tool that was created as a user interface for experiment preparation (mainly, configuring the testbed hardware) and execution. Then we presented RUNE, which is an alternative for SpringOS in experiment scenarios that the latter cannot handle directly. In particular, RUNE is intended for use in connection with the emulation of ubiquitous network systems.

Chapter 12 detailed the way in which QOMET and StarBED are integrated using the support tools on StarBED to create the synergistic entity that is QOMB, thus consolidating the building components in order to create a new type of testbed. After looking at the architecture of QOMB, we then explained the integration with the two experiment-support tools for StarBED, namely SpringOS and RUNE. For each of these two tools, we presented a simple example experiment that illustrated all the steps that need to be carried out in order to perform an experiment with any of the two solutions. That chapter ended with a general discussion of QOMB, and a comparison of QOMB against equivalent approaches for wireless network experiments.

In Chapter 13, we demonstrated the wide spectrum of applications of a wireless network emulation testbed such as QOMB, and in the same time the usefulness of the technique of network emulation in general. For this purpose we presented first several WLAN emulation experiments performed on QOMB. These experiments focused, in turn, on VoIP performance assessment, on a motion planning algorithm for autonomous robots, and on the evaluation of a routing protocol (OLSR). The second part of that chapter was dedicated to a series of active RFID tag experiments, as an illustration of the ubiquitous network system emulation capabilities of QOMB. As these experiments were done in the framework of the development of a pedestrian localization system, we also summarized the key points of that project. Then, we described the emulation framework of QOMB that made possible these experiments. Finally, we presented several categories of active RFID tag experimental results that we obtained on QOMB, emphasizing the opportunities provided by such a testbed for ubiquitous network system evaluation and optimization.

14.2 Practical Advice

We believe that practical information is the most useful to those who want to enter for the first time the world of network emulation. This is why we end this book with a series of advices for those readers interested in starting to use network emulation in their activity. While it is of course impossible to foresee all potential needs for emulation-based network experiments, we identified three use cases that we consider the most probable, namely

(1) a small company
(2) a large company
(3) a research group

In the following sections, we shall present the typical requirements associated with each of the three use cases above, and we shall propose the network emulation solutions that we see as most fitted for these scenarios.

14.2.1 *Small Company*

A small company may be developing network software that it would like to push as quickly as possible to market, so as to gain market share from its competitors and perhaps even a competitive advantage. The application probably addresses a limited problem that the company, nevertheless, envisages as important enough for its customers. Possible examples include communication applications, e-commerce, and so on. Note that even when the application itself does not have direct network functionality, it may still include such support for purposes such as communicating usage statistics to the company, for automatic updates, and so on.

From the network point of view, the requirements for our hypothetical application would be to effectively use the network to communicate a moderate amount of data between two end-user clients, or between an end-user client and the company server, in a manner which is robust enough to potential network impairments.

Given these requirements, we propose the use of a software network emulator solution, which we expect is capable of support-ing the expected moderate amount of traffic, and can introduce the necessary network degradation for testing the application in a scenario corresponding to two remote locations, between which network conditions may be less than perfect in terms of delay, packet loss, and bandwidth limitations.

As a consequence, a possible experiment setup would be that shown in Fig. 14.1. The two end nodes "Client A" and the "Client/Server B"[2] communicate with each other through the software network emulator that is installed on a dedicated workstation. The application under test is installed on the two end nodes. The network emulation software is configured so as to reproduce several typical scenarios such as

- low delay and low packet loss
- low delay and high packet loss
- high delay and low packet loss
- high delay and high packet loss

In all cases bandwidth limitations can also be introduced, depending on what are the expected conditions for the end users. For instance, to test the possibility of using the application over an

---

[2] Node "B" can be either identical to "A", hence another application client, or provide some sort of service the node "A", hence a server.

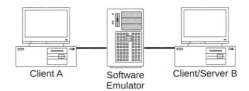

Figure 14.1. Suggested setup for use of a software network emulator by a small company.

ADSL modem, an appropriate rate limitation configuration of the network emulator should be used.

Such simple scenarios should be sufficient for most needs and should give application developers an idea about how their product would behave in a wide range of network conditions. Note that while we focused on small companies in this section, everything we discussed also applies to the case of private developers, or any other kind of users that may be interested in network application performance evaluation.

Depending on their financial capabilities and whether they would like to receive technical support, the category of users concerned by this use case have the choice between a free software emulator, such as Dummynet or NetEm, or a commercial software emulator, such as Shunra VE Cloud or Desktop, or PacketStorm Communications Tornado, which we described in detail in the corresponding chapters, Chapter 4 and Chapter 5, respectively. Simena NE100 also meets the requirements of the presented scenario, even though given the fact that it is an integrated solution, it may come at a slightly higher cost. A company may, nevertheless, consider that the higher cost is compensated by the fact that no setup is required in this case for the workstation used to run the network emulation software in the other cases.

14.2.2 *Large Company*

A large company is probably developing a more complex network system compared with a small company. Examples include various kinds of managements systems (e.g., ERM), cloud computing applications, etc. Requirements that derive from such application

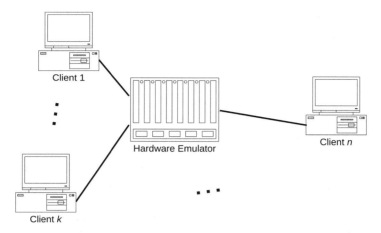

Figure 14.2. Suggested setup for use of a hardware network emulator by a large company.

complexity are a larger amount of traffic, a larger number of nodes, as well as more intricate interactions between these nodes when compared with the previous use case.

As a consequence, a software network emulator may not be sufficient to thoroughly evaluate such complex applications, mainly because of limitations in terms of supported throughput and the complexity of the network scenarios it can reproduce. Therefore, we propose the use of a hardware network emulator for the typical goals of large companies.

A possible setup for this use case is shown in Fig. 14.2. We assume that the experiment involves a number of *n* clients (which can represent either end-user desktops or application servers) that are connected to a hardware network emulator appliance. Although we depicted direct connections between all clients and the network emulator, if the number of ports of the appliance is insufficient, network switches can be used to aggregate the traffic produced by clients, so as to extend the scale of the experiment. Moreover, while we depicted all clients as desktop PC, some of them can also be other kind of devices, such as hardware systems (e.g., hardware traffic generators) that are required to perform the intended experiment, or that may be even under test themselves.

The application that is being test is considered to be installed on the *n* clients (including the use of hardware solutions). The hardware network emulator is configured to create the required complex network topology, and the composite network degradation effects that correspond to it. As the complexity of the setup increases, the complexity of the configuration step is also more significant, and users must make sure that the scenarios they will evaluate indeed cover the range of conditions they expect to encounter in the target production network.

We have reviewed in the second part of this book a large number of commercial network emulators that are suited for the use cases presented here, such as the Shunra VE Appliance, the PacketStorm Communications Hurricane and E series, the Simena PTC3000 and NE series, the Apposite Technologies Linktropy and Netropy series, or the Anue Systems GEM (see Chapter 5). The most appropriate of these alternatives must be decided by the company based on its requirements in terms of execution speed, network emulation capabilities, and, perhaps, cost.

14.2.3 *Research Group*

Researchers have usually different interests compared with commercial companies. They will typically not test already developed products but rather new ideas that are still under development. Moreover, researchers may be interested in a lower-level evaluation of the system they develop, requiring realistic but controllable network conditions. Research experiments may also be carried out on larger scales that those performed by companies, often with the Internet as a target. Peer-to-peer systems and distributed file systems are but a few examples that enter in this category.

We envisage that there are two possible solutions for the types of experiments a research group may intend to perform, depending on whether the most important requirement concerns modeling accuracy or experiment scale.

14.2.3.1 When modeling comes first

One type of situation is when modeling comes first, in the sense that researchers want to be able to make experiments with networks that

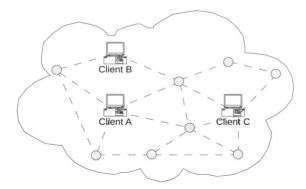

Figure 14.3. Suggested setup for use of a simulator-based network emulator by a research group.

were thoroughly and accurately modeled down to a very detailed level, so that they can fully understand the internal behavior of the system they develop.

For such a case, we deem that emulation-capable network simulators are the most appropriate solution, especially given the fact that the researchers do probably already have experience with those network simulators. In Fig. 14.3 we show one of the many scenarios possible with such a tool, in which a few real nodes (clients "A", "B", and "C") are completely embedded into a simulated network that is intended as an accurate replica of the target real network for the developed application. We estimate that in many cases this approach comes as a natural continuation of the simulation-only experiments that may have been carried out by researchers, a continuation meant to validate an initial prototype implementation of the developed protocol or system.

While we have discussed several simulator-based network emulation solutions in Chapter 6, we believe that for general-purpose experiments the commercial variants, such as the system-in-the-loop module of OPNET Modeler, or EXata network emulator are most usable. If certain restrictions on the execution platforms are not a problem, then NCTUns, with its many features, can be a viable solution, for both academic and commercial environments.

On the other hand, the Ns-2 emulation features do not seem mature enough yet for such experiments.[3]

14.2.3.2 When scale comes first

The other important scenario is when experiment scale is the most significant requirement. Simulator-based network emulation does not have the necessary scalability properties in terms of number of nodes and amount of traffic for being used in such a context. Therefore, in large-scale scenarios, only a network emulation testbed can provide the necessary resources to perform the experiments.

In Chapter 7, we have introduced three testbeds that could be used for the purpose of such large-scale experiments. Thus, for experiments in an isolated network, Emulab is the first choice, whereas for experiments distributed over the Internet, PlanetLab is the most suited alternative. For wireless network related research, obviously ORBIT is the best solution. To these three testbeds, we add those presented in the third part of this book: first, the large-scale network experiment testbed, StarBED, which can be considered an equivalent of Emulab (although StarBED exceeds Emulab by more than double in size) and, second, QOMB, which is adding wireless network emulation support to StarBED and, hence, is an alternative to ORBIT.

---

[3] Recent communications we had with Ns-3 developers indicate that the emulation features of this network simulator are being actively developed, and Ns-3 based emulation may soon become an applicable alternative.

Bibliography

1. Ahn, J., Danzig, P. B., Liu, Z., and Yan, L. (1995). *Evaluation of TCP Vegas: emulation and experiment*, in Proc. of the ACM SIGCOMM, Cambridge, Massachusetts, August 1995, pp. 185–195.

2. Ahrenholz, J., Danilov, C., Henderson, T. R., and Kim, J. H. (2008). *CORE: a real-time network emulator*, in Proc. of IEEE Military Communications Conference (MILCOM), San Diego, USA, November 16–19, 2008.

3. Anue Systems, Inc., *Ethernet Network Emulators*, http://www.anuesystems.com/Products_NetworkEmulator_Ethernet.shtml.

4. Anue Systems, Inc., *Network Emulation Case Studies*, http://www.anuesystems.com/Resources_NetworkEmulator_CaseStudies.shtml.

5. Apposite Technologies, Inc., *Network Emulation Product Lines*, http://www.apposite-tech.com/products/index.html.

6. Augusto, J. C., and McCullagh, P. (2007). Ambient intelligence: concepts and applications, *International Journal on Computer Science and Information Systems*, vol. 4, no. 1, 2007, pp. 1–28.

7. Bavier, A., Bowman, M., Chun, B., Culler, D., Karlin, S., Muir, S., Peterson, L., Roscoe, T., Spalink, T., and Wawrzoniak, M. (2004). *Operating system support for planetary-scale services*, in Proc. of the 1st Symposium on Network Systems Design and Implementation (NSDI'04), March 2004.

8. Bavier, A., Feamster, N., Huang, M., Peterson, L. and Rexford, J. (2006). *In VINI veritas: realistic and controlled network experimentation*, in Proc. of the 2006 Conf. on Applications, Technologies, Architectures, and Protocols for Computer Communications (SIGCOMM'06), New York, USA, 2006, pp. 3–14.

9. Bellard, F., *QEMU open source processor emulator*, http://www.qemu.org/.

10. Beuran, R. (2004). *Mesure de la qualite dans les reseaux informatiques (Measuring Quality in Computer Networks)*, Ph.D. thesis, CERN-

THESIS-2005-004, Université Jean Monnet, Saint-Etienne, France, and University Politechnica of Bucharest, Romania, July 2004.

11. Beuran, R., Chinen, K., Latt, K. T., Miyachi, T., Nakata, J., Nguyen, L. T., Shinoda, Y., and Tan, Y. (2006). Application performance assessment on wireless ad hoc networks, in Asian Internet Engineering Conference (AINTEC 2006), Springer-Verlag LNCS 4311, Bangkok, Thailand, November 28–30, 2006, pp. 128–138.

12. Beuran, R., and Ivanovici, M. (2004). *User-Perceived Quality Assessment for VoIP Applications*, technical report (delivered to U4EA Technologies), CERN-OPEN-2004-007, CERN, Geneva, Switzerland, January 2004.

13. Beuran, R., Ivanovici, M., Dobinson, B., Davies, N., and Thompson, P. (2003). *Network Quality of service measurement system for application requirements evaluation*, in Proc. of Intl. Symp. on Performance Evaluation of Computer and Telecommunication Systems (SPECTS 2003), Montreal, Canada, July 20–24, 2003, pp. 380–387.

14. Beuran, R., Nguyen, L. T., and Shinoda, Y. (2010). *QOMB wireless network emulation testbed: evaluation and case study*, in 5th ACM International Workshop on Wireless Network Testbeds, Experimental Evaluation and Characterization (WiNTECH 2010), in conjunction with MobiCom 2010, Chicago, USA, September 20–24, 2010.

15. Beuran, R., Nguyen, L. T., Miyachi, T., Nakata, J., Chinen, K., Tan, Y., and Shinoda, Y. (2009). *QOMB: A Wireless Network Emulation Testbed*, IEEE Global Communications Conference (GLOBECOM 2009), Honolulu, Hawaii, USA, November 30–December 4, 2009.

16. Beuran, R., Nakata, J., Okada, T., Kawakami, T., Chinen, K., Tan, Y. and Shinoda, Y. (2010). Emulation framework for the design and development of active RFID tag systems, *Journal of Ambient Intelligence and Smart Environments (JAISE)*, vol. 2, no. 2, April 2010, pp. 155–177.

17. Beuran, R., Nguyen, L. T., Latt, K. T., Nakata, J. and Shinoda, Y. (2007). *QOMET: A Versatile WLAN Emulator*, in Proc. of IEEE Intl. Conf. on Advanced Information Networking and Applications (AINA 2007), Niagara Falls, Ontario, Canada, May 21–23, 2007, pp. 348–353.

18. Beuran, R., Nakata, J., Okada, T., Nguyen, L. T., Tan, Y. and Shinoda, Y. (2008). *A Multi-purpose Wireless Network Emulator: QOMET*, 22nd IEEE International Conference on Advanced Information Networking and Applications (AINA 2008) Workshops, FINA 2008 symposium, Okinawa, Japan, March 25–28, 2008, pp. 223–228.

19. Candela Technologies, Inc., *LANforge ICE WAN/Network Emulator*, http://www.candelatech.com/lanforge_v3/datasheet.html#ice.

20. Carbone, M., Cecchetti, G, Rizzo, L., Checconi, F. and Ruscelli, A. (2007). *Wireless link emulation in OneLab*, in Proc. of Intl. Workshop on Real Overlays And Distributed Systems (ROADS), Warsaw, Poland, July 2007.

21. Carbone, M. and Rizzo, L. (2009). *Dummynet Revisited*, Technical Report, University of Pisa, Italy, 31 May 2009.

22. Carson, M. and Santay, D. (2003). *NIST Net: a Linux-based Network Emulation Tool*, ACM SIGCOMM Computer Communication Review, vol. 33, no. 3, pp. 111–126, 2003.

23. Conchon, E., Garcia, J, Perennou, T. and Diaz, M. (2007). *Improved IP-level Emulation for Mobile and Wireless Systems*, in Proc. of IEEE Wireless Communications and Networking Conference (WCNC07), Hong Kong, China, March 2007.

24. Davies, N. (2003). *Delivering Predictable Quality in Saturated Networks*, technical report, Predictable Network Solutions, September 2003.

25. De, P., Raniwala, A., Sharma, S. and Chiueh, T.-C. (2005). *Design considerations for a multihop wireless network testbed*, IEEE Commun., vol. 43, no. 10, October 2005, pp. 102–109,

26. D-ITG, Distributed Internet Traffic Generator. http://www.grid.unina.it/software/ITG/

27. Engel, M., Smith, M., Hanemann, S. and Freisleben, B. (2004). *Wireless ad-hoc network emulation using microkernel-based virtual Linux systems*, in Proc. of the 5th EUROSIM Congress on Modeling and Simulation, 2004, pp. 198–203.

28. Fall, K. (1999). *Network emulation in the Vint/NS simulator*, in Proc. of IEEE Symposium on Computers and Communications, 1999, pp. 244–250.

29. Garcia, J., Conchon, E., Perennou, T. and Brunstrom, A. (2007). *KauNet: Improving Reproducibility for Wireless and Mobile Research*, in Proc. MobiEval Workshop at ACM MobiSys 2007, San Juan, Puerto Rico, June 2007.

30. Global Environment for Network Innovations (GENI) Project. http://www.geni.net/.

31. Globus Grid Toolkit. http://www.globus.org/.

32. Gokturk, E. (2007). *A stance on emulation and testbeds, and a survey of network emulators and testbeds*, in Proc. of 21st European Conference

on Modelling and Simulation (ECMS 2007), Prague, Czech Republic, June 4–6, 2007.

33. Guffens, V. and Bastin, G. (2005). *Running virtualized native drivers in user mode linux*, in Proc. of USENIX 2005 Annual Technical Conf., 2005.

34. Guruprasad, S., Ricci, R. and Lepreau, J. (2005). *Integrated network experimentation using simulation and emulation*, in: Proc. of 1st Intl. Conf. on Testbeds and Research Infrastructures for Development of Networks and Communities (TRIDENTCOM 2005), 2005.

35. GNU Radio Home Page. http://gnuradio.org/redmine/wiki/gnuradio.

36. Haeberlen, A., Dischinger, M., Gummadi, K. P. and Saroiu, S. (2006). *Monarch: a tool to emulate transport protocol flows over the Internet at large*, in Proc. of the 6th ACM SIGCOMM on Internet measurement (IMC'06). New York, NY, USA, 2006, pp. 105–118.

37. Hemminger, S. (2005). *Network Emulation with NetEm*, in Proc. of the Linux Australia Conference (linux.conf.au 2005), Canberra, Autralia, April 2005.

38. Huang, X. W., Sharma, R. and Keshav, S. (1999). *The ENTRAPID protocol development environment*, in Proc. of the Eighteenth Annual Joint Conf. of the IEEE Computer and Communications Societies (INFOCOM'99), vol. 3, March 1999, pp. 1107–1115.

39. Huang, Y. L., Tygar, J. D., Lin, H. Y., Yeh, L. Y., Tsai, H. Y., Sklower, K., Shieh, S. P., Wu, C. C., Lu, P. H., Chien, S. Y., Lin, Z. S., Hsu, L. W., Hsu, C. W., Hsu, C. T., Wu, Y. C., Leong, M. S. (2008). *SWOON: a testbed for secure wireless overlay networks*, in Proc. of. Workshop on Cyber Security Experimentation and Test 2008 (CSET'08), July 28, 2008.

40. Hokuriku Research Center, National Institute of Information and Communications technology, *QOMET Wiki*, https://www.starbed.org/qoala/twiki/bin/view/QOALA/QOMET

41. InterWorking Labs, Inc., *Maxwell Network Emulator*, http://www.maxwelltester.com/.

42. Internet Automobility Laboratory, *Dummynet Extension EDN*, http://www.ial.jp/software.html.

43. Iperf Home Page at SourceForge. http://sourceforge.net/projects/iperf/.

44. iTrinegy, Ltd., *iTrinegy Network Emulators*, http://www.itrinegy.com/network-emulators/network-emulator-overview.html.

45. International Telecommunication Union, Telecommunication Standardization Sector (2001). *ITU-T Recommendation P.862: Perceptual*

evaluation of speech quality (PESQ), an objective method for end to end speech quality assessment of narrow-band telephone networks and codecs, ITU-T, February 2001.

46. Ivanovici, M. (2005). *Network Quality Degradation Emulation — An FPGA-based Approach to Application Performance Assessment*, PhD Thesis, University "Politehnica" Bucharest, Bucharest Romania, 2005.

47. Ixia, *Modern Networks Testing and Compliance*, http://www.ixiacom.com/products/index.php.

48. Jansen, S. and McGregor, A. (2005). *Simulation with real world network stacks*, in Proc. of WSC'05, 2005, pp. 2454–2463.

49. Jiang X. and Xu, D. (2003). *vBET: a vm-based emulation testbed*, in Proc. of the ACM SIGCOMM workshop on Models, methods and tools for reproducible network research (MoMeTools'03), New York, NY, USA, 2003, pp. 95–104.

50. Johnson, D., Stack, T., Fish, R., Flickinger, D. M., Stoller, L., Ricci, R. and Lepreau, J. (2006). *Mobile Emulab: A robotic wireless and sensor network testbed*, in Proc. of IEEE INFOCOM 2006, Barcelona, Spain, April 23–29, 2006.

51. Judd, G. and Steenkiste, P. (2004). *Repeatable and realistic wireless experimentation through physical emulation*, SIGCOMM Comput. Commun. Rev., vol. 34, no. 1, pp. 63–68, 2004.

52. Kamp, P.-H., Watson, R. N. M. (2000). *Jails: Confining the omnipotent root*, in Proc. of 2nd Int. Conf. on System Administration and Networking (SANE 2000), Maastricht, The Netherlands, March 22–25, 200.

53. Kaul, S., Gruteser, M., and Seskar, I. (2006). *Creating Wireless Multihop Topologies on Space-Constrained Indoor Testbeds Through Noise Injection*, in Proc. of 2nd International Conference on Testbeds and Research Infrastructures for the Development of Networks and Communities (Tridentcom 2006), Barcelona, Spain, March 1–3, 2006.

54. Kayssi, A. and El-Haj-Mahmoud, A. (2004). *EmuNET: a real-time network emulator*, in Proc. of the 2004 ACM symp. on Applied computing (SAC'04), New York, NY, USA, 2004, pp. 357–362.

55. Kojo, M., Gurtov, A., Manner, J., Sarolahti, P, Alanko, T. and Raatikainen, K. (2001). *Seawind: A Wireless Network Emulator*, in Proc. of GI/ITG Conference MMB 2001, Aachen, Germany, September 2001.

56. Kropff, M., Krop, T., Hollick, M., Mogre, P. S. and Steinmetz, R. (2006). *A Survey of Real-World and Emulation Testbeds for Mobile Ad hoc Networks*, TridentCom 2006.

57. Legendre, F., Borrel, V., De Amorim, M. D. and Fdida, S. (2006). *Reconsider microscopic mobility modeling for self-organizing networks*, IEEE Communications Magazine, 2006.

58. Liljenstam, M., Liu, J., Nicol, D., Yuan, Y., Yan, G. and Grier, C. (2005). *RINSE: The real-time immersive network simulation environment for network security exercises*, in Proc. of PADS'05. Washington, DC, USA, 2005, pp. 119–128.

59. Linux VServers Project. http://linux-vserver.org/.

60. Luo, Q., Ni, L. M., He, B., Wu, H. and Xue, W. (2004). *MEADOWS: modeling, emulation, and analysis of data of wireless sensor networks*, in Proceeedings of the 1st int. workshop on Data management for sensor networks (DMSN'04), New York, NY, USA, 2004, pp. 58–67.

61. Mahadevan, P., Rodriguez, A., Becker, D. and Vahdat, A. (2005). *MobiNet: A Scalable Emulation Infrastructure for Ad Hoc and Wireless Networks*,in Proc. of 2005 workshop on wireless traffic measurements and modeling (WiTMeMo '05), Berkeley, CA, USA, 2005, pp. 7–12.

62. Mahrenholz D. and Ivanov, S. (2004). *Real-Time Network Emulation with ns-2*, in Proc. of 8th IEEE International Symposium on Distributed Simulation and Real Time Applications (DS-RT'04), 2004, pp. 29–36.

63. MEMSIC Wireless Modules. http://www.memsic.com/products/wireless-sensor-networks/wireless-modules.html.

64. Miyachi, T., Chinen, K. and Shinoda, Y. (2006). *StarBED and SpringOS: Large-scale General Purpose Network Testbed and Supporting Software*, in Proc. of Intl. Conf. on Performance Evaluation Methodologies and Tools (Valuetools 2006), ACM Press, Pisa, Italy, October 2006.

65. Mosberger D., and Peterson, L. L. (1996). *Making Paths Explicit in the Scout Operating System*, in Proc. of the 2nd Symposium on Operating Systems Design & Implementation (OSDI 1996), Seattle, WA, USA, Oct 1996, pp. 153–167.

66. Nakata, J., Miyachi, T., Beuran, R., Chinen, K., Uda, S., Masui, K., Tan, Y., and Shinoda, Y. (2007). *StarBED2: Large-scale, Realistic and Real-time Testbed for Ubiquitous Networks*, 3rd International Conference on Testbeds and Research Infrastructures for the Development of Networks & Communities (TridentCom 2007), Orlando, Florida, USA, May 21–23, 2007.

67. NCTUns 6.0 Network Simulator and Emulator Home Page. http://nsl.csie.nctu.edu.tw/nctuns.html.

68. NetEm Home Page. http://www.linuxfoundation.org/collaborate/workgroups/networking/netem.

69. NetFPGA Home Page. http://netfpga.org/.

70. Netperf Home Page. http://www.netperf.org/netperf/.

71. Nguyen, L. T., Beuran, R. and Shinoda, Y. (2011). An Interference and Load Aware Routing Metric for Wireless Mesh Networks, *International Journal of Ad Hoc and Ubiquitous Computing (IJAHUC)*, vol. 7, no.1, 2011, pp. 25–37.

72. Nicol, D. M., Liljenstam, M. and Liu, J. (2005). *Advanced concepts in large-scale network simulation*, in Proc. of the 37th Winter Simulation Conference (WSC 2005), December 2005.

73. NIST Net Home Page. http://snad.ncsl.nist.gov/nistnet/.

74. Nordstrom, E., Gunningberg, P. and Lundgren, H. (2005). *A testbed and methodology for experimental evaluation of wireless mobile ad hoc networks*, in Proc. of TRIDENTCOM'05, 2005.

75. Nussbaum, L. and Richard, O., *A Comparative Study of Network Link Emulators*, in: Proc. of the 12th Communications and Networking Simulation Symposium (CNS'09), San Diego, USA, March 22–27, 2009.

76. Okada, T., Nakata, J., Beuran, R., Tan, Y. and Shinoda, Y. (2008). *Large-scale Simulation Method of Mobile Robots*, 2nd International Symposium on Universal Communication (ISUC 2008), Osaka, Japan, December 15–16, 2008, pp. 309–314.

77. Olsr.org Project. *Olsrd: An adhoc wireless mesh routing daemon*, http://www.olsr.org/.

78. Omnicor, *NetDisturb*, http://www.omnicor.biz/Products/Ethernet TestSystems/tabid/99/Default.aspx.

79. OpenVZ Home Page. http://wiki.openvz.org/Main_Page.

80. OPNET Technologies, *OPNET Modeler*, http://www.opnet.com/.

81. OPTICOM (2008). *PEVQ: Advanced Perceptual Evaluation of Video Quality*, White Paper, 2008.

82. PacketStorm Communications, http://www.packetstorm.com/.

83. Perennou, T., Conchon, E., Dairaine, L. and Diaz, M. (2004). *Two-stage wireless network emulation*, in Proc. of the Workshop on Challenges of Mobility (WCM 2004), August 2004.

84. Peterson, L., Anderson, T., Culler, D. and Roscoe, T. (2002). *A Blueprint for Introducing Disruptive Technology into the Internet*, in Proc. of the 1st ACM Workshop on Hot Topics in Networking (HotNets'02), October 2002.

85. PlanetLab Europe. *The Onelab2 Project*, http://www.onelab.eu/.

86. PlanetLab Home Page. http://www.planet-lab.org/.

87. Polley, J., Blazakis, D., McGee, J., Rusk, D. and Baras, J. S. (2004). *ATEMU: a fine-grained sensor network simulator*, in Proc. of the First Annual IEEE Communications Society Conf. on Sensor and Ad Hoc Communications and Networks (SECON 2004), October 2004, pp. 145–152.

88. Pongor, G. (1993) *OMNeT: Objective Modular Network Testbed*, in Proc. of the International Workshop on Modeling, Analysis, and Simulation On Computer and Telecommunication Systems (MASCOTS '93), La Jolla, San Diego, CA, USA, January 17–20, 1993, pp. 323–326.

89. Postel, J. (1987). *TCP and IP bake off*, IETF RFC 1025, September 1987.

90. ProtoGENI Home Page, http://www.protogeni.net/trac/protogeni.

91. Puzar M. and Plagemann, T. (2005). *NEMAN: A network emulator for mobile ad-hoc networks*, in Proc. of ConTEL 2005, 2005.

92. Ramachandran, K., Kaul, S., Mathur, S., Gruteser, M., Seskar, I. (2005). *Towards Large-Scale Mobile Network Emulation Through Spatial Switching on a Wireless Grid*, in Proc. of the Workshop on Experimental Approaches to Wireless Network Design and Analysis (E-Wind), in conjunction with ACM SIGCOMM 2005, Philadelphia, PA, USA, August 22–26, 2005.

93. Riley, G. F., Fujimoto, R. M., Ammar M. H. (1999). *A generic framework for parallelization of network simulations*, in Proc. of Seventh International Symposium on Modeling, Analysis and Simulation of Computer and Telecommunication Systems (MASCOTS'99), October 1999.

94. Rizzo, L. (1997). *Dummynet: A simple approach to the evaluation of network protocols*, ACM SIGCOMM Computer Communication Review, 27(1):31–41, 1997.

95. Robinson, S. (2004). *Simulation: The practice of model development and use*, Wiley, March 2004.

96. Scalable Network Technologies. *QualNet Developer*, http://www. scalable-networks.com/products/qualnet/.

97. Scalable Network Technologies. *EXata Software Virtual Network*, http://www.scalable-networks.com/exata/.

98. Scalable Network Technologies. *Parallel Capabilities*, http://www. scalable-networks.com/products/parallel-processing/.

99. Shunra, Inc., *Shunra Virtual Enterprise (Shunra VE)*, http://www. shunra.com/ve-suite-overview.

100. Simena, Inc., *Simena Network Emulator Series*, http://www. simena.net/NetworkEmulator.htm.

101. Simena, Inc., *Simena Portable test Center*, http://www.simena. net/PTC3000.htm.

102. Simmonds, R., Bradford, R. and Unger, B. (2000). *Applying parallel discrete event simulation to network emulation*, in Proc. of the fourteenth workshop on Parallel and distributed simulation (PADS'00). Washington, DC, USA, 2000, pp. 15–22.

103. Snort Home Page. http://www.snort.org/.

104. Spirent Communications, Inc., *SmartBits: Award-winning traffic generation & analysis*, http://www.spirent.com/Solutions-Directory/ Smartbits.aspx

105. University of Southern California, Information Sciences Institute. *The ns-2 Network Simulator*, http://nsnam.isi.edu/nsnam/index.php/.

106. University of Southern California, Information Sciences Institute. *The ns-3 Network Simulator*, http://www.nsnam.org/.

107. Telcordia Technologies, Inc. and Candela Technologies, Inc., *WISER — Wireless IP Scalable Network Emulator*, http://wiser.research. telcordia.com/.

108. University of Utah, School of Computing. *Emulab — Total network testbed*, http://www.emulab.net/.

109. Vahdat, A., Yocum, K., Walsh, K., Mahadevan, P., Kostic, D., Chase, J. and Becker, D. (2002). *Scalability and accuracy in a large-scale network emulator*, ACM SIGOPS Operating Systems Review, 36: 271–284, 2002.

110. Vaidya, N. H., Bernhard, J., Veeravalli, V. V., Kumar, P. R. and Iyer, R. K. (2005). *Illinois wireless wind tunnel: a testbed for experimental evaluation of wireless networks* in Proc. of ACM SIGCOMM workshop on experimental approaches to wireless network design and analysis (E-WIND), Philadelphia, Pennsylvania, USA, August 22–26, 2005, pp. 64–69.

111. Wang, S. Y., Chou, C. L., Huang, C. H., Hwang, C. C., Yang, Z. M., Chiou, C. C. and Lin, C. C. (2003). *The Design and Implementation of the NCTUns 1.0 Network Simulator*, in Computer Networks, vol. 42, issue 2, June 2003, pp. 175–197.

112. Wang, S. Y. and Liao K. C. (2006). *Innovative Network Emulations using the NCTUns Tool*, in Computer Networking and Networks, Nova Science Publishers, 2006.

113. White, B., Lepreau, J., Stoller, L., Ricci, R., Guruprasad, S., Newbold, M., Hibler, M., Barb, C., and Joglekar, A. (2002). *An integrated experimental environment for distributed systems and networks*, in Proc. of 5th

Symposium on Operating Systems Design & Implementation (OSDI 2002), Boston, USA, December 9–11, 2002, pp. 255–270.

114. Wiles, B. C., and Walker, J. *Speak Freely 7.6a*, http://www. speak-freely.org.

115. Wireless Information Network Laboratory, Rutgers University. *ORBIT — Wireless Network Testbed*, http://www.orbit-lab.org/.

116. Ymatic, Inc., http://www.ymatic.co.jp.

117. Zec, M., and Mikuc, M. (2004). *Operating system support for integrated network emulation in IMUNES*, in Proc. of First Workshop on Operating System and Architectural Support for the On Demand IT Infrastructure (OASIS), Boston, USA, 2004.

118. Zheng P. and Nil, L. M. (2003). *EMPOWER: a network emulator for wireline and wireless networks*, in Proc. of IEEE INFOCOM 2003, San Francisco, USA, 2003.

119. Zhou, J., Ji, Z., and Bagrodia, R. (2006). *TWINE: a hybrid emulation testbed for wireless networks and applications*, in Proc. of IEEE INFOCOM 2006, Barcelona, Spain, April 23–29, 2006.

Index

2-hop topologies 242
3-hop topologies 242
G.1050 128, 135, 136, 157, 161,
    164

abstractions 208, 223
active node placements 240
active RFID 356, 360
  tag communication 286,
      289–290, 360
  tag communication
      protocol 365
  tag emulation 359
  tag emulation framework 359
  tag experiments 336, 356–357,
      359, 361, 363, 365, 372
  tag firmware 360, 363
  tag micro-controller 360
  tag prototype system 356
  tag system 356, 359
  tag wireless communication 285
  tags 298, 314–315, 342,
      356–360, 362–363, 365–366,
      372
actuators 262, 298, 315
Ad hoc Protocol Evaluation
    (APE) 267
ad-hoc routing algorithms 213
ad hoc scripting solutions 80
ad hoc wireless networks 348
adaptive protocol 96
adjusted deltaQ parameters 300
ADSL modem 374

Agilent ESG 241
Ambient Intelligence (AmI) 279
AmI see Ambient Intelligence 279
AmI devices 279
analytical equations 28
analytical modeling 3, 27–29, 33,
    37–39, 368
analytical simulation 178
analytical simulation methods 178
anechoic chamber 267
Anue Systems 3, 26, 49, 54,
    153–155, 157–160, 369
  claims 160
  ethernet network emulators
      153, 376
  products 153
Anue XGEM 160, 163–167
Anue XGEM emulator 163
AODV 178, 185, 195, 202–203,
    353
AODV routing 193
APE see Ad hoc Protocol Evaluation
AppleTalk 48, 126
application-layer protocols 181,
    189, 195, 202
application performance 43, 45,
    93, 104–105, 110–113, 138,
    143–144, 353
  analysis features 106
  degradation 113
  evaluation 123
  issues 105
  thresholds 111

Application Performance Analysis
  Package 110
application QoE 280–282
Apposite Netropy 160, 163–167
Apposite Technologies 3, 43, 45,
  54, 57, 138–139, 141, 143,
  145, 147–149, 151, 160, 369
  claims 145
  lines 151
  product family 138, 302
Apposite Technologies
  Linktropy 150, 376, 253, 264
Apposite Technologies
  Netropy 149, 151, 160
Apposite Technologies
  Netropy 151, 160
arbitrary-size networks 185
arbitrary waveform generator 241
ARP 174, 189, 202–203
ARP IPv4 202
ARPANET 1
associate QOMET node 334
ATEMU 262, 272
Atheros 210, 218, 237
Atheros AR5212 236
ATLAS 280
AYID32305 357

backbone networks 212
background link utilization
  feature 163
background noise 267
background traffic 76, 146,
  149–150, 268
background traffic models 281
background traffic utilization 140
bandwidth 1, 9, 26, 44, 57
  constraints 112
  control 153, 163
  control XGEM 155
  cost 127
  limitations 21, 42, 45, 48, 55,
    83–84

requirements 127, 347
  restrictions 43
bandwidth-hungry 141
bandwidth thresholds 156
bandwidth throttle 119
Berkeley Packet Filter (BPF) 175
bi-directional emulation 130,
  135–136, 167
bi-directional packet transfer 44
bit error injection 131
bit error insertion 123–124
bit error probability 96
bit error rate 106, 119, 135, 140,
  145–146, 156, 289
BitTorrent applications 203
black box 15
bluetooth 179, 246
  cards 237
  interfaces 247
BPF *see* Berkeley Packet Filter
browser-based GUI 155
browser-based interface 144–145
browser control interface 119
buffers 18, 105, 347
building network simulators 46
building network topologies 189
bursts 94, 119
  effects 163
business-critical storage 26
byte mode 112

captured network packets 175
captured trace file 176
captured traces 61
captured traffic 122, 159
cascaded headers 130
CAWIS *see* Centralized Arbitrary
  Waveform Injection
  Subsystem
CBQ *see* Class-Based Queueing
CBR sessions 193
CCT *see* Critical Channel Traversing
CDMA 179

Centralized Arbitrary Waveform
  Injection Subsystem (CAWIS)
  241
centralized emulation 64, 88, 98,
  115
  approach 97, 139, 258
  execution 64–65, 69
CERN 3, 280
circular motion 293
Cisco IOS 79
Class-Based Queueing (CBQ) 98
CLI *see* command-line interface
client-server model 200
client-server scenarios 106
cluster computing 200
CoDeeN 225
cognitive radio networking
  experiments 233
command line 90, 95
command-line arguments
  values 332
command-line interface (CLI) 129,
  135–136, 140, 145–146, 151,
  167
  support 167
command-line tools 285, 295, 299,
  371
commercial network
  emulators 103–104,
  106–108, 110, 112, 114, 116,
  118, 120, 122, 124, 126, 128,
  130, 132, 160
commercial network
  simulators 30
commercial simulators 30
commercial software
  emulators 52, 374
commercial software network
  emulator 194
Common Open Research Emulator
  (CORE) 42
common operational picture 188
companion software product 126
complex hardware 264

complex link-level emulator 56
complex mechanisms 239
complex multi-hop network
  topologies 240
complex network performance
  scenarios 90
complex network phenomena 60
complex network scenarios 114,
  159, 165
complex network situations 115
complex network structures 107
complex network system 374
complex network topologies 43,
  139, 165, 168, 259
complex networking scenarios 25
complex networks 56, 148, 177,
  185
complex orchestration 326
complex propagation 360
complex scenarios 25, 177, 183,
  185, 323, 368
complex setups 183–184
complex virtual network 184
complex wireless network
  scenarios 321
complexity 33, 50, 59–60, 376
composite network degradation
  effects 376
computer-based execution 72
computer-based network
  applications 334
computer-based wireless network
  technologies 294
computer-based wireless
  networks 325
computer clusters 54, 186, 192,
  194
computer-executable code 31
CONDUIT 338–339
conduits 315–318, 336–38,
  365–366
configurable attenuators 267
configurable impairments 153
configurable mix 233

configurable parameters 98, 242,
  353
configurable topologies 304
configuration change 48
configuration files 310, 314, 337
configuration parameters 313
configuration settings 93, 99
configuration step 376
configuration system 234
configuration tasks 154, 325
conformance 8, 174
congestion 43, 45, 48, 60, 84, 87
  conditions 91, 140, 146
  constraints 44
  control 98
  effects 95, 106, 115–116
  emulation 131, 163
  loss 45
  threshold 15, 92
connection 4, 8–9, 28, 49, 54–56
  outages 140, 146
  topology 128
Connection Managers 190, 202
container-based virtualization 214
contention 89, 241, 244, 288,
  300–301
  information 300
  management 228
contention-dependent adjustment
  300
contention-free communication
  299
controlled environment 26, 35
controlled experiments 279
controlled interference 235
controlled mobility conditions
  267
controlled network impairments
  221
controlled real conditions 266
copper Gigabit Ethernet interfaces
  142, 144
CORE *see* Common Open Research
  Emulator

core router 211
core technology 44, 194
CPU 213–216, 307–308
  cores 193
  frequency 22
  power 195
  resources 176
  scheduling mechanisms 215
  type 193
CRC 156
Critical Channel Traversing (CCT)
  268
critical performance indicators
  190
critical performance metrics 187
critical server resources 110
critical traffic 138
CSV format 129
customized operating system 53
customized OS images 238
customized performance metrics
  190
cyber warfare support 191

D-Link 218, 309
D-Link DWL-AG530 210
daemon-launching command 355
DARPA 170
data link layer 290, 342
  parameters 291
  protocol model 291
data-link layer, model 300
data link network layer 289
data packets 48, 126, 172
database 208, 234, 238–239
database integration 46
DDoS *see* distributed denial of
  service
degree of control 254, 272
degree of realism 254, 272
delay accuracy 86
delay amounts 156
delay control 142

delay distributions 93, 99
Delay Doubler 156
delay emulation 254
delay nodes 211, 216
delay profiles 89, 101
delay tolerant networks (DTN)
    233
delay variation 56, 95, 156
deltaQ 285–287, 289, 292–294,
    299–300, 370–371
    library 287–291, 293–294,
        298–300, 351–352, 370
    parameters 300
destination network protocol
    ports 119
destination ports 132
destination space 318
DHCP protocol 311
digital network replica 48, 187
directional antennas 291–293
discrete-event simulation 178,
    180, 268
discrete small-scale mobility
    scenarios 245
disruptive technologies 225
distance vector protocols 203
distributed architectures 194, 200
distributed data centers 106
distributed denial of service
    (DDoS) 191
distributed emulation 64, 68–69,
    93, 195
    approach 52, 256
    execution 71
    mechanism 195
    paradigm 301
    scenarios 60
    solutions 269, 271
    tool 114
distributed execution 66, 88, 168,
    177, 185
    approach 70
    approaches 66
    capabilities 264

features 189
    mechanism 283
Distributed Internet Traffic
    Generator 77, 239
distributed intervals 155
distributed management scheme
    230
distributed network emulation
    system 42
distributed random variation 292
distributed simulation 179
distributed storage 47, 222
distributed testbed environment
    228
distributed virtualization 223–224,
    226
    mechanisms 231
    task 224
distribution mechanism 326
DRD 91–92
DS3 122
DSDV 195, 202
DSL modems 90
DSR 195, 202–203
DTN *see* delay tolerant networks
Dummynet 3, 11, 42, 47, 52, 57,
    60, 67, 83–89, 92, 98–101,
    295–296, 304, 321–322,
    368–369
    command-line manual 85
    packet 87
    pipes 85
    queues 86, 88
dynamic condition emulation 140,
    146
dynamic condition variations 167

E-model 347
ECN *see* explicit congestion
    notification
ECN congestion flag 92
ECN-enabled packets 92
electromagnetic waves 292

embedded applications 72
embedded devices 334
embedded systems 298
EMPOWER 42, 62, 269, 271
Emulab 42, 63, 205–206, 245
  architecture 208
  control system 219
  experiment 216, 218
  hardware 220
  mechanisms 213
  software 80, 206, 223
  user interface 207
  virtualization technique 215
emulation platform 2, 8, 12, 362
emulation servers 70
emulation-side network 71
emulation testbeds 3, 368
emulation tools 3, 42, 50, 64, 79,
  255, 294, 368
end experiment execution 325
ENIAC 1
error-free seconds (EFS) 26
Ethernet 44, 107, 122, 150, 157
EXata 47, 62, 187
explicit congestion notification
  (ECN) 92

FER *see* frame error rate
FIFO (first-in, first-out) 13, 95
FIFO-based queueing 98
FPGA 53
FPGA-based Approach to
  Application Performance
  Assessment 281
FPGA-based digital signal
  processor 267
FPGA-based implementation 302
frame error rate (FER) 289–290,
  359
frame error rate model 290
frame overhead 140
free emulators 50–51, 368
free software emulators 52, 374

FTP 23, 181, 189, 195, 202–203
full-mesh networks 106

gateways 59, 180, 354–355
Gaussian distribution 14, 156
GEM 54, 153, 157–158, 167
  ethernet network emulators 157
  features 157
  network emulators 157
  products 49
GENI *see* Global Environment for
  Network Innovation
gentle RED (GRED) 87, 98
gentle red algorithm 87
Global Environment for Network
  Innovation (GENI) 232
GRED *see* gentle RED
grid node radio interface 244
grid topology 243
grid virtualization 234
ground link utilization 140, 146
GSM 179
GUI 90, 114, 129, 144, 186, 194,
  200–201
GUI-based debugging 179

Hurricane 42, 54, 118, 165, 167
  models 167
  network emulators 122
  products 42, 121
Hurricane II 118
Hurricane series 54, 59, 120–121
hybrid approach 68, 280
hybrid simulation 178

ICMP 181, 189, 195, 202–203
ICMPv6 181, 194, 202
ICT 2
Illinois Wireless Wind Tunnel
  (iWWT) 267
IMUNES 42–43, 263

INE *see* iTrinegy Network
  Emulator 43
INE for Windows 43, 62
information technology (IT) 1
interfaces 8, 94, 120, 157, 174
IP address 155, 196, 332, 337, 341
IP checksum 156
IP Firewall (IPFW) 84–85
IP Network Emulator (IPNE) 47,
  187
IP phones 20
iperf command 332
iperf tool 349
iperf traffic generation command
  355
IPFW *see* IP Firewall
IPNE *see* IP Network Emulator
iproute2 94
IPTV 131, 141
IPX 48, 126, 246
iSCSI 122, 131
ISP 27
IT *see* information technology
iTrinegy Network Emulator
  (INE) 43
ITUT Recommendation 347
iWWT *see* Illinois Wireless Wind
  Tunnel

kernel 44, 86, 95, 194
  clock 99
  extensions 226
  module extension 45, 90
  network protocol stack 197

LANforge-ICE 43, 52
Large Hadron Collider (LHC) 280
LBNL packet 175
LCD 136, 162, 167
LHC *see* Large Hadron Collider
link latency 141

link-layer emulator actions 295,
  297
link-layer frames 175
link-level emulation 50, 56–57
link-level network emulation,
  capabilities 304
link-level network emulator 56,
  295
Linktropy 43, 139, 146
  devices 138
  models 152
  network emulators 143
  products 152
Linktropy and Netropy models 151
Live-Sim-Live 181
  approach 185
  scenario 181–182
local area network (LAN) 10, 110,
  212, 243
log-distance model 292
log-distance path loss model 286,
  292, 328
low bandwidth 118
low-fidelity models 255

MAC 43, 162, 165, 240
  filtering 244
  layer 156, 239–240, 301
  protocols 273
madwifi 218, 240
MANET *see* mobile ad hoc
  networks
Maxwell 43
MEADOWS 262
mean opinion score (MOS) 120,
  347
MEF-18 157, 161, 164
MICA2 mote 213
Miniaturized Wireless Network
  Testbed (MinT) 268
MiNT *see* Miniaturized Wireless
  Network Testbed

mobile ad hoc networks (MANET) 179, 233, 355
Mobile Emulab 221, 267
mobile networks 179, 188, 245, 282, 303
mobile robotic wireless 213
mobile robots 221, 245
mobile topologies 241
Mobile WiMAX 278
MobiNet 269, 271
ModelNet 44, 70, 269
Monarch 265, 272
MOS *see* mean opinion score
multi-hop network topologies 239
multi-hop routing protocols 298
multi-hop topologies 242
multi-hop wireless networks 353
multi-layer model 290
multi-level emulation layers 315
multi-link configurations 142
multi-link emulation 135–136
multi-path 165, 245, 360
multimedia transmission performance 128
MyPLC 223, 228

National Science Foundation (NSF) 170
NCTUns 3, 44, 194–196
NEMAN 264
net-centric systems 188
Net Tool Optimizer 159
NetDisturb 44
NetEm 3, 44, 83, 93, 95–99, 101, 295, 304, 369, 374
NetFPGA 212–213, 246–247
Netropy 45, 145
netstat 196
network connectivity 1
network emulation 2, 5
network emulation techniques 50, 368

Network Emulator (NE) 3, 10, 41, 43
network interface cards (NICs) 19
network interface drivers 175
network intrusion techniques 191
network links 55, 113, 159, 197–198, 231, 354
network model emulation 136
network parameters 56, 108, 163
network performance 27, 89, 111, 356
network problems 109, 133
network profile 156, 166, 256
network QoS 280–281
network quality degradation 9–10, 56
network services 47, 105, 222
network simulation 2, 11, 27, 30–33, 37, 46, 49, 179, 187, 262, 368
network technologies 106–107, 115, 143, 195, 272, 289, 303, 322
network traffic 9, 20, 28, 57, 64–65, 69, 75–76, 105, 122
NICs *see* network interface cards
NIST Net 3, 45, 57, 83, 89–93, 98–99, 101, 265, 322
Node Agent 238–239
Node Manager 226
node mobility 32, 267, 293
    emulation 287
    models 286
node name 329
node orientation 293
node power cycling 208
noise generation 240–241, 244–245
    antennas 236, 242
    subsystem 241
    system 242
noise power 242, 289–290
Ns-2 3, 45, 169, 171
Ns-3 46, 170

NSF *see* National Science
   Foundation

OLSR *see* Optimized Link State
   Routing
OMF *see* ORBIT management
   framework
OML *see* ORBIT measurement
   framework & library
omni-directional 291–292
OneLab 84
OpenBSD 263
OpenDHT 225
OpenRISC processor emulator for
   IEEE 336
operating system kernel 43, 85,
   197
OPNET 180, 185, 343
   emulation features 181
   modeling environment 181
   models 181
   simulation 180
OPNET Modeler 3, 46, 178, 180,
   182
OPNET Modeler Wireless
   Suite 179
OPNET Technologies 46, 178, 183,
   191
OPTICOM 348
optimal end-user experience 105
optimal transmission range 364
Optimized Link State Routing
   (OLSR) 178, 185, 189, 287,
   298, 353
ORBIT 46, 231, 244–245, 249
   emulates mobility 243
   hardware 235
   nodes 236, 244
   noise generation system 244
   wireless network 80
ORBIT management framework
   (OMF) 234, 237–238

ORBIT measurement framework &
   library (OML) 239
ORBIT radio grid 235, 241, 248
ORBIT Traffic Generator
   (OTG) 239
OSPF support 166
OTG *see* ORBIT Traffic Generator

packed network protocol
   stacks 263
packet analyzer tool 122
packet collision 336
packet conversion 180
packet correlation 237
packet corruption 96, 156, 164
packet delay 156, 182, 290
packet duplication 45, 48, 91, 96,
   106, 119, 123, 150–151, 156
packet FIFO 98
packet filtering 119, 121, 131,
   146, 155, 164, 241
Packet Flow Switch
   (PFS) 137–138
Packet impairment 119, 121, 156,
   158
packet jitter 154
packet listing 122
packet loss 9, 42–43, 45, 55–57,
   83–84, 95–96, 106–107,
   112–113, 116, 123–124,
   133–134, 141–142, 152–153,
   297, 346
packet loss concealment
   techniques 346
packet mode 112
packet modifiers 121
packet re-ordering 119
packet sink 119, 124
PacketStorm 47
PacketStorm Communications 3,
   42, 47, 54, 59, 117
PacketStorm e series 120
PacketStorm emulators 47, 125

PacketStorm family 118
PacketStorm Series 118
patent-pending technology 128
pause frames 155, 163
PC emulators 12
PC-oriented architecture 314
Perceptual Evaluation of Speech
    Quality (PESQ) 21, 347–348
Perceptual Evaluation of Video
    Quality (PEVQ) 23
PESQ *see* Perceptual Evaluation of
    Speech Quality
PEVQ *see* Perceptual Evaluation of
    Video Quality
PFS *see* Packet Flow Switch
ping 189, 202, 349
PlanetLab 47, 55, 63, 80, 207
    design 229
    developers 224–225, 228
    functionality 226
    infrastructure 227
    nodes 213
    slices 224, 226, 228
PlanetLab Central 80
Portable Test Center (PTC) 54,
    127, 133–134, 136–138,
    163–164
protocol 2, 23, 28, 34
    assessment 23, 25, 368
    evaluation 301
    implementations 14, 90, 173,
        262–263, 291
    mode 172–174
    modules 200
    performance evaluation 342
    processing 173
    stack 84, 199, 263, 269
    uses 357
prototype localization system
    357–358, 361–362
PSCapture 118, 125
PTC *see* Portable Test Center

qdiscs 94
QEMU 8
QoE *see* quality of experience
QoE metrics 120, 166, 345
QOMB 4, 47, 63, 272, 277, 305
    architecture 323, 371
    components 277, 284
    components QOMET 346
    experiment host 332
    functionality 366
    wireless network emulation
        301, 341
QOMET 278, 283, 285–286, 290,
    301
    chanel library 335, 359
    command 300, 325
    command-line tool 299
    deltaQ 345, 351, 359–360
QOMET on StarBED 284, 321–322,
    324
QoS *see* quality of service
Quadrupler 156
quality of experience (QoE) 22,
    115, 162, 281
quality of service (QoS) 106,
    115–116, 162, 166
QualNet 47, 187, 191, 343
QualNet Developer 3, 47, 63, 186,
    201
queue management 112, 116
    algorithms 87, 113
    tail 151

rack-mount chassis 154, 157
radio grid 232–233, 245
Random Early Detection (RED) 87
random mobility 193
random offset 96
real active RFID tags 361
real communication conditions
    359
real device processor 336
real distributed application 196

real equipment 36–38, 257, 282
real-life evaluation 249
real-life IP networks 196
real-life networks 195–196
real network applications 75, 253, 353
real network conditions 165, 253, 265, 272
real network interfaces 197, 268, 271
real nodes 214, 258–259, 377
real packets 172–175, 180
real system 19, 28–29, 34, 36, 49, 257
real-time execution 17, 29, 33, 185
real-time flow 261, 273
real-time graphs 118, 125
real-time packet modifications 119, 129
real-time scheduler 33, 172, 174, 176
Real-time Ubiquitous Network Emulation 48, 283, 299, 304, 306, 314–320, 323–324, 334–335, 337, 339–342, 371
real wireless network interfaces 245, 264, 283
real-world conditions 138, 141
real-world entities 46, 171
real-world environments 2
real-world setting 233
real-world testing 2–3, 10, 21, 27, 33, 39, 49, 368
real-world trials 2, 18, 34, 252
real-world Unix machines 44, 196
realistic client workload 224, 230
realistic environments 7, 20, 292
realistic experiments 244, 262, 315
realistic high-speed background traffic 137
realistic network conditions 76, 113, 121, 183

realistic scenarios 22, 25, 346, 348
received signal strength indicator (RSSI) 241
RED *see* Random Early Detection
RedHat 219
remote access 22, 226, 304, 308
remote end-users 105, 108, 110–111, 114
remote experimentation 212–213
remote host 265
RF interferences 267
RF-shielded room 359
RINSE 268
RIP 195, 202–203
robot experiments 351–353
robot motion-planning algorithm 288, 352
router intercepting packets 93
router mode operation 157
routing 23, 45, 170, 224, 263
    capabilities 105
    centers 222
    functionality 211
    information 126
    information module 298
    metrics 354–355
    protocol assessment 59
    protocol evaluation 346, 353
    protocol support 287
    tables 70, 215, 244, 298
RS-232 122, 141, 147
RSSI *see* received signal strength indicator
RUNE architecture 318, 340
RUNE-based experiment topology 315
RUNE-based experiments 318, 341
RUNE Manager 317–319, 340–341
RUNE Master 316–319, 340–341
RUNE spaces 335, 338, 341, 366

SAN *see* storage-area network
satellite 43, 45, 264
    fade 140, 146
    networks 106–107, 109, 143,
        152, 179, 184
    systems 179
scheduling algorithms 84, 179
SDR *see* software-defined radio
Select Nodes with Fixed
        Interference (SNFI) 242
SFP 120, 148, 150–151, 159
Shunra 3, 11, 59, 79, 103
Shunra VE *see* Shunra Virtual
        Enterprise
Shunra VE Cloud 57, 104,
        111–113
Shunra VE Desktop Professional
        114
Shunra VE Desktop Standard
        113–114
Shunra Virtual Enterprise 48, 104
Sim-Live-Sim 181–182, 185
Simena 3, 48, 54, 59, 126, 129
    network emulators 127,
        130–132, 135
    products 130–131
    traffic generators 137
Simena markets 135, 137
Simena NE 48, 57, 374
Simena PTC 48, 160, 163–166
simulated networks 46, 171, 178,
        180
simulated nodes 44, 196, 200, 214
simulated packets 174, 180
simulated scenarios 187
simulation 2–3, 27, 30, 33, 90, 169
    capabilities 47
    engine 169, 177, 180, 185–186
    execution 33
    experiments 2, 32, 37, 187
    framework 46
    functionality 169
    host 198
    machine 200

    tool 47, 186
simulation setup 2
simulator-based emulation 184,
        268
simulators 30, 33, 46, 63, 170
SITL *see* System-in-the-Loop
SNFI *see* Select Nodes with Fixed
        Interference
SNR 242
software-defined radio (SDR) 207,
        233
software emulators 43, 51–53,
        145, 168
software network emulator 51,
        54, 64–65, 107, 260, 373–375
SpringOS 283, 304, 306, 309
    mechanisms 323, 366
    software 310
    syntax 326
StarBED 48, 55, 283, 303
    architecture 305
    development 303–304
    experiment switches 313
    hosts 334, 353
    infrastructure 305–306, 323
storage-area network (SAN) 109
street topology 287, 293, 355
System-in-the-Loop (SITL) 46,
        179, 182–184, 202
System-in-the-Loop module 46,
        179

TCP 23, 45, 97, 203
    agents 174
    flags 132
    server 197–199
    source 132
TCP Reno 10
TCP Vegas 10
testbeds 2, 54–55, 205
thought experiments 27
topology-level emulation 50,
        57–59

topology level emulator 57–59, 177, 185, 194
Tornado 48, 52, 54, 118, 122
traceroute 189, 195, 202–203
  commands 196

ubiquitous network systems 280
UDP 24, 119, 175, 178, 181, 189
Universal Software Radio Peripheral (USRP) 207, 233
UPQ *see* user-perceived quality
USART 360
User Mode Linux (UML) 263
user-perceived quality (UPQ) 22, 77, 280, 345, 347–348
USRP *see* Universal Software Radio Peripheral

variability 29
variable network parameters 60
video tele-conferencing (VTC) 346
VINI project 263
virtual emu 189
Virtual Machine Monitor (VMM) 226–227
virtual network 14–15, 78, 181, 184
  devices 58, 98
  driver 263
  environment 105
  interfaces 215, 243, 247, 264, 302
  testbeds 231
  topology 70, 255
virtual networks, spanning 248
virtual nodes 43, 207, 214
virtual representations 33, 57
virtual street environment 348, 354
VLAN 119, 122, 128, 135
VMM *see* Virtual Machine Monitor

Voice over Internet Protocol (VoIP) 21–22
VoIP *see* Voice over Internet Protocol
VPN 304
VPN technology 308
VTC *see* video tele-conferencing

wall attenuation 292
WAN *see* wide area network
WAN bandwidth limitation 110
WAN degradation 110
WAN delay 110
WAN-emulated delay 95
WAN emulation 42, 47, 104, 118
WAN emulation experiments 125
WAN emulation products 43, 45, 48
WAN emulation software 48, 122
WAN emulator 10, 139
WAN optimization 109
wave propagation 289
web traffic generation 24
weighted-fair queueing algorithm 83
white Gaussian noise signals 241
Wi-Fi 207, 221, 264, 285, 294, 301, 325
  access 233
  cards 210
  emulation 323
  interfaces 207
  nodes in Emulab 217
wide area networks (WAN) 10, 45, 48, 93, 105, 122
WiMAX 278, 285
wire-speed network emulation 127
wireless network emulation 4, 47, 247, 253
  experiments 282, 324–325
  support 378
  testbeds 249, 264, 344

wireless network experiments
247, 249, 267, 280
Wireless Suite 179
Wireless Suite for Defense 179
WISER 49
WLAN 43, 122, 278, 285, 345
  communication conditions 349,
    355
  connections 279
  emulation 272
  experiments 345, 347, 349,
    351, 353, 355

networks 366
technology 278

xDSL 45, 143
Xen 69, 216
XFP 145, 159
XGEM 154–157, 166

ZigBee 179, 278
ZX-Spectrum platforms 8